Exploration of the
Valley of the Great Salt Lake

Exploration of the Valley of the Great Salt Lake

Howard Stansbury

With an Introduction by Don D. Fowler

SMITHSONIAN INSTITUTION PRESS
Washington, D.C.   London

Reprinted 1988, with new Introduction by Don D. Fowler, in
the series Exploring the American West

© Smithsonian Institution   1988
Introduction

New material edited by Jeanne M. Sexton

Originally issued 1852 as Exploration and Survey of the Valley
of the Great Salt Lake of Utah, including a Reconnoissance of a
New Route through the Rocky Mountains. By Howard Stansbury, Captain,
Corps Topographical Engineers, U.S. Army.

Library of Congress Cataloging-in-Publication Data

Stansbury, Howard.
    Exploration of the Valley of the Great Salt Lake.

    (Exploring the American West)
    Reprint. Originally published: Exploration and
survey of the Valley of the Great Salt Lake of Utah,
including a reconnoissance of a new route through the
Rocky Mountains, 1852. With new introd.
    1. Utah—Description and travel. 2. Great Salt Lake
Region (Utah)—Description and travel. 3. West (U.S.)—
Description and travel—1848-1860. 4. Natural
history—Utah. 5. United States—Exploring expeditions.
I. Title. II. Series.
F826.S73 1988   917.8′042   88-1968
ISBN 0-87474-889-5

British Library Cataloguing-in-Publication Data is available

ISBN 0-87474-889-5

The paper in this book meets the guidelines for permanence and
durability of the Committee on Production Guidelines for Book
Longevity of the Council on Library Resources.

Cover: First View of Great Salt Lake Valley From a Mountain
Pass, from Stansbury's *Exploration and Survey of the Valley
of the Great Salt Lake of Utah* ... (1852).

Contents

Publisher's Statement

In its Exploring the American West series the Smithsonian Institution Press is undertaking the reprint of rare and out-of-print reports originally prepared by our nation's first government and military explorers. Now considered classics of western discovery and exploration, these reports gave the American people and federal policy makers their first glimpse of that vast region beyond the Mississippi River that was to become part of the United States. Many of these official reports began as private journals the explorers kept as they recorded their observations and surveys. Often written under the most adverse conditions, around campfires with frostbitten fingers or under siege by swarms of flies and mosquitoes, these reports convey the frustration and jubilation that were the twin companions of the western explorers. Enhancing the value of these reports are drawings and maps that are based on sketches made in the field by the illustrators who usually accompanied these expeditions. Some of these young men went on to distinguished careers as mapmakers, engravers, and artists; others sacrificed their lives in their dedication to science and art. Whether written by such giants of western exploration like John C. Frémont, whose name became a household word, or by those who remained obscure army officers known only to students of western history, like Howard Stansbury, these reports are today an integral part of the library of western Americana. Not only do they provide insight into the motives of these explorers but they also bring to light their unique contributions to the westward movement. And to the general reader, these handsomely illustrated reports still convey the excitement and lure of the West that so fascinated and attracted the people of the nineteenth century.

Introduction

Stansbury's expedition to the Great Salt Lake Valley in 1849–50 was one of many extraordinary assignments in western American exploration carried out by members of the U.S. Army Corps of Topographical Engineers in the decades preceding the Civil War. President Thomas Jefferson set the precedent for federally sponsored exploration of the American West when he sent Lewis and Clark into, and beyond, Louisiana Territory in 1803. From the outset, both official and unofficial parties of exploration functioned as advance elements of American expansion into Spanish-Mexican and British territories. Once Lewis and Clark passed beyond Louisiana Territory and into the British-controlled Oregon country, Lewis and Clark were, de facto, diplomatic spies. In 1806, U.S. Army Lt. Zebulon Pike was sent to the southern Rockies and wound up being arrested as a spy by the Spanish government when he and his men entered the territory of New Mexico Province.

During the War of 1812, the U.S. Army created a topographical division, assigned to make maps, but soon also assigned to design and direct public works projects, as well as to explore the ever-expanding West. The first major western expedition by U.S. Army topographical engineers was led by Lt. Stephen Long to the foot of the Rocky Mountains in 1819. In 1838, the division was reorganized into the Corps of Topographical Engineers, commanded by Col. James J. Abert. Most of Abert's engineers were the "best and the brightest" from West Point, the top few from each year's class. Stansbury did not attend West Point, but Abert nonetheless enlisted him in the corps in 1838. He was promoted to captain in 1840.

Born in 1806 in New York City, Howard Stansbury was educated as a civil engineer and worked for several years on a variety of harbor, canal, and railroad projects around the Great Lakes and in Virginia. After joining the army, he returned to work around the Great Lakes, as well as on the harbor facilities at Portsmouth, New Hampshire. In April 1849 Colonel Abert assigned Stansbury to survey the Great Salt Lake and explore the surrounding region. First Lt. John W. Gunnison was assigned to assist him. Gunnison, born in 1812 in New Hampshire, had graduated high in his class at West Point in 1833. His first assignments were in the 1830s guerilla clashes between the U.S. Army and fugitive Indians in Florida called the Seminole Wars. In 1838 he participated in the Removal of the Cherokee people from Tennessee and adjacent regions to Indian Territory, along the tragic "Trail of Tears." In 1839 he transferred to the Corps of Topographical Engineers, working in Georgia and around the Great Lakes.

It is useful to consider the context in which Stansbury and Gunnison undertook their expedition. Between December 1845 and February 1848, by the annexation of Texas, the agreement with Great Britain over the Oregon country, and the treaty ending the Mexican-American War, United States territory increased by more than 1,200,000 square miles. In 1847, the Mormons made their exodus from Missouri to what would become Utah. In April 1848, news of gold in California reached the East. As Stansbury and Gunnison prepared to leave for the West, the great gold rush of 1849 was heating up.

Talk of a transcontinental railroad had begun in the early 1840s. After 1846, and the de facto acquisition of the Southwest, California, and the Oregon country, the question became, which route would the railroad follow? Bitter North-South sectional rivalry soon erupted over which part of the country would get, and thereby profit from, the transcontinental railroad route. In the early 1850s, Congress directed the Corps of Topographical Engineers to create the Pacific Railroad Surveys to examine several potential routes through the northern, central, and southern tiers of states. But even before the official Pacific Railroad Surveys, the Corps of Topographical Engineers was active in "opening" the vast new territory. They were assigned to explore, to map out wagon roads, as well as potential railroad routes, and to study the natural history of the country. They made the first systematic observations of the flora, fauna, geology, climate, and the Indians in much of the Great Plains and the Far West. They did so on numerous expeditions, and left a monumental legacy of Reports of what they did and observed. Stansbury's expedition was, thus, a significant part of the post–1846 effort of western exploration by the Corps of Topographical Engineers.

Stansbury and Gunnison were not the first government, or quasi-government, explorers to reach the Valley of the Great Salt Lake. In 1831, Capt. Benjamin L. E. Bonneville, an army engineer, had resigned his commission, ostensibly to go West and enter the fur trade. But he carried with him orders from the War Department that seem to have made him an "unofficial" spy in British and Mexican territories. (Historians still disagree as to the exact nature of Bonneville's activities. Bonneville established a fort north of the Great Basin. He hired mountain man Joseph Walker and sent him and a party to the Great Salt Lake and beyond, across the Great Basin and into California. The path taken by Walker's party through present-day northern Nevada became the principal emigrant route to California after 1848. Bonneville's explorations were made famous by Washington Irving's 1837 book *The Rocky Mountains: or Scenes, Incidents and Adventures in the Far West, Digested from the Journal of Capt. B. L. E. Bonneville.* . . . In 1843–44, another topographical engineer, John C. Frémont, saw the Great Salt Lake during his trek westward. His expedition's ultimate purpose was clearly, but more openly, in the vein of those led by Lewis and Clark, Pike, and Bonneville. Frémont was the first to recognize that the Great Basin (actually some 120 valley-basins divided by mountain ranges) was an area of internal drainage: no rivers therein flowed to the sea. Frémont also discovered and named Pyramid Lake in western Nevada on the same expedition.

While Stansbury's primary assignment was to survey the Great Salt Lake and explore the region around it, he was also to seek a better wagon road between Fort Bridger in Wyoming and Salt Lake City, and to look at the country in terms of a potential route for a transcontinental railroad. His expedition did not begin auspiciously. Cholera was raging in Missouri when he started. Gunnison apparently had it, and began the trip in bed aboard a spring wagon. As California gold fever increased, many of the men deserted and headed for the "Diggings." When the party arrived in Salt Lake City, the Mormons feared the soldiers were there to spy, or to wreak government reprisal against them. But Stansbury gained Mormon leader Brigham Young's confidence, and indeed came to have considerable admiration for the Mormons, as his *Report* attests. Gunnison too was sympathetic to the Mormons. His 1852 book *The Mormons, or Latter-Day Saints, in the Valley of the Great Salt Lake, a History of Their Rise and Progress, Peculiar Doctrines, Present Conditions and Projects* presents a fair and objective view of the Mormons. But Stansbury's and Gunnison's apologies went largely unheeded in the inflammatory times of the 1850s. By 1857, relations between the Mormons and the United States had been fanned into an impasse, and President James Buchanan sent a contingent of the U.S. Army to Utah to quell the Mormon "insurrection." It was the first major maneuver in a government campaign against Mormon polygamy and independence that did not cease until the Mormon church officially renounced plural marriage in the 1890s. In the history of this forty-year battle over the "Mormon question," and all the heated rhetoric that fueled it, Stansbury's and Gunnison's moderate and generally objective views of early Mormon life and practices in Utah stand out.

In 1853 Gunnison, now a captain, returned to Utah, this time leading one of the Pacific Railroad Survey parties. He was assigned the 38th parallel route through the Central Rocky Mountains and on across the Great Basin. In late October 1853 his party reached Sevier Lake, Utah, southwest of the Great Salt Lake. There in an attack by Pahvant Ute Indians, Gunnison and six others, including the artist Richard Kern, who had worked with several Corps of Topographical Engineers parties, were killed and mutilated.

Stansbury's *Report* was submitted to the army and ordered printed as a congressional document in 1852. It became immediately popular and was reprinted several times in the following years by the Lippincott publishing firm of Philadelphia. Some of the popularity undoubtedly was due to Stansbury's description of the Mormons and the lives they had established for themselves in the Great Basin. In the decade following, Stansbury returned to engineering work around the Great Lakes. At the onset of the Civil War he was assigned duties as a mustering officer, retired briefly, and then reentered the army, serving as mustering and disbursing officer in Madison, Wisconsin, until his death in 1863.

Stansbury's *Report* reflects both the person and his accomplishments. He clearly had a keen eye and a lively wit. His droll description of the symbiotic underground household arrangements of prairie dogs, rattle-snakes, and burrowing owls is engaging. His descriptions of the Indian people he encountered are both sympathetic and ethnographically useful to later anthropologists. While Frémont, and before him, Joseph Walker and other mountain men, had skirted portions of the perimeter of the Great Salt Lake, Stansbury was the first to successfully encircle the entire lake, with great effort, as he graphically relates in his *Report*. He was the first to point out that the Great Salt Lake is but a remnant of a much larger body of water, "a vast *inland* sea," as he called it. Three decades later, the geologist Clarence King would recognize that Frémont's Pyramid Lake is the remnant of prehistoric Lake Lahontan, another vast body of water that existed in the Great Basin during Ice Age times. A second government geologist, Grove Karl Gilbert, would name Stansbury's inland sea prehistoric Lake Bonneville, for the intrepid captain. One of the Ice Age terraces of Lake Bonneville is called the Stansbury Terrace. Stansbury and Gunnison named islands in the Salt Lake after themselves, and one after Frémont. Gunnison is also remembered by a county, a town, and a river in Colorado, and a town and a reservoir in Utah.

The system of triangulation used by Stansbury and Gunnison to map the Great Salt Lake region was the first application of the procedure by the Corps of Topographical Engineers in the West, and among the first in North America. It was a marked improvement over other methods then in use, although Stansbury's descriptions of the struggles to establish the fixed points indicate the difficulties involved. Maj. William Helmsley Emory, of the Corps of Topographical Engineers, used the procedure with great success during the United States-Mexican Boundary Survey of the 1850s. It was the system adopted by the four "Great Surveys" of the 1870s, the U.S. Geographical and Geological Surveys led by Lt. George Wheeler, Clarence King, F. V. Hayden, and John Wesley Powell which succeeded the Corps of Topographical Engineers in western exploration after the Civil War. The transcontinental railroad route that Stansbury recommended—up the Platte River, across southern Wyoming, and especially the route he found through the tangled topography of the Wasatch Mountains into the Great Salt Lake Valley—was ultimately the route chosen. Farther west it followed Walker's path down the Humboldt River in Nevada. On May 10, 1869, the last spike was driven at Promontory Point, Utah, a place Stansbury had explored during his circuit of the Salt Lake. Finally, Stansbury's objective, yet sympathetic, portrayal of the Mormons' lives, beliefs, and first two years in their "Great Basin Kingdom" was recognized at the time as a major statement.

Stansbury's *Report* is reprinted here without Appendix G, Meteorological Observations, which can be found in the original volume. His *Report* remains an important historic and cultural document of the great saga of the exploration and settlement of the American West. It is a great pleasure to have it made available once more.

Don D. Fowler
University of Nevada, Reno
September 1987

Exploration of the
Valley of the Great Salt Lake

FORT UTAH ON THE TIMPANOGAS. — VALLEY OF THE GREAT SALT LAKE.

Ackerman Lith 379 Broadway N.Y

SPECIAL SESSION,}   𝕾𝖊𝖓𝖆𝖙𝖊.   { EXECUTIVE.
March, 1851. }   { No. 3.

"

EXPLORATION AND SURVEY

OF THE

VALLEY

OF THE

GREAT SALT LAKE OF UTAH,

INCLUDING

A RECONNOISSANCE OF A NEW ROUTE THROUGH THE ROCKY MOUNTAINS.

BY HOWARD STANSBURY,

CAPTAIN CORPS TOPOGRAPHICAL ENGINEERS,
U. S. ARMY.

PRINTED BY ORDER OF THE SENATE OF THE UNITED STATES

PHILADELPHIA:
LIPPINCOTT, GRAMBO & CO.
1852.

BUREAU TOPOGRAPHICAL ENGINEERS, }
19th *April*, 1852. }

SIR:

I have the honour to submit a copy of CAPTAIN STANSBURY'S Report of his Expedition to the Salt Lake, called for by a resolution of the Senate of the 12th of March, 1851.

Respectfully, Sir,

Your obedient servant,

J. J. ABERT,

Col. Corps Top. Eng'rs.

HON. C. M. CONRAD, *Secretary Department of War.*

WAR DEPARTMENT, }
Washington, April 19th, 1852. }

HON. W. R. KING, *President of the Senate.*

SIR:

IN compliance with a resolution of the Senate, passed March 12th, 1851, I have the honour to transmit herewith " A Copy of the Report of CAPTAIN HOWARD STANSBURY, of the Corps of Topographical Engineers, of his Exploration of the Valley of the Great Salt Lake."

I have the honour to be,

Very respectfully,

Your obedient servant,

C. M. CONRAD,

Secretary of War.

Printed by T. K. & P. G. Collins.

INTRODUCTION.

In preparing this Report of the Exploration of the Valley of the Great Salt Lake, I have occasionally availed myself of the notes and journals of the other members of the expedition, where they tended to elucidate facts of which I was not personally cognizant. Generally, those here given are the result of my own observation. It is a subject of much regret that the exigencies of the service so hastened our departure, as to give but little time for preparations so necessary to the proper outfit of a party about to engage in an extensive exploration. The instruments that could be obtained upon so short a notice, were not of a character suited to the purposes for which they were required; and the want of such facilities proved the occasion of no little vexation and delay. The pressure upon the Bureau of Topographical Engineers would allow of the detail of but a single officer to aid me—a force entirely inadequate to the satisfactory performance of the multifarious and arduous duties required in the course of so long, and so widely-extended, an examination. The illness of that officer, during the whole of the journey from the Missouri to Green River, deprived me altogether of his much-needed services, and threw upon myself, alone, the whole burden of that portion of the reconnoissance.

In a part of the Survey of the Utah Valley, we were aided by Lieut. G. W. Howland, of the regiment of Mounted Rifles, who was detailed from the command at Cantonment

3

Loring, for the purpose; but who, before its completion, was required to rejoin his regiment, for service on the Pacific coast.

In the Department of Natural Science, from my very limited time, I was not successful in securing the services of a competent assistant. Yet, although as much has not been accomplished as I had anticipated, it is hoped that some additional light has been thrown upon the Geological formation and Natural History of these almost unknown regions. The papers of Professors Baird, Haldeman, Torrey, and Hall, together with the analyses of Dr. Gale, will not be without interest to the lovers of science. To these gentlemen, and to Messrs. Girard & Peale, I am much indebted for the labours which, from a regard to the general interests of science, they have bestowed toward rendering the present report more complete and satisfactory.

In what has been said respecting the Mormon community, I have endeavoured frankly to present the impressions produced upon my mind by a somewhat intimate acquaintance of a year's duration with both rulers and people. The intelligence of their organization into a Territorial Government, had not reached the valley when we left it. How far the change in their relations to the country, may, as has been asserted, have revolutionized the feelings of the people, it is impossible for me to say. But no representations, that have yet been made public, have served in the least to alter my expressed opinion of their character for either love to the country, or loyalty to the government. Since the return of the expedition, it has appeared evident that the nature of the domestic relations of the Mormons has been very generally misapprehended. It seems that the "spiritual wife system," as it has been very improperly denominated, has been supposed to be nothing more nor less than the unbridled license of indiscriminate intercourse between the sexes, either openly practised by all, or indulged, to the invasion of individual rights, by the spiritual leaders. Nothing can be further from the real'state of the case. The tie that binds a Mormon to his second, third, or fourth wife, is just as strong, sacred, and indissoluble, as that which unites him to his first. Although this assumption of new marriage bonds be called "*Sealing*," it is contracted, not secretly, but under the solemn sanctions of a religious ceremony, in the presence, and with the approbation and consent of relatives and friends. Whatever may be thought of the morality of this practice, none can fail to perceive that it exhibits a state of things entirely different from the gross licentiousness which is generally thought to prevail in this community, and which, were it the case, would justly commend itself to the unmingled abhorrence of the whole civilized world. The recent acquittal of a Mormon Elder for shooting the seducer of one of his wives, on the ground that the act was one of justifiable homicide, fully corroborates the truth of this remark, and shows in how strong a light the sacredness and exclusive character of such relations are viewed by the Mormons themselves.

The route pursued by the expedition on its return, through a pass in the mountains hitherto unknown, will, perhaps, lead to further investigation of that remarkable depression lying between the Park Mountains and the South Pass. That a feasible route may be traced through this depression has been satisfactorily demonstrated; and the saving in distance cannot but prove an object of importance, either in the establishment of a post route, or in the construction of a railway communication across the continent. The development of the inexhaustible mineral resources of the coal basin of the Green River valley, may be found, and at no very distant period, to go far toward lessening the obstacles which at present exist in the settlement of a country so destitute of other fuel. It is to be hoped that the government will not discontinue the further examination of these most interesting regions. From the heads of the Arkansas to the northern boundary of the republic, lies a field possessing mineral and agricultural resources sufficient, were they more fully known and explored, for the sustenance of a population equal to that of the original thirteen states of the Union. Constituting, as it does, a sort of neutral ground between widely separated portions of this vast country, what can be more obviously desirable than that its character should be more fully known, its hidden sources of wealth developed, and rendered available to the enterprise of our ever advancing population?

In conclusion, I take much pleasure in acknowledging the efficient and faithful services of my friend and assistant, Lieut. J. W. Gunnison, of the Corps of Topographical Engineers. To high professional skill, he added energy, judgment, and an untiring devotion to the interests of the expedition, which very materially contributed to its success. Whilst confined to winter quarters in Salt Lake City, he paid particular attention to the religious doctrines and practices of the Mormon Church, the results of which, as I understand, he is about publishing to the world. The subject will doubtless prove of great interest to the theologian, and, indeed, to all who have watched, with any attention, the progress, in this country, of the various extravagant theories, civil and religious, which form so marked a characteristic of the present age.

CONTENTS.

8 CONTENTS.

CHAPTER VIII.

CHAPTER IX.

APPENDIX A.

10   CONTENTS.

APPENDIX B.

APPENDIX C.

ZOOLOGY.

APPENDIX D.

BOTANY.

APPENDIX E.

GEOLOGY AND PALÆONTOLOGY.

APPENDIX F.

CHEMICAL ANALYSES.

LIST OF ILLUSTRATIONS.

STANSBURY'S REPORT.

CHAPTER I.

Washington, March 10, 1852.

COLONEL JOHN J. ABERT,
Chief of Bureau of Topographical Engineers.

SIR:—I have the honour to submit to the Bureau of Topographical Engineers the following report of the results of an expedition, organized in obedience to your orders of April 11, 1849, having for its object a survey of the Great Salt Lake, and an exploration of its valley.

Your instructions required me to report to the commanding officer of the regiment of Mounted Rifles, at Fort Leavenworth, on the 10th of May following, and directed me to accompany those troops on their route to Oregon as far as Fort Hall, at which point I was to separate from the command and prosecute the examinations required. Owing to causes beyond my control, and of which the bureau is already aware, I did not reach Fort Leavenworth until after the departure of the Rifle Regiment from that post, and was consequently obliged to make such change in my arrangements as the circumstances required. The necessary outfit and provisions were obtained from the proper departments of the army, and the party enlarged and well armed, to enable it to protect itself from any danger or depredation to which it might be exposed from tribes of roving or hostile Indians. I wish here to express my obligation to Colonel Sumner, the commanding officer at Fort Leavenworth, and to the quartermaster, Major Ogden, as well for the prompt and efficient aid rendered by them as for the kind interest they evinced in the success of the expedition. Every facility was cheerfully accorded, and every thing conducive to our comfort most liberally supplied. We were much delayed, however, by the heavy drafts made upon the resources

13

of the post for outfits and transportation furnished to several heavy trains for Oregon, New Mexico, and California, as well as by a panic occasioned by exaggerated reports of the existence of the cholera at the post; which caused the desertion of forty teamsters and mechanics in one night. Not a hand was to be hired, nor could the quartermaster furnish me with a single teamster. I was consequently obliged to send an express to Kansas for the necessary additional force.

Before leaving Fort Leavenworth, we were joined by a small party of emigrants for California, who desired to travel in our company for the sake of protection, and who continued with us as far as Salt Lake City. This proved a fortunate arrangement, since we thereby secured the society of an excellent and intelligent lady, who not only, by her cheerfulness and vivacity, beguiled the tedium of many a monotonous and wearisome hour, but, by her fortitude and patient endurance of exposure and fatigue, set an example worthy the imitation of many of the ruder sex.

The cholera had for a considerable time been raging on the Missouri; and as we passed up, fearful rumours of its prevalence and fatality among the emigrants on the route daily reached us from the plains. On the day we left Fort Leavenworth, one member of our little party was carried to the hospital in a state of collapse, where he died in twenty-four hours. The only officer attached to my command had been ill for several weeks, with severe attacks of intermittent fever, which now merged into chronic dysentery, and he was, in consequence, unable to sit on his horse, or to do duty of any kind. These were rather discouraging circumstances for an outset; but, at length, on the 31st day of May, our preparations being completed, we commenced our journey, my own party consisting in all of eighteen men, five wagons, and forty-six horses and mules; while that of Mr. Sackett, our fellow-traveller, contained six persons, one wagon, one travelling carriage, and fifteen animals. Lieutenant Gunnison, being too ill to travel in any other manner, was carried on his bed, in a large spring wagon, which had been procured for the transportation of the instruments. The weather, in the morning, had been dark and lowering, with occasional showers, but it cleared off about noon; the camp broke up; the wagons were packed, and we prepared to exchange, for a season, the comforts and refinements of civilized life, for the somewhat wild and roving habits of the hunter and the savage. My party consisted principally of experienced *voy-*

ugeurs, who had spent the best part of their lives among the wilds of the Rocky Mountains, and to whom this manner of life had become endeared by old associations. We followed the "emigration road," (already broad and well beaten as any turnpike in our country,) over a rolling prairie, fringed on the south with trees. The hills consisted principally of carboniferous limestone, in apparently horizontal strata, which in places formed quite prominent escarpments. Our first day's journey was only of six miles; but we were now fairly embarked, and things gradually assumed the appearance of order and regularity.

Although the route taken by the party has been travelled by thousands of people, both before and since we passed over it, I have thought that some brief extracts from the daily journals of the expedition might not be without interest; for, although nothing very new may perhaps be elicited, still it is not improbable that they will convey, to such as peruse them, a more correct idea of what the thousands have had to encounter who have braved this long journey in search either of a new home in Oregon, or of that more alluring object—the glittering treasure of California.

Friday, June 1.—Bar. at sunrise, 20.86; Ther. 63°. The road for the first few miles wound along the fence of what appeared to be a large, neglected Indian farm, following for about nine miles the dividing ridge between the waters of the Missouri and those of the Kansas, with deep ravines inclining to the northeast. The ridge terminated in a steep hill, at the bottom of which we found Walnut Creek, running to the south. By an escarpment on the west side, the rock was found to be of the same character as that passed over yesterday. At 3½ o'clock, we descended by a steep and somewhat dangerous road, to the valley of a small and beautiful stream running north, upon the left bank of which we encamped, near the edge of a wood, fringing the stream, in which black-walnut, white-oak, and hickory predominated. A short distance from the camp, to the north, are high limestone bluffs, without trees.

In the course of the afternoon we passed the travelling-train of a Mr. Allen, consisting of about twenty-five ox-teams, bound for the land of gold. They had been on the spot several days, detained by sickness. One of the party had died but the day before of cholera, and two more were then down with the same disease. In the morning early, we had met four men from the same camp, returning on foot, with their effects on their backs, frightened at the danger and disgusted already with the trip. It was here that we first saw a train "*corralled.*" The wagons were drawn up in the form of a circle and chained together, leaving a small opening at but one place, through which the cattle were driven into the enclosed space at night, and guarded. The arrangement is an excellent one, and rendered impossible what is called, in Western phrase, a "stampede"—a mode of assault practised by Indians for the purpose of carrying off cattle or horses, in which, if possible, they set loose some of the animals, and so frighten the rest as to produce a general and confused flight of the whole. To a few determined men, wagons thus arranged form a breastwork exceedingly difficult to be carried by any force of undisciplined savages.—Occasional showers during the day. Evening clear and pleasant, with a bright moon. Day's travel, twelve miles.

Saturday, June 2.—Bar. 29.17; Ther. 64°. The general course to-day has been north-west, over a rolling prairie country, indented by deep ravines, formed by numerous small streams flowing into the Missouri, which runs eight or ten miles to the north-east. In crossing a steep ravine in the forks of one of these affluents of that river, a part of one of the wagons was broken, the repair of which occupied the remainder of the day, and obliged us to encamp on the left bank of the stream, the bluff of which was quite steep. Near the top of the bank was a stratum of shale about two feet thick; the overlying limestone being considerably undermined by disintegration: over the limestone was a layer of light-coloured friable sandstone. In the shale, no fossils were discovered, but the limestone contained stems of encrinites. The strata appeared to be horizontal. Grass and water are here very abundant, and fine springs are to be found on the south side of the stream, which is richly wooded. Day's travel, seven miles.

Sunday, June 3.—Bar. 29.01; Ther. 80°. Camp not moved to-day. The cliff on the north side of the creek was traced for about a mile up the stream. The shale continues horizontal. In some parts it was dark, and apparently carboniferous, but no fossils were discovered in it. Above it the limestone was sandy and ferruginous, and the upper layers contained many fossils,—spirifer, productus, &c.,—mixed with small shells. The cliff was from one hundred and fifty to two hundred feet high, facing north-west.

Monday, June 4.—Bar. 29.18; Ther. 65°. The road in the morning was very sinuous, from its following the crest of a high ridge to avoid the spurs and ravines on the right. We are now fairly on the broad open prairie; the air fresh, cool, and delightful; the view on all sides very extensive. In the afternoon we were met by a small band of Sauk Indians, who presented a paper, written by some philanthropic emigrant, representing that as we were now passing through their country, consuming their grass, water, and wood, (the latter of which was very scarce) they wished to receive something by way of remuneration, whether money, biscuit, (of which they are very fond,) or tobacco. They were rather a fine-looking body of men, and seemed quite peaceably disposed. They were evidently on the look-out for the different companies as they passed, with the purpose of levying contributions. They accompanied us to camp, and received some biscuit and tobacco, with which they seemed well satisfied.

The formation passed over to-day has been the same as that observed heretofore, except that the shales appear to be rather more predominant, and the limestone more ferruginous, and perhaps more siliceous. In a deep ravine the shales were very evident, being in some places washed out to a great extent from the overlying limestone, which presented large tabular massès, in place, in which no dip was discovered.

Tuesday, June 5.—Bar. 29.17; Ther. 70°. The country traversed to-day has been principally rolling prairie, rising gradually for about six miles; our road, following the crest of a ridge, with heads of ravines from the north and the south interlocking, was rendered both crooked and undulating. After tracing this winding track for some time, we entered the main emigration road from Kansas. Up to this point the road has been very good—smooth, hard, and dry, and free from abrupt descents or ascents. The country around us is entirely destitute of trees; not so much as a twig is to be seen; all is bald, naked prairie, with sweeping undulations of the surface, as if a heavy ground-swell of the ocean had been suddenly arrested and converted, by the wand of some enchanter, into fixed and solid soil.

Rain came on about noon, with occasional showers, until nearly sunset, when it cleared off, with high wind from the south. Ferruginous and slaty limestones were occasionally exposed in the ravines, very fossiliferous, containing principally testacea. Some stems of crinoideæ were also found in the rock, in place. Plover and prairie hens were now seen very frequently; the former, however, for the first time, and very shy. In the afternoon, we met a

2

small party of travellers, with a sick man in a wagon. They proved to be returning emigrants, who, after proceeding as far as Fort Kearny, had lost heart, sold out all they had, (their flour and bacon at one cent per pound,) and were now slowly and sadly wending their way back to their homes. They assured us that many more were in the same melancholy case. Day's march, fourteen miles.

June 6.—Camp up by 4 A. M.   Bar. 28.75; Ther. 70°.   Wind south-east; clouds heavy and threatening.   It shortly commenced raining hard, and continued until nearly noon.   The ground to-day has been strewed with pebbles of granite, quartz, and porphyry, and also with large blocks of porphyritic granite.   On the tops of the hills, limestone again appeared; it was non-fossiliferous, and rather sandy.   About five miles from camp we crossed a small stream, from which were procured some specimens of spirifer. Under this rock was a non-fossiliferous stratum and then shale. The upper stratum was not in place.   In the afternoon we passed a melancholy memento of disappointed hope and blasted enter-prise—four freshly-made graves of emigrants, who had died by the way, and were here left on the wide waste, with not a name to pre-serve their remembrance.   How different such a fate from the high and sanguine prospects with which they had set out!

In the evening a heavy thunder-storm from the south-east, with rain and violent wind.   Day's travel, twenty miles.

June 7.—Bar. 28.43; Ther. 68°.   The travelling to-day is heavy, in consequence of the rains of yesterday.   The road lies through a rolling prairie and upon a ridge dividing the waters of the Missouri from those of the Big Blue river, a tributary of the Kansas.   Met a Mr. Brulet, a French trader, from Fort La-ramie, with a large train of wagons, laden with packs of buffalo-robes, bound for St. Louis.   He had been forty days on the road, and had met not less than four thousand wagons, averaging four persons to a wagon.   This large number of emigrants appeared to him to be getting along rather badly, from their want of experi-ence as to the proper mode of travelling on the prairies, to which cause much of the suffering experienced on these plains is doubt-less to be ascribed.   We availed ourselves of his offer to carry back letters to our friends at home.

In the course of the morning, passed the fresh grave of a poor fellow whose last resting-place had been partially disturbed by the wolves.   They had burrowed a large hole near the head, which,

however, had been subsequently filled up with sticks by some com-
passionate traveller. It was an affecting object, and no good omen
of what might be looked for, should any of us fall by the way in
our long and arduous journey. Upon a ridge near our noon halt,
was found considerable detritus of primitive rocks, scattered over
the surface of the ground, and many boulders of granite. Above
this lay the limestone, the lower strata of which appeared to be
composed of honey-comb limestone; the upper strata were more
sandy and without fossils. After a march of seventeen and three-
fourths miles, encamped on the left bank of what our guide called
Legerette Creek. The banks, at the crossing, were high and steep,
and afforded some very good sections of limestones interspersed
with shales. A road had been made, with no little trouble, by the
emigrants, down the banks on each side, and the crossing was tolerably good. The stream is thirty feet wide by one foot deep, and
flows with a bold and rapid current into the Missouri. The strata,
exposed by a section at the crossing, the direction of which was
S. S. E. and N. N. W., were limestones with strata of shales, conformable, with a marked dip of 12° to the west, and containing a
considerable number of fossils, productus, spirifer, &c. Our camp
for the night is situated on the edge of a beautifully broad and
level prairie, nearly elliptical in form, almost encircled by this
lovely stream, whose banks are fringed with the richest foliage:
noble old oaks, elms, and walnuts overhang the water, with a background of rising hills covered with grass and flowers.

Friday, June 8.—Bar. at sunrise, 28.79; Ther. 68°. Wind
north-east, cool and delightful. A small party, with a single
wagon, drove into camp just as we were leaving the ground. They
had formed part of a company from St. Louis, had proceeded
within sixty miles of Fort Kearny, but had quarrelled, and become disgusted with the trip and with each other, and had separated. These persons were on their return to St. Louis. They
gave discouraging accounts of matters ahead. Wagons, they said,
could be bought, upon the route of emigration, for from ten to fifteen dollars apiece, and provisions for almost nothing all. So
much for arduous enterprises rashly undertaken, and prosecuted
without previous knowledge or suitable preparation! What else
could be expected? The road to-day has been quite circuitous,
ranging from S. by W. to W. by N. We have been following the
ridge dividing the two main forks of Legerette Creek, just above
the junction of which we encamped last night. Extensive grassy

slopes descended from the road on each side of us as we gradually ascended the ridge. From our elevated position, the course and windings of either branch of the stream could plainly be traced by the fringes of rich timber which clothed their banks, while the dull uniformity of the prairie was agreeably relieved by the ravines of numerous tributary waters, extending almost to the crest of the ridge over which we travelled, and wooded to their very heads. As we continued to rise with the country, the graceful undulations of the naked hills and hollows contrasted agreeably with the waving lines of hickory and oak that marked the course of each little rivulet until it joined its destined stream, and formed together a landscape which, for extent and rich picturesque beauty, cannot easily be surpassed. The country generally begins to present a more sandy appearance than heretofore, and the rock to be composed of extremely friable materials, from the decomposition of which results much sand impregnated with iron and shale, together with a great deal of gravel. The examination of a ravine near the morning's camp, the north side of which was very precipitous and about a hundred and fifty feet in height, exhibited a section from N. to S. of the upper strata of rocks, which were in this direction horizontal, but with a dip to the west. The strata consisted of layers of shales, sand, and detritus of older rocks, mixed with sand—all very friable. In the bottom, limestone again appeared. On a hill opposite, the limestone was found cropping out with a dip to the west. The country to-day has presented a different aspect from that heretofore passed over; being intersected by deep ravines, most of which are heavily wooded to near the summit of the ridge. We encamped at the head of one of these, in a handsome grove of timber, after a drive of seventeen and a half miles.

Saturday, June 9.—Bar. 28.66; Ther. 63°. Morning cool and sky overcast. The road continued to ascend for a few miles, when we crossed the Big Vermilion, (a tributary of the Big Blue,) which heads a mile to the N. E. The crossing is miry. In the afternoon, encamped on the right bank of the Big Blue, near a spring of fine water, on the margin of a level prairie, bordered with huge trees, under the welcome shade of which we pitched our tents after a fatiguing march of twenty-six miles.

The stream is here about seventy yards wide and three feet deep, flowing with a bold current, and is tolerably well wooded. We found the trees and stumps on its banks carved all over with the names of hundreds of emigrants who had preceded us, the dates of their passing, the state of their health and spirits, together with an occasional message for their friends who were expected to follow. Such a record, in the midst of a wide solitude like this, could not but make a strong and cheering impression on every new-comer, who thus suddenly found himself, as it were, in the midst of a great company of friends and fellow-travellers. On the left bank was the freshly-made grave of a French trader, whose name was well known to most of our *voyageurs*. It was heaped up with earth and covered longitudinally with heavy split logs, placed there to prevent the depredations of the wolves; the whole being surmounted by a wooden cross, with the name of the deceased and the usual significant abbreviation, I H S, carved rudely upon it. We had passed six graves already during the day. Melancholy accompaniments they are of a road silent and solitary at best, and ill calculated to cheer the weary, drooping wayfarers. Our encampment was pleasantly situated under the spreading branches of some large oaks, with a spring of pure, cold water near at hand—the latter an item which we soon afterward learned to value beyond all price. Just above us was a wagon with a small party of emigrants. They had lost most of their cattle on the journey; and the father of three of them having died on the road, they, in conformity with his dying wishes, were now on their return to the settlements. A short distance beyond these, we found another small company, who had been encamped here for twelve days on account of the illness of one of their comrades. They also were on their return. Had we been going out on a private enterprise, discouragements were not wanting as well from the dead as the living.

Since crossing the Vermilion, the character of the country has changed from that of a high and rolling prairie to a comparatively flat and elevated plateau, with the drains much broader and not so depressed as heretofore. The soil is much deeper, the trees larger and more numerous, and the water cooler and more abundant. White sandstone, light-coloured shales, some flints, and a few fossils, were passed during the day. At the crossing of a small branch, about two miles before reaching the Big Blue, the rock exhibited a section from north to south, nearly horizontal, with perhaps a slight dip to the south. It consisted of white limestone and strata of flint, with some imperfect fossils. The general surface of the rock is worn into escarpments in the shape of bastions,

with numerous terraces rising one above the other, having a striking and picturesque effect. Some shales are interspersed among
the chalky limestone. Here also were seen several small boulders
of red granite. Some good-sized catfish were caught in the Blue
by the men, during the night.

Sunday, June 10.—Bar. 28.82; Ther. 70°. The camp rested,
it having been determined, from the commencement of the expedition, to devote this day, whenever practicable, to its legitimate
purpose, as an interval of rest for man and beast. I here beg to
record, as the result of my experience, derived not only from the
present journey, but from the observation of many years spent in
the performance of similar duties, that, as a mere matter of pecuniary consideration, apart from all higher obligations, it is wise to
keep the Sabbath. More work can be obtained from both men
and animals by its observance, than where the whole seven days
are uninterruptedly devoted to labour.

Very early in the morning it was discovered that three horses
from our herd, and one from a neighbouring encampment, had
been stolen during the night, and that so adroitly as not to occasion
the slightest noise, although our animals were all picketed in the
very centre of the camp and within a few feet of the tents. Search
was forthwith made for the trail of the robbers, which was soon
found, and ascertained to be that of Indians. Two parties of
scouts were despatched in pursuit. In the mean time, the ammunition chests were opened, additional cartridges served out, arms
examined and reloaded, the men practised in shooting at a mark,
and every preparation made to guard against a repetition of the
outrage. In a few hours one of the parties, under Archambault,
the guide, an experienced hunter and mountaineer, returned, but
without the animals. They had crossed the Blue at the ford, and
followed the trail of the Indians about six miles, but here the latter had recrossed, and taken to the hard open prairie, where all
further trace of them was lost, and the pursuit in consequence
given up. They found, however, the spot where the Indian party
had encamped the day previous, marked by the fragments of an
ox they had just stolen from a neighbouring train. They had
taken two; one they had killed and devoured, leaving in their
haste the yoke and hide of the slaughtered animal, together with
a small portion of the meat, while they made off with the horses,
and drove the other ox before them. The robbers were Pawnees,
and had evidently been watching ever since our arrival, as they

had selected the very best horses in both trains, all of which, to make the matter worse, happened to be private property. Effective measures should certainly be taken to punish and thereby prevent the occurrence of these outrages by a band of savages, who, although receiving a large annuity from the national treasury, take every opportunity to prey upon those under the protection of the government. Several large catfish and some soft-shelled turtle were caught in the stream by the men. The rich bottom in the rear of the camp produces strawberries of fine quality in the utmost profusion; the men gathered them by hatfuls. Two very large terrapins were also found here on the prairie.

In the afternoon, the advance of a train from St. Joseph, belonging to Messrs. Bissonet and Badeau, bound on a trading expedition among the Sioux, passed the camp and halted on the bluff beyond. Mr. Bissonet, who is an old trader and appears to be well acquainted with the country, informed me that the stream called by our guides the Legerette is in fact the Nemaha; and that the streams called by Frémont, Great and Little Nemahas are the waters of Turkey Creek, and flow into the Blue to the north of the road. A section of about one hundred feet high, in a ravine on the south side of the river, showed the strata to be horizontal from north to south, with a dip of ten degrees to the west. The order of superposition was as follows:—Lower, most visible, red clay and sand; gray shales; blue limestone; gray limestone, and flint; white sandstone. They all contained fossils except the clay. A species of mallow and *Œnothera* occurred on the bottoms of the streams, with *Digitalis* and *Loasa nitida*. Phlox, once abundant, is becoming scarce.

Monday, June 11.—Bar. 28.56; Ther. 65°. At half-past five o'clock, a most violent storm of wind and rain set in, and raged with great fury for three hours. The tents were prostrated, and the baggage much wetted by the rain. Several large trees were blown down, and one fell across an emigrant wagon close by us. The owners, who had sought refuge in it from the tempest, narrowly escaped with their lives. About nine, it cleared, and the tents were raised to allow them to dry. Eight miles from the Blue, we struck the emigration road from Independence. Here we found a company of seventy or eighty persons, with some twenty wagons, on their way to California, among whom I recognised several former *compagnons de voyage* on the Missouri. After crossing Ketchum's Creek, encamped a short distance to the right of the road,

on one of the head branches of Turkey Creek, the channel
of which appeared to be cut deeply into the detritus of a sandstone slightly ferruginous.   Near the Blue, the highest rock observed was ferruginous sandstone, and during the day an imperfect section exposed shaly limestone and white sandstone.   Our
course has lately been rising with the country, and we have been
traversing a sort of plateau, having, however, no very marked
ridges, but being intersected in all directions by ravines, the sides
of which have but a moderate slope and little fall, with water
standing in pools.   Passed six graves to-day.   Day's march, seventeen and a-quarter miles.

Tuesday, June 12.—Bar. 28.64; Ther. 63°.   Breakfast at four.
In ten and a half miles crossed the west branch of Turkey Creek,
and halted to noon on the bank of Wyeth's Creek, six miles beyond.   The crossing here is bad and rocky, and the grass poor,
having been eaten close by the trains which had preceded us.
The afternoon was oppressively hot and close, the wind being
from the eastward, with every appearance of rain.   We have been
in company with multitudes of emigrants the whole day.   The
road has been lined to a long extent with their wagons, whose
white covers, glittering in the sunlight, resembled, at a distance,
ships upon the ocean.   We passed a company from Boston, consisting of seventy persons, one hundred and forty pack and riding
mules, a number of riding horses, and a drove of cattle for beef.
The expedition, as might be expected, and as is too generally the
case, was badly conducted: the mules were overloaded, and the manner of securing and arranging the packs elicited many a sarcastic
criticism from our party, most of whom were old and experienced
mountain-men, with whom the making up of a pack and the loading of a mule amounted to a science.   We passed also an old
Dutchman, with an immense wagon, drawn by six yoke of cattle,
and loaded with household furniture.   Behind, followed a covered
cart containing the wife, driving herself, and a host of babies—
the whole bound to the land of promise, of the distance to which,
however, they seemed to have not the most remote idea.   To the
tail of the cart was attached a large chicken-coop, full of fowls;
two milch-cows followed, and next came an old mare, upon the
back of which was perched a little, brown-faced, barefooted girl,
not more than seven years old, while a small sucking colt brought
up the rear.   We had occasion to see this old gentleman and his
caravan frequently afterward, as we passed and repassed each

other, from time to time, on the' road. The last we saw of him was on the Sweetwater, engaged in sawing his wagon into two parts, for the purpose of converting it into two carts, and in disposing of every thing he could sell or give away, to lighten his load.

Œnothera, with its bright yellow flowers, was frequent in the landscape, both to-day and yesterday, with *Amorpha* and *Artemisia*. The prairie-rose is becoming quite abundant.

Near Wyeth's Creek, a section showed the upper rocks, near the top of a ridge, to consist of dark ferruginous sandstone, under which were white clayey shales, the soil being formed principally by decomposed sandstone.

After travelling twenty-six miles, we encamped on the level bank of Walnut Creek—a tributary of the Little Blue, with a tolerable supply of grass and water. Near this encampment, a small section showed the formation to consist of red sandstone, apparently horizontal, very friable, and containing traces of organic remains, but none recognisable. Under the sandstone were traces of shale, light-coloured and very sandy. Black iron-ore was discovered in the sandstone.

Wednesday, June 13.—About two o'clock in the morning, the camp was suddenly aroused by the bursting upon it of a most furious storm. The wind blew a hurricane, the rain fell in torrents, while the thunder and lightning were terrible and incessant. Fortunately the camp had been pitched in a sheltered spot, or it must have been entirely blown away by the tempest: as it was, the tents were prostrated by the wind, and preserved with much difficulty. Our men were exposed to all its fury for several hours. At length, however, the sky partially cleared, but the lowering enemy seemed still to linger, as if meditating another attack. The morning proved exceedingly hot and close; the barometer continued to fall. Our poor mules having been picketed within the lines all night, and consequently exposed to the storm, seemed dejected, tired, and hollow; and altogether the camp seemed weary and dispirited. The weather looked so very doubtful that we did not move until half-past two o'clock; the men being until then engaged in drying their bedding, which had been thoroughly soaked by the rain. An immense number of black beetles and other insects swarmed around the camp last evening. Attracted by the light, they annoyed us beyond measure, and could be heard all night, pattering against the tents like large drops of rain in a heavy shower.

Amorpha, Commelina, and *Artemisia* are still abundant, but the phlox is disappearing. In the bottom of the creek a species of larkspur and wild-onion abound; our men used the latter freely, and we found them quite palatable in flavouring our bean-soup. Shortly after resuming the march, we reached the dividing height between a tributary of Emigrant's Creek and Sandy Creek, another affluent of the Little Blue. The view here was extensive and very beautiful. The Sandy and its numerous small tributaries could be distinctly traced in all their sinuous courses, by their dense bordering foliage, now turned up by the wind, and contrasting strongly with the encircling bluffs that stood out against the sky, without a single bush or twig to relieve the sight. Indeed, the appearance of a tree, in all these regions of naked prairie, is to the traveller a certain indication of the presence of water; and in con-sequence, numerous tracks are to be seen, leading off from the main road to some sheltered and sequestered grove, affording the welcome indulgence of shade, wood, water, and grass to the weary emigrant and his still more wearied beasts. Elsewhere, during the long fatiguing day, shade there is none; unless, indeed, it be beneath his wagon, which to him is literally his home. In it he carries his all, and it serves him as tent, kitchen, parlour, and bed-room, and not unfrequently as a boat, to ferry his load over an otherwise impassable stream. Many have no other shelter from the storm during the whole journey, and most of these vehicles are extremely tight, roomy, and comfortable. Encamped after a short march of five miles, on the right bank of the Sandy. In the afternoon we met four men from Fort Laramie, who informed us that a large band of some six hundred Pawnees had become so very troublesome to the emigrants between the Blue and Fort Kearny, that a force had been despatched from that post to drive them off. A small party had also been discovered a few miles back, lurking under a cliff of rocks, a short distance south of the road, doubtless on the watch for another chance to steal our horses. We were on our guard, however. The camp was formed by drawing the wagons into a semi-circle, resting on the stream, with the tents pitched alternately between them, except those of the officers, which were placed on the bank and faced the enclosure. Within this all the animals were carefully picketed, and a strong guard, well armed, set at dusk. These precautions doubtless saved us from molestation. The formation to-day consisted of white and red sandstones, principally the latter, being evidently the sandstone formation above the carboniferous series.   The white sandstone was very fossiliferous.

Thursday, June 14.—Ther. at sunrise, 66° ; Bar. 28.58. Heavy dew; wind N. W., quite fresh and cool.   Leaving Little Sandy, the road follows the ridge between it and the Little Blue, over decomposed red sandstone.   Halted to noon on the right bank of the Big Sandy, a tolerably bold stream when the water is high; but at present it stands only in pools, on a bed of white sand two hundred feet in width.   The afternoon march was on the south side of the ridge, which forced us to cross the heads of numerous ravines and small runs putting into the Blue, upon one of which we encamped, having accomplished twenty-one miles.   We met to-day, for the first time, several new plants, indicating an approach to regions of a different and less fertile character than those we had hitherto traversed.   The aloe and the prickly-pear were found in the sand-hills, as were the *Commelina* and the *saxifrage*.   The prairie-rose, *Amorpha, Œnothera,* and *Artemisia* abound.   A blue lupine and a white mallow were also gathered.

In the afternoon we met Major Belger, of the quartermaster's department, on his return from Fort Kearny, with an escort of dragoons.   He had fallen in with a band of five hundred Pawnees, who, however, did not attack him.   He confirmed the rumour that a force had been sent from the fort after them.   A fight had taken place on the north side of the Platte, between the Indians and two parties of emigrants, in which the former were defeated, with the loss of their chief, five others killed, and six wounded; the whites having one man wounded and a horse killed.   A large number of plover were seen to-day.

Monday, June 18.—Bar. 28.13 ; Ther. 86°.   We have been travelling for the last three days up the valley of the Little Blue. Where we first struck it, the stream is eighty feet wide, apparently deep, very crooked, with a swift current.   It is fringed, sometimes on one side, sometimes on the other, with a narrow belt of cotton-wood and willows.   The valley presents a tolerably uniform appearance, bounded by ridges, seldom more than a mile or two apart, the intervening bottoms sloping gradually down to the river.   The grass is generally very abundant, and *prêle* (the common scouring-rush) is found in great plenty.   Our mules ate it with avidity.

In the morning we passed a government ox-train, laden with provisions for the new post about to be established in the neighbourhood of Fort Hall.   It consisted of thirty-one heavy wagons, four hundred oxen, (five or six yoke to each team,) and about forty men. At night the wagons are drawn into a circle, in the open plain, away from any covert, and chained together by the wheels, leaving a small space. The cattle are driven, after feeding, into the enclosure thus formed, when the aperture is closed for the night, and a guard set. A very formidable little field-work is thus easily and rapidly constructed. In the morning and middle of the day the cattle are turned loose to graze, and a day-guard is detailed for their protection. This is the general mode adopted by travellers on the plains for the security of themselves and their property.

The valley of the Little Blue has not presented any great novelty in the way of flowers. The only new plants met with have been a lupine, the flower of which, of a bright purple, rises directly from the root; the plant is totally leafless. A splendid variety of the mallow, of a bright carmine colour, its trailing stems sending up flowers in little patches of a few yards square, presented a rich and beautiful appearance, enlivening the monotony of the prairie by its brilliant hues. The aloe occurred in some places in abundance; and there were a few cacti, and a species of a leguminous plant was met with, having a flower of a pale purple colour, resembling a vetch; also a species of pale blue digitalis.

Yesterday, being Sunday, was devoted to rest. Most of the people, however, availed themselves of the opportunity to take a hunt, as we had killed no game up to this time. In fact, we had had no opportunity, the game having been driven from the vicinity of the travelled route by the unintermitted stream of emigration which had already passed over the road. The result of their efforts was accordingly not very magnificent, the whole party bringing in only a duck, a musk-rat, a large snapping-turtle, and one miserably poor little antelope. The constant use of salt meat, without vegetables, had affected us all with a cutaneous irritation, to be allayed only by the use of fresh meat; and hence the arrival of this antelope, poor as it was, was hailed by our *voyageurs* with lively satisfaction. The little carcass was cut up and divided among the several messes, a portion being sent to our travelling companions; and it was amusing to see how soon every one was sedulously engaged in preparing this most welcome addition to our usual homely fare. The scene was picturesque: the camp-fires blazed in every direction, while around each might be seen a busy little group, boiling, roasting, and baking, in happy anticipation of their venison dinner; the mules, meanwhile, filled to repletion with the rich grass of the prairie, lay stretched and rolling upon the grass in lazy enjoyment, exempt for one happy day from the harness and the whip.

After travelling up the Blue for about twelve miles, we left it and crossed the ridge dividing its waters from those of the Nebraska or Platte River. The character of this ridge is that of an extensive level plateau, or table, with slight undulations: the soil is composed of sand and clay, having occasionally water standing on it in pools, which, however, are dry most of the summer. On arriving at the western edge of the plateau, the country became more elevated, and presented a range of small hills of a sandy reddish clay, with a sharp outline toward the river, forming the "coast of the Nebraska," and also constituting the bluff bounding the river valley on the south. From this elevated position the valley presented a lovely appearance. The bottom was as level as a floor, covered with short fresh grass of the richest green, without a shrub or bush to interrupt the view. Beyond this verdant carpet of two miles in breadth, flowed the river of which we had heard so much, while a dense growth of large timber, covering Grand Island, which lay immediately before us, formed a fit framework for this lovely picture of calm and quiet beauty.

Archambault, our guide, told me that the last time he had passed this spot, the whole of the immense plain, as far as the eye could reach, was black with herds of buffalo. Now, not so much as one is to be seen; they have fled before the advancing tide of emigration. Driven from their ancient and long-loved haunts, these aboriginal herds, confined within still narrowing bounds, seem destined to final extirpation at the hand of man. The prairie bottom of the Platte is here elevated but a very few feet above the river in its present stage, which, however, is higher than usual. The appearance of the water is precisely that of the Mississippi and Missouri, of a muddy white, and its current is, like theirs, constantly boiling and eddying in restless turbulence. It is quite shallow, as its name, both in Indian and French, indicates, so that I found no difficulty in riding my mule over to the island, at the head of which we encamped for the night, after a march of thirty-two miles.

In the course of the morning we passed the remains of a Pawnee village, recently abandoned. The band to which it belonged was probably the same before mentioned as having been driven off by the troops from Fort Kearny. Near it, several large mushrooms, the first we had seen, were found. Cacti were met with during the day, also the purple mallow, as well as a small red species, the perfume of which is very sweet, resembling that of heliotrope. Dwarf *Artemisia* was also abundant. The measured distance from Fort Leavenworth to this point, by the usually travelled route, is two hundred and ninety-six miles.

Tuesday, June 19.—Ther. at 5 o'clock, 70°. Men and animals much fatigued by the journey of yesterday. We travelled up the Platte fifteen miles, and encamped within two miles of Fort Kearny, on the bank of the river, for the sake of water and grass. Wood for cooking could be procured only by wading the river, and bringing it from the opposite side on the shoulders of the men. After encamping, rode up to the fort, and called upon the commanding officer, Colonel Bonneville, whose adventures among the Rocky Mountains are so well known to the world. He received us very courteously, offering us every facility in his power in furtherance of our progress. We remained at this post until the afternoon of the 21st, to recruit the mules, get many of them shod, and to procure such necessary supplies as could be obtained. The post at present consists of a number of long low buildings, constructed principally of adobe, or sun-dried bricks, with nearly flat roofs; a large hospital-tent; two or three workshops, enclosed by canvas walls; storehouses constructed in the same manner; one or two long adobe stables, with roofs of brush; and tents for the accommodation of the officers and men. There are stationed here two companies of infantry and one of dragoons. I was told that the hail-storms had been very frequent this season and quite destructive, cutting down the weeds and stripping the trees of their foliage.

Lieutenant Gunnison being still quite feeble, and unable to ride on horseback, I purchased for his use a little spring-carriage, which had been left here by a party of emigrants. Such abandonments are very common; most of these sanguine and adventurous companies, by the time they get thus far, beginning to find out that they have started on their journey with more than they can contrive to carry. In order to lighten their load, most of them dispose of every thing they can possibly spare, and at almost any price. Flour and bacon, for example, had been sold as low as one cent per pound; and many, being unable to sell even at that price, had used their meat for fuel. The pack company from Boston, which had passed us on the route, and which we found encamped here on our arrival, left before our departure. As they had been entirely unaccustomed to the operation of packing, their mules, as was to be expected, were in a most horrible condition, with galled backs and sides that made one shudder to behold. The proper mode of arranging the load of these suffering animals is an art taught only by experience. These people, though belonging to a race famous for foresight and calculation, had, like others from less thrifty and managing portions of the Union, been selling and giving away all they could dispense with. While encamped here we have had several severe thunder storms, accompanied with heavy rains and violent winds.

CHAPTER II.

FROM FORT KEARNY TO FORT LARAMIE.

Thursday, June 21.—Having taken leave of our kind and hospitable friends at the fort, we overtook our own train, which had been sent ahead in the morning, and found them encamped on the bank of the Platte, after a drive of twenty-five miles. Lieutenant Gunnison, who had gone before in his little wagon, by some means missed the camp in the darkness, and did not arrive, which gave me no little uneasiness, lest the exposure should prove detrimental in his very delicate state of health. We discovered, however, in the morning, that he had found good quarters at an emigrant encampment on the road.

The character of the Platte valley for the last forty miles is that of a flat prairie, composed of sand and clay, in which, when the latter predominates, water is found standing in small pools, but when the sand is most abundant, the water passes through it like a sieve and is quite drained away. Hence we have passed innumerable little wells, dug to a depth of from two to four feet. The water is generally clear and cool, but much of the sickness on this route has been attributed to its use. The soil thrown out is sandy, though not unfrequently having a mixture of clay. The water thus obtained is evidently the result of infiltration from the higher levels or bluffs, which, in this hidden manner, discharge their surplus moisture into the river. The bluffs on the opposite side of the river, near Fort Kearny, are apparently formed of pure sand, and are much higher, and appear to be more wooded, than on the south side of the stream. About twenty miles above the fort, the character of the bluffs on the south side seemed changed, and presented a more gradual slope to the river; the soil contained more clay, and, at a distance of a mile back from their escarpment, they were cut up by constant ravines with banks precipitous and, in some instances, perpendicular. In one spot, such was the tenacity of the soil, that an upright mass of earth in the form of a column had been left by the waters. Here were found fossils of a character similar to those obtained at the point where we first entered the valley: they were, however, in a very friable and decomposed state.

Sunday, June 24.—Bar. 27.56; Ther. 83. Our journey for the last two days has been up the valley of the Platte, which, in some places, is more than a mile in width. From one spot I counted upward of twenty islands, which, being densely covered with green willows and cotton-woods, presented, in contrast with the naked monotonous country through which we were passing, a perfect picture of refreshing beauty. From the fact that the islands in the river are, for the most part, covered with trees, the almost total absence of this feature in the landscape of the valley must be attributed, in part at least, to the fires which periodically sweep over the country in the autumn, destroying every thing before them. On our return by this same route, in the fall of 1850, the country, for more than three hundred miles, had been completely devastated by these conflagrations, insomuch that our animals came near perishing for want of herbage. The north side of the river does not appear to suffer so much from this cause; which may, in part, arise from the direction of the prevailing winds. Encamped on the bank of the Platte, fifty-six miles above Fort Kearny. The bluffs bounding the valley were of clayey soil, cut up by deep ravines, in many instances nearly perpendicular, their character becoming bolder as we advanced. The soil is richer and contains more clay. The plants seen were *Tradescantia*, the purple mallow, (the root of which resembles the parsnip, and is used by the Indians for food,) the small yellow *Œnothera*, and a pretty, small stellate-flowered plant. Over large portions of the bottom, no flowers were met with; on the high ground, red mallow, *Mimosa, Linum,* a white *Mimulus,* and a sort of larkspur. The aloe was flowering in abundance on the face of some very steep bluffs.

Monday, June 25.—Ther. at sunrise, 64°; Bar. 27.52.   The bluffs on our left, which are about two miles distant, are assuming a much more broken appearance than heretofore, being cut up into peaks and ridges in the most picturesque manner.   Upon examination they were found to be composed of sandy clay, intersected by precipitous ravines, the sections of which presented strata slightly differing in colour and hardness.   The fossils collected were some teeth, apparently of an animal of the lizard tribe, and the *femur* either of a bird or a small lizard; the head of the bone and nearly the entire shaft measured three and a-half inches, but the latter crumbled on removing it.   Both of these were found in place.   Remains also were seen of what appeared to be bones, fully four or five inches in circumference, but in so friable a state that it was impossible to remove them from their matrix or accurately to determine their form.   Other fossils were found, but in a very imperfect state.   The sections showed that the strata were perfectly conformable to those already passed, the dip being about 12° to the south-west, and the north-west sections horizontal.   These deep and precipitous ravines are doubtless the result, on an extended scale, of the action of water, and satisfactorily explain the muddy character of the Platte and the Missouri, into which washings from these bluffs have been carried for ages.

Tuesday, June 26.—In the morning we crossed the dry bed of a small stream having its banks well covered with trees, the first we had met with since entering the valley of the Platte, now a distance of one hundred miles.   In the afternoon we overtook the pack-train of the Boston company, which had left Fort Kearny the day before we did.   They had seen about a hundred buffaloes crossing the river, and having succeeding in killing one, were no little elated at their good luck.   We had not as yet been so fortunate as to discover a single one, a circumstance that proved a source of great annoyance to our hunters, in whose mind the association of "the plains" with buffalo-meat was fixed and inseparable, and who, consequently, by no means relished their almost exclusive confinement to salt pork.   They were now on the *qui vive,* anxiously anticipating the feasts to which they had constantly looked forward.   No buffalo however, were seen to-day, the herds having been frightened from the road.

Encamped six miles above the point of junction of the two forks of the Platte, on the bank of a small stream of running water with a sandy bottom, the first that had blessed our vision since

3

leaving the Blue. This little creek, running parallel with the South Fork, winds its very sinuous way, without bank or shrub or bush to mark its course, until it discharges its waters into the river several miles below. The bluffs on our left continue to present the same wild forms, being also clothed in many places with trees, among which the white-cedar appeared to predominate. Owing to the sandy nature of the soil, no fossils were found in a perfect state, except two varieties of shells: some imperfect remains of teeth were also seen, but in too frail a condition to be preserved. About six miles below the Forks, the bluffs presented a rougher appearance than those passed early in the day. The principal ravines did not appear to extend very far back, but were of considerable width, and intersected by others which came into them from every direction. Their sides were very steep, rising in some cases to the height of two hundred feet; and so entirely was the surface of the ground intersected and cut up, that it was difficult to find a spot of even a few yards square that did not enter into the formation of some one of them. The prodigious quantity of earth that has been removed by the action of water cannot be imagined without witnessing the scene here presented. The soil composing the hills, although mixed more or less with clay, is sandy, and occasionally assumes the character of a very friable sandstone. Opposite the Forks, however, the formation of the bluffs again alters, and begins to assume a more undulatory and less precipitous appearance, not so much traversed by ravines. This change is occasioned by the cropping out of a stratum of a whitish sandstone. The bluffs passed to-day must, at a period long back, have extended much closer to the river than where we now find them, having, in fact, been gradually washed into it, leaving the valley much broader, and, to a certain extent, one of denudation.

Carduus, Cactus with a large sickly-looking yellow flower, *Amorpha, Tradescantia,* a small sunflower, and a species of milk-plant were here found. The *Amorpha* is beginning to bloom. The vetch, with its purple clusters, is met with, but seems of a different species from that seen heretofore, and has not so much foliage.

Wednesday, June 27.—To-day the hunters killed their first buffalo; but, in order to obtain it, had to diverge some four or five miles from the road, and to pass back of the bluffs, the instinct or experience of these sagacious animals having rendered them shy of approaching the line of travel. This has not always been the case, for it is a well-attested fact, that when the emigration first commenced, travelling trains were frequently detained for hours by immense herds crossing their track, and in such numbers that it was impossible to drive through them. In many instances it was quite difficult to prevent their own loose cattle from mingling with the buffaloes, of which they did not seem to be at all afraid. The eyes of our French *voyageurs* fairly glistened as they rode into camp laden with the meat, and their arrival was hailed with a general shout of congratulation. The long-desired spoil was soon divided, and a busy scene ensued of roasting, boiling, and making *boudin*, which is a sort of sausage, boiled and eaten hot: when skilfully prepared, it forms a most excellent dish. Huge marrow-bones might now be seen roasting most temptingly by fires made of *bois de vache*, and a new spirit seemed to be infused into the entire party by this return to their favourite diet. Although, in such a company, it would have been rank treason to utter the opinion, yet I could not help thinking at the time, that the fat of this meat, which our men were devouring with so much *gusto*, had a somewhat rank and disagreeable flavour; and I must, in truth, confess that I was not a little disappointed by a dish of which I had received such glowing accounts. I found afterward, indeed, that such was the opinion, not only of us green ones, but even of our mountain connoisseurs themselves, although, at the time, they did all they could to persuade us that it was most excellent; for the animal killed was a " bull," whose flesh is eaten only when no other can be obtained, whence the males are very seldom killed when the " cows" can be procured.

The rock, where it cropped out in the bluffs, was composed of white or gray sandstone, similar to that previously passed; in some places strata of an ochreous marl were met with, and in one spot, twelve miles above the Forks, a stratum of gypsum. The fossils were in too imperfect a state to be identified. The small sunflower was seen in great abundance, and also buffalo-grass. Innumerable buffalo-trails were crossed, leading from the river through the ravines between the bluffs, to the country beyond, some of which were well beaten, and pressed nearly a foot deep into the soil.

Thursday, June 28.—Morning bright and pleasant. Ther. at sunrise, 59°; Bar. 27.18. The day proved fine, notwithstanding the threatening appearance of rain last night, with a cool and refreshing wind from the north. The Boston train, which had kept ahead of us, was seen crossing the South Fork—an operation which they effected apparently without difficulty; but I preferred to follow still further the main road, which soon led us up one of those points of heavy sand-bluffs which here put down directly to the river, being cut up in the most fantastic manner by precipitous, wide, and abrupt ravines of white sand. Keeping back of the heads of these, we again turned down to the river, and halted to noon on the bank of the Platte. To-day, buffalo were seen from the road, for the first time, feeding in large detached herds, scattered over the prairies like huge droves of cattle. The sight, to those of us who had never beheld these animals, was exceedingly interesting, and reminded me of the herds I had seen spread for miles over the lovely and fertile valley of Mad River, in Ohio. There must have been several thousands within our view, grazing in peaceful security. The effect upon our hunters, and, in fact, upon the whole party, was that of sudden and most intense excitement, and a yearning, feverish desire to secure as much as possible of this noble game. Archambault, the guide, had started early in the morning for the bluffs to hunt, taking with him another man, both mounted. About two o'clock they returned, loaded down with the choice pieces of three fat cows, which they had killed. After we had advanced a mile on the afternoon's march, a large band of these animals was discovered directly ahead and near the road. The opportunity was too tempting to be resisted. There was no prospect of getting buffalo above, as they were evidently travelling south; and I determined therefore, to remain where we were during this and the following day, and to send out and secure as much meat as possible before crossing the South Fork. A halt was accordingly made at once, the hunters sent forward, and the afternoon occupied in drying the meat brought in during the morning. Our men, however, failed in approaching the great herd before they took the alarm and vanished. The result of to-day's work, nevertheless, was five killed, of which four were secured and brought into camp. On the succeeding day three more were killed. The flesh thus obtained was forthwith cut into thin strips, dried over a fire on a willow frame, and packed into sacks for future use.

Saturday, June 30.—Ther. at sunrise, 61°; Bar. 27.03; with heavy fog. The road, all the morning, continued at the foot of the gently sloping bluff of the Platte, with a wide level bottom, the uniformity of its surface unbroken by a single bush. A large island was passed, of about six miles in length, by two and a-half in width, level as a floor, with here and there a clump or grove of timber on either margin. A small herd of buffalo was descried in the river, wading about among some small islands in search of grass.

We passed to-day through a large village or settlement of the prairie-dog, (*Arctomys ludoviciana*,) extending in length not less than half a mile. These little animals are very shy, and, at the least approach of a stranger, hie themselves with all speed to their holes, in which they partly bury their bodies, leaving only their heads visible just above the surface of the ground, where, so long as the alarm lasts, they keep up a continual barking. The note somewhat resembles the bark of a small puppy, but is nevertheless so peculiar as to be instantly recognised ever afterward, by any one who has once distinctly heard it. They are very hard to get, as they are never found far from their holes; and when shot, fall immediately into them, where they are generally guarded by a rattlesnake—the usual sharer of their subterranean retreat. Several were shot by us in this situation, but when the hand was about to be thrust into the hole to draw them out, the ominous rattle of this dreaded reptile would be instantly heard, warning the intruder of the danger he was about to incur. A little, white, burrowing owl also (*Stryx cunicularia*) is frequently found taking up his abode in the same domicile; and this strange association of reptile, bird, and beast seem to live together in perfect harmony and peace. I have never personally seen the owl thus housed, but have been assured of the fact from so many, so various, and so credible sources, that I cannot doubt it. The whirr of the rattlesnake I have heard frequently when the attempt was made to invade these holes, and our men at length became afraid to approach them for this purpose.

The march, to-day, was prolonged to an unusually late hour, as I was in hopes of reaching the ford of the South Fork before night, but finding this impracticable, we encamped on the bank of the river where the prairie was hard and level, with plenty of excellent grass and water. With the exception of a few small willows growing on the opposite side, and a large cotton-wood or two a few miles up the river, serving to mark the point for crossing, no trees were to be seen. We were fortunate enough, however, to find three or four old lodge-poles, left by a passing band of Sioux, which, eked out by *bois de vache* for fuel, served to give us a capital roast of buffalo-meat, which, wearied as we were by a march of fourteen hours in the burning sun, proved a most welcome and acceptable refreshment.

The formation over which we have passed the last two days has been composed of beds of sand and sandy shales. No rock has been met with; and wherever a section of the soil was obtained, it presented layèrs of sand containing small proportions of argillaceous matter. The general profile of the hills is rounded and undulatory. Rock, apparently in regular strata, is to be seen in the opposite bluffs, which are bolder and approach the river more nearly than on the south side.

Sunday, July 1.—Ther. at 9 o'clock, 81°; Bar. 26.74. The day being very warm and fine, advantage was taken of it to dry more thoroughly the meat we wished to preserve. Our breakfast this morning, which was spread out on the ground, with a piece of India-rubber cloth for a table, under the shade of one of the wagon-covers, consisted, for five persons, of two buffalo-tongues and the hump of a fat cow, nearly the whole of which was consumed. The flesh of a fat buffalo-cow is perhaps the best beef that can be eaten, wholly free from the rank flavour which marks the fat of the male: it is at once juicy, tender, nutritious, and very digestible, added to which it has a *game* flavour which renders it far superior to the very best beef of the States. It may, in fact, be not improperly denominated "*game beef.*"

This was the first time that any of my mess had partaken of that famous dish, the "*hump,*" and the quantity disposed of was the best proof of the intense relish with which it was enjoyed. This and the tongue, tender-loin, bass, and marrow-bones are considered the choice parts of the carcass, and, where the animals are plenty, no other parts are taken, the residue being left on the ground for the wolves. Some idea may be formed of the great digestibility of this species of food, as well as of the enormous quantities devoured at a single meal, from the fact that the regular daily allowance or ration for one employee in the Fur Company's service is eight pounds, the whole of which is often consumed. It is true, however, that an old mountaineer seldom eats any thing else. If he can get a cup of strong coffee, with plenty of sugar, and as much buffalo-meat as he can devour, he is perfectly happy and content, never feeling the want either of bread or vegetables.

A partial examination was made to-day of the north bank of the river. The rocks which had attracted attention yesterday were distant about four hundred yards from the stream and very much weathered, presenting a broken surface, owing to some of the strata having disintegrated faster than others. The perpendicular section of the rocks was seen in place.   The bluff was intersected by ravines, many of which also exposed vertical sections. The strata were nearly horizontal, with perhaps a slight slip to the west, and very fossiliferous, some of them being composed of encrinital remains.   The hills were about one hundred and fifty feet in height, and consisted of the following strata:—On the surface, a yellow shale, containing encrinites and grit; layers of loose detritus and quartzose conglomerate; brown shale and sand, the former containing wood and bones; white sandstone, the exposed surface marked by ripples; calcareous sandstone; sandy limestone, composed principally of remains of stems of encrinites, none of the central portions of which were found, (this layer was some feet thick, and was traced fully a mile;) whitish sandstone; botryoidal limestone.   The fossils found were the remains of encrinites, which were abundantly diffused through the different strata, with the exception of the detritus.   Some bones occurred, but in a very imperfect state: a large flat bone was found imbedded in sandy shale, and endeavours were made to get it out, which did not succeed.   The part exposed presented a segment of a circle from twelve to sixteen inches in diameter.   About half a mile below this point was a peak formed by large masses of encrinital limestone; and at a point still lower down, the same formation was found, the whole being crowned by a white marl, containing encrinites and grit.   At this point were discovered the remains of the bones of some large animal, only imperfect specimens of which could be procured, for want of the means of extracting them. One fragment was seen, fully seven inches in circumference; and a tooth, exposed for a length of five inches, was broken in the attempt to get it out.   The condyle of the jaw and what was supposed to be the foot of some reptile were secured.

Monday, July 2.—Ther. at sunrise, 68°; Bar. 26.63.   After travelling up the river for fourteen miles, it was determined to make the crossing of the South Fork by fording.   In preparation for this movement, one of the wagons, as an experimental pioneer, was partially unloaded, by removing all articles liable to injury from water, and then driven into the stream; but it stuck fast, and the ordinary team of six mules being found insufficient to haul it through the water, four more were quickly attached, and the crossing was made with perfect safety, and without wetting any thing. In the same manner were all the remaining wagons crossed, one by one, by doubling the teams, and employing the force of nearly the whole party wading alongside to incite and guide the mules, lest, from some sudden eccentricity, to which those animals are so constantly prone, a wagon might be capsized or precipitated into a hole. The water was perfectly opake with thick yellow mud, and it required all our care to avoid the quicksands with which the bottom is covered. The labour was excessive, on both men and animals, as the river was nearly half a mile wide, and the current from recent rains ran with great rapidity and force. Wading such a stream breast-deep four or five times, with such treacherous footing, was very exhausting, and we were glad to encamp, immediately after crossing, upon the left bank. Both man and beast suffered more from this day's exertion than from any day's march we had yet made. About one and a-half miles above the crossing a new Indian lodge was seen standing entirely alone. A fact so unusual excited our curiosity: upon going to the place, it was found to contain the body of an Indian (probably a chief) raised upon a low platform or bier, surrounded by all the implements believed by these simple children of the forest to be necessary for his use in the spirit-land. The lodge was carefully and securely fastened down at the bottom, to protect its charge from the wolves. It was an affecting spectacle. His last battle fought, his last hunt over, here he lay in the solitude of death, abandoned by wife and child, and all he loved, yet surrounded by the tokens of their parting care, the rude proofs of a love that followed him to an unknown hereafter. We are now, by our measurements, four hundred and seventy-nine miles from Fort Leavenworth, and one hundred and eighty from Fort Kearny.

Tuesday, July 3.—Morning cool and delightful; Ther. at sunrise, 71°; Bar. 26.59; Wind S. W., fresh and bracing. To-day we crossed the ridge between the North and South Forks of the Platte, a distance of eighteen and a-half miles. As we expected to find no water for the whole of this distance, the India-rubber bags were filled with a small supply. The road struck directly up the bluff, rising quite rapidly at first, then very gradually for twelve miles, when we reached the summit, and a most magnificent view saluted the eye. Before and below us was the North Fork of the Nebraska, winding its way through broken hills and green meadows; behind us the undulating prairie rising gently from the South Fork, over which we had just passed; on our right, the gradual convergence of the two valleys was distinctly perceptible; while immediately at our feet were the heads of Ash Creek, which fell off suddenly into deep precipitous chasms on either side, leaving only a high narrow ridge, or backbone, which gradually descended, until, toward its western termination, it fell off precipitately into the bottom of the creek. Here we were obliged, from the steepness of the road, to let the wagons down by ropes, but the labour of a dozen men for a few days would make the descent easy and safe. The bottom of Ash Creek is tolerably well wooded, principally with ash and some dwarf cedars. The bed of the stream was entirely dry, but toward the mouth several springs of delightfully cold and refreshing water were found, altogether the best that has been met with since leaving the Missouri. We encamped at the mouth of the valley, here called Ash Hollow. The traces of the great tide of emigration that had preceded us were plainly visible in remains of camp-fires, in blazed trees covered with innumerable names carved and written on them; but, more than all, in the total absence of all herbage. It was only by driving our animals to a ravine some distance from the camp, that a sufficiency for their subsistence could be obtained.

The two slopes of the ridge dividing the main forks of the Platte, at the point where we crossed it, differ from each other in a remarkable manner. On that toward the South Fork, the valleys are wide and long, with gracefully curved lines, gentle slopes, and broad hollows. In numerous instances, these hollows are without drainage, owing to which large circular or oval basins are formed, in the bottoms of which water collects, forming quite extensive ponds or lakes : these, however, disappear during the summer, leaving their beds clothed with a rich, luxuriant growth of herbage. On the opposite side of the summit the features of the country present a striking contrast. Almost immediately after crossing the point of "divide," we strike upon the head waters of Ash Creek, whence the descent is abrupt and precipitous. Immediately at your feet is the principal ravine, with sides four or five hundred feet in depth, clothed with cedar : into this numerous other ravines run, meeting it at different angles, and so completely cutting up the earth, that scarcely a foot of level ground could be seen. The whole surface consisted of merely narrow ridges, dividing the ravines from each other, and running up to so sharp a crest that it would be difficult for any thing but a mountain-goat to traverse their summits with impunity. Never before had I seen the wonderful effects of the action of water on a grand scale more strikingly exemplified.

The soil on the top of the ravine seemed to consist of decomposed sand-rock, among which, however, were found some pieces of silicious limestone, with traces of encrinites. In one of the lateral ravines, a complete section of the rock was obtained. It was composed of layers of white sandstone, calcareous sandstone, sand, sand and clay, and granitic and quartz detritus, cemented by calcareous rocks. The only fossils found were the remains of encrinites, which existed in almost all the strata; and in some the quartzose portion of the rock was composed of their stems. Toward the lower part of the gorge was a bed or layer of marl, in which were the remains of what very much resembled the seeds of a plant. All the strata were horizontal. On examining them at the mouth of the hollow, on the following day, a stratum was found of botryoidal limestone, consisting of oblong pieces of magnesian limestone, cemented by a calcareous rock, and also another bed of sandy marl, containing remains of the seeds already mentioned, together with some oblong bodies, which were probably those of encrinites.

Heavy thunder, wind, and rain, during the night.

Wednesday, July 4.—At 9 A. M., Bar. 26.76; Ther. 68°. This being a national festival, I determined to spend the day here and celebrate it as well as our limited means would permit. A salute was fired morning and evening, and a moderate allowance of grog served out to the men, which, with a whole day's rest and plenty of buffalo-meat, rendered them quite happy. We had observed yesterday, on the opposite side of the river, a number of Indian lodges, pitched on the bank; but the total absence of any living or moving thing about them induced us from curiosity to pay them a visit. In order to do this it was necessary to cross the river, here nearly a mile in breadth, with a strong, rapid current. I was afraid to risk any of the animals, as the bottom was known to be very treacherous and full of quicksands; so it was determined we should wade it. Having stripped to our drawers, we tied our shirts and moccasins around our necks to keep them dry, and, accompanied by five or six of the men, commenced the passage. The water was up to our middle, and the strong and constant pressure of the current rendered our efforts to bear up against it very fatiguing. We struggled on, but very slowly, from the yielding nature of the sandy and marly bottom, which was immediately washed from beneath the foot every time it was placed on the ground. If we stood still in the same spot, even for a short time, the bottom would be so rapidly excavated from beneath us, that a hole of sufficient depth would be formed to render swimming necessary. After continuing these tedious and laborious efforts until we had nearly reached the opposite shore, on advancing a single step we found ourselves in water beyond our depth, (the channel of the river running close to the bank,) and the shirts we had so carefully endeavoured to keep dry were in a moment thoroughly soaked. We made out, however, to scramble ashore.

I put on my moccasins, and, displaying my wet shirt, like a flag, to the wind, we proceeded to the lodges which had attracted our curiosity. There were five of them, pitched upon the open prairie, and in them we found the bodies of nine Sioux, laid out upon the ground, wrapped in their robes of buffalo-skin, with their saddles, spears, camp-kettles, and all their accoutrements, piled up around them. Some lodges contained three, others only one body, all of which were more or less in a state of decomposition. A short distance apart from these was one lodge which, though small, seemed of rather superior pretensions, and was evidently pitched with great care. It contained the body of a young Indian girl of sixteen or eighteen years, with a countenance presenting quite an agreeable expression: she was richly dressed in leggings of fine scarlet cloth, elaborately ornamented; a new pair of moccasins, beautifully embroidered with porcupine quills, was on her feet, and her body was wrapped in two superb buffalo-robes, worked in like manner. She had evidently been dead but a day or two; and to our surprise a portion of the upper part of her person was bare, exposing the face and a part of the breast, as if the robes in which she was wrapped had by some means been disarranged, whereas all the other bodies were closely covered up. It was, at the time, the opinion of our mountaineers that these Indians must have fallen in an encounter with a party of Crows; but I subsequently learned that they had all died of the cholera, and that this young girl, being considered past recovery, had been arrayed by her friends in the habiliments of the dead, enclosed in the lodge alive, and abandoned to her fate—so fearfully alarmed were the Indians by this, to them, novel and terrible disease. But the melancholy tale of this poor forsaken girl, does not end here. Her abandonment by her people, though with inevitable death before her eyes, may perhaps be excused from the extremity of their terror; but what will be thought of the conduct of men enlightened by Christianity, and under no such excess of fear, who, by their own confession, approached and looked into this lodge while the forsaken being was yet alive, and able partially to raise herself up and look at them, but who, with a heartlessness that disgraces human nature, turned away, and, without an effort for her relief, left her alone to die! Which company deserved the epithet of savages, the terrified and flying red men, or the strong-hearted whites who thus consummated their cruel deed?

Leaving this melancholy scene, we recrossed the river and returned to our encampment, where preparations had been made for a Fourth of July dinner. Although deprived of the vegetable luxuries upon which our Eastern friends were doubtless feasting, still our bill of fare would not have been unacceptable even to an epicure. Buffalo-soup, buffalo-ribs, tender-loin, and marrow-bones roasted, boiled ham, stewed peaches, and broiled curlew, relished with a couple of bottles of cool claret, (which had beeen carefully preserved for the occasion,) and crowned by a cup of coffee and a segar, made a meal which, notwithstanding the cup was of tin and our table the greensward, we thought not entirely unworthy of the day. In the evening two men came into camp and requested our hospitality: they had been emigrants, but were on their return to the States disgusted, having fallen out with their company by the way.

Thursday, July 5th.—Bar. 26.67. Ther. 56°. We commenced our journey to-day up the North Fork of the Platte. The road winds along the bottom under the bluffs. The lower stratum consists of yellow clay, capped by cliffs of sandstone and silicious limestone, about two hundred feet in height. This formation was traced uninterruptedly for about twenty miles. The limestone appeared to contain no fossils—at least, none were discovered. Toward the end of the day's march the clay was left uncovered by the limestone, presenting bald eminences destitute of the least vegetation, which, from the action of the weather, had been worn into various curious and isolated peaks, of forms extremely picturesque. Encamped on the bank of the river, after a tedious march of twenty-three miles. Just above us, was a village of Sioux, consisting of ten lodges. They were accompanied by Mr. Badeau, a trader; and, having been driven from the South Fork by the cholera, had fled to the emigrant-road, in the hope of obtaining medical aid from the whites. As soon as it was dark, the chief and a dozen of the braves of the village came and sat down in a semicircle around the front of my tent, and, by means of an interpreter, informed me that they would be very glad of a little coffee, sugar, or biscuit. I gave them what we could spare. They told us there was another and larger band encamped about two miles above, many of whom were very sick with the cholera: they themselves had been afflicted with it, but had in a great measure recovered, although they were in great dread of its return. As soon as they were told I had a doctor, or "medicine-man," with me, and received assurances that some medicines should be prepared for them, and left with the trader, (who had married among them,) they expressed much delight, and returned to their village, where, soon after, the sound of the drum and the song, expressive of the revival of hope, which had almost departed, resounded from the "medicine lodge," and continued until a late hour of the night. In the mean time, I directed a quantity of medicine to be prepared, with the necessary directions for using it. The following morning we paid a visit in passing, to the upper village, which contained about two hundred and fifty souls. They were in the act of breaking up their encampment, being obliged to move farther up the river to obtain fresh grass for their animals. A more curious, animated, and novel scene I never witnessed. Squaws, papooses, dogs, puppies, mules, and ponies, all in busy motion, while the lordly, lazy men lounged about with an air of listless indifference, too proud to render the slightest aid to their faithful drudges. Before the lodge of each brave was erected a tripod of thin slender poles about ten feet in length, upon which was suspended his round white shield, with some device painted upon it, his spear, and a buckskin sack containing his "medicine" bag. It reminded me forcibly of the scenes of Ivanhoe and the Crusaders, and impressed me with the singularity of the coincidence in the customs of what were then the most refined nations of the world, with those of these wild and untutored savages. The cholera had been quite bad among them, and was still raging. I visited nearly every lodge, in company with the doctor and Mr. Bissonette the trader, and medicine was administered to all who required it. It was touching to witness the moral effect produced by the mere presence of a "medicine-man" upon these poor wretches. They swallowed the medicine with great avidity, and an absolute faith in its efficacy, which, I have little doubt, saved many a life that would otherwise have been lost. I shall never forget one poor fellow, a tall, fine-looking young man of about twenty-five. He had been sick three days, and we found him sitting on the ground, his blanket drawn closely around him, and his chin resting upon his knees, the image of despair,—very quiet, but the expression of his countenance showing that he had made up his mind that he must die. To add to his despondence, a young man from the next lodge had just been carried out and buried. The doctor examined him closely, and then requested the interpreter to tell him that the worst was past, and that, with care and attention, he would soon entirely recover. Never did I behold any thing like the change which, in an instant, came over the expressive countenance of this poor savage. His face flushed, the fire came into his eyes, and a radiant smile of confidence and hope, which was beautiful to behold, broke through the previous gloom. He raised his eyes, till now sternly fixed upon the ground, gently smote his hands together, turned his head toward his squaw, who was standing behind him, and in a low and silvery tone communicated to her the joyful news. It was to him a perfect resurrection from the dead; for he seemed now to entertain no doubt of his recovery, but received the assurance of the doctor as if it had been the fiat of fate. It was a moving sight, and although we could not understand a single word that passed, the whole scene was perfectly intelligible. After administering to all who stood in need, a quantity of medicine was left with Mr. Bissonette, with the necessary directions.

The whole village was much revived by this visit from the "medicine-man," and expressed much thankfulness, and a strong desire that he should remain among them. As this was obviously impossible, we continued our journey, accompanied for several miles by the people of both villages. The whole scene was unique in the highest degree. The road was strewn for miles with the most motley assemblage I ever beheld, each lodge moving off from the village as soon as its inhabitants were ready, without waiting for the others. The means of transportation were horses, mules, and dogs. Four or five lodge-poles are fastened on each side of the animal, the ends of which trail on the ground behind, like the shafts of a truck or dray. On these, behind the horse, is fastened a light framework, the outside of which consists of a strong hoop bent into an oval form, and interlaced with a sort of network of rawhide. Most of these are surmounted by a light wicker canopy, very like our covers for children's wagons, except that it extends the whole length, and is open only at one side. Over the canopy is spread a blanket, shawl, or buffalo-robe, so as to form a protection from the sun or rain. Upon this light but strong trellice-work, they place the lighter articles, such as clothing, robes, &c., and then pack away among these their puppies and papooses, (of both which they seem to have a goodly number;) the women, when tired of walking, get upon them to rest and take care of their babies. The elasticity of the poles makes the motion easy and pleasant. I afterward saw an old Indian, that had been crippled in one of the skirmishes which so often occur among these tribes, whose only mode of locomotion was a contrivance of this kind, from which he could not move without assistance.

The dogs also are made to perform an important part in this shifting of quarters. Two short, light lodge-poles are fastened together at the small end, and made to rest at the angle upon the animal's neck, the other end of course, trailing upon the ground. Over his shoulders is placed a sort of pad, or small saddle, the girth of which fastens the poles to his sides, and connects with a little collar or breast-strap. Behind the dog, a small platform or frame is fastened to the poles, similar to that used for the horses, upon which are placed lighter articles, generally puppies, which are considered quite valuable, being raised for beasts of burden as well as for food and the chase. I was informed by Mr. Bissonette, that many tribes, having no horses or mules, use dogs altogether in moving their villages. We saw a large number of these animals, with their sharp noses and wolflike ears, thus harnessed, and trotting along as if it were an occupation to which they were perfectly accustomed. The whole duty of taking down and putting up the lodges, packing up, loading the horses, arranging the lodge-poles, and leading or driving the animals, devolves upon the squaws, while the men stalk along at their leisure; even the boys of larger growth deeming it beneath their dignity to lighten the toils of their own mothers.

The whole band halted about ten o'clock on the bank of the river, but several of the old men and the chief of the village continued with us until our noon halt. I invited the latter to lunch with us, which he did to his entire satisfaction, devouring as much meat as the whole mess beside, and I afterward espied him seated at one of the messes of the men, as earnestly engaged in laying in an additional supply as if he had not eaten for a week. The Indian, in fact, from his wandering habits and uncertain mode of existence, acquires the faculty of laying in, when opportunity offers itself, a store of food against the fast that may follow, thus approximating the instincts of other wild denizens of the forest.

After crossing a few running streams, we encamped near a number of springs of soft, cold, sandstone water, which proved very grateful after the hot and dusty journey of the day.

The banks on this side of the river have presented little of interest, the surface generally consisting of rolling prairie, gradually rising to the summit of the hills, which are at a considerable distance from the stream. On the opposite side, the cliffs are precipitous, displaying sections of horizontal beds of apparently the same rock already noticed. About two miles from our noon halt the rock was exposed close to the river and but little above its level. It consisted of layers of sandstone, with detritus, magnesian limestone, sand, and clay. Some fossils were collected and remains of encrinites were observed. On entering the bottom of the North Fork, we found the white *Œnothera*, a large flower, growing with but a single flower-stem. Lupines are still found in considerable numbers, together with phlox and some species of sunflower. The heads of the ravines were clothed with pine and cedar. The growth of the latter tree appears to be diminishing; for while numerous dead trees lay strewn along the bottoms, but few living ones were found growing on the hills.

Saturday, July 7.—Ther. at sunrise, 59° ; Bar. 26.55. This morning we caught a view of the celebrated "Chimney Rock," and also of the "Court-house," which latter consisted of two bald elevations, similar in formation to that already passed, to which the *voyageurs*, most of whom are originally from St. Louis, had given this name, from a fancied resemblance to a well-known structure in their own city.

In riding out from the road to visit this curious formation, we found the main bluff of the river to be about five miles distant, the intervening country consisting of rolling hillocks covered with grass. In our ride we crossed the dry sandy bed of a stream, about two hundred and fifty feet in width, which, in the rainy season, must discharge a large quantity of water. It had little or no bank, and, from the appearance of drift-wood far out on the prairie, must overspread a large surface in the spring. A mile and a-half from this creek we came upon another, called on the maps " Dry Creek," but known among the mountain-men as " Lawrence's Fork," from the fact that a man of that name had been killed on it by the Sioux. The Court-house was but a few hundred yards beyond this stream, which was about thirty feet wide and two or three feet deep, flowing with a free, bold, and tolerably rapid current: it had cut its bed through the blue clay, with a few narrow layers of sand. I attempted to cross it, but the bottom consisted of a stiff marly mud, into which the feet of the animals sank rapidly, and could with difficulty be withdrawn. Fearful of miring them down, I gave up the attempt, and thus lost the opportunity of examining this celebrated seat of justice more closely. Upon the bank, where we attempted to cross, I found a large block of what proved to be *lignite,* and near by a lump of what was thought to be oolitic clay, from which several species of fresh-water shells were taken. The lignite had evidently been brought down by the creek, as many large masses of it were seen lying in the water and strewn along the banks. Should this substance be found in any quantity in the hills to the south, it may have a very important bearing upon the future settlement of this region; one of the great obstacles to which, even when water can be commanded, is the total absence of timber sufficient for fuel. Could lignite be found in sufficient quantity for this purpose, many spots in this extensive valley might be settled to advantage, and would thus furnish stations where the emigrant and mail trains might find shelter, protection, and provisions. I should have directed a more extended examination, but the objects contemplated by the expedition had been already too much delayed to justify it.

After passing the Court-house, a large butte, to the right of the Chimney Rock, was before us the whole afternoon, and presented so remarkable a resemblance to the capitol at Washington, with its dome in the centre and its wings on either side, that it was the subject of remark with all of our company who had ever seen that building. The resemblance was very strong, and I could not but wonder that it had not elicited remark from some previous traveller; since, compared with the far-famed Chimney Rock, it is a much larger and more imposing object.

After a warm drive of twenty-five miles, we encamped within five miles of the Chimney Rock, upon a point, or rather knoll of land, overlooking the prairie toward the Platte, here about a mile distant. Directly at the foot of the bluff is a most lovely spring, which comes bubbling up from the ground in a clear, pellucid stream, affording abundance of the coldest and most delicious water we had yet found. (Temperature, $52\frac{1}{2}°$.) Here we spent the following day, which was the Sabbath. No wood was to be obtained nearer than the bluffs, and I was obliged to despatch a wagon thither to procure sufficient for cooking purposes. The hunters went out early, and returned about ten o'clock, with as

4

much meat as two pack-mules could carry—their riding-mules also
being loaded with the same welcome freight. They had killed three
elk and an antelope. Ther. in the sun, with fresh breeze, at $12\frac{1}{2}$
o'clock, $98\frac{1}{2}°$.

Monday, July 9.—Ther. at sunrise, 55°; Bar. 26.26; Wind N.
W. I determined this morning to examine more particularly the
curious bluffs or range which extends from the Court-house to
Chimney Rock, and on beyond nearly to Scott's Bluffs. Riding
south from the road for a distance of about five miles over an open
prairie, cut up in every direction by hollows and little short ridges,
we arrived at a pass or gorge through what appeared to be the
main bluff, or southern boundary of the Platte valley. The cliffs
on either side of the pass were about thirty feet high, and presented
a section of clay, sandy clay, and calcareous sandstone. In some
places, projecting from the side of the cliff, were rounded layers of
the latter rock, disposed in a vertical direction, presenting the appearance of the vertebræ of some large animal. On reaching the
summit of the pass, I found that this range, instead of being the
main bluff bounding the Platte valley, was only a high ridge separating it from that of Lawrence's Fork. The latter stream here
runs about north-east, through a broad, level prairie, four or five
miles wide, bounded by a high bluff on its southern side, and discharges itself into the Platte many miles below; the stream forks
just above, and a high, broad ridge, similar in its character to that
we had just crossed, divided the two branches, the valleys of which
seemed to extend a considerable distance to the west. A few trees
were seen on the farther one. In the pass, two handsome varieties of *Digitalis* occurred, both of a blue colour, one with glabrous
leaves, and flowers of a bright blue, the other with pubescent leaves,
and flowers not so bright; a dwarf white chrysanthemum was also
found in the same locality. I hoped to find some more specimens of
lignite on this stream, which is the same that washes the base of the
Court-house lower down, where that substance was seen yesterday.
I accordingly rode out to it. It was here a beautiful bubbling brook,
flowing with a rapid current over sand and rolled stones, brought
down from the Court-house ridge in immense quantities. No
lignite was discovered at this spot, although I have little doubt that
it exists higher up, near the sources of this little stream.

The south side of the ridge, which we followed until nearly opposite the Chimney Rock, presents the same fantastic appearance as does that fronting the Platte valley, being worn by the

weather into jutting, round abutments and castellated towers. At this point the ridge is two miles wide, very much broken, and the side so steep that it was impossible to keep the saddle while ascending. Descending the north slope, we were guided through a series of narrow and extremely intricate ravines by a well-worn buffalo-trail into the plain below. Before us was the Chimney Rock, a point on this route so well known and so often described. In the strata of clay, sand, sandstones, and siliceous limestones, over which we have been travelling for the last three days, the clay is most predominant in this vicinity and to the eastward of Scott's Bluff. The partial disintegration of these strata has in some places given to the bluffs the most curious shapes, and among others, that of the Chimney Rock. This singular conformation has been, undoubtedly, at one time, a portion (probably a projecting shoulder) of the main chain of bluffs bounding the valley of the Platte, and has been separated from it by the action of water. It consists of a conical elevation of about one hundred feet high, its sides forming an angle of about 45° with the horizon; from the apex rises a nearly circular and perpendicular shaft of clay, now from thirty-five to forty feet in height. The cone has, I think, been formed by the disintegration of the softer portion of the bluff arranging itself at its natural angle in a conical form, while the remainder of the earth has been carried away by the floods and distributed over the plain, leaving the broad valley which is at present found between it and the main bluff. The Chimney, being composed of more tenacious materials, has been left standing in a vertical position, and has been worn into its present circular form by the gradual action of the elements. That the shaft has been very much higher than at present, is evident from the corresponding formation of the bluff, as well as from the testimony of all our *voyageurs*, with whom it was for years a landmark or beacon visible for forty or fifty miles, both up and down the river. It is the opinion of Mr. Bridger that it was reduced to its present height by lightning, or some other sudden catastrophe, as he found it broken on his return from one of his trips to St. Louis, though he had passed it uninjured on his way down. Its vicinity has long been a favourite encamping ground for the emigrants, as there are springs of water near and the grass is tolerably good. In crossing over from the valley of Lawrence's Fork, it was noticed that the ridge had been at one time covered with a tolerably dense growth of cedar. These trees have nearly all died, and their trunks are strewn over the ground. Young pines, however, are rapidly taking their place. What could have caused this singular phenomenon? In former years the valley of the Platte was similarly covered with these dead cedars, brought down by the freshets, but now there are none to be found, they having all been converted into fuel by the emigrants. Three miles from the Chimney Rock, the road gradually leaves the river for the purpose of passing behind Scott's Bluff, a point where a spur from the main ridge comes so close to the river as to leave no room for the passage of teams. There was no water between these two points, a distance of more than twenty miles, and we were consequently obliged to go on until nine o'clock, when we encamped at the bluff, on a small run near a delicious spring, after having been in the saddle sixteen hours without food, and travelled thirty-one and a-half miles. The march was a severe one upon the animals, as they were in harness, after the noon halt, for seven successive hours, without water. The afternoon was oppressively hot, and the gnats and musquitoes almost insufferable. There is a temporary blacksmith's shop here, established for the benefit of the emigrants, but especially for that of the owner, who lives in an Indian lodge, and had erected a log shanty by the roadside, in one end of which was the blacksmith's forge, and in the other a grog-shop and sort of grocery. The stock of this establishment consisted principally of such articles as the owner had purchased from the emigrants at a great sacrifice and sold to others at as great a profit. Among other things, an excellent double wagon was pointed out to me, which he had purchased for seventy-five cents. The blacksmith's shop was an equally profitable concern; as, when the smith was indisposed to work himself, he rented the use of shop and tools for the modest price of seventy-five cents an hour, and it was not until after waiting for several hours, that I could get the privilege of shoeing two of the horses, even at that price, the forge having been in constant use by the emigrants. Scott's Bluff, according to our measurement, is five hundred and ninety-six miles from Fort Leavenworth; two hundred and eighty-five from Fort Kearny, and fifty-one from Fort Laramie.

Thursday, July 12.—Bar. 26.13; Ther. at sunrise, 53°. We arrived to-day at Fort Laramie, and encamped a short distance above, on Laramie's Fork, a fine, rapid stream, about fifty yards wide. Here we remained until the 18th, recruiting our animals, getting them shod, repairing our wagons, and making the necessary

FORT LARAMIE.

Ackerman Lith 379 Broadway NY

arrangements for continuing our journey. I here unpacked one of the barometers which I had taken charge of for the Smithsonian Institution, to be left at this post. It had stood the journey admirably, was in perfect order, and was gladly received by Lieutenant Woodbury, of the corps of Engineers. Observations also were made for the latitude of the post, which placed it in lat. 42°.12′ 38.″ 2, long. 104° 31′ 26″.

Fort Laramie, formerly known as Fort John, was one of the posts established by the American Fur Company for the protection of their trade. Its walls are built in the usual style of such structures, of adobe or unburnt brick. The company sold it to the United States Government; and their people, when we arrived, were temporarily encamped near the ford of the creek, having recently surrendered the possession of the post to the troops, whom we found engaged in preparing for its extension and in the erection of additional quarters, under the superintendence of Lieutenant Woodbury. It is garrisoned at present by two companies of Infantry and one of Mounted Rifles, under command of Major Sanderson, of the latter corps, by whom we were received with the greatest courtesy, and promptly furnished with such supplies as were within the resources of his command. I procured here fifteen additional mules, and our stock now consisted of fifty-six mules, five horses, four steers for beef, and two milch-cows, one of which we had found on the prairie, abandoned or lost by her owners.

The country has risen considerably since leaving Scott's Bluff, and the general flora indicates a much drier atmosphere: the grasses especially are brown and burned up wherever the earth is not directly moistened by proximity to some stream. The soil around Fort Laramie appears to be sterile, owing no doubt to the extreme dryness of the air and the almost total absence of dews. The great quantity of coarse conglomerate, too, which, by its disintegration, leaves the surface covered with gravel, must operate as a great impediment to cultivation. The rocks, however, contain the elements of fertility, being composed of limestone, clay, and sand; and I have no doubt that, with the aid of irrigation, the bottom lands of Laramie Creek might be made to produce most abundant crops. Hay is cut about eight miles up the stream in quantity sufficient for the wants of the garrison.

A short excursion of some seven miles up the Laramie river, showed that the sections of the bluffs presented strata of sandstone conglomerate, formed, in some cases, of the detritus of sandstone and calcareous rocks, cemented in an argillaceous matrix. The general direction of the strata was nearly horizontal, but there were evident local displacements, caused apparently by subterraneous upheavings. In some cases the strata were declined as much as 30°, and in opposite directions, within a short space. In many places large quantities occurred of the fragments of primary rocks, resulting, most probably, from the decomposition of conglomerate: the sandstone was often good, although generally too scaly for building purposes.

CHAPTER III.

FROM FORT LARAMIE TO FORT BRIDGER.

Wednesday, July 18.—Taking leave of our friends at Fort Laramie, we continued our journey this morning. The next place where we shall meet with a human habitation will be Fort Bridger, on Black's Fork of Green River, distant about four hundred miles.

While the train followed the travelling track, I took a road nearer the river, and examined a quarry which the workmen from the fort are here opening. The strata exposed in the bluffs were principally gray sandstone, with some thin calcareous layers, the general dip being south and south-west about 17°. On the opposite bank of the river, which is high and covered with pine, the inclination appeared to be much greater. The fossils were quite imperfect. The only ones that could be descried were abundant remains of encrinites. The limestone at the quarry is dark, carboniferous, with conchoidal fracture, and slightly fœtid. It lies in layers of six or eight inches thick, and is immediately overlaid by slaty shales and gray sandstone. A considerable number of *Productus semi-reticulatus* was found in it, as well as in the sand between the layers: some specimens of a large sort of oyster lay in a nearly horizontal position. Some imperfect fossils were also obtained from the sandstone. The general surface is formed of strata of grayish sandstone and clay, the former varying in hardness, some being very friable, while others are exceeding hard, especially some which were slightly coloured by oxide of iron.

Near the quarry was a spring of pure cold water. A vein of trap, about six inches wide, passed perpendicularly through the quarry, and had evidently affected the rocks on either side. Leaving this spot, we struck across to the south, and joined the camp, which had been pitched just below a large warm spring that comes bubbling out of the ground and forms immediately a small stream. Temperature of the spring, 71°.

Above the mouth of Warm Spring Creek, the hills become increased in height, and a lofty range runs north by west, evidently thrown up by internal convulsions, the strata having a considerable dip to the south-west. The banks of the Platte where it cuts through the range are apparently perpendicular, and from a distance appeared to be composed of red sandstone. The general dip of the rocks, where not disturbed, seems still to be toward the south-west, though very slight.

Auguste Tesson, one of my very best men, was taken sick to-day with something very like the cholera.

Thursday, July 19.—Bar. 25.68; Ther. 80°. Leaving the valley of the Warm Spring Branch, the road crosses over to a branch of Bitter Creek, an affluent of the Platte, down the valley of which it winds until it reaches the main stream. We followed this valley the whole day, crossing the stream several times, and encamped on its left bank after a short march of ten and a-half miles. We were detained here the following day by the extreme illness of Auguste, who was unable to be removed. We passed to-day the nearly consumed fragments of about a dozen wagons that had been broken up and burned by their owners; and near them was piled up, in one heap, from six to eight hundred weight of bacon, thrown away for want of means to transport it farther. Boxes, bonnets, trunks, wagon-wheels, whole wagon-bodies, cooking utensils, and, in fact, almost every article of household furniture, were found from place to place along the prairie, abandoned for the same reason. In the evening, Captain Duncan, of the Rifles, with a small escort, rode into camp. He had left Fort Laramie in the morning, and was in hot pursuit of four deserters, who had decamped with an equal number of the best horses belonging to the command.

Bitter Creek is a fine clear stream, about fifty feet wide, with a swift current, and seems, from the great heaps of drift-wood piled up on its banks, to discharge a large quantity of water in the spring.

Upon examining the bluff on the opposite side of the stream, the strata were found to be composed of sandstone and clay with sand. There was also a layer of sulphate of lime about four inches thick and crystalline. In some of the layers of sandstone there were ripple-marks of water; others were thickly studded with oval bodies about the size of pigeons' eggs. Other strata were formed of more compact sandstone, not in layers but in irregular shaped masses, as if composed of bones, much resembling what we had remarked near Chimney Rock. Some fossils were collected, but in not a very perfect state. In some of the sandstones there were evidently a great many, but in the more friable they were rotten; and in others the stone, in the endeavour to get them out, split in every direction. A crystalline mass of what was thought to be sulphate of lime was also found, with dark crystals interspersed. The top of the hill was covered with masses of primitive rock, probably from the decomposition of conglomerate. The hunters brought in the choice parts of three fat buffalo-cows to-day, which fairly loaded down their pack-mules. The meat was estimated to weigh upward of one thousand pounds.

Saturday, July 21.—We followed up the dry bed of a fork of Bitter Creek for three or four miles, when it crosses over a high ridge and descends precipitously into a narrow ravine forming the heads of a branch of Horse-shoe Creek. Following down this ravine, which gradually widens into a broad valley, walled in by steep bluffs, much cut by ravines and entirely destitute of timber, we reached Horse-shoe Creek, a beautiful stream of running water, clear, soft, and very cool. There are two tracks here, one crossing below the junction of the two forks, two hundred yards to the right, the other crossing both forks. The latter was taken, and after crossing the western forks, we followed up its valley for a couple of miles, over some very high, rolling country, and crossing over to the valleys of two dry sandy beds, came to a branch seven miles from Horse-shoe Creek, upon the left bank of which we encamped.

All the dry beds we have passed to-day give evidence of discharging large quantities of water, which, at the melting of the snows, descend from the Black Hills, a range immediately on our left. Their channels are full of rolled primary rock, feldspar, and white and pink quartz, brought down by the spring torrents. Upon the top of the dividing ridge between Bitter Creek and

SCENE IN THE BLACK HILLS.. BITTER CREEK VALLEY.

Horse-shoe, we passed some enormous blocks of granite, lying upon the surface, some of which were cubes of twenty feet.

The road, as usual, was strewn with fragments of broken and burnt wagons, trunks, and immense quantities of white beans, which seemed to have been thrown away by the sackful, their owners having become tired of carrying them farther, or afraid to consume them from danger of the cholera. The commanding officer at Fort Kearny had forbidden their issue at that post on this account. Stoves, gridirons, moulding-planes and carpenters' tools of all sorts, were to be had at every step for the mere trouble of picking them up.

The next day, being Sabbath, was passed in camp, during which hourly observations both of the thermometer and barometer were made, commencing at six o'clock. We are fifty miles from Fort Laramie.

In descending the ridge into the valley of Horse-shoe Creek, a section of a stratum of reddish clay was exposed, some distance above the bottom, surmounted by a large and coarse sandstone. On the banks of the Horse-shoe, there was a perpendicular section of about one hundred feet of a stratum of clay and sandy limestone. The rock seemed very fossiliferous, but, owing to its fracturing in all directions, few specimens could be obtained. The peaks to the left seemed to be of reddish clay, so far as could be judged from their appearance and the manner of their disintegration. A considerable change has taken place in the flora as the country begins to ascend. Since leaving Fort Laramie, a variety of geranium has been frequent upon the borders of the streams. A small-leaved Œnothera, white, and the blue Digitalis, were also found. On the north side of the ridge, some plants were seen which we had not met with before; Azalea; a small white Œnothera, on a tall stem, the flowers not more than a line and a-half in diameter; two species of Potentilla, yellow, and two or three varieties of Campanula.

Monday, July 23.—Ther. 47°. Ascending from the valley of the run where we had encamped, the road winds along a high, undulating ridge, for several miles, with very deep, precipitous ravines heading on each side, thus rendering our course very sinuous. The road then descends for about a mile and a-half into the broad valley of a run which has been on our left for three or four miles, and follows its dry bed until it strikes another fork coming in from the left, with a fine stream of running water, and a broad bottom, covered with willows of a large size. Our course this morning has been about parallel with the range of the Black Hills, the base of which could frequently be seen from the more elevated portions of the road. The valley of the Platte also was to be seen far in the distance to the north. Crossing La Bonté Creek, encamped near a fine spring, after a fatiguing march of twenty-four miles.

In passing along the ridge, the only rock exposed consisted of coarse sandstone, with a decided dip to the north-east of 15°, and beds of clay were interposed between the strata. On descending from the ridge into the valley of the fork, some siliceous limestone was found, from which a few fossils were collected. In the same locality were masses of sandstone of a reddish colour. On the side of a ravine to the left of the road, the same sandstone appeared to crop out. After crossing this stream, the geological character of the country changed materially. The soil assumed a red colour, being composed principally of red sandstones and shales. To the left rose a high crest or ridge crowned with gray and red sandstone, which was very hard. The general direction of this ridge was N. N. W. and S. S. E., and it was manifestly formed by the upheaving of the strata, the dip being at least 45° to the north-east, while the south-west face of the rocks was very precipitous. At nearly the highest point of the ridge, a small ravine occurred, containing a layer of coal shale, apparently overlaid by dark shales, and layers of red clay and light slaty shales. The portions of these strata which were exposed were in so decomposed a state that no fossils could be obtained except very imperfect ones.

In the valley of La Bonté Creek, the soil was found to be formed by the decomposition of highly ferruginous rock. Before the crossing of this stream, a ravine exposed a layer of gypsum, which was very fine and white, and of considerable thickness. Overlying it were layers of red sandstone and shales, conformable with the apparent dip of the sandstones forming the crest. A mile or two beyond the La Bonté, the gray sandstone was seen cropping out, overlying the red sandstone, and with a considerable dip to the north. Above these were layers of red and light shales and impure carboniferous limestone, from which a number of fossils (*Avicula monotis*, and *Cardinia*) were collected. The limestone seemed to be composed, to a great extent, of shells: in the more sandy and slaty shales the fossils were not so numerous. To the left were some eminences composed of the more resisting sandstones, the same as those forming the crest of the ridge, and which seemed to be the result of some force from beneath. The rocks were so broken that no indication could be obtained of their stratification. About one mile from La Bonté, the ridge on the left became lower, and the dip of the rocks was evidently less. They are composed of gray and white sandstone, clayey shales and clay, from which some few fossils were collected.

The formation over which we have been travelling to-day seems to have been the result of the upheaving of the underlying strata, and the direction of the force would appear to have been from N. N. W. to S. S. E. It is not improbable that the trap and red sandstone seen on the Platte about twelve miles above Fort Laramie is the result of the same action, as that point would be in about the direction in which such a line would strike the river. The formation of the high ridges seen on the north side of the Platte is undoubtedly owing to the same cause. The strata observed to the right of the road before leaving the valley of the La Bonté were not conformable with those on the ridge, but had a slight dip to the south-east. They consisted of clay and coarse sandstone, and were analogous to those passed in the early part of the day. There can be but little doubt that they have been deposited since the elevation of the ridge.

Tuesday, July 24.—Ther. at sunrise, 49°. Temperature of the spring the same. The road to-day passes over a rolling country, being spurs of the Black Hills. We crossed the dry beds of several small streams, skirted, in some instances, with willows, box-elder, wild-cherry bushes, and occasionally with some large cotton-woods, until we reached the river La Prêle. At this spot the mules were watered only, it being impossible to procure a blade of grass for them all the day. Consequently, we were obliged to continue on some four miles farther, until we reached the Platte, where we encamped in a pretty little grove of large cotton-woods, with but a very scanty supply of grass. The artemisia seemed, to-day, to have taken complete possession of the country; and what little grass once grew along the road has been literally *burned out* by the passing emigrants.

Upon arriving at the encamping ground, it was found, to our great grief, that the barometer was broken. It had been firmly fixed in an upright position, in the small spring-carriage, and carefully strapped to one of the stancheons; but in coming down a steep and rough ravine, it must have received a jar that snapped the tube in two. The rates of the two chronometers, which were in the same wagons, were, however, unchanged. The large spring-wagon, containing all the instruments, came near meeting with a fatal accident to-day, by the breaking of a breast-chain while descending a steep hill, at the foot of which was a very precipitous ravine, and it was only saved from destruction by the promptitude and presence of mind of one of the men.

The hills over which we passed to-day were composed of coarse sandstone and conglomerate, with a slight dip to the south. From the summit of some hills to the left of the road, a view was obtained of the ridge we had passed over yesterday. It terminated in some low hills. To the W. S. W. of this ridge, and parallel to it, about twelve or fifteen miles distant, was another higher ridge, of which Laramie Peak appeared to be the most easterly elevation. Toward the west was yet another, running north-west, the soil at the base of which was formed from the decomposition of the red sandstone and shales. On the ridge itself were found white and red sandstone, very hard, and foetid dark limestone, the same as that observed at the quarry near Fort Laramie. The dip was here fully 60° to north-east. Some fossils, *Terebratula* and *Productus*, were collected here, principally from the limestone. The strata in the valley appeared to consist of sandstone and shales, and were not conformable with the rocks forming the ridge. These rocks, nevertheless, were found cropping out in some places. On descending into the valley of the Platte, we passed a section of some gray sandstone, with, perhaps, some dark shales, probably carboniferous.

Wednesday, July 25.—Morning bright and cool. Brisk wind from north-west. A distance of five miles up the Platte, over a sandy soil, brought us to Deer Creek, a bright, clear stream, running pleasantly through a large grove of timber, principally cotton-wood. Judging from appearances, this spot has been a favourite camp-ground for the emigrants. Property of every description was strewn about in all directions, and in much greater quantities than we had yet seen. Just above the mouth of this stream, there was a ferry over the Norh Fork of the Platte, at which I determined to cross the train. The means employed for this purpose were of the rudest and simplest kind. The ferry-boat was constructed of seven canoes, dug out from cotton-wood logs, fastened side by side with poles, a couple of hewn logs being secured across their tops, upon which the wheels of the wagons rested. This rude raft was drawn back and forth by means of a rope

CROSSING OF THE PLATTE MOUTH OF DEER CREEK.

Ackermann Lith. 379 Broadway N.Y.

stretched across the river, and secured at the ends to either bank. Frail and insecure as was the appearance of this very primitive ferry-boat, yet all the wagons were passed over in the course of two hours, without the slightest accident, although many of them were very heavily laden. The animals were driven into the stream and obliged to ferry themselves over, which they did without loss, although the river was now somewhat swollen by late rains and the current extremely rapid and turbid. The ferrymen informed me that an emigrant had been drowned here, the day before, in essaying to swim his horse across, which he persisted in attempting, notwithstanding the earnest entreaties and warnings of his friends. They told us that this man made the twenty-eighth victim drowned in crossing the Platte this year; but I am inclined to believe that this must be an exaggeration. The charge for ferriage was two dollars for each wagon. The price, considering that the ferrymen had been for months encamped here, in a little tent, exposed to the assaults of hordes of wandering savages, for the sole purpose of affording this accommodation to travellers, was by no means extravagant.

A short distance above where the road crosses Deer Creek, coal was found cropping out of the bluff on the left bank of the stream. Ascending the creek, the direction of which was about north by west, the strata were inclined at an angle of about three degrees, but not at right angles to the dip, which appeared to be north by east. The coal was lying on a stratum of white sandstone of considerable thickness; above it were some dark shales; and above these, gray sandstones, in which latter were found fossils of *Sigillaria*, and, in those under the coal, stems of *Calamites*; but as the only examples that could be obtained were from rocks which had been exposed to the action of the weather, they were imperfect. The stratum of coal was three or four feet thick, and resembled the cannel coal very much; but as the only specimens obtained were very much weathered, this could not be ascertained with certainty. As the strata rose, the coal could be traced ascending the hills on the side of the bank, and the deeper underlying rocks became more fully exposed. They consisted of sandstones, varying in colour from red to gray, and containing many fossils, principally vegetable.

The road, after crossing the river, runs mostly on the side of the bluffs, which here approach much nearer than on the south side. They consist of reddish sandstone, containing some curious fossils. Among these were perfectly rounded masses, fully a foot in diameter, and others of stone apparently contorted like a rope tied into knots; they all appeared to have been attached to a stem. The formation, on the left side of the river, consists of sandstone with some beds of clayey shales and slaty shales. Salt was found efflorescing on the rocks in two or three places, and this was the case also on the opposite side, at the coal-beds on Deer Creek. Artemisia was almost the only vegetation, and great difficulty was experienced in obtaining enough grass to subsist our animals. The soil appears very barren, more from the absence of moisture than from the character of its constituents; as even the alluvial bottoms exhibit the same destitute and naked features. The road, since crossing, has been through deep sand, making the travel extremely slow and fatiguing. Day's march, fifteen and a-half miles.

Thursday, July 26.—Early this morning we passed a small island in the river, promising a welcome supply of grass for our wearied animals, which for the last three days have had very little to eat, and begin to exhibit the effects of this want of nourishment. Having afforded them a hearty meal, we continued up the valley to a high bluff running to the river: we crossed it and encamped in a deep valley beyond, where some pools of standing water afforded drink for our stock. The grass was quite sufficient. Some of the pools were so highly impregnated with salt as to be quite unpleasant to the taste.

The general character of the formation is the same as that of yesterday—sandstone and shales: coal was found in two places, the first near the island where we nooned, and again about five miles beyond. In both cases the overlying strata were shales and clay; and that beneath, sandstone. The dip has been mostly to the north; but, where the coal was last seen, the strata were found dipping to the south-west, at an angle of about 20°. They then became horizontal, and in about half a mile the dip was again to the north. Some specimens of shale, with impressions of leaves, were collected, and also some crystallized carbonate of soda.

Friday, July 27.—Morning bright and cool. The road for the greater part of the day has been through deep, heavy white sand, of which the hills seem to be chiefly composed. Turning off from the river, we left the road for the purpose of finding grass, and encamped directly behind the Red Buttes, five miles distant from the river, on the margin of a small lake or pond, formed by numerous little springs of very cold and excellent water.   Grass was found on a neighbouring hillside sufficient for our animals.

The road to-day passed over from the Platte, crossing a spur of of the mountains.   Above this point, a high range of hills, which had been observed running to the north-west, inclined rather more to the north side of the river, which here forces a passage for itself through a gorge of the mountain.   The strata there presented were of red sandstone and shales, whence the name of " Red Buttes."   The rocks were inclined at an angle of about 25°, with a dip to the west, as were also the strata on the north side. The sections presented were of sandstones, white or red, shales, slaty shales, and clay.   Considerable quantities of nitrate and carbonate of soda were found on the surface.

To-day we find additional and melancholy evidence of the difficulties encountered by those who are ahead of us.   Before halting to noon, we passed eleven wagons that had been broken up, the spokes of the wheels taken to make pack-saddles, and the rest burned or otherwise destroyed.   The road has been literally strewn with articles that have been thrown away. Bar-iron and steel, large blacksmiths' anvils and bellows, crow-bars, drills, augers, gold-washers, chisels, axes, lead, trunks, spades, ploughs, large grindstones, baking-ovens, cooking-stoves without number, kegs, barrels, harness, clothing, bacon, and beans, were found along the road in pretty much the order in which they have been here enumerated.   The carcasses of eight oxen, lying in one heap by the roadside, this morning, explained a part of the trouble.   I recognised the trunks of some of the passengers who had accompanied me from St. Louis to Kansas, on the Missouri, and who had here thrown away their wagons and every thing they could not pack upon their mules, and proceeded on their journey·   At the noon halt, an excellent rifle was found in the river, thrown there by some desperate emigrant who had been unable to carry it any farther.   In the course of this one day the relics of seventeen wagons and the carcasses of twenty-seven dead oxen have been seen.   Day's march, twenty-four miles.

Saturday, July 28.—Morning bright and pleasant, but at 9 A. M. the wind rose from the south-west, and blew almost a hurricane the whole day, tearing up the sand and gravel, and dashing it into our faces, as we rode, with such violence as to cause sensible pain.   It was impossible to look up for a moment, as the eyes became immediately filled with sand, so that the teamsters were obliged to fasten their handkerchiefs over their faces to enable them to see where they were going. This has been the most disagreeable day's travel we have yet experienced; for the wind, in addition to its furious violence, was so very hot and dry as to render respiration, from the great rarefaction, quite difficult. The throat and fauces became dry, the lips clammy and parched, and the eyes much inflamed from the drifting dust. A pair of green goggles partially remedied this latter annoyance; and I would advise every one who contemplates a journey across these sandy plains, to provide himself with several pairs before starting. They afford great relief from the incessant glare of a bright sun, to which he may make up his mind to be constantly exposed during the whole of his weary route. With all our efforts, owing to these opposing causes, our day's march was only eighteen miles, and we encamped on the head of a spring, one hundred and sixty-four miles from Fort Laramie and forty-four miles from the ferry, and remained at this camp over Sunday.

The country, all the way from the crossing of the Platte, is a dry, sterile, and dreary desert. The artemisia constitutes nearly the whole growth, and what little grass had come up has been completely eaten off by the hundred thousand animals that have passed before us. Thirty-one head of dead cattle were passed on the roadside to-day, and on the bank of a small drain, where the efflorescence of alkaline matter was very abundant and rendered the water nauseously offensive, nine oxen lay dead in one heap. They had been poisoned, doubtless, by the water. Our accompanying friends occupied a portion of Sunday in selecting such articles as they could best spare, and threw them away to lighten their load, their animals beginning to fail quite sensibly. The day was cool, with a fresh breeze from the north. Thermometer at sundown, 52°; and at 10 P. M. 44°.

Monday, July 30.—Ther. at sunrise, 29°. Morning very cold. Ice, half an inch thick, had formed during the night in the water-buckets, and a faint white-frost was visible on the ground. To-day we crossed over to the Sweetwater River, descending into its valley by the side of a small tributary, whose course was nearly south, and encamped on the left bank of this beautiful little stream, a mile below Independence Rock. The river is about seventy feet wide, from six to eighteen inches in depth, with a uniform and tolerably rapid current of clear, transparent water.

In the valley of the tributary opposite our noon halt, some

masses of igneous rocks, granite and serpentine, protruded considerably above the soil. The direction of the dike was from north to south. The strata through which they protruded did not appear to be disturbed, nor were any specimens of metamorphic rocks found near them, although, had such existed, their presence would have been indicated, as being more resisting than the sandstone of which the surface rock is generally composed. Wherever any sections of the latter have been obtained, they were found to be either coarse white or gray sandstone, and clay, with coarse conglomerate. Some distance below this dike, the igneous rocks again became visible, and at this point portions of white sandstone were found overlying the lower parts of the rock, and apparently in horizontal layers. The surface of the ground in the vicinity, where water had apparently stood, was coated with a white saline substance, a portion of which was collected.

The same substance has been observed within the last two days on the surface in those localities where water has evaporated. Near our encampment this evening, large masses of igneous rock protrude in every direction, but the sandstone near them does not appear to have been disturbed.

Few or no flowers have been met with on this portion of the route, owing, in part, to the dryness of the atmosphere, (due to our increasing elevation,) and in part to the occurrence of frosts during the summer months.

Tuesday, July 31.—Ther. at sunrise, 40°. Leaving camp we continued up the valley of the Sweetwater, and passed the far-famed "Independence Rock," a large rounded mass of granite, which has frequently been described by travellers. It was covered with names of the passing emigrants, some of whom seemed determined, judging from the size of their inscriptions, that they would go down to posterity in all their fair proportions. A short distance beyond was a range of granite hills, stretching entirely across the valley, and continuous with a range extending to the north. Through this range the Sweetwater passes in a narrow cleft or gorge, about two hundred yards in length, called the "Devil's Gate." The space between the cliff, on either side, did not in some places exceed forty feet. The height was from three to four hundred feet, very nearly perpendicular, and, on the south side, overhanging. Through this romantic pass the river brawls and frets over broken masses of rock that obstruct its passage, affording one of the most lovely, cool, and refreshing retreats from

5

the eternal sunshine without, that the imagination could desire. It is difficult to account for the river having forced its passage through the rocks at this point, as the hills, a very short distance to the south, are much lower, and, according to present appearance, present by no means such serious obstacles as had been here encountered. It is probable, that when the cañon was formed, stratified rocks obstructed it in that direction, and that these rocks have since disappeared by slow disintegration. The granite rocks of the pass were traversed in many places by dikes of trap, which were in some instances twenty feet thick, whose direction was east and west. South of the pass, at its eastern extremity, stratified rocks, consisting of conglomerate, were observed, in a nearly horizontal position, without exhibiting the least evidence of having been disturbed by the igneous rocks around which they were placed; indeed, they could be traced in close contact with the granite, without any displacement of the strata, proving that their formation must have been subsequent to that of the granite, from the disintegration of which they were composed. The conglomerate is of the same character as that which was observed before coming upon the carboniferous rocks. The rocks were not observed to have any marked dip. It is highly probable that they belong to a period subsequent to that in which the carboniferous rocks were formed, and that the eruption of granite took place after the latter formation, but before that of the conglomerate. No dikes of trap were observed in the granite, except in the immediate vicinity of the Devil's Gate.

After passing this remarkable cañon, we enter upon a broad level valley, bounded on each side by ranges of mountains, their summits broken into curious peaks and eminences entirely destitute of vegetation. Between these winds the Sweetwater, with a current more gentle than heretofore, its banks covered with grass. An accident occurring to one of the wagons, the remainder of the day was consumed in its repair. Thermometer at sunset, 70°.

Wednesday, August 1.—Ther. at sunrise, 33°. Frost during the night; morning clear, calm, and very beautiful. The road passing occasionally through deep, heavy sand, continued up the right bank of the Sweetwater, which, for the greater part of the morning, flowed at the foot of a long, high range of granite bluffs, with here and there a stunted cedar growing from the crevices in the rocks. The valley is here nearly two miles wide, with rolling hills between the two mountain ranges, which bound it on either side and form its limits. The artemisia seems to have taken complete possession of the soil, growing five or six feet high, with twisted stems, resembling somewhat in their texture the ground cedar of the New England coast. At the Devil's Gate I noticed some, quite seven feet high and nine inches in diameter. The Wind-River Mountains were seen on the horizon—their sides, for a third part of the distance down from their summits, glistening with snow, in the rays of the morning sun, like burnished silver. They presented a very beautiful object.

About a dozen burnt wagons and nineteen dead oxen were passed to-day along the road; but the destruction has been by no means as great as upon the North Fork of the Platte and the crossing over to the Sweetwater.

In the morning we passed what at a distance appeared to be a small lake or pond, frozen over and covered with a very light fall of drifting snow. The illusion was perfect, and was maintained to the last moment, even when riding up to its very margin. It was found to be a slight depression, about four hundred yards long, by one hundred and fifty in width, covered with an efflorescence of carbonate of soda, deposited on the ground from the evaporation of the water which had held it in solution. This substance, indeed, covers a large portion of the country, and is quite abundant on the banks of the river. The emigrants use it in mixing their bread, and prefer it to the salæratus of the shops for that purpose.

On the south range of mountains, about fifteen miles above the Devil's Gate, a ravine, formed by a small stream, exposed a section of the rocks. The strata evidently belonged to the carboniferous system, and had been acted upon by heat. The limestone was in some instances converted into marble, and other specimens afforded examples of its partial change. It belonged to the dark slaty-coloured variety, such as had been found at the quarry near Fort Laramie, and has since been seen wherever the lower beds have been tilted up. The red and white sandstone had also been affected by heat, their structure being more crystalline. The dip was to the south, and was very great, varying from 70° to 80°, and some of the lower beds of the red sandstone were nearly vertical. The sequence of the strata seemed to be exactly the same as had been observed near the Red Buttes. On the west surface of the hills, which were precipitous, and covered to a great extent with pine, dark bands of soil were observed, having the appearance of being formed by the decomposition of carbonaceous matter, which however must have been altered by heat. It is highly probable that these beds have been tilted up by some granite rock, although none appeared on the surface, being probably covered up by the secondary beds which have been deposited since the eruption took place. The valley between the hills and the river gradually rose, and where the rocks had been protruded must have been at a considerable elevation above the latter. They were composed of white and gray sandstones, evidently fossiliferous, but the fossils were in so decomposed a state that no specimens, with the exception of some imperfect encrinital stems, could be obtained. The beds were nearly horizontal, and were analogous to the same formation over which we had been passing all along the Platte. Toward the close of our march to-day, the summit of one of these lower hills was found to be composed of clay similar to that of the Chimney Rock, and to the formations in that vicinity. The elevations, though not so marked as to peculiarity of form, resembled them in their general features. The rocks on the north side of the river are still granitic.

Encamped, after a march of twenty-one and a-half miles, on the right bank of the river, which is here growing smaller and the current more gentle. In the course of the day we passed a party of eight wagons from Iowa, bound to the land of gold. A number of women and children were of the party, and application was made for medical attendance upon one of the former, who was about being confined.

Friday, August 3.—Ther. at sunrise, 31°. The rocky ridges gradually disappeared as we followed up the valley of the Sweetwater, occasionally crossing long and lofty spurs which would not admit of our passing between them and the river. The soil is very barren, producing only the artemisia, and two or three varieties of grass ; a species of *Iris*, which is quite abundant, the *Linum ceruleum*, a yellow *Potentilla*, a scarlet star-shaped flower, with tubular corolla, and *Œnothera hispida* were seen in the bottoms.

The character of the valley for the last two days has been analogous to that of the Platte below Fort Laramie. The last of the granite was passed yesterday. The hills on both sides of the river have since been formed of sandstones and clay, the latter of which forms the irregular outline of the bluffs above Ash Hollow, and in many instances presenting a similar appearance when it is found on the tops of the hills. The strata seemed perfectly horizontal. At our nooning point yesterday, the carboniferous rocks were found rising up at a considerable angle, but no section was obtained. The only rock exposed was the red sandstone, which had been rendered partially crystalline by the action of heat. The surrounding rocks had not been disturbed. Some beds of very coarse conglomerate were seen cropping out near the river.

In the course of the day, Captain Duncan, of the Rifles, who had passed us at Bitter Creek on the 19th of July, in pursuit of deserters, came into camp, having followed his men to within fifty miles of Fort Bridger. He had come upon them at daylight, while they lay asleep, disarmed them, secured their horses, and was now on his return, having taken also another man who had deserted previously—so that he had five in all. The pursuit was one of great hardship, privation, and fatigue, and the energy and perseverance with which it had been continued was the subject of admiration with all. Encamped on the Sweetwater, at a point where the road leaves it to avoid a cañon above, which is impassable for wagons for several miles. March, in the last two days, forty miles.

Saturday, August 4.—Morning clear and cool. Leaving the train to follow the beaten track, which makes a short cut over the hills, I determined to follow up the cañon of the Sweetwater. The stream, as I had anticipated, was shut up between lofty, rocky eminences, coming down directly to the water at an angle of from 45° to 60°, along the sides of which we scrambled, sometimes walking and leading our mules over crags where it was impossible to ride, crossing and recrossing the stream ever and anon, to enable our animals to get along at all. A short distance after entering the cañon, the red sandstone was found cropping out at an angle of 45°, with a dip to the north; and a little farther on the crystalline rocks appeared, forming the sides of the cañon. The prevailing rock was gneiss; but sienite and granite were found in some places constituting the principal bulk of the formation. A narrow bottom occasionally gave room for some fine groves of large aspens, the sight of which, after our long and dreary ride without a particle of shade, was truly refreshing. The bed of the river was filled with large boulders and fragments of rock which had fallen from the cliffs above, among which the waters foamed and fretted with a gurgling murmur, which, when contrasted with the flat, silent waters of the Platte, was very pleasant to the ear. It reminded one of the clear, purling streams we had left at home.

The river here is truly a mountain-stream, with great fall, rapid current, and water as clear as crystal, of the temperature of 55°. On emerging from the district of primary rocks, we came upon the stratified, which were formed of micaceous, slaty shales, and red sandstone, all evidently metamorphic: their beds were inclined at an angle of from 40° to 70° to the north. Veins of quartz were observed in them in some places. Trap dikes were very frequent in the crystalline rocks. The surface rock on the hills in the vicinity appeared to be a continuation of the same shaly formation. The aspen, beech, willow, and cotton-wood were found growing on the bottoms, and on the hills cotton-wood, pine, and cedar. Sage hens, (*Tetrao urophasianus*,) a species of grouse, were seen in great numbers, and the men shot as many as we could conveniently carry. They are very good eating, and some of the older ones were larger than a full-grown barn-door fowl.

In the afternoon, we met the mail from Great Salt Lake City, with upward of six thousand letters, and were glad to avail ourselves of the opportunity to write to our friends. Camp on Sweetwater. Day's march, twenty-three miles.

Monday, August 6.—Leaving the valley of the Sweetwater, we crossed this morning through the South Pass over to the head branches of Sandy Creek, an affluent of the Colorado, or Green River of the West, and nooned at the "Pacific Springs," at the foot of the pass, on the western side. This celebrated depression through the Rocky Mountains is now so well known that any further description of it would be superfluous. That of Frémont conveys a very accurate idea of the locality, which has nothing remarkable in its features. The water at the Pacific Springs is not very good, but is quite cold. It is a favourite camping ground of the emigrants on account of the grass. Encamped for the night on the banks of Dry Sandy, where we had to dig in the bed of the stream for water; but a very scanty supply was obtained; and the grass moreover was so scarce that our animals were allowed to run loose all night under the protection of the guard, instead of being picketed as usual. In the afternoon, one of our best mules died from the bite of a snake. In the morning her jaws and fauces had been observed to be very much swollen, and before sundown she became so weak that we were obliged to release her from the wagon, when she lay down by the side of the road and in a short time expired.

Between the Sweetwater and the South Pass, the soil for some four or five miles presented the same disintegrated dark shales as had been observed on the other side of the river. It then became more sandy, and portions of weathered marble were found on the surface. On ascending some low hills on the left of the road, and within about a mile of the Pass, marble was found in place, containing a considerable incrustation of silex. It evidently cropped out on the south side of these hills, on the top of one of which was found a stratum of gray sandstone, in which the remains of encrinites were observed. It was quite horizontal, not conformable with the marble under it, and was undoubtedly a continuation of the secondary formation which had been observed up the whole valley of the Sweetwater. On the left of the road, and a few miles distant, were some high hills, which, from their appearance, seemed to be capped by the reddish clay which forms the isolated masses in the valley of the Platte. Shortly after passing the summit we found a stratum of apparently metamorphic clay, horizontal, with an east and west direction. Over this were strata of gray sandstone, horizontal, or with a slight dip to the east. Descending the western side of the Pass, the soil was composed principally of red sand. No rocks were visible. About a mile from Dry Sandy, some masses of rock were observed on the right of the road, standing up like pillars; they were found to be composed of a coarse sandstone, of an ochrey colour. Under them were white and red shales, apparently horizontal. The surface of the ground appeared to be the result of the decomposition of this ochrey rock.

I witnessed, at the Pacific Springs, an instance of no little ingenuity on the part of some emigrant. Immediately alongside of the road was what purported to be a grave, prepared with more than usual care, having a headboard on which was painted the name and age of the deceased, the time of his death, and the part of the country from which he came. I afterward ascertained that this was only a *ruse* to conceal the fact that the grave, instead of containing the mortal remains of a human being, had been made a safe receptacle for divers casks of brandy, which the owner could carry no farther. He afterward sold his liquor to some traders farther on, who, by his description of its locality, found it without difficulty.

Wednesday, August 8.—In our march, yesterday, to the Little

Sandy, where we encamped, nothing of interest was observed. In Little Sandy the same strata as had occurred previously were found, with a dip of 8° to the south. A section of the rock in the vicinity, exposed on the top the same ochrey-coloured sandstone, and then red shales. From the shales were obtained some remains of plants, but the rock was in so decomposed a state that they could not be identified. On the road, some fragments of limestone were found on the surface, containing fossils, but we could not secure any specimens. From Little Sandy to Big Sandy, artemisia covers the whole face of the country, which has a dreary, barren aspect. Near our camp of this morning, a small section presented thin laminated white sandstones and clayey shales; and from the appearance of the country for several miles, this must have been the character of the rocks. Twelve miles from the Little Sandy, on descending a ravine, fossiliferous trunks of large trees, some of them nearly two feet in diameter, were observed upon the ground: the interior of some of these was hollowed out, but concentric rings were noticed near the circumference, and, in some specimens, longitudinal fibres were found in the interior. The bark appeared to be marked in places for the attachment of leaves of *Cycadeœ*, but they were all much weathered. The rocks on the river-bank were white compact sandstone, disposed in thin lamellæ, sandy and clayey shales, and a gray compact limestone, breaking with a conchoidal fracture. Some large portions of trunks of trees were protruding from the cliff, imbedded in apparently arenaceous shales. Some few specimens of fossils (*Nautilus* and *corals*) were collected, but, on account of the weathered state of the rocks, they were necessarily imperfect. The limestones contained but few fossils.

Thursday, August 9.—Our road to-day lay along the right bank of Big Sandy, until we reached Green River, which we crossed above the junction, and encamped a couple of miles below. The increased altitude, and the consequent dryness of the atmosphere, had so shrunk the woodwork of many of our wagon-wheels, that various expedients had to be resorted to, in order to prevent them from falling to pieces. To-day one of the wheels of the instrument-wagon, that precious and important portion of our train, became so weak from this cause that I was forced to take out nearly all the load, and distribute it among the other teams, to enable us to reach camp with it. We picked up a pair of wheels belonging to some emigrant-wagon, but they would not answer; so we were obliged to wedge up the wheel as well as we could, and to sink it in the river during the night, to swell the wood.

The bluffs on Big Sandy presented several sections. The strata consisted of thin layers of clayey shales, argillaceous gray limestones, and of crystallized sulphate of lime. These strata were seldom more than two or three inches in thickness, the layers of gypsum being about half an inch. There were also thin laminæ of dark slaty shales above the gray limestone. Remains of plants were found, and also some imperfect shells. Near the junction of Big Sandy with Green River some large nodules of ferruginous sandstone were observed, and near them the remains of trees of a large size. The dip was about 5°, a little to the west of south. Upon Green River we came upon a layer of brownish clay, of considerable thickness; and from the appearance of the hills on our right, it is probable that they are formed by the weathering of this bed of clay. Green River, or the Colorado of the Gulf of California, is here a fine, bold, clear stream, discharging a large quantity of water. In its bed are found rounded stones, consisting principally of detritus of primary rocks. Day's march, only thirteen miles.

Friday, August 10.—After travelling about four miles, the road leaves Green River and crosses over a ridge dividing it from Black's Fork, one of its tributaries, upon the left bank of which we encamped, with abundance of grass, and wood obtained from the willows which here fringed its banks. The Uintah mountains were distinctly seen far to the south, their sides glittering with snow in the rays of the setting sun.

In a ravine of the western bluff of Green River valley, the rocks were partially exposed, particularly some strata of hard white sandstone. They consisted of sandstone in laminæ, about fifteen inches thick, and layers of argillaceous shales, and argillaceous limestone, made up principally of shells. There were evidently, also, some strata of conglomerate, formed chiefly of serpentine, sienite, and trap. Among the rounded pebbles found near the top of the ravine was one of dark fœtid limestone, partially converted into marble, and precisely similar to the metamorphic limestone observed flanking the granite chain in the vicinity of the South Pass. A specimen of fossil wood was also found, which appeared to have been partially converted into lignite. The strata were, as far as could be judged, horizontal, and a section on the opposite side of the valley showed the same sandstone maintaining about the same level. If there was any dip, it was to the south, although certainly not so great as had been observed in the strata since leaving the South Pass. Quite a number of fossils were collected here. The character of the soil in the valley of Green River would indicate a considerable preponderance of argillaceous elements in the rocks. The ridge between it and Black's Fork afforded an imperfect section of the rocks. They were, however, mostly covered by clay. The less decomposed rock consisted of white and slaty sandstone, a coarse-grained grayish sandstone, and a thin stratum of limestone. But few fossils could be collected, the surface of the rocks being almost entirely concealed by blue clay—the result of the disintegration of strata which seemed to compose the greater portion of the mass. The strata were very nearly horizontal, although a slight dip to the north was suspected. Common salt was found on some of the stones. The layer of limestone was near the top of the rocks.

Saturday, August 11.—Ther. at 6 o'clock, 40°. A drive of thirty-two miles, during which we crossed Ham's Fork and Black's Fork three times, brought us to Fort Bridger—an Indian trading-post, situated on the latter stream, which here branches into three principal channels, forming several extensive islands, upon one of which the fort is placed. It is built in the usual form of pickets, with the lodging apartments and offices opening into a hollow square, protected from attack from without by a strong gate of timber. On the north, and continuous with the walls, is a strong high picket-fence, enclosing a large yard, into which the animals belonging to the establishment are driven for protection from both wild beasts and Indians. We were received with great kindness and lavish hospitality by the proprietor, Major James Bridger, one of the oldest mountain-men in this entire region, who has been engaged in the Indian trade, here, and upon the heads of the Missouri and Columbia, for the last thirty years. Several of my wagons needing repair, the train was detained five days for the purpose, Major Bridger courteously placing his blacksmith-shop at my service.

In a ravine to the right of the ford of Ham's Fork, on the north bank, white sandstone was found cropping out, and here some specimens of very perfect shells were collected. Under the sandstone were argillaceous shales, and above them apparently a thin stratum of limestone and rolled pebbles. The general surface of the country appeared to be the result of the disintegration of argillaceous

FORT BRIDGER. BLACK'S FORK OF GREEN RIVER

Ackerman Lith. 379 Broadway NY

rocks and some sandstones, the former greatly predominating. In some places, layers of blue and red clay, of considerable thickness, were observed, and also gray argillaceous limestone; but owing to the surface of the rocks being covered by the clay detritus, no complete sections of them were obtained, nor were any fossils found in them. Farther on, upon Black's Fork, a ridge was crossed in which the different layers of the rocks were quite apparent. Here two strata of coarse reddish sandstone, which disintegrated but slowly, were prominent. They were separated by layers of limestone, shales, and clay. The shales were so nearly horizontal that no dip could be ascertained. Following the valley of Black's Fork, we passed, in the afternoon, strata of green and white sandstone, whitish shales, and clay, but too much decomposed to afford us any fossils. In the valley were found some blocks of limestone, wholly made up of the debris of shells. The valley of Black's Fork, in the vicinity of Bridger's Fort, is three or four miles broad, and many of the numerous little branches into which the stream is divided are handsomely fringed with thickets of cotton-wood. The soil is composed of the detritus of the surrounding rocks, and huge blocks of metamorphic rock, and some trap and serpentine, are found upon the surface. At the fort we were shown a piece of rock, evidently volcanic, in the cells of which were contained some particles of gold. It was stated that it had been found in the bed of Black's Fork in the vicinity. If so, it must have been washed down from the Uintah chain of mountains, a lofty range to the south, in which the stream heads. These mountains were at this time covered with snow for a considerable distance from their summits; but of their lithological formation no opinion could be formed, as their great distance precluded all opportunity of examining them. The strata of the hills around the fort were nearly horizontal, and consisted of gray limestone, clayey and slaty shales, and sandstones. Some few miles up the stream, sections of these rocks were found, from which some fossils were obtained. In the beds of the stream were found rounded rocks, composed principally of metamorphic sandstone, and some marble. The same rocks were seen in horizontal strata on the hills.

From Fort Bridger there are now two routes as far as the Humboldt or Mary's River, where they again unite. The old road strikes Bear River, follows down its valley by the Soda Springs to Fort Hall, whence it pursues a south-westerly course to the Humboldt. By this route a northing of nearly two degrees is made, and the road, consequently, is much lengthened. The other route was laid out by the Mormon community in 1847, and conducts the emigrant to their city, in the southern part of the Salt Lake valley, causing him to vary from the line of his direction rather more than a degree southwardly : this he has to recover by a direct north course to the crossing of Bear River near the north end of the lake, whence he proceeds in a north-west direction, until he intersects the old road from Fort Hall. I was desirous of ascertaining whether a shorter route than either of these could not be obtained by pursuing a direct course to the head of the lake, or to the point where Bear River enters its basin through the Wahsatch range from Cache Valley. If practicable, such a trace would save the emigration the great detour that has to be made by either of the present routes, and would have a direct bearing upon the selection of a site for the military post contemplated for this region. I had ascertained that this selection had not yet been made, the officer designated for that purpose having determined to winter his command in temporary quarters, in the vicinity of Fort Hall. A glance at the map will show the importance of this "cut-off" to the travel for either Oregon or California. I therefore determined to make the examination myself, accompanied by Major Bridger, and to send forward the train to Salt Lake City by the Mormon road, under the command of Lieutenant Gunnison, whose health had become so far established as to enable him to resume his seat in the saddle. The train left, accordingly, on the 16th; but as we returned to this point by the same route the following year, I defer for the present any description of it. I was myself detained until the 20th, by the absence of the partner of Major Bridger, who was on a trip to Salt Lake City, and without whose presence Major B. did not deem it prudent to leave the fort. As the examination was intended to be a mere reconnoissance, without instruments, a couple of men, with as many pack-mules, a little flour and bacon, with some ground coffee, and a blanket a piece, comprised all the preparation it was thought needful to make, taking care, however, that the little party should be well armed.

CHAPTER IV.

FROM FORT BRIDGER TO GREAT SALT LAKE CITY.

Monday, August 20.—We followed the Mormon road for several miles, and then took a " cut-off" leading more to the north, crossing the dividing ridge between the waters of Muddy Fork, an affluent of Green River, and those of Bear River, which falls into the Great Basin. We crossed the broad valley of Tar-Spring Creek, a tributary of Bear River, where the two roads join. The " cut-off" has been abandoned on account of an almost impassable hill at the dividing ridge. This, and another almost equally steep, are the only objections to this route, the rest of the way being excellent. Leaving the Mormon road at the crossing of Bear River, we followed down its valley six miles, as far as Medicine Butte, an elevated knob in the valley. This is a spot well known among the Indians, as that to which they were formerly in the habit of repairing to consult their oracles, or " medicine-men," who had located their " medicine lodge" in the vicinity of this little mountain. The route of a road to reach the north end of Salt Lake should pursue a nearly west course from Bridger's Fort to this Butte, a distance of about thirty miles; the country, according to the representations of our guide, who has passed over it many times, being extremely favourable.

At our encampment on Bear River, near this Butte, abundance of speckled trout were caught, resembling in all respects the brook trout of the States, except that the speckles are black instead of yellow. An ox, which had strayed from some unfortunate emigrant, was found on the bank of the stream, in such capital condition that he was shot for food, and such portions as we could not carry with us were most generously presented to a small encampment of Shoshonee Indians, whose wigwams were erected among the bushes on the opposite side of the stream. It was curious to see how perfectly every portion of the animal was secured by them for food, even the paunch and entrails being thoroughly washed for that purpose. The squaws acted as the butchers, and displayed familiar acquaintance with the business, while the men lounged about, leaning lazily upon their rifles, looking listlessly on, as if it were a matter in which they were in no manner interested. They had quite a large number of horses and mules, and their encampment betokened comparative comfort and wealth.

The bottom of Bear River is here four or five miles in breadth, and is partially overflowed in the spring: the snow lies upon it to the depth of four feet in the winter, which prevents the Indians from occupying it during that season of the year, for which it would otherwise be well adapted.

In leaving Fort Bridger, we passed over horizontal lias beds. About six miles to the north of the road, the country appeared to be much broken up, and not solely by the action of water. The strata seemed dislocated and inclined, presenting much the same appearance as those near Laramie. Near this point, Frémont states that he found coal, which probably has been thrown up here. At Ogden's Hole, on the eastern slope of the Wahsatch Mountains, we found the ranges of hills to be composed of the carboniferous strata, thrown up at a very considerable angle; and at Bear River, near our encampment of to-day, they were almost perpendicular, the later strata being deposited by their side in an almost horizontal position, with a very slight dip to the southeast. At this latter point, the older sandstones were cropping out at an angle of 35°; and on the opposite side of the river, the same strata were seen with a dip in the contrary direction, the valley being evidently an anticlinal axis.

Wednesday, August 22.—Crossing the broad valley of Bear River diagonally, we forded that stream, and struck over a point of bluff into a valley, the course of which being too much to the south for our purpose, we passed over to another, and followed it to its head, where it opens upon a long ridge, running to the south-west. Instead of following the ridge, (which I afterward found should have been done,) we crossed over two more ridges into a third valley, in which was a small rapid stream running into Bear River. Fearful of getting too far south, I ascended the western bluff of this stream, in hopes of finding a valley or ridge the course of which would give us more westing; but the country, in that direction, was so much broken that we were forced still farther to the south, and struck upon the heads of Pumbar's Creek, a tributary of the Weber River, which latter discharges its waters into the Great Salt Lake. This valley, our guide insisted, would lead us in the right direction, and it was concluded to follow it down,

which we did for about four miles, and bivouacked for the night.
We continued down this valley until the middle of the following
day, when, instead of the broad open appearance which it had at
first presented, it soon began to contract, until it formed a cañon,
with sides so steep that it was scarcely passable for mules. A
blind Indian-trail wound along the hillside, at an elevation of
several hundred feet above the stream, into which a single false
step of our mules would instantly have precipitated us. It required no small exertion of nerve to look down from this dizzy
height into the yawning gulf beneath. After following the cañon
some ten miles, we came to a broad valley coming into it from the
left, which the guide declared headed in the ridge from which we
had descended yesterday, and to the eastward of the route we had
taken. As all prospect of a road by the valley of Pumbar's
Creek was now out of the question, I determined to follow up this
valley and ascertain whether a route could not be obtained in that
direction. This was accordingly done, and we found it to be as
the guide had stated. This branch of Pumbar's Creek, which we
called Red Chimney Fork, from the remarkable resemblance of
one of the projections of the cliffs to that object, we found to
have a very moderate descent from the ridge to its mouth, with
plenty of room for a road, requiring but little labour to render
it a good one. The timber is small and consists of oak, black-
jack, aspen, wild-cherry, service-berry, and box-elder of large size.
In many places it is quite abundant.

On Pumbar's Creek, the hills were composed of strata of marble and metamorphic sandstone, inclined at an angle of 80° to the
north-east. Lower down, the horizontal strata were found lying
by the side of these inclined rocks. On Red Chimney Fork, the
strata were nearly horizontal, consisting principally of layers of
red sandstone conglomerate, formed from metamorphic rocks with
calcareous cement, and white sandstone with layers of conglomerate interposed. Near its junction with Pumbar's Creek, strata
of slaty shales occurred, cropping out at an angle of 70°.

Below the Red Chimney Fork, the valley of Pumbar's Creek
opens sufficiently to allow the passage of a road through the bottom; but, as its course was leading us from our intended direction, we availed ourselves of a ravine, which, a mile below, comes
into it from the north-west, and followed this up to its head, thus
attaining the height of the general level of the country. The
ascent is quite regular, but the road would have to be *made* all

the way up, and a considerable quantity of small cotton-wood timber cut out. The upper strata on this branch appeared to be
nearly analogous to those met with on Red Chimney Fork. We
followed this ridge or table in a north-west direction for several
miles, when we became involved among numerous ravines which
ran to the south, and were too deep and abrupt to be available.
In order to avoid them, the trace must be thrown so much to the
north, that even were a road practicable up to this point, it would
be entirely too crooked; and great difficulty, moreover, would have
to be encountered in crossing the immense ravines which lay at
the eastern base of the ranges bordering the Salt Lake. Some of
these ravines run down into Ogden's Creek, and others into Bear
River below the point at which we crossed it. Time would not
admit of my pursuing the examination farther in this direction.
My train had left Fort Bridger several days before me, and would
be awaiting my arrival at Great Salt Lake City to commence the
survey which was the more immediate object of the expedition.
I, therefore, although with the greatest reluctance, concluded to
make the best of my way to the lake, passing through Ogden's
Hole, and thence crossing the high range dividing it from Salt
Lake Valley, by a pass which the guide informed me existed there.
We accordingly changed our course, and turning down a steep, narrow ravine for wood and water, encamped. The night was very cold,
and ice formed in the buckets nearly an inch thick. We constructed
a semicircular barricade of brush to keep off the wind, and, by the
aid of a large fire of pine-logs, passed the night very comfortably.

The soil on the ridge passed over to-day, seemed formed principally from red sandstone, and the boulders are primitive. The
country is much better wooded, the timber being willow, aspen,
and, in the ravines, tall firs and pines. The geranium was abundant: two or three yellow *compositæ* and asters were observed.

Sunday, August 26.—Morning very cold. Ther. at sunrise,
16°. Our provisions being nearly exhausted, I determined to go
on for at least a part of the day, although contrary to my usual
practice, this being the first Sabbath on which any travelling has
been done since the party left the Missouri. After following some
miles down the ravine upon which we had encamped, we struck
upon an Indian lodge-trail, leading either to Cache Valley or to
Ogden's Hole. This we followed in nearly a southerly direction,
crossing many deep hollows and very steep ridges, up which we
had to scramble, leading our mules, (it being impossible to ride,)

until we struck upon the head of a broad, green, beautiful valley, with an even, gentle descent, which led us, in about three miles, down to Ogden's Creek, just before it makes a cañon, previous to entering Ogden's Hole. There we encamped for the remainder of the day, with abundance of excellent grass, wood, and water. The same alternations of red and white sandstone appeared here as were seen on the Red Chimney Fork.

Just before descending into this valley, we had observed from the high ground, the smokes of numerous Indian signal fires, rising in several directions—an intimation that strangers had been discovered in their country. A strict watch was therefore maintained during the night, lest our animals should be stolen. Wild cherries were found in tolerable abundance, and the trail was strewn over with their smaller branches, thrown away by the Indians, who had evidently passed only a day or two before, in considerable numbers.

Monday, August 27.—We followed down Ogden's Creek about a mile, when we found that the broad valley was shut up between two ranges of hills, or rather mountains, leaving a flat, low, level bottom, densely covered in places by willows, through which the stream meanders from side to side, for three miles, washing alternately the base of either range. After passing through this cañon, the ridge separated, and before us lay a most lovely, broad, open valley, somewhat in the shape of a crescent, about fifteen miles long, and from five to seven miles in width, hemmed in on all sides, especially on the south and west, by lofty hills and rocky mountains, upon the tops and sides of which the snow glistened in the rays of the morning sun. The scene was cheering in the highest degree. The valley, rich and level, was covered with grass; springs broke out from the mountains in every direction, and the facilities for irrigation appeared to be very great. Ogden's Creek, breaking through its barriers, flows in a crystal stream at the base of the mountains on the south, for rather more than half the length of the valley, when it forces a passage through the huge range which divides this " gem of the desert" from the Salt Lake Valley, by a cañon wild and almost impassable. On the north, a beautiful little brook, taking its rise in the elevated ground separating this from Cache Valley, washes the base of the western hills, and joins Ogden's Creek just before it enters the cañon, after passing through which the latter discharges its waters into the Weber River, a tributary of the Great Salt Lake. Numerous bright little streams of pure running water were met with in abun-

6

dance, rendering this the most interesting and delightful spot we had seen during our long and monotonous journey.

Rather more than half-way between the cañon of Ogden's Creek and the north end of the valley, a pass is found by which a crossing of the mountain into the Salt Lake Valley can be effected. The ascent of the western side is, for the first four or five hundred yards, very abrupt and rocky, and would require a good deal of grading to render a road practicable; but after this, little or no labour would be necessary, except to cut away the brush, which, in places, is quite thick. The length of the pass is about three miles, and the height of the range through which it makes the cut, from eight hundred to a thousand feet above the valleys on each side. The valley of Ogden's Creek, or Ogden's Hole, (as places of this kind, in the nomenclature of this country, are called,) has long been the *rendezvous* of the North-west Company, on account of its fine range for stock in the winter, and has been the scene of many a merry réunion of the hardy trappers and traders of the mountains. Its streams were formerly full of beaver, but these have, I believe, entirely disappeared. Some few antelope were bounding over the green, but the appearance of fresh "Indian sign" accounted for their scarcity.

During our ride through the valley we came suddenly on a party of eight or ten Indian women and girls, each with a basket on her back, gathering grass-seeds for their winter's provision. They were of the class of "root-diggers," or, as the guide called them, "snake-diggers." The instant they discovered us, an immediate and precipitate flight took place, nor could all the remonstrances of the guide, who called loudly after them in their own language, induce them to halt for a single moment. Those who were too close to escape by running, hid themselves in the bushes and grass so effectually, that in less time than it has taken to narrate the circumstance, only two of them were to be seen. These were a couple of girls of twelve or thirteen years of age, who, with their baskets dangling at their backs, set off at their utmost speed for the mountains, and continued to run as long as we could see them, without stopping, or so much as turning their heads to look behind them. The whole party was entirely naked. After they had disappeared, we came near riding over two girls of sixteen or seventeen, who had "cached" behind a large fallen tree. They started up, gazed upon us for a moment, waved to us to continue our journey, and then fled with a rapidity that soon carried them beyond our sight.

In the pass through which we entered Ogden's Hole, the carboniferous rocks were again found, thrown up at an angle of 70° or 80°, with a dip to the north-east. On the western side of the high range of hills which extended to the north-west and formed the eastern boundary of Ogden's Hole, the edges of the strata cropped out as if a great fault had been formed at the point of elevation. No debris of primitive rock were discovered, nor was any observed in place during the whole journey from Bridger's Fort. In the pass leading to Salt Lake, through the Wahsatch range, the rock were metamorphic. Some beautiful specimens of marble were observed, and also some white crystalline sandstones. The strata again appeared on the western side of the range, and were inclined to the north-east about 70°. The chain evidently was not formed on a central axis. No fossils were collected during this part of the journey, as we travelled rapidly, and the means of transporting them were necessarily limited.

Descending the pass through dense thickets of small oak-trees, we caught the first glimpse of the GREAT SALT LAKE, the long-desired object of our search, and which it had cost us so many weary steps to reach. A gleam of sunlight, reflected by the water, and a few floating, misty clouds, were all, however, that we could see of this famous spot, and we had to repress our enthusiasm for some more favourable moment. I felt, nevertheless, no little gratification in having at length attained the point where our labours were to commence in earnest, and an impatient longing to enter upon that exploration to which our toils hitherto had been but preliminary.

Emerging from the pass, we entered the valley of the Salt Lake, and descending some moderately high table-land, struck the road from the Mormon settlements to the lower ford of Bear River, whence, in two or three miles, we came to what was called Brown's Settlement, and rode up to quite an extensive assemblage of log buildings, picketed, stockaded, and surrounded by out-buildings and cattle-yards, the whole affording evidence of comfort and abundance far greater than I had expected to see in so new a settlement. Upon requesting food and lodging for the night, we were told to our great surprise that we could not be accommodated, nor would the occupants sell us so much as an egg or a cup of milk, so that we were obliged to remount our horses; and we actually bivouacked under some willows, within a hundred yards of this inhospitable dwelling, turning our animals loose, and guarding them all night, lest, in search of food, they should damage the crops of this surly Nabal. From a neighbouring plantation we procured what we needed ; otherwise we should have been obliged to go sup-perless to bed. I afterward learned that the proprietor had been a sort of commissary or quartermaster in Colonel Cook's Mormon Battalion, in California, and had some reason to expect and to dread a visit from the civil officers of the United States, on ac-count of certain unsettled public accounts; and that he had actually mistaken us for some such functionaries. Subsequent acts of a similar nature, however, fully evinced the ungracious character of the man, strongly contrasted as it was with the frank and generous hospitality we ever received at the hands of the whole Mormon community.

The following day we reached the City of the Great Salt Lake, and found that the train had arrived safely on the 23d, and was now encamped near the Warm Springs on the outskirts of the city, awaiting my coming.

The result of the reconnoissance we had thus completed was such as to satisfy me that a good road can be obtained from Fort Bridger to the head of the Salt Lake ; although I incline to the opinion that it should pass farther north than the route taken by me, entering the southern end of Cache Valley, probably by Black-smith's Fork, and leaving it by the cañon formed by Bear River in making its way from that valley into the lake basin. A more minute examination than the pressure of my other duties allowed me time to make will, I think, result in the confirmation of this view and the ultimate establishment of this road. Should such prove to be the case, it will, in addition to shortening the distance, open to the emigration, at the season they would reach it, the inex-haustible resources of Cache Valley, where wood, water, abundance of fish, and the finest range imaginable for any number of cattle, offer advantages for recruiting and rest possessed by no other point that I have seen on either side of the mountains.

Before reaching Great Salt Lake City, I had heard from various sources that much uneasiness was felt by the Mormon community at my anticipated coming among them. I was told that they would never permit any survey of their country to be made; while it was darkly hinted that if I persevered in attempting to carry it on, my life would scarce be safe. Utterly disregarding, indeed giving not the least credence to these insinuations, I at once called upon BRIGHAM YOUNG, the president of the Mormon church and the governor of the commonwealth, stated to him what I had heard, explained to him the views of the Government in directing an exploration and survey of the lake, assuring him that these were the sole objects of the expedition. He replied, that he did not hesitate to say that both he and the people over whom he presided had been very much disturbed and surprised that the Government should send out a party into their country so soon after they had made their settlement; that he had heard of the expedition from time to time, since its outset from Fort Leavenworth; and that the whole community were extremely anxious as to what could be the design of the Government in such a movement. It appeared, too, that their alarm had been increased by the indiscreet and totally unauthorized boasting of an *attaché* of General Wilson, the newly-appointed Indian Agent for California, whose train on its way thither had reached the city a few days before I myself arrived. This person, as I understood, had declared openly that General Wilson had come clothed with authority from the President of the United States to expel the Mormons from the lands which they occupied, and that he would do so if he thought proper. The Mormons very naturally supposed from such a declaration that there must be some understanding or connection between General Wilson and myself; and that the arrival of the two parties so nearly together was the result of a concerted and combined movement for the ulterior purpose of breaking up and destroying their colony. The impression was that a survey was to be made of their country in the same manner that other public lands are surveyed, for the purpose of dividing it into townships and sections, and of thus establishing and recording the claims of the Government to it, and thereby anticipating any claim the Mormons might set up from their previous occupation. However unreasonable such a suspicion may be considered, yet it must be remembered that these people are exasperated and rendered almost desperate by the wrongs and persecutions they had previously suffered in Illinois and Missouri; that they had left the confines of civilization and fled to these far distant wilds, that they might enjoy undisturbed the religious liberty which had been practically denied them; and that now they supposed themselves to be followed up by the General Government with the view of driving them out from even this solitary spot, where they had hoped they should at length be permitted to set up their habitation in peace.

Upon all these points I undeceived Governor Young to his entire satisfaction. I was induced to pursue this conciliatory course, not only in justice to the Government, but also because I knew, from the peculiar organization of this singular community, that, unless the "President" was fully satisfied that no evil was intended to his people, it would be useless for me to attempt to carry out my instructions. He was not only civil governor, but the president of the whole Church of Latter-Day Saints upon the earth, their prophet and their priest, receiving, as they all firmly believed, direct revelations of the Divine will, which, according to their creed, form the law of the church. He is, consequently, profoundly revered by all, and possesses unbounded influence and almost unlimited power. I did not anticipate open resistance; but I was fully aware that if the president continued to view the expedition with distrust, nothing could be more natural than that every possible obstruction should be thrown in our way by a "masterly inactivity." Provisions would not be furnished; information would not be afforded; labour could not be procured; and no means would be left untried, short of open opposition, to prevent the success of a measure by them deemed fatal to their interests and safety. So soon, however, as the true object of the expedition was fully understood, the president laid the subject-matter before the council called for the purpose, and I was informed, as the result of their deliberations, that the authorities were much pleased that the exploration was to be made; that they had themselves contemplated something of the kind, but did not yet feel able to incur the expense; but that any assistance they could render to facilitate our operations would be most cheerfully furnished to the extent of their ability. This pledge, thus heartily given, was as faithfully redeemed; and it gives me pleasure here to acknowledge the warm interest manifested and efficient aid rendered, as well by the president as by all the leading men of the community, both in our personal welfare and in the successful prosecution of the work.

CHAPTER V.

EXPLORATION OF A ROUTE FROM GREAT SALT LAKE CITY TO FORT
HALL, AND RECONNOISSANCE OF CACHE VALLEY.

MATTERS being thus satisfactorily adjusted, as the provisions
which had been laid in at the beginning of the journey were nearly
exhausted, I left the city on the 12th of September, with teams
and pack-mules, for Fort Hall, to procure the supplies for the party
which had been forwarded to that post by the supply-train attached to Colonel Loring's command; and at the same time to
carry out that portion of my instructions which directed me to explore a route for a road from the head of Salt Lake to Fort Hall.
The main party was left under the command of Lieutenant Gunnison, with instructions to commence the survey upon a basis already
laid down. I was accompanied on this trip by Mr. John Owen,
the sutler of the regiment of Mounted Rifles, and Mr. T. Pomeroy,
a merchant from St. Louis, on his way to California. Our route,
as far as the crossing of Bear River, near the head of the lake, was
that usually pursued by emigrants passing through Salt Lake City
to California. It skirts the eastern shore of the lake throughout
its whole length, from north to south, as far as the ford, where
the road turns off to the west. As the country passed over in this
part of the journey is embraced within the limits of the survey, it
requires, at present, no farther notice.

From the crossing, the emigrant road pursues a W. N. W. course,
until it intersects that from Fort Hall. The ford of Bear River
at this point is not very good. The banks are high and steep on
both sides, and the stream, which is about two hundred and fifty
feet wide, is quite rapid. The bottom is a hard, firm gravel. In
the spring and early part of summer, the waters are too high to
admit of fording, and temporary ferries become necessary. Leaving the emigrant road at this point, our route may be described,
generally, as following up the Malade (called by Frémont the
Roseaux) to its head; thence crossing a high dividing ridge, we
fall upon the heads of the Pannack, a tributary of the Port Neuf,
(which latter is an affluent of Lewis's Fork of the Columbia,) and

following down its valley to within five miles of Fort Hall, we cross the Port Neuf, and passing over a wide level plain, reach that celebrated trading-post. But this line is deserving of notice rather more in detail. About two miles above the ford, Bear River, in emerging from Cache Valley, breaks through the chain forming the eastern boundary of the valley of Salt Lake. The range, which here sinks quite suddenly, for a short distance to the south of the cañon or gate through which the river has forced its passage, consists of low, rounded hills, which present no trace of rock on the surface. The river indeed appears to cut through rock, but an opportunity did not occur to ascertain this by actual observation. After crossing and following up its right bank for two and a-half miles, we left the river, and struck into a broad and beautiful valley, formed by the Roseaux, or Malade, which, flowing from the north, discharges itself into Bear River some miles below the ford. The valley is five or six miles wide, and its western boundary is formed by a chain of high, rounded hills, being the continuation of a lofty rocky promontory, projecting into the north end of the Lake. The eastern boundary of this valley is formed by the continuation, in a northern direction, of the Wahsatch range, which divides it from the Bear River and Cache Valley. Ascending the valley, these mountains rise to a considerable height, the strata dipping to the north-east, and the direction of the chain inclining to the west. The valley of the Malade is extremely level, free from underbrush, with very little artemisia, and affords ground for an excellent wagon-road. Water to-day was found in quantities sufficient for the animals, at points conveniently distributed, and grass was abundant. Several fine springs were passed, in which the water was cold and clear. Continuing up the valley until four o'clock, we came to a superb little stream, coming out of the eastern mountain, running with great swiftness over a bed of breccia, and discharging a large quantity of clear, cold water. The fall was great and the quantity of water ample for the irrigation of a very large farm, for which the lay of the land offers great facilities. Here we encamped, with plenty of fine grass. Distance from the city, one hundred and three miles; and from Bear River ford, twenty-four and a-half.

Thursday, September 20.—Our march to-day was only eleven miles, owing to the necessity of making a road across a small stream with steep banks, which comes through a depression in the eastern hills, through which a road from Sheep Rock, near the

Soda Springs, had been partially explored by Mr. Owen, whose wagons had come through it some two weeks since, on their way to Salt Lake City. He describes the country as rough and rolling, with several high and steep ridges to be crossed. The road to-day has been level, with wood and water abundant. Encamped on the left bank of the Malade, here six feet wide and two feet deep.

Friday, September 21.—Following up the left bank of the Malade for four miles, we crossed a small swift fork coming in from the north-east, affording abundance of water for irrigating a considerable extent of its valley on each side. The valley of the Malade is becoming gradually narrower and the hills lower. Crossing another fork from the east, we strike upon "Hedspeth's Cut-off," which leads from Sheep Rock, near the Soda Springs, to the Mormon road at Goose Creek. Distance, one hundred and twenty-five and a-half miles.

The valley of the Malade seems to be formed principally of whitish clay, in which, however, no good section was found, so that it is uncertain whether it presents any stratification. Occasionally ridges of limestone and conglomerate push out from the side of the mountains; and in one instance the river was found flowing over a bed of breccia. The rock on the west side of the valley consisted of dark compact limestone, with a dip of 20° to the south-west. Shortly after reaching the Cut-off, a belt of high hills extended across the valley from east to west, composed of dark limestone containing a considerable number of fossils. These hills we ascended by one of the handsomest passes I had seen in the country. The inclination in no instance exceeds 5°; the soil is hard and porous; the natural road perfectly drained. The length of the pass is four miles, from the summit of which we descended to the east fork of the Malade, upon which we encamped, with intensely cold, pure water, willows for firewood, and good grass. In the pass some specimens of obsidian and volcanic debris were collected, evidently of secondary formation, and not conformable with the limestone ridges. Trachytic rock was also found on the side of the stream, forming a considerable hill, and overlaid by dark limestone.

Saturday, September 22.—Directly after starting, crossed the east fork of the Malade, and still following the Cut-off, the track of which is hard and well beaten, we ascended another pass, in a north direction, very similar in its character to that we came up yesterday. From the top of this pass, which is the dividing ridge between the Malade and the waters of the Port Neuf, the road descends by a gentle slope to the dry bed of a small stream, which forms a narrow gorge; emerging from which, and proceeding north, we descended to a small stream forming one of the heads of a branch of the Port Neuf. It flows at the foot of a spur of the range of hills which constitute the dividing ridge between it and the Pannack, (another affluent of the Port Neuf,) and rises in a broad valley lying to the westward of the road. It is bounded on the west by a high range of hills extending to the southward, and in that direction forming the "divide" between the waters of the Malade and those of the Pannack.

The secondary or lower hills in this valley seem to be composed principally of white clay containing volcanic debris. Crossing the stream, we left the cut-off altogether, and turning to the left, crossed over this ridge, which, where we crossed it, is very high and steep, and a mile and a-half in width. Descending its western slope, we struck upon the heads of one of the main forks of the Pannack, down which an excellent road can be obtained without difficulty, the descent being moderate and the ground generally level.

Descending the valley of this stream, we encamped on its right bank with plenty of grass, fine cool water, and a profusion of willows for fuel. Day's march, fifteen miles.

At the dividing ridge between the waters of the Port Neuf and the Malade, the direction of the stratification has evidently changed. Near the south end of the pass, an escarpment of dark limestone is seen on the eastern side, lying on and conformable with layers of feldspathic rock. A short distance farther on, the same rock is again seen, overlaying the dark limestone, and with a dip of about 50° to the north-east. From this point the centre of elevation, consisting evidently of this hypogene rock, appears to take a direction to the north-west, striking the chain of hills continued from the west side of the valley of the Malade. It is plainly to be seen that this has been a region of great disturbance, which did not cease until a period subsequent to the deposition of the secondary rocks that repose on the limestones, although not conformable with them. Passing this ridge, several high conical hills were observed on the right, which seemed to be formed of secondary rocks, the stratification of which was apparently much more horizontal than that of the, limestones. The dividing ridge between the Port Neuf and the Pannack is composed of dark limestones, altered shales, and veins of the same feldspathic rock noticed in the pass. The strata were inclined east by north, at an angle of 70°. The ridge seems to run a little west of north, until it disappears in the valley of the Snake River. Upon the summit of this " divide" was found what was at first thought to be altered coal, but upon farther examination it appeared to be an aluminous rock, containing but a small trace of carbonate of lime. Its colour was black, hardness greater than that of feldspar, and the form a rhombic prism. The limestone was crystalline, and contained numerous specimens of shells and corals, but in so altered a state that it was impossible to determine them.

The length of the fork of the Pannack which we descended is sixteen miles. It pursues a westerly direction, until it joins the main stream, which latter flows from the southward, through what appeared to be a well-defined valley. The ground for a road is excellent, with only one or two exceptions, which are not of a serious character.

On descending the dividing ridge in which it heads, the rocks were hidden by a black, rich soil; occasional boulders of granite were seen on the surface, but no section could be obtained until we came to a gorge about five miles down the valley. Here the river cuts through a much lower ridge of hills, composed of limestone, dipping to the east, at an angle of about 63°: below this the stream has cut its bed through secondary hills formed of argillaceous sandstone and clay, both of which are white, and mixed with pieces of obsidian and occasional boulders of serpentine: still lower down the valley, a section in a ravine to the right of the road, discovered some rocks which might almost be considered cretaceous; alternating with white argillaceous sandstone, they contained a considerable quantity of organic remains, principally coral, but so much altered by heat that it was impossible to determine them with precision. The dip of these strata was about 40° north-east. The beds were covered by the remains of disaggregated conglomerate, composed principally of porphyry and granite. Proceeding down the stream, metamorphic sandstones, crystallized almost to the whiteness of white quartz, were found, forming escarpments of the lower hills; a short distance below this point, a ridge of hills, composed of limestone, shales, and red sandstone, extended across the valley; they were all much inclined, with a dip to the east. At this point, where the river cuts a passage through this chain, a mass of feldspathic rock was seen. The dip

of these strata and also of the crystalline sandstone was about
E. S. E., at an angle of from 60° to 70°.

From the junction of the two forks, the valley changes its direction to the N. N. W., which it maintains until it merges in that of
the Port Neuf, a distance of eighteen miles; it becomes broader, the
bottoms are high, hard, very level, and entirely covered with artemisia.   Coarse red metamorphic sandstone was found on the side
of the valley at this point, with a considerable dip to the north-east.
Clayey shales also occurred; and, from the appearance of the soil,
a great deal of argillaceous rock, must exist in the vicinity.   Five
miles below the forks, a remarkable isolated hill stands on the
western side of the valley, called by the traders the " Windmill
Rock."   Here a dike of trap was met with, running north-east and
south-west, forming the axis of a chain extending across the valley,
and of which the isolated hill seemed to form a part.   The dike
constituted the summit of a high hill on the east side of the river:
on the west side, the same rock was found, but not so high.   Metamorphic sandstone (red) was found overlaying the trap, and what
appeared to be porous basalt was found in considerable abundance:
no section of the stratification of the sandstone could be obtained.

Beyond this point, the valley of the Pannack gradually sinks
down into that of the Snake River.   The hills that enclose it are
not high, and seem formed almost wholly of white clay; at least,
this was the only soil exposed, even in some very deep ravines.
The same character of soil is found on the whole country this side
of Snake River.

Twelve miles from the forks, we leave the Pannack, which there
makes a curve to the westward, around the point of a ridge which
is quite low, and the ascent gentle and regular.   Upon reaching
the level of the table-land, nothing was to be seen, as far as the
eye could reach, but the eternal artemisia, which had taken complete possession of this barren, dreary waste, and extended quite
to the Port Neuf.   Upon reaching this stream, we struck upon
the emigrant road by Fort Hall to California; and descending a
bluff, or rather a cliff, two hundred feet in height, and composed
entirely of argillaceous soil, we crossed the Port Neuf and entered the valley of the Columbia.   From the top of the bluff, an
extensive level plain, clothed with grass, is spread out before us,
like a beautiful picture; while the fringe of heavy timber, stretching far away to the north and west, indicates the position of
Lewis's Fork of the great river of the West.   Five miles to the

north, Fort Hall, with its whitewashed walls, is plainly in view. The "Three Buttes" rise in the distance, while the Port Neuf, with its bright, sparkling waters, flows at our feet. The scene was one of surpassing beauty, and richly repaid us for our dreary ride across the desert plain of sage.

The Port Neuf, where we forded it, is a fine, clear, bold stream, one hundred yards wide and three feet deep, with a moderately rapid current and pebbly bottom. The plain between it and Snake River presents a level bottom, formed principally of decomposed vegetable mould, reposing on sandy loam and gravel. Numerous springs of cold, pellucid water, abounding in speckled trout of delicious flavour, break out in every direction, giving rise to many little streams, which rapidly increase in size and afford great facilities for irrigation as well as for the construction of mills. Passing over this delightful plain, we left Fort Hall on our left, and five miles beyond it terminated our journey, at Cantonment Loring, our point of destination.

I was most courteously received by Lieutenant-Colonel Andrew Porter and the officers of his command, which consisted of two companies of the regiment of Mounted Rifles, left here by Colonel Loring on his way to Oregon, with the view of selecting a permanent post for the protection of the vast emigration across the continent. The troops were quartered in tents, but were busily engaged in the erection of quarters, of a more substantial character, for the winter.

The result of this exploration *has been to demonstrate the entire practicability of obtaining an excellent wagon-road from Fort Hall to the Mormon settlement upon the Great Salt Lake.* With the exception of the ridge dividing the waters of the Pannack from those of another affluent of the Port Neuf, the line traced is unexceptionable, and offers facilities for the best natural road I ever saw. Although when we passed there had not been even a track broken, so favourable is the surface of the country that I transported my provisions over it without the slightest difficulty, loading my wagons with not less than thirty-five hundred pounds each. The ridge referred to can, by a little labour, be rendered easy to cross; and even as it is, offers but little obstruction. In seasons of high water, Bear River and the Port Neuf would have to be crossed by ferries; or, should the travel ever demand it, timber for the construction of bridges could be obtained in the vicinity of both localities.

The supply-train from Fort Leavenworth, with my provisions, had not arrived at the post, as I expected, and I was consequently detained until the 6th of October, when, having obtained them, I set out on my return. The frank and generous hospitality we received during our stay at the post demands a grateful acknowledgment.

Returning, I was accompanied by Colonel Porter, with a small escort, as far as the crossing of Bear River. He was desirous that we should make conjointly a reconnoissance of Cache Valley, to ascertain its fitness for the location there of a permanent military post.

Following the same route which I had taken when coming up, we arrived at Bear River on the evening of the 11th, and encamped. The examination of Cache Valley occupied several days. Crossing over the range of low, rounded hills through which Bear River has cut a passage, we entered this beautiful and picturesque valley, which was then covered with a profusion of rich green grass, and adorned and diversified by numerous clumps of willows. Our attempt to cross it directly was frustrated by meeting with a deep, quiet stream, called the Muddy, which rises in the hills dividing the southern end of the valley from Ogden's Hole, and winds through the tall grass without banks, until it discharges its waters into Bear River, just before that stream enters the valley of the Salt Lake. We were in consequence driven some eight miles to the south, and effected our crossing where the valley is full of swampy springs, affording abundance of good sweet water, and excellent grass. Speckled trout of large size abounded in the streams. After crossing the Muddy, we skirted the eastern side of the valley for thirty-five miles in a northerly direction, crossing successively Blacksmith's Fork, Logan's Fork, High Fork, Gros Bois, and Rush Creek, all tributaries of Bear River, which latter stream traverses the valley from the north, until it breaks through the range forming its western boundary and enters that of the lake. The streams on the east side take their rise in a heavy range running to the north and constituting the eastern limit of the valley, which has an average width of about ten miles. The cañons which they form before leaving the mountains abound in timber, consisting principally of cotton-wood, with some maple. They afford desirable facilities for irrigation, presenting at the same time advantageous sites for the erection of mills. These ravines abound in fine timber in quantities sufficient for fuel and building purposes.

As the object of the reconnoissance was principally to ascertain what were the capabilities of this valley to afford sustenance for a military post, if established in its vicinity, the examination was but a general one, and was not directed to the selection of any particular portion of it for such a purpose. At the time the reconnoissance was made, all the information that could be obtained from the oldest mountain-men, induced both Colonel Porter and myself to believe that it was one of the most eligible spots in the whole country for wintering stock. It had been a rendezvous for the American Fur Company for many years, and stock had been wintered there by them with great advantage. The snow was seldom deep, and the cattle not only retained their flesh, but grew fat during the winter. So flattering were the appearances, and so great the advantages offered by this lovely valley, that nearly the whole number of cattle and mules belonging to the cantonment were, upon the return of Colonel Porter to that post, driven down here under the care of a proper guard, to be wintered. The season, however, proved unusually severe; the snow fell in the valley to a depth unprecedented; and more than one-half of the herd, in which were included some of my own animals, perished in consequence. The fact of the liability of the valley to a similar occurrence in future will doubtless have its due influence in finally deciding upon its eligibility as the best site for a post in the vicinity of Salt Lake.

The soil of the valley is very rich, being principally alluvial, with a great deal of vegetable mould. Facilities for irrigation are very great, and water could be commanded to a large extent for farming purposes. Any amount of hay might be cut without in the least interfering with the range for cattle. The only objection to this, as a most desirable spot for settlement, is the danger from snow; and even this might be in a great degree obviated, by the erection of suitable sheds for protection of the stock during the more severe portions of the seasons. These seldom last beyond a few weeks.

Should the road to which I have already adverted be established from Fort Bridger, through the valley of Blacksmith's Fork, it would at once attract to it the travel to Oregon and California; a fact which would have its due weight in the selection of a site for a military post for the protection of this part of the country.

The advance of the season precluded the making of much geological examination beyond the immediate vicinity of the route travelled, which led through the valley at the base of the ranges. The only rocks met with were those composing the lower hills,

which consisted principally of conglomerates overlaying some argillaceous sandstones and beds of white and red clay. The conglomerates on the lower hills were formed principally of dark limestone,
much worn. On the higher benches, large boulders of feldspar
were found. Albite and serpentine also occurred, and metamorphic sandstones, some of which were very beautifully veined, as if
the strata had been disturbed before they had hardened.

Returning to the southern end of the valley, we again struck the
Muddy, and followed it up to where it forks, amid the hills forming
the "divide" from Ogden's Hole. The eastern fork makes an impassable cañon, but we followed up the west fork about four miles,
whence we crossed the Wahsatch range, and descended into a beautiful, level, circular valley, about a mile in diameter, hemmed in by
an amphitheatre of lofty and steep mountains. Several fine springs
head in this singular little hollow, which uniting and emerging on
the south-west side, form the head of Box-elder Creek, a tributary
of the Salt Lake. The pass or gorge through which this little
stream rushes down the mountain to the plains below is steep,
rugged, and very narrow, being in places scarcely passable for
mules. I had hoped it would afford a passage over the range for
wagons, but this I soon found to be impracticable. Descending
this wild pass for about two miles, we reached the lake valley, and
repaired to our camp on Bear River.

In crossing the Wahsatch range at this point, the lower hills on
the eastern side were composed of broken conglomerate. Large
boulders of serpentine were met with on the surface, and also altered sandstones and limestones. Ascending from Cache Valley,
the dark limestones were found cropping out, but the surface was
so completely covered with vegetable soil that no section could be
obtained. The limestones seemed to form the summits of the highest
elevation of the range, but as we passed through the deep gorge
of Box-elder Creek, this could not be positively ascertained. No
trap was observed, but large boulders of granite were seen in the
sides of the pass. The rocks had been so much worn, and the
surface was so covered by fallen masses, that no section of the
stratification was visible.

CHAPTER VI.

RECONNOISSANCE OF THE DESERTS AROUND THE WESTERN SHORES OF
THE GREAT SALT LAKE.

THE two following days were busily occupied in making preparation for an exploration around the western shore of the lake,
which I desired to complete previous to entering upon a more
minute survey of its waters. The expedition was deemed necessary, to enable me as well to ascertain its general features as to
gain some knowledge of the means and appliances necessary to
carry on the survey with safety and expedition. By the old mountain-men such a reconnoissance was considered not only hazardous
in the highest degree, but absolutely impracticable, especially at
so late a season of the year. In this opinion they were confirmed
by the representations of the Indians, who represented water to
be extremely scarce and the country destitute of game. It was
affirmed that the contemplated circuit had been repeatedly attempted by old and experienced trappers, in search of beaver, but
always without success; the adventurers being invariably obliged
to return with the loss of most of their animals. This was discouraging; but in addition to these objections, it was known that
mortal offence had been taken by the Shoshonee or Snake Indians,
(through whose country we would be obliged to pass,) arising from
a gross and wanton outrage which had been a short time before
inflicted upon them by a company of unprincipled emigrants, by
whom their women had been most brutally treated, and their
friends murdered while attempting to defend them. Fears were
entertained lest, in the wilds of this inhospitable region, where
foot of white man had never trod, we should fall a sacrifice to the
just vengeance of those infuriated savages.

Having determined, however, that the examination was necessary
to enable me to carry out the instructions of the department, I resolved to proceed, or at least to make the attempt. My preparations were simply to kill a beef and dry as much of the flesh as we
could carry upon our pack-mules; since it would have been unsafe to
risk the existence of the party upon the chances of killing game by

7

the way. We also provided ourselves with three India-rubber bags, of the capacity of five gallons each, and a small keg, for transporting water across the desert; some sacks of flour, a small tent without poles, a tent-fly, and a blanket to each man. In addition, each person carried a few pounds of fresh beef attached to his saddle, which might be used before resorting to our store of dried meat. Thus equipped and well armed, we set out on the afternoon of the 19th of October, the little party numbering five men and sixteen mules. The provision-train for the surveying party was sent forward by the emigrant road, on the east side of the lake, under Lieutenant Howland, with orders to report to Lieutenant Gunnison at Salt Lake City. Colonel Porter had left us the day previous, on his return to Cantonment Loring.

From the ford of Bear River we followed the emigrant road westward for about four miles, which brought us to the Malade River. The crossing here was very difficult, and we found it impossible to get our animals over with their packs on, because of the depth of water; they were accordingly unloaded and dragged or driven over, one at a time, and some of them came near being swamped in the soft, sticky mud composing the bottom. The men were obliged to strip, and carry the packs over on their heads, the lighter articles being thrown across. Wood was very scarce: we had but artemisia-bushes and a few charred sticks found amid the ashes of the extinguished fires left by the emigrants. These were, however, sufficient for cooking purposes. Grass there was none; and we began already to have some foretaste of the hardships to which our poor animals were about to be exposed. The night was cold; thermometer 22°. As wood could not be obtained even for tent-poles, we contented ourselves with stretching our weary bodies upon the ground, and, wrapped in our blankets, slept soundly till the morning.

The bottoms of Bear River and the Malade are composed of white clay, in which no trace of organic remains was discovered. The current of the Malade is here slow, and the water brackish and nauseous.

Saturday, October 20.—Ther. at daylight, 26°. Continued on the emigrant road about four miles, when we left it and turned more to the southward, with the intention of doubling a lofty promontory that puts into the lake from the north, and forms the western boundary of the Malade valley. In about a mile we came upon three or four beautiful springs of clear, bright water: they were gushing out from a rocky point, (of dark limestone and coarse argillaceous sandstone, with a dip of about 20° to the east,) and unite to form a branch which runs southward some miles, and then sinks in the sand, before reaching the lake. The water was, however, warm, brackish, and entirely unfit for drinking. Following down this stream for several miles, we struck on a succession of bare, level plains, composed of white clay and mud, with occasionally pieces of limestone and obsidian scattered on the surface. These dreary plains were occasionally separated from each other, by patches of salt grass and scattered clumps of artemisia. They had apparently formed, at some remote period, a part of the lake, and it is probable were partially covered during the freshet months. Some portions of the ground were still moist, and too soft to admit the passage of our mules without danger of miring. Where dry, the surface was hard and smooth.

In the afternoon, as I felt apprehensive of being overtaken by night without water for our animals, we turned more to the westward, and directed our steps toward the promontory range previously mentioned. Before reaching it, however, we came upon a small stream, fifteen feet wide and a foot deep, but it was quite salt, and almost unfit to drink; yet, as we had no prospect of finding better, we were fain to bivouac on its bank for the night. Artemisia was abundant, furnishing plenty of excellent fuel, although it reminded me somewhat of the scriptural phrase, "crackling of thorns under a pot," so constantly did the fire require replenishing. Day's travel, twenty-two miles.

Sunday, October 21.—Ther. at daybreak, 27°. There being neither grass nor water at this point, we left it early, and made in a south-west direction for the foot of the mountain, travelling over a hard, even surface of dry mud, as level as a floor and without a particle of vegetation of any kind. Before reaching the base of the hills, we descried some Indians at a distance, who, as soon as they discovered us, commenced a most rapid and precipitate flight. As they were on foot, I despatched the guide after them at full gallop to bring them to a parley, being desirous of obtaining from them some information, and if possible, to prevail upon some of them to act as guides through the unknown regions before us. The man overtook them at the foot of the mountain, when several of them, finding their retreat about to be cut off, halted, and advanced upon him with their guns presented, but were restrained from firing by an old Indian, who seemed to act as their chief.

As soon as they perceived the rest of our party moving toward them from the plain, the whole band, consisting of some six or eight men and half a dozen squaws, retreated incontinently up the mountain, and in a few minutes totally disappeared, nor did we see them again. As we continued to advance, we passed through their encampment, which they had abandoned in such haste that they left every thing as it was at the moment of their flight— the kettle was boiling over the fire, and a good gun rested against a bush. We left all untouched, and did not even dismount, as we knew they were watching us from behind the rocks, and I was desirous of convincing them of our peaceable disposition.

Following down the eastern base of the promontory for about two miles, we encamped on a small spring-branch, coming down from the mountains, furnishing very tolerable water and plenty of grass— refreshment most welcome to our jaded and famished animals, which had not had a full meal for nearly two days. At the Indian camp there was a spring, but the water, although abundant, was salt and unfit for use. Temperature of the spring, 84°. The mountain or main promontory seemed to be composed of limestone, altered shales, and sandstones: it rises from fifteen hundred to two thousand feet.

Monday, October 22.—Ther. at sunrise 25°. Morning clear and calm. The Salt Lake, which lay about half a mile to the eastward, was covered by immense flocks of wild geese and ducks, among which many swans were seen, being distinguishable by their size and the whiteness of their plumage. I had seen large flocks of these birds before, in various parts of our country, and especially upon the Potomac, but never did I behold any thing like the immense numbers here congregated together. Thousands of acres, as far as the eye could reach, seemed literally covered with them, presenting a scene of busy, animated cheerfulness, in most graceful contrast with the dreary, silent solitude by which we were immediately surrounded.

Our course until noon was south, along the base of the high promontory which puts into the lake from the north. On our left, for about three miles from our encampment, was an isolated knob or hill, separated from the main range by a grassy plain. It consisted of limestone and slaty shales, in the former of which were some small caves. The rocks were thrown up at a very high angle, and in some places were perpendicular, and rested, as far as could be ascertained, on a primitive formation below. Toward the southern end of the

FIRST VIEW OF GREAT SALT LAKE VALLEY.   FROM A MOUNTAIN PASS

Ackerman Lith 379 Broadway NY

PANORAMIC VIEW FROM ROCK GATE CAMP LOOKING N E

CROSS BEAR RIVER BAY GREAT SALT LAKE

WEST END OF FREMONT'S ISLAND, AND PART OF ANTELOPE ISLAND FROM ALUM BAY.

promontory, the limestones disappeared, and the surface rock was formed of conglomerate composed chiefly of the older sedimentary rocks, and some boulders of serpentine and porphyry. Upon examining several isolated masses of this, it was found that each stone (principally rounded pebbles of quartz) was surrounded by a crystalline layer of satin spar, as if it had formed a nucleus around which the lime had crystallized. In about ten miles we reached the southern extremity of this high rocky range, where it juts into the lake. Within this distance we passed five or six springs, some of them with very good water, bursting from the foot of the mountain. Innumerable salt and sulphur springs break out of the bank all along, but are soon lost in the broad sand and mud flat which lies between the banks and the water. This flat is about two miles broad, entirely without vegetation, and has, I think, been slightly covered by the lake in the spring and summer. Both yesterday and to-day, considerable quantities of small drift-wood was seen lying on the sands—a fact which favours this opinion.

The mirage along the lake shore, and above the moist, oozy plains, has been, for the last two days, very great, giving rise to optical illusions the most grotesque and fantastic, and rendering all estimate of the distance or form of objects vague and uncertain. Two miles farther we reached a small rill of brackish, indifferent water, upon which we bivouacked, fearing to go on, lest we should be left without any.

The evening was mild and bland, and the scene around us one of exciting interest. At our feet and on each side lay the waters of the Great Salt Lake, which we had so long and so ardently desired to see. They were clear and calm, and stretched far to the south and west. Directly before us, and distant only a few miles, an island rose from eight hundred to one thousand feet in height, while in the distance other and larger ones shot up from the bosom of the waters, their summits appearing to reach the clouds. On the west appeared several dark spots, resembling other islands, but the dreamy haze hovering over this still and solitary sea threw its dim, uncertain veil over the more distant features of the landscape, preventing the eye from discerning any one object with distinctness, while it half revealed the whole, leaving ample scope for the imagination of the beholder. The stillness of the grave seemed to pervade both air and water; and, excepting here and there a solitary wild-duck floating motionless on the bosom of the lake, not a living thing was to be seen. The night proved perfectly serene, and a young moon shed its tremulous light upon a sea of profound, unbroken silence. I was surprised to find, although so near a body of the saltest water, none of that feeling of invigorating freshness which is always experienced when in the vicinity of the ocean. The bleak and naked shores, without a single tree to relieve the eye, presented a scene so different from what I had pictured in my imagination of the beauties of this far-famed spot, that my disappointment was extreme.

Tuesday, October 23.—Ther. at daylight, 37°. Morning clear and calm; the lake and mountains to the eastward yet wrapped in mist. The west side of the extremity of the promontory is composed of porphyry, interspersed with seams of white quartz, which veined it in the most beautiful manner. The quartz veins in some instances were several feet thick. These rocks, evidently in place, rose boldly, forming escarpments looking to the south-west, with a dip, apparently to the north, of about 50°. Decomposed limestone, containing organic remains, and also trap rock, were here observed. The ground near our encampment was covered with a species of *Astragalus,* the seed-pods of which were covered by a substance resembling cotton, and presented the appearance of oval white balls, about the size of a robin's egg. I afterward found this plant upon most of the islands of the lake.

Rounding the point of the promontory, the shore of the lake trends off to the northward, forming several picturesque little bays with bold rocky headlands. After travelling about nine miles, we came to several springs of good and most welcome water, and we stopped to refresh our animals and to noon. The finding of this water was entirely unexpected, as, from the representations of an old Shoshonee Indian, made to us before leaving Bear River, I did not look for any for two days, and had in consequence dismounted one of the men to enable us to carry the more vessels, all of which had been filled before leaving our camp in the morning. I went down to the shore of the lake to taste of the water: it was as salt as very strong brine, and clear and transparent as diamond. A large flock of gulls was swimming about near the shore. After feasting our animals upon the grass that grew among the tall rushes and canes around the spring, we continued along the shore of the lake for about nine miles farther, and succeeded in discovering three springs within that distance, at the last of which we halted for the night.

After doubling the southern end of the promontory, the broad flats, which had characterized the shore at its eastern base, entirely disappeared, and the water, although apparently shallow, came nearly up to the base of the hills. Near the margin of the lake it is not safe in all places for animals to pass, as the almost constant exudations of salt water from the edge of the grass, undermine the surface, rendering the narrow intervening beach treacherous and miry. The water to the westward appears bold and deep; and enough has been seen to convince me that a large sail-boat will be absolutely indispensable in the contemplated survey, for the supply of the different parties with provisions and water. Wood there is none. Fuel for cooking, can, however, be generally obtained from the artemisia which abounds almost everywhere; but timber for the construction of the triangulation stations, will, in most instances, have to be transported by water, or hauled down from the cañons of the mountains.

The rocks observed were porphyry, gneiss, dark slaty shales, and metamorphic sandstone, dipping to the north-east. After proceeding some miles to the north, dark limestones with white marble veins occurred, alternating with clayey shales. The rocks on this side of the promontory are much more rugged than on the other, or eastern slope, presenting numerous lofty escarpments where they crop out, the dip being to the east. A cactus, with very long prickles, was observed near our morning camp; and at the spring where we nooned, a small jointed cane trailed on the ground, in some instances to a distance of more than thirty feet. The men made excellent pipe-stems of this material. The spring where we encamped for the night was an oval hole or pit, with perpendicular sides, about fifteen feet long, six broad, and four deep. The water was tolerably good: a small spring, rising at the base of the hill, ran into the lake close by. These springs afterward afforded us nearly all the water used upon the survey of the west shore of the lake; but a voyage of fifty miles was frequently necessary to obtain a supply even for a few days.

Wednesday, October 24.—Clear and calm. Ther. at daylight, 19°; sunrise, 24°. Continuing our journey up the lake-shore, we shortly came to a brackish spring, where there had been a camp of Indians the night before. We had thought last night that we saw their fires, but they had fled, alarmed probably by the report of some guns that had been discharged in our camp. A quantity of some species of seeds they had been beating out lay in small heaps around, and I found an old water-bottle they had left in their haste. It was ingeniously woven of a sort of sedge-grass, coated inside with the gum of the mountain pine, by which it was rendered perfectly water-tight. I afterward saw some similarly shaped vessels, and made of the same material, that would hold nearly two gallons.

As nothing was to be gained by rigidly following the lake-shore, I determined to cut across the projecting points, keeping the general features of the lake in view. At this point we came upon a low range of basaltic hills, extending some miles west of the mountains which continued to the northward, and presenting a steep escarpment on the lake, where we again struck it. This lower series of hills extended also to the north, and we followed along their base for many miles, the range gradually falling off to the east as we advanced. The general soil was white clay, formed from the decomposition of the rocks. At three o'clock, having travelled eighteen miles without water, we halted, removed the packs from the backs of our weary beasts, and served out from our scanty store a pint of water to each mule, which the famished creatures eagerly drank from a tin pan. We remained here a couple of hours, to allow them to graze on some tolerably good bunch-grass, when we again saddled up at sundown, and continued our journey, determined to go on till water should be found, or at least as long as the animals could travel. At ten o'clock we reached a small sluggish stream, containing some water entirely too salt for our use, but which the poor animals drank with great avidity, having been without for more than twelve hours. Here we lay down for the night, both man and beast much fatigued with the day's march.

The country passed over to-day has been barren, desolate, and forlorn to the last degree. Artemisia has prevailed to the exclusion of all other vegetation. Not the note of a bird nor the chirp of an insect was to be heard. A solitary crow and one grasshopper were the only living things seen during the whole day's march.

Thursday, October 25.—Ther. at sunrise, 24°. We had an opportunity this morning of seeing fully the ground over which we had passed the night previous. It consisted of an oval flat of clay and sand, some four or five miles broad from east to west, and extending double that distance toward the north; bounded on both sides by lofty hills, with high mountains in the background. North of the flat the ridge was much lower, and it appeared as if there were a pass or depression through it, leading to another valley or plain beyond. Three streams came down from this low ridge, and, flowing to the southward, either sank into the sand or discharged themselves into the lake, which we now judged to be some six or

VIEW LOOKING NORTH WEST FROM PROMONTORY POINT GREAT SALT LAKE.

eight miles to the southward, the flat extending in that direction to the water's edge.   Two of these streams (all of which were salt) we crossed without much difficulty ; but the third, on the western side of the flat, was impassable, and we had to ascend it for three miles before we could obtain a crossing.   On the west side of this latter branch comes in a small tributary, in the bed of which, near its source, a beautiful spring, ten feet wide, bubbles up from the bottom, with a column of water rising in its centre six inches in diameter.   The water was clear as crystal, but salt and sulphurous, which latter quality might account for the numerous tracks of the antelope around its margin, as that animal is known to delight in waters of this character.

This extensive flat appears to have formed, at one time, the northern portion of the lake, for it is now but slightly above its present level.   Upon the slope of a ridge connected with this plain, thirteen distinct successive benches, or water-marks, were counted, which had evidently, at one time, been washed by the lake, and must have been the result of its action continued for some time at each level.   The highest of these is now about two hundred feet above the valley, which has itself been left by the lake, owing probably to gradual elevation occasioned by subterraneous causes.   If this supposition be correct, and all appearances conspire to support it, there must have been here at some former period a vast *inland* sea, extending for hundreds of miles ; and the isolated mountains which now tower from the flats, forming its western and south-western shores, were doubtless huge islands, similar to those which now rise from the diminished waters of the lake.

In passing over this mud-plain, the glare from the oozy substance of which it is composed was extremely painful to the eyes. Leaving it behind us, we ascended a ridge to the west of it, two or three miles broad, passing over some remains of shales and altered limestone with conglomerate, the crest being composed of porous trap, underlying the sedementary rocks, and cropping out to the west.   It may be remarked here, that the general direction of all the ridges noticed in this region is north and south, and they terminate most frequently in sharp, bold promontories, to the south.   A herd of antelope was seen on this ridge, numbering about a hundred, but too wild to be approached.

Descending its western slope, we came into another plain, somewhat similar to the last in form, but much more extensive in all directions, and densely covered with artemisia.   Over this desolate, barren waste, we travelled until nearly dark, when we reached a rocky promontory, constituting the southern point of a low ridge of hills jutting into the plain from the north. The rock was porous trap, in which no stratification could be made out. The mules having been without water or grass the whole day, and our stock of the former being insufficient to give them even their stinted allowance of one poor pint, we halted for a couple of hours, and drove them upon the side of the mountain to pick what they could get from the scanty supply of dry bunch-grass that grew in tufts upon its side. The prospect of water now began to be rather gloomy; and I was obliged to put the party upon allowance, lest we should be left entirely destitute. At eight o'clock we replaced the packs upon our mules, all of which began to show the effects of their unusual abstinence, and rode on till near midnight by the light of the moon, in a south-westerly direction, over a country similar to that we had traversed during the day; when, finding the indications of water growing less and less promising, and that our animals were nearly worn out, we halted, and, covered with our blankets, we lay down on the ground till morning, regardless of a heavy shower that fell during the night.

Friday, October 26.—The poor animals presented this morning a forlorn appearance, having been now without a drop of water for more than twenty-four hours, during eighteen of which they had been under the saddle, with scarcely any thing to eat. I now began to feel somewhat anxious. Should our mules give out before we could reach the mountains west of us, to which I had determined to direct our course as speedily as possible, we must all perish in the wilderness. Sweeping the horizon with a telescope, I thought I discovered something that looked like willows to the north-west, distant about four or five miles. Reanimated by this gleam of hope, we saddled up quickly and turned our steps in that direction. We soon had the lively satisfaction of finding our expectations confirmed; for, arriving at the spot, we found, after some search, a small spring welling out from the bottom of a little ravine, which having with some labour been cleaned out, we soon enjoyed a plentiful, most needed, and most welcome supply of excellent water for all.

The whole party being much exhausted from their long absti- nence and unceasing exertions, we halted here for the day, to afford opportunity for our animals to recruit their wasted strength upon the plentiful supply of grass which grew all around us.

Old decayed wigwams, constructed of willows, indicated that this spot had long been a favourite place of resort for the Indians, for the same reason, doubtless, which rendered it so welcome to ourselves.

On the summit of a ridge south-west of our halting-place, large masses of magnetic iron ore were discovered, some of which were partially encased in basaltic rock. In the ravine whence the spring broke out, were found pebbles of alabaster, obsidian, and other rocks, apparently the result of the disintegration of beds of conglomerate, none of which, however, was seen in place.

Saturday, October 27.—Ther. at sunrise, 35°. Resuming our journey, we took a course south by east, which led us past the ridge upon which we had halted two nights before. The formation was porous trap, and the direction of the ridge north by west and south by east. We then passed along the base of a range of low hills, composed apparently of trap and basalt. After travelling ten miles, we came to a range of higher hills extending northwest and south-east. Here the dark limestone was again observed, but the stratification could not be ascertained. We then passed, in a southerly direction, through deep sand, along what at one time had been the beach of the lake, as drift-wood was frequently seen lying on the sands that stretch out to the eastward for many miles. In one instance a drifted cotton-wood log was seen, lying near what had evidently been the water-line of the lake, as thick as the body of a man. On our right was a high ridge or promontory, with a narrow bottom sloping down to the edge of the flat.

The soil here was not so clayey as heretofore, being composed in many places of calcareous sand and decomposed conglomerate. Some masses of the latter were seen, resembling exactly that met with on the eastern side of the promontory range putting out into the lake. The country to-day has been similar to that passed over previously—dry, barren, and entirely destitute of water. We dug a well some five feet deep on the edge of the flat, which soon filled with water. The mules crowded around the hole, and seemed to watch the process of our labour, as if sensible of the object of our exertions, but upon tasting the water, refused to drink, although they had been travelling the whole day without a drop. Day's march, about sixteen miles.

Sunday, October 28.—Our little stock of water had become so reduced that we were compelled to forego our coffee this morning, and the most rigid economy in the use of the former was strictly enforced. We were on the road very early, and followed for several miles, down the edge of the sand at the foot of the range of hills on our right, when we ascended it, taking a course south-west by west, and passing over beds of conglomerate, which presented a stratification almost horizontal. The ridge was about five miles wide, stretching off to the southward, and about five hundred feet above the level of the beach. The soil consisted of decomposed conglomerate, and was much cut up by deep ravines. On the west side, volcanic rock was again met with.

Leaving the ridge, we entered upon a plain or sort of bay, partly covered with artemisia, and partly (to the westward) with mud and salt. It appeared to be bounded on the west, about thirty miles distant, by a high mountain-range, extending far to the northward, upon an eastern spur of which I judged we had encamped on Friday. The plain contained several island mountains, rising from it as from the water. To one of these, distant about twelve miles south-west by west, we directed our course and reached it about an hour before sunset. Here we stopped for a short time to prepare our scanty supper, and to give the mules a chance to pick a little grass, which was scarce and dried up. Not a drop of water had we met with the whole day; but at noon I had ordered a pint to be served out to each animal. Before arriving at this spot, one of the poor creatures "gave out," and we thought we should have to leave him to the wolves, but he afterward partially recovered, and another pint of water being given him, he went on. The rocky island, at the north end of which we halted, extended many miles to the southward, and was apparently surrounded on all sides by the mud-plain. One of the party ascended it, but could see nothing of the lake, nor any appearance of water in any direction. The rocks were formed of altered clayey and sandy shales, and strata of conglomerate, all of which had been much contorted, but evidently at different periods, as they were not conformable.

It now became a matter of serious importance to find water for the mules, as they had been without for nearly forty hours, most of the time under the saddle, and almost without food. Nothing, therefore, remained but to go on as far as possible during the night, so as to reach the western ridge bounding this basin as early the following day as practicable. We accordingly saddled up about dark and proceeded on the same course, directing our steps toward another island in the plain, which appeared to be about fifteen miles distant. The night was quite cold, and the moon shone as bright as day. Our course lay over a flat of damp clay and salt mud, in many places soft and deep, which made the travelling slow and laborious. All trace of vegetation had vanished, and even the unfailing artemisia had disappeared. The animals were so tired and weak that the whole party was on foot, driving our herd before us. The mule which had given out in the afternoon was now unable to proceed, and had to be abandoned in the midst of the plain, where it no doubt perished. Many others showed symptoms of extreme exhaustion, so that their packs had to be shifted and lightened repeatedly. I began to entertain serious fears that I should not be able to reach the mountain with them; nor was I certain that when we did reach it we should be able to find water in time to save their lives. The night was consequently passed in a state of great anxiety. We continued on until after midnight, crossing occasionally some little drains of salt water coming from the north, when we reached a small isolated butte, which was only a pile of barren rocks, with scarce a blade of grass upon it. Wood or water there was none; so, although the night was quite cold, we laid ourselves down, fireless and supperless, upon the sand, wearied to exhaustion by a continuous march of eighteen hours. The only sign of vegetable life to be seen here was a small chenopodeaceous plant, without leaves, but having long prickles. The artemisia had entirely disappeared. On each side of us, to the north and the south, was a rocky island or butte, similar in character to the one near which we had halted, but much larger.

Monday, October 29.—On awaking early, we found the mules gathered around us, looking very dejected and miserable. They had searched in vain for food, and were now in nearly a starving condition. Before us, indeed, lay the mountain where we hoped to find both food and water for them, but between lay a mud-plain fifteen or twenty miles in extent, which must be crossed before we could reach it. I was much afraid the animals were too weak to succeed in the attempt, but it was our only hope. We set out, the whole party on foot, pursuing the same general course of south-west by west that we had followed yesterday.

The island, at the foot of which we had slept last night, presented sections of sandstones and shales, which appeared to be of comparatively recent origin. They had evidently been somewhat altered by heat, but not to any great extent. At the north-east point of the island on our left, the strata were inclined at an angle of 70° to north-east. No fossils were found in them. Near the western side of this rocky protrusion, I observed what appeared to have been an ancient crater, forming three-fourths of an inverted cone, open to the north-west, around which were sections of shales and sandstones, very much contorted, and dipping in opposite directions on opposite sides. The lower part of the cone was filled with claystone. No volcanic rocks were found at the point where we crossed these islands, but decomposed conglomerate and alabaster occurred in considerable quantities.

The first part of the plain consisted simply of dried mud, with small crystals of salt scattered thickly over the surface. Crossing this, we came upon another portion of it, three miles in width, where the ground was entirely covered with a thin layer of salt in a state of deliquesencce, and of so soft a consistence that the feet of our mules sank at every step into the mud beneath. But we soon came upon a portion of the plain where the salt lay in a solid state, in one unbroken sheet, extending apparently to its western border. So firm and strong was this unique and snowy floor, that it sustained the weight of our entire train, without in the least giving way or cracking beneath the pressure. Our mules walked upon it as upon a sheet of solid ice. The whole field was crossed by a network of little ridges, projecting about half an inch, as if the salt had expanded in the process of crystallization. I estimated this field to be at least seven miles wide and ten miles in length. How much farther it extended northward I could not tell; but if it covered the plain in that direction as it did where we crossed, its extent must have been very much greater. The salt, which was very pure and white, averaged from one-half to three-fourths of an inch in thickness, and was equal in all respects to our finest specimens for table use. Assuming these data, the quantity that here lay upon the ground in one body, exclusive of that in a deliquescent state, amounted to over four and a-half millions of cubic yards, or about one hundred millions of bushels.

At two o'clock in the afternoon we reached the western edge of the plain, when to our infinite joy we beheld a small prairie or meadow, covered with a profusion of good green grass, through which meandered a small stream of pure fresh running water, among clumps of willows and wild roses, artemisia and rushes. It was a most timely and welcome relief to our poor famished animals, who had now been deprived of almost all sustenance for more than sixty hours, during the greater part of which time they had been in constant motion. It was, indeed, nearly as great a relief to me as to them, for I had been doubtful whether even the best mule we had could have gone more than half a dozen miles farther. Several of them had given out in crossing the last plain, and we had to leave them and the baggage behind, and to return for it afterward. Another day without water and the whole train must have inevitably perished. Both man and beast being completely exhausted, I remained here three days for refreshment and rest. Moreover, we were now to prepare for crossing another desert of seventy miles, which, as my guide informed me, still lay between us and the southern end of the lake. He had passed over it in 1845, with Frémont, who had lost ten mules and several horses in effecting the passage, having afterward encamped on the same ground now occupied by our little party.

During our stay here, it rained almost every day and night. The salt plain, which before had glistened in the sunlight like a sheet of molten silver, now became black and sombre; the salt, over which we had passed with so much ease, dissolved, and the flat, in places, became almost impassable. We had encamped at the eastern base of a range of high mountains, stretching a great distance to the north, and terminated, three miles below, in an abrupt escarpment, called Pilot Peak: upon the lofty summit of which rested a dark cloud during the whole of our stay. For three miles from the base the ascent is gradual, the surface being covered with gravel and boulders of granite, feldspathic rock, and metamorphic sandstones, all evidently waterworn. Higher up the mountain, the only stratified rocks seen were micaceous schists and slaty shales, intersected in various directions by veins of quartz, and very much displaced. The general dip was north by east from 70° to 80°. Proceeding south a few miles along the mountain, the same stratified rocks were again noticed, evidently much altered by heat, being interspersed with veins of granite and quartz. Dwarf cedar was growing here, and, higher up the mountain, dwarf pine; in the bottom, white and red willow, and *Equisetum*.

In a nook of the mountain, some Indian lodges were seen, which had apparently been finished but a short time. They were constructed in the usual conical form, of cedar poles and logs of a considerable size, thatched with bark and branches, and were quite warm and comfortable. The odour of the cedar was sweet and refreshing. These lodges had been put up, no doubt, by the Shoshonee Indians for their permanent winter-quarters, but had not yet been occupied. The savages had been in the neighbourhood to collect the nuts of the pine-tree, called here piñon, for food, but what they left had been destroyed by insects. While at this camp, one of our best mules was stolen. A couple of men, whom I had sent back across the plain to search for a revolver that had been lost in our last night march, reported, on their return to the camp, that they had discovered the tracks of two Indians on our trail, and had seen their fires in the mountains. These stealthy depredators must have followed us at a distance and watched their opportunity to plunder. The only wonder is that they did not steal more than a single mule; for the country was so utterly desolate, that we never once thought that any human being would ever be found where we had passed, except from absolute necessity, and consequently the vigilance of our night-guard was relaxed. Snow fell the night before we left this camp, and covered the ridge about halfway down from its summit.

Friday, November 2.—Ther. at sunrise, 19°. As we were aware that immediately before us lay another desert plain, without wood, water, or grass, for seventy miles, some little preparation was necessary before undertaking to cross it. This consisted simply in baking bread and cooking meat enough to last us through, and in packing upon our mules as much grass as they could carry, which we had cut, a handful at a time, with our hunting-knives. We had only vessels sufficient to carry twenty gallons of water—a small supply for so many men and animals. The mules, however, were now much recruited by their rest, and we started in good spirits. Following the western edge of the mud-plain at the foot of the range for three miles, we came to the southern point of the mountain, where there had been an encampment of emigrants, who had taken this route from Salt Lake City in 1848. There were here several large springs of excellent water, and the encampment had apparently been quite a large one. The usual destruction of property had taken place. Clothes, books, cases of medicine, wagon-wheels, tools, &c., lay strewn about, abandoned by their owners, who had laboriously brought them two thousand miles only to throw them away.

The route from the Salt Lake to this point was first taken by Colonel Frémont, in 1845. A year afterward, it was followed by a party of emigrants under a Mr. Hastings, whence its present name of "Hastings's Cut-off." A portion of his company, which had followed at some distance behind him, becoming belated in crossing the Sierra Nevada Mountains, a number of them perished, and the remainder were reduced to the revolting necessity of living upon the bodies of their dead comrades, until they were rescued by relief from Sutter's Fort.

The road to California from this point follows around the southern end of the ridge, passes to the north of another high mountain, and thence on to the head of Humboldt's or Mary's River.

Leaving the springs, we crossed, once more, though in an opposite direction, the same mud-plain over which we had been obliged to pass in order to reach the mountain. It was twelve miles in width; and now, in consequence of the recent rains, was soft and slippery—all the salt having disappeared, except a few crystals left in some old wagon-tracks. The travelling was in consequence heavy and laborious. After crossing, we passed, by a gentle ascent, over a neck of land which connected the high ridge on our left, at the north end of which we had bivouacked on the 29th, with another and broader one to the south, and which latter turned off considerably to the south-west. Here we halted for a short time, to give our mules their last chance to pick a little bunch-grass which grew in thin scattered tufts on the mountain-side.

The strata, at this point, were very much contorted, as at the northern end of the same protruded ridge, inclining in all directions. The higher hills were composed of dark limestone, traversed in various directions by veins of white marble, some of which were of considerable thickness. The dip was to the north-west, 65°. Over the limestone were beds of conglomerate, not conformable; the lower layers of which, or those in immediate contact with the limestone, consisted of portions of the rock that had not been waterworn. Lower down, near the base of the hill, was found a coarse, imperfect oolitic limestone, dipping about 50° to north-west, and under these some sandstone, not conformable, and imperfect.

After halting an hour, we pursued our journey along the eastern base of this isolated mountain or butte, where the dark limestone was again seen, with gypsum, conformable and at right angles with the strata. Some six miles farther on, we passed another isolated butte, upheaved through the level mud-plain, containing what appeared to be another crater, analogous to that seen on the northern end of the ridge, open to the eastward, with the strata dipping in every direction. The main butte appeared to be, at this end, about ten miles wide from east to west, and had manifestly been very much disturbed.

From this point we travelled on until past midnight, over a level mud-plain, lighted by the rays of the moon, which struggled through a mass of dark and threatening clouds. The wind was fresh and cold, and the mud soft and tenacious, making the travelling very slow and fatiguing. During the night, we passed five wagons and one cart, which had stuck fast in the mud, and been necessarily left by their owners, who, from appearances, had abandoned every thing, fearful of perishing themselves in this inhospitable desert. Great quantities of excellent clothing, tool-chests, trunks, scientific books, and, in fact, almost every thing, both useless and necessary on a journey of this kind, had been here left strewn over the plain. Many articles had not even been removed from the wagons. The carcasses of several oxen lying about on the ground satisfactorily explained the whole matter. In attempting to cross the plain, the animals had died from exhaustion and want of water, and the wagons and their contents had of course to be abandoned.

About one o'clock in the morning, we halted in the midst of the plain, enticed by the sight of a broken ox-yoke, the remains of a barrel, and part of an old wagon-bed, which served for fuel sufficient to boil a little coffee, of which all hands stood very much in need. The mud was ankle-deep; and the only place upon which we could spread down a blanket to sleep was around some scattering bushes of artemisia, where the wind had collected a little sand, presenting a spot rather higher and not so wet as the mud-flat around. The whole scene was as barren, dreary, and desolate as could be well imagined. We gave the mules a portion of the grass that had been packed upon them in the morning, and two pint-cups of water each—the only liquid they had tasted during the day. We then fastened them up as well as we could to the artemisia-bushes, and, wrapping ourselves in our blankets, lay down to wait for the morning. The night was windy and quite cold, and the poor mules kept up such a pitiful and mournful cry, that we were but little recruited by our night's rest.

It may well be supposed that there were few attractions to detain us long on this spot. We had exhausted our fuel last night, and there was nothing with which to cook breakfast; so we started quite early without any, pursuing the same general course through the heavy mud. The wind, uninterrupted by any obstacle, blew hard over the level plain; and although the thermometer stood at only 47°, yet it was very cold, and brought into requisition all appliances for preventing the escape of animal heat. In the course of the morning, we passed a spot where some emigrants had made a large "cache" of such things as they could not carry. But it had been constructed in such a bungling manner, that it had easily been discovered and robbed: twelve ox-yokes remained in a heap on the ground. After travelling until noon, we came to a low ridge of hills running nearly north and south. We sheltered ourselves behind it, and finding plenty of artemisia, kindled a fire, and boiled our coffee, which, with a piece of bread and cold bacon, constituted our first and only meal for the day.

Our poor animals looked wretchedly, and two of them giving out before reaching the ridge, were with great difficulty driven up. As they had been without water for twenty-four hours, except the cupful which had been served out to them last night, after filling a few canteens for our own use, the remainder of our little stock was divided among them.

The ridge was composed of porous trap. The hills were higher toward the north, where they were connected with a range which seemed to form a spur from the mountains east of us. They gradually diminished to the south, not extending more than a mile or two in that direction.

Before us, distant about twelve miles, was a high mountain-range, on the eastern side of which, the guide informed me, there was a spring with plenty of water. I had hoped to be able to cross it to-day, but the state of our animals was such that it proved impracticable, since it was dark before we reached its western base. I the less regretted this, as in the course of the afternoon we had found several little pools of rain-water, from which the mules drank with great avidity and to repletion. The ascent to the range was gentle, and we encamped at the mouth of a narrow, winding pass through it, amid plenty of large cedar-trees and very large artemisia—a welcome sight, as the day had been cold and blustering, and there was every prospect of a heavy storm. Large fires were soon blazing, and every one was tired enough at once to seek his blanket, without going to the trouble of preparing the evening meal. Indeed, there was little or nothing to prepare; our bread was all gone, and there was not water enough either to make bread or coffee, and none could be sought for in the dark. The two mules that had failed in the morning, again gave out before reaching the mountain, and had finally to be abandoned.

Sunday, November 4.—Ther. 33°. Upon rising we found it snowing hard, and the ground covered to the depth of two inches. It soon ceased, however, and before night had melted in the plain, although the neighbouring mountains continued all whitened by it. After much search, water was found in a deep ravine near by; and grass was tolerably abundant, though dry and hard. As the mules were nearly exhausted and much stiffened by their journey across the deep mud-plains, I determined to remain here for the day, to recruit them. A couple of men were sent back afoot, to try and recover those left yesterday: they returned, after dark, bringing with them one only; the other had strayed from the road, and all efforts to recover it were vain. It was the third lost on this trip.

A deep ravine at the foot of the mountain presented sections of the strata. The lowest exposed was dark limestone with white veins, inclined to the south-east, at an angle of 85°; in fact, almost vertical. Ascending the ravine, the limestone was found to be overlaid by red sandstone, and this again by clayey shales. All these rocks had been altered by heat. No organic remains were found in the sandstones or shales, but some corals were seen in the limestone. The rocks were all veined with white marble. Large crystalline nodules of this substance were found, which assumed the form of *arragonite*. Some specimens of iron ore were also found, apparently a carbonate, but not in place. Ther. at noon, 37°; sunset, 31°.

Monday, November 5.—Ther. 23°. Morning clear and quite cold. Crossed the mountain through the pass. The snow was about two inches deep and the ground frozen hard. Followed down the eastern slope for about two miles, when we came to a spring-branch issuing from a gorge of the mountains where there was plenty of green grass—the first full supply our animals had enjoyed for several days.

The only rocks observed in crossing the mountain were limestones, containing remains of encrinites and corals. A wide dike of trap formed the crest; and, on the eastern side, another dike was seen running north by east, and south by west, forming the summit of a lower ridge. The limestones were tilted up almost vertically, but as the surface of the ground was covered with snow, the nature of the strata and their direction could not be very accurately ascertained. A piece of altered coal was found at the eastern base of the mountain, but not in place. The lower hills were covered with conglomerate not conformable.

Leaving the spring, our true course lay about east, to strike the southern point of another range ten miles distant, and forming the eastern boundary of a broad, green, intervening valley, which extended northward to the southern shore of the Great Salt Lake, and was covered with grass, the first we had seen since leaving Pilot Peak. It was shut in toward the south by a range of comparatively low hills, connecting the two mountain ranges that formed its eastern and western boundaries. A direct course could not be taken for this point, owing to numerous springs, which rendered the valley in that direction marshy and wholly impassable. We were consequently forced many miles to the southward, and obliged to make a circuit of more than a semicircle to gain the opposite side. We followed down the western base of the mountain for two or three miles, passing a fine spring, with good grass, near which we encamped for the night, among some dwarf cedars, that both furnished us with fuel and afforded a protection against the wind, which blew fresh and cold from the north-west. Ther. at sunset, 43°.

Tuesday, November 6.—Ther. at sunrise, 30°. Continued our journey in a northerly direction, along the western base of the mountain, for twelve miles, when we reached its northern extremity, which was about a mile and a-half wide, and terminated in bold escarpments five or six hundred feet high. One of these resembled, in a remarkable manner, a huge castle, the vertical walls of which were not less than three hundred feet in height.

Before reaching this point of the mountains, I remarked, on our left, in the middle of the valley, a curious, isolated mass of rocks, resembling a small fortification or redoubt : it was surrounded by marshy meadow-land, and could, in case of need, be defended by a small force against almost any number of Indians. Numerous springs broke out from the mountain and at the edge of the prairie ; but they were all saline, with a temperature of 74°, and totally unfit to drink. To this place we gave the name of " Spring Valley." Near the point of the mountain was a very large spring, which discharged its waters northward into the lake. The water was very salt, nauseous, and bitter, with a temperature of 70° ; notwithstanding which it swarmed with innumerable small fish, and seemed to be a favourite resort for pelicans and gulls.

In a shallow ravine near our morning camp, limestone was found cropping out, with a dip of 80° to the north-west. This rock was seen as we followed the range, appearing at the spurs ; and dikes of trap were observed, forming peaks farther back up the mountainside. The ridge gradually became less elevated as we proceeded toward the point, where the stratified rocks (limestone and shales) were found in a horizontal position. Along the northern termina-

tion of the range, the strata were again found to be much displaced and almost vertical. They were composed of limestone
and shales, overlaid in some places by conglomerate. Salt springs
were very numerous in this locality.

After doubling the point, we came upon another valley, similar
to the one through which we had just passed, and from which it was
divided by the ridge or mountain just described. Our true course
here, also, was to cross this valley in an easterly direction, and
strike the northern point of another range where it terminates immediately on the southern shore of the Salt Lake, now plainly
visible; but the numerous salt springs, as in the case of that
passed yesterday, rendered a straight course impracticable. Consequently, after following the eastern base of the ridge about
six miles to the south, we began gradually to diverge from it to the
eastward, and at dark encamped in the prairie, near a noble spring
of fresh, cold water, with abundance of excellent grass, and an extensive grove of large willows for fuel. A fierce gale sprang up
from the south-east, which kept us in a constant state of alarm
during the night, lest we should be burned in our beds from the
tall dry grass taking fire. It had in fact kindled several times,
and the flame was extinguished with some difficulty, rendering a
strict watch necessary until morning. This valley is called " Tuilla
Valley" by the Mormons, and forms an excellent pasturage for
numerous herds of cattle, wintered here by them under the charge
of keepers. The grass is very abundant, and numerous springs are
found on both sides of it.

On the eastern side of the mountain, which divides it from
Spring Valley, the same geological appearances occur as were seen
yesterday at the point of the range and on its western side. The
limestones were thrown up at a very great angle, and in some
places the strata were perpendicular.

Another mule gave out to-day, and was necessarily abandoned.
Ther. at sunset, 43°.

Wednesday, November 7.—Ther. at sunrise, 47°. Starting
early in the morning, we crossed to the eastern side of the valley,
followed the base of the mountain to its northern extremity, and
reached the shores of the Great Salt Lake near Black Rock,
whence we crossed the valley of the Jordan, over sterile artemisia
plains, and reached the city in the afternoon—being the first party
of white men that ever succeeded in making the entire circuit of
the lake by land. Attempts had, in early times, been made to

circumnavigate it in canoes, by some trappers in search of beaver; but they all proved unsuccessful, from want of fresh water.

The examination just completed proves that the whole western shore of the lake is bounded by an immense level plain, consisting of soft mud, frequently traversed by small, meandering rills of salt and sulphurous water, with occasional springs of fresh, all of which sink before reaching the lake. These streams seem to imbue and saturate the whole soil, so as to render it throughout miry and treacherous. For a few months, in midsummer, the sun has sufficient influence to render some portions of the plain, for a short time, dry and hard: in these intervals the travelling over it is excellent; but one heavy shower is sufficient to reconvert the hardened clay into soft, tenacious mud, rendering the passage of teams over it toilsome, and frequently quite hazardous.

These plains are but little elevated above the present level of the lake, and have, beyond question, at one time formed a part of it. It is manifest to every observer, that an elevation of but a few feet above the present level of the lake would flood this entire flat to a great distance north and south, and wash the base of the Pilot Peak range of mountains, which constitute its western boundary; thus converting what is now a comparatively small and insignificant lake into a vast inland sea. This extensive area is, for the most part, entirely denuded of vegetation, excepting occasional patches of artemisia and greasewood. The minute crystals of salt which cover the surface of the moist, oozy mud, glisten brilliantly in the sunlight, and present the appearance of a large sheet of water so perfectly, that it is difficult, at times, for one to persuade himself that he is not standing on the shore of the lake itself. High rocky ridges protrude above the level plain, and resemble great islands rising above the bosom of this desert sea.

The mirage, which frequently occurs, is greater here than I ever witnessed elsewhere, distorting objects in the most grotesque manner, defying all calculation as to their size, shape, or distances, and giving rise to optical illusions almost beyond belief. With the exception of the two valleys lying at the south end of the lake, the country is, as a place of human habitation, entirely worthless. There is, however, one valuable use to which it may and perhaps will be applied: its extent, and perfectly level surface, would furnish a desirable space on which to measure a degree of the meridian.

CHAPTER VII.

Upon my arrival at Salt Lake City, I found that the camp, under Lieutenant Gunnison, was then about sixty miles to the southward, upon Utah Lake. I accordingly joined him as soon as possible. The work, during my absence, had been carried forward by that officer with energy, industry, and judgment.

I had hoped, from the representations which had been made to me of the mildness of the two previous winters, that we should be able to keep the field the greater part, if not the whole of the season; but, in the latter part of November, the winter set in with great and unusual severity, accompanied by deep snows, which rendered any farther prosecution of the work impracticable. I was therefore compelled to break up my camp, and to seek for winter quarters in the city. These were not obtained without some difficulty, as the tide of emigration had been so great that houses were very scarce, and not a small portion of the inhabitants, among whom was the president himself, were forced to lodge portions of their families in wagons.

Upon terminating the field-work for the season, I despatched three men, one of whom was my guide and interpreter, with a small invoice of goods, to trade for horses among the Uintah Utahs, with directions to await my orders at Fort Bridger. Reports afterward reached us that a bloody fight had taken place between the Sioux and the Yampah Utahs, which latter tribe reside in the vicinity of the Uintahs, and great fears were entertained that the little party had been cut off by one or the other of the contending tribes. Such a calamity, aside from the loss of life, would have been of serious consequence to the expedition, as the horses I expected to obtain were almost indispensable to the return of the party to the States, the number of our animals having been much diminished by death and robbery.

It may as well be mentioned here, that the party thus despatched subsequently joined me in the spring, as soon as the melting of the snows rendered communication with Fort Bridger prac-

STATION EAST END OF THE BASE LINE.

Ackerman Lith. 379 Broadway N.Y.

ticable, bringing with them a drove of twenty-five horses. They had met with very rough usage from the Indians, having been robbed of a number of their horses, beside the whole of what remained of their goods, and narrowly escaped with their lives.

From the report by Lieutenant Gunnison of his operations during my absence, I make the following synopsis.

A thorough exploration was made, with the view of ascertaining the points for such a base line as would best develop a system of triangles embracing both the Salt Lake and Utah valleys.

A line was selected, and carefully measured by rods constructed for the purpose, and tripod stations erected over the termini, which were marked by metal points set in wooden posts sunk flush with the surface of the ground. The length of the base is thirty-one thousand six hundred and eighty feet.

Fourteen principal triangulation stations were erected, consisting of large pyramidal timber tripods, strongly framed, to be covered, when required for use, by cotton cloth of different colours, according to the background. The triangles extended to the south shore of Utah Lake, and embraced an area of about eighty by twenty-five miles.

A survey and sounding had been made of the Utah Lake, and also of the river connecting it with Salt Lake: this operation requiring a line to be run of one hundred and twenty-six miles, principally by the back angle, with the theodolite.

Although such a result, from less than two months' labour, would be entirely satisfactory under ordinary circumstances anywhere, and would reflect credit on the energy and capacity of the officer in charge of the work, yet it may be remarked that it would be very unfair to judge of it by a comparison with similar results obtained in the Eastern States. There, all the accessories to such a work, especially water and timber, are abundant, and generally at a convenient distance: here, on the contrary, both are very scarce and hard to be obtained. All the water, for instance, used both for cooking and drinking, that was consumed on the base line, (requiring seven days of incessant labour in its measurement,) had to be transported upon mules from the river, which lay a mile east of its eastern terminus; and the force employed in the erection of most of the triangulation stations had to be supplied in a like manner. But the principal difficulty was the scarcity of timber. Wood grows nowhere on the plains; all the wood used for cooking in camp, and all the timber, both for posts on the base line and for the construction of the stations, had to be hauled from the mountains, in many cases fifteen or twenty miles distant, over a rough country without roads.   Almost every stick used for this purpose cost from twenty to thirty miles' travel of a six-mule team.   This, together with the delays of getting into the cañons, where alone the timber can be procured, cutting down the trees, and hauling them down the gorges by hand to the nearest spots accessible to the teams, involved an amount of time and labour which must be experienced before it can be appreciated.   All this had to be done, however, or the prosecution of the work would have been impracticable.

Before leaving the Salt Lake City for Fort Hall, I had engaged the services of Albert Carrington, Esq., a member of the Mormon community, who was to act as an assistant on the survey.   He was without experience in the use of instruments; but, being a gentleman of liberal education, he soon acquired, under instruction, the requisite skill, and, by his zeal, industry, and practical good sense, materially aided us in our subsequent operations.   He continued with the party until the termination of the survey, accompanied it to this city, and has since returned to his mountain home, carrying with him the respect and kind wishes of all with whom he was associated.

The winter season in the valley was long and severe.   The vicinity of so many high mountains rendered the weather extremely variable ; snows fell constantly upon them, and frequently to the depth of ten inches in the plains.   In many of the cañons it accumulated to the depth of fifty feet, filling up the passes so rapidly that, in more than one instance, emigrants who had been belated in starting from the States, were overtaken by the storms in the mountain gorges, and forced to abandon every thing, and escape on foot, leaving even their animals to perish in the snows.   All communication with the world beyond was thus effectually cut off; and, as the winter advanced, the gorges became more and more impassable, owing to the drifting of the snow into them from the projecting peaks.

We remained thus shut up until the third of April.   Our quarters consisted of a small unfurnished house of unburnt brick or adobe, unplastered, and roofed with boards loosely nailed on, which, every time it stormed, admitted so much water as called into requisition all the pans and buckets in the establishment to receive the numerous little streams which came trickling down

from every crack and knot-hole. During this season of comparative inaction, we received from the authorities and citizens of the
community every kindness that the most warmhearted hospitality
could dictate; and no effort was spared to render us as comfortable as their own limited means would admit. Indeed, we were
much better lodged than many of our neighbours; for, as has been
previously observed, very many families were obliged still to lódge
wholly or in part in their wagons, which, being covered, served,
when taken off from the wheels and set upon the ground, to make
bedrooms, of limited dimensions it is true, but yet exceedingly
comfortable. Many of these were comparatively large and commodious, and, when carpeted and furnished with a little stove, formed
an additional apartment or back building to the small cabin, with
which they frequently communicated by a door. It certainly argued
a high tone of morals and an habitual observance of good order and
decorum, to find women and children thus securely slumbering in
the midst of a large city, with no protection from midnight molestation other than a wagon-cover of linen and the ægis of the law.
In the very next enclosure to that occupied by our party, a whole
family of children had no other shelter than one of these wagons,
where they slept all the winter, literally out of doors, there being
no communication whatever with the inside of their parents' house.

The founding, within the space of three years, of a large and
flourishing community, upon a spot so remote from the abodes of
man, so completely shut out by natural barriers from the rest of
the world, so entirely unconnected by watercourses with either of
the oceans that wash the shores of this continent—a country offering no advantages of inland navigation or of foreign commerce, but,
on the contrary, isolated by vast uninhabitable deserts, and only
to be reached by long, painful, and often hazardous journeys by
land—presents an anomaly so very peculiar, that it deserves more
than a passing notice. In this young and progressive country of
ours, where cities grow up in a day, and states spring into existence in a year, the successful planting of a colony, where the
natural advantages have been such as to hold out the promise of
adequate reward to the projectors, would have excited no surprise;
but the success of an enterprise under circumstances so at variance
with all our preconceived ideas of its probability, may well be considered as one of the most remarkable incidents of the present
age.

A brief reference to the early history of this people, and to the events and motives which led to their planting such a settlement in the midst of a barren wilderness, may not be without interest.

The City of the Great Salt Lake, the capital of the settlement, was founded in 1847, by a religious community of people known among us by the name of Mormons, but who style themselves the "Latter-day Saints of the Church of Jesus Christ." It is situated in lat. 40° 46′ north, and long. 112° 6′ west, at the foot of the western slope of the Wahsatch Mountains, an extensive chain of lofty hills, forming a portion of the eastern boundary of what is known in our geography as the "Great Basin."

The origin of this new religious sect in our country is well known, and therefore it will only be necessary to advert to it very briefly. It was first organized in 1830, under the auspices of *Joseph Smith*, the founder; and, after a temporary residence in Kirtland, Ohio, was removed to Jackson county, Missouri, where by divine revelation "the saints" were directed to build a magnificent temple, the pattern of which was to be revealed from on high. The corner-stone of this edifice was laid, but the builders were eventually driven from the State by an armed mob. They next removed to Illinois, where, upon the bank of the Mississippi, they built a flourishing city, which they called Nauvoo. They lived here until 1844, when they became obnoxious to the inhabitants of that State also, and were finally attacked by an enraged multitude, and their prophet, Joseph Smith, and his brother Hyrum, murdered in the jail of Carthage. During the year 1845, these persecutions continued; and threats of greater outrages being held out, the Mormons found their situation no longer tolerable within the boundaries of that State, and at length, in a solemn council, determined to abandon their homes in their city of Nauvoo, and to seek, in the wilds of the Western wilderness, a spot remote from the habitations of men, where, secure from lawless violence, they might worship according to the rites of the new religion they had introduced.

Into the particular causes which led to the expulsion of the Mormons from Missouri and Illinois it is not the province of this report to inquire. The facts have long been before the country, and its judgment has been passed upon them; but the results of the persecutions to which they were subjected have been as curious as they were wholly unlooked-for.

The Mormons having resolved to emigrate, preparations for the journey were immediately commenced, by hastily and at much

GREAT SALT LAKE CITY - FROM THE NORTH.

Ackerman Lith 379 Broadway, N.Y.

sacrifice exchanging such property as they could dispose of for animals, wagons, and breadstuffs; and in the beginning of February, 1846, a large proportion of the community crossed the Mississippi from Nauvoo, and formed a rendezvous near Montrose, in Iowa. Here they remained, exposed to intense cold and deep snows, until March, when, being joined by several hundred wagons and a large number of women and children, they organized their company under the guidance of *Brigham Young*, president of the church, and successor of Joseph Smith their founder and seer.

In their progress westward, through the northern part of Missouri, they were again driven from that State, by violent threats, into the southern borders of Iowa, whence, after much hardship and suffering, they reached, in the course of the summer, the banks of the Missouri, beyond the limits of the States. Here they enclosed land and planted crops, leaving some of their number to reap the fruits, which were to be applied to the sustenance of other companies, that were to follow as soon as they should be able to provide the means. They were about crossing the river to pursue their journey westward, when an officer of the United States Government presented himself, with a requisition for five hundred men to serve in the war with Mexico. This demand, though sudden and unexpected, was promptly and patriotically complied with; but in consequence, the expedition was broken up for the season. Those that remained, being principally old men, women, and children, prepared to pass the winter in the wilds of an Indian country, by cutting hay and erecting log and sod huts, and digging as many caves as time allowed and their strength enabled them.

During this winter, owing to the great privations incident to such a life, and to the want, in many instances, of the most common necessaries, great numbers sickened and died: their cattle, too, were stolen by the Indians, or perished by starvation.

In the succeeding spring of 1847, the people were again organized for their journey; and on the 8th of April, a pioneer company, consisting of one hundred and forty-three men, seventy-two wagons, and one hundred and seventy-five head of horses, mules, and oxen, with rations for six months, agricultural implements and seed-grain, manfully set out in search of a home beyond the Rocky Mountains.

Pursuing their route up the left bank of the Platte, crossing at Fort Laramie, and passing over the mountains at the South Pass, the advanced guard at length reached the valley of the Great Salt Lake, on the 21st of July. On the 24th, the presidency and the main body arrived. A piece of ground was selected, consecrated by prayer, broken up, and planted; and thus, in 1847, was formed the nucleus of what, in 1850, was admitted as a Territory of the Union, and which bids fair ere long to present itself at the door of the national legislature for admission as one of the States of the confederacy.

In a short time after the arrival of the pioneer company, ground was surveyed and laid out into streets and squares for a large city; a fort or enclosure was erected, of houses made of logs and sun-dried brick, opening into a large square, the entrance to which was defended by gates, and formed a tolerably secure fortification against Indian attacks. In October following, an addition of between three and four thousand was made to their number, by the emigration of such as had been left behind, and the fort was necessarily enlarged for their accommodation. Agricultural labours were now resumed with renewed spirit; ploughing and planting continued throughout the whole winter and until the July following, by which time a line of fence had been constructed, enclosing upward of six thousand acres of land, laid down in crops, besides a large tract of pasture land. During the winter and spring, the inhabitants were much straitened for food; and game being very scarce in the country, they were reduced to the necessity of digging roots from the ground, and living upon the hides of animals which they had previously made use of for roofing their cabins, but which were now torn off for food. But this distress only continued until the harvest, since which time provisions of all kinds have been abundant.

This year, (1848,) a small grist-mill was erected, and two saw-mills nearly completed. The following winter and spring, a settlement was commenced on the banks of the Weber River, a bold, clear stream which breaks through the Wahsatch Mountains, forty miles north of the city, and discharges its waters into the Salt Lake.

Upon Ogden Creek, an affluent of the Weber, a city has since (1850) been laid out, and called Ogden City, and is already surrounded by a flourishing agricultural population.

In the autumn, another large immigration arrived under the president, Brigham Young, which materially added to the strength of the colony. Building and agriculture were prosecuted with renewed vigour. Numerous settlements continued to be made wherever water could be found for irrigation. A handsome council-house was commenced, to be built of red sandstone procured

STREET IN GREAT SALT LAKE CITY _ LOOKING EAST.

Ackerman Lith? 379.Broadway,N.Y.

from the neighbouring mountain, and two grist-mills and three saw-mills, added to those already in operation. The winter of this year was much more severe than the preceding one, and snow fell on the plain to the depth of ten inches.

In the following spring (1849) a settlement was commenced, and a small fort built near the mouth of the Timpanogas or Provaux, an affluent of Lake Utah, about fifty miles south of the city. During this summer, large crops of grain, melons, potatoes, and corn were raised, and two more saw-mills erected.

The colony had now become firmly established, and all fear of its ability to sustain itself were, from the overflowing abundance of the harvest, set at rest. Nothing could be more natural than that the people should turn their attention to the formation of a system of civil government. Hitherto they had been under the guidance of their ecclesiastical leaders only, and justice had been administered upon principles of equity simply, enforced by the government of the church alone. This would answer very well while the community remained small, and consisted only of those who acknowledged the binding force of spiritual rule in matters purely temporal also. But, as the colony increased, it was not to be expected that it would continue to consist solely of members of the church, willing to submit to such a jurisdiction, without the sanctions of an organized civil government.

A convention was therefore called "of all the citizens of that portion of Upper California lying east of the Sierra Nevada mountains, to take into consideration the propriety of organizing a Territorial or State government."

The convention met at Great Salt Lake City, on the 5th of March, 1849, and on the 10th adopted a constitution, which was to remain in force until the Congress of the United States should otherwise provide for the government of the territory.

It "ordained and established a free and independent government, by the name of the STATE OF DESERET;" fixed the boundaries of the new State; provided for the election of governor, senators, representatives, and judges: all of whom, as well as the other officers created by it, were required to take an oath to support the constitution of the United States. On the 2d of July, the legislature, created by the organic law, met, elected a delegate to Congress, and adopted a memorial to that body, in which, among other things, they state that "the inhabitants of the State of Deseret, in view of their own security, and for the preservation of the constitutional right of the United States to hold jurisdiction there, have organized a provisional State government, under which the civil policy of the nation is duly maintained." "That there is now a sufficient number of individuals residing within the State of Deseret to support a State government." They therefore asked "that, if consistent with the constitution and usages of the Federal Government, the constitution accompanying the memorial be ratified, and that the State of Deseret be admitted into the Union on an equal footing with other States"—"or such other form of civil government established, as Congress in its wisdom and magnanimity might award."

A constitution and petition for a *Territorial* organization had been previously forwarded to Congress; but in consequence of information received afterward, a memorial for a State government was substituted in its room. Such is a brief sketch of the origin and progress of this colony, and the condition in which we found it upon our arrival in August, 1849.

A city had been laid out upon a magnificent scale, being nearly four miles in length and three in breadth; the streets at right angles with each other, eight rods or one hundred and thirty-two feet wide, with sidewalks of twenty feet; the blocks forty rods square, divided into eight lots, each of which contains an acre and a-quarter of ground. By an ordinance of the city, each house is to be placed twenty feet back from the front line of the lot, the intervening space being designed for shrubbery and trees. The site for the city is most beautiful: it lies at the western base of the Wahsatch Mountains, in a curve formed by the projection westward from the main range, of a lofty spur which forms its southern boundary. On the west it is washed by the waters of the Jordan, while to the southward for twenty-five miles extends a broad level plain, watered by several little streams, which, flowing down from the eastern hills, form the great element of fertility and wealth to the community. Through the city itself flows an unfailing stream of pure, sweet water, which, by an ingenious mode of irrigation, is made to traverse each side of every street, whence it is led into every garden-spot, spreading life, verdure, and beauty over what was heretofore a barren waste. On the east and north the mountain descends to the plain by steps, which form broad and elevated terraces, commanding an extended view of the whole valley of the Jordan, which is bounded on the west by a range of

HOT SPRING - THREE MILES FROM GREAT SALT LAKE CITY.

rugged mountains, stretching far to the southward, and enclosing within their embrace the lovely little Lake of Utah.

On the northern confines of the city, a warm spring issues from the base of the mountain, the water of which has been conducted by pipes into a commodious bathing-house; while, at the western point of the same spur, about three miles distant, another spring flows in a bold stream from beneath a perpendicular rock, with a temperature too high to admit the insertion of the hand, (128° Fahr.) At the base of the hill it forms a little lake, which in the autumn and winter is covered with large flocks of waterfowl, attracted by the genial temperature of the water.

Beyond the Jordan, on the west, the dry and otherwise barren plains support a hardy grass, (called bunch-grass,) which is peculiar to these regions, requiring but little moisture, very nutritious, and in sufficient quantities to afford excellent pasturage to numerous herds of cattle. To the northward, in the low grounds bordering the river, hay in abundance can be procured, although it is rather coarse and of an inferior quality.

The facilities for beautifying this admirable site are manifold. The irrigating canals, which flow before every door, furnish abundance of water for the nourishment of shade-trees, and the open space between each building, and the pavement before it, when planted with shrubbery and adorned with flowers, will make this one of the most lovely spots between the Mississippi and the Pacific. One of the most unpleasant characteristics of the whole country, after leaving the Blue River, is the entire absence of trees from the landscape. The weary traveller plods along, exposed to the full blaze of one eternal sunshine, day after day, and week after week, his eye resting upon naught but interminable plains, bald and naked hills, or bold and rugged mountains: the shady grove, the babbling brook, the dense and solemn forest, are things unknown here; and should he by chance light upon some solitary cotton-wood, or pitch his tent amid some stunted willows, the opportunity is hailed with joy, as one of unusual good fortune. The studding, therefore, of this beautiful city with noble trees, will render it, by contrast with the surrounding regions, a second " Diamond of the Desert," in whose welcome shade, like the solitary Sir Kenneth and the princely Ilderim, the pilgrim, wayworn and faint, may repose his jaded limbs and dream of the purling brooks and waving woodlands he has left a thousand miles behind him.

The city was estimated to contain about eight thousand inhabit-

9

ants, and was divided into numerous wards, each, at the time of our visit, enclosed by a substantial fence, for the protection of the young crops : as time and leisure will permit, these will be removed, and each lot enclosed by itself, as with us. The houses are built, principally, of adobe or sun-dried brick, which, when well covered with a tight projecting roof, make a warm, comfortable dwelling, presenting a very neat appearance. Buildings of a better description are being introduced, although slowly, owing to the difficulty of procuring the requisite lumber, which must always be scarce and dear in a country so destitute of timber.

Upon a square appropriated to the public buildings, an immense shed had been erected upon posts, which was capable of containing three thousand persons. It was called " *The Bowery*," and served as a temporary place of worship, until the construction of the Great Temple. This latter is to surpass in grandeur of design and gorgeousness of decoration all edifices the world has yet seen; and is to be eclipsed only by that contemplated in Jackson county, Missouri, —to be erected when " the fulness of time shall come," and which will constitute the head-quarters or central point, whence light, truth, and the only true religion shall radiate to the uttermost parts of the earth. A mint was already in operation, from which were issued gold coins of the Federal denominations, stamped, without assay, from the dust brought from California.

The provisional State government, with all the machinery of executive, legislative, and judicial functionaries, was in regular and harmonious action, under the constitution recently adopted. The jurisdiction of the " State of Deseret" had been extended over and was vigorously enforced upon all who came within its borders, and justice was equitably administered alike to " saint" and " *gentile*"—as they term all who are not of their persuasion. Of the truth of this, as far at least as the gentiles were concerned, I soon had convincing proof, by finding, one fine morning, some twenty of our mules safely secured in the public pound, for trespass upon the cornfield of some pious saint; possession was recovered only by paying the fine imposed by the magistrate and amply remunerating the owner for the damage done to his crops. Their courts were constantly appealed to by companies of passing emigrants, who, having fallen out by the way, could not agree upon the division of their property. The decisions were remarkable for fairness and impartiality, and if not submitted to, were sternly enforced by the whole power of the community. Appeals for

BOWERY, MINT, & PRESIDENT'S HOUSE GREAT SALT LAKE CITY.

Ackerman Lith: 379 Broadway N.Y.

protection from oppression, by those passing through their midst, were not made in vain; and I know of at least one instance in which the marshal of the State was despatched, with an adequate force, nearly two hundred miles into the western desert, in pursuit of some miscreants who had stolen off with nearly the whole outfit of a party of emigrants. He pursued and brought them back to the city, and the plundered property was restored to its rightful owner.

While, however, there are all the exterior evidences of a government strictly temporal, it cannot be concealed that it is so intimately blended with the spiritual administration of the church, that it would be impossible to separate the one from the other. The first civil governor under the constitution of the new State, elected by the people, was the president of the church, Brigham Young; the lieutenant-governor was his first ecclesiastical counsellor, and the secretary of state his second counsellor: these three individuals forming together the " presidency" of the church. The bishops of the several wards, who, by virtue of their office in the church, had exercised not only a spiritual but a temporal authority over the several districts assigned to their charge, were appointed, under the civil organization, to be justices of the peace, and were supported in the discharge of their duties, not only by the civil power, but by the whole spiritual authority of the church also. This intimate connection of church and state seems to pervade every thing that is done. The supreme power in both being lodged in the hands of the same individuals, it is difficult to separate their two official characters, and to determine whether in any one instance they act as spiritual or merely temporal officers.

The establishment of a civil government at all, seems to me to have been altogether the result of a foreseen necessity, which it was impossible to avoid. As the community grew in numbers and importance, it was not to be expected, as has been before remarked, that the whole population would always consist solely of members of the church, looking up to the presidency, not only as its spiritual head, but as the divinely commissioned and inspired source of law in temporal matters and policy also. It became necessary, therefore, to provide for the government of the *whole*, by establishing some authority which could not be disputed by any, and would exercise a control over them as citizens, whether they were members of the church or not; and which, being acknowledged and recognised by the Government of the United States, would be supported by its laws and upheld by its authority. The civil government, therefore, was wholly precautionary, and only for such gentiles as might settle among them, the power and authority of the church over its members being amply sufficient where they alone were concerned. In the organization of the civil government, nothing could be more natural than that, the whole people being of one faith, they should choose for functionaries to carry it into execution, those to whom they had been in the habit of deferring as their inspired guides, and by whom they had been led from a land of persecution into this far-off wilderness, which, under their lead, was already beginning to blossom like the rose. Hence came the insensible blending of the two authorities, the principal functionaries of the one holding the same relative positions under the other. Thus the bishop, in case of a dispute between two members of the church, would interpose his spiritual authority as bishop for its adjustment, while in differences between those not subject to the spiritual jurisdiction, and who could not be made amenable to church discipline, he would act in the magisterial capacity conferred upon him by the constitution and civil laws of the State. Thus the control of the affairs of the colony remained in the same hands, whether under church or state organization; and these hands were, in a double capacity, those into which the constituents had, whether as citizens or as church-members, themselves chosen to confide it.

The revenue of the new State seemed to partake of the same double character; the treasures of the church being freely devoted, when necessary, to the promotion of the temporal prosperity of the body politic. These are derived from a system of tithing, similar to that of the ancient Israelites. Each person, upon profession of his faith, and consequent reception into the bosom of the church, is required to pay into "the treasury of the Lord" one-tenth of all that he possesses; after which, he pays a tenth of the yearly increase of his goods; and in addition contributes one-tenth of his time, which is devoted to labour on the public works, such as roads, bridges, irrigating canals, or such other objects as the authorities may direct. The whole amount thus collected goes into the coffers of the church, and is exacted only from its members. A tax is also laid upon property as with us, which is levied upon all, both "saint" and gentile, and which constitutes the revenue of the civil government. All goods brought into the city, pay as the price of a license, a duty of one per cent., except spirituous liquors, for

which one-half of the price at which they are sold is demanded:
the object of this last impost being avowedly to discourage the introduction of that article among them. It has, indeed, operated
to a great extent as a prohibition, the importer, to save himself
from loss, having to double the price at which he could otherwise
have afforded to sell. The result of this policy was, when we were
there, to bring up the price of brandy to twelve dollars per gallon,
of which the authorities took six; and of whisky to eight dollars,
of which they collected four dollars. The circulating medium is
principally gold of their own coinage, and such foreign gold as is
brought in by converts from Europe.

Notwithstanding this heavy, and as it would be to us, insupport-
able burden upon industry and enterprise, nothing can exceed the
appearance of prosperity, peaceful harmony, and cheerful content-
ment that pervaded the whole community. Ever since the first
year of privation, provisions have been abundant, and want of the
necessaries and even comforts of life is a thing unknown. A design was at one time entertained (more, I believe, as a prospective
measure than any thing else) to set apart a fund for the purpose
of erecting a poorhouse; but after strict inquiry, it was found that
there were in the whole population but two persons who could be
considered as objects of public charity, and the plan was consequently abandoned.

This happy external state, of universally diffused prosperity, is
commented on by themselves, as an evidence of the smiles of Heaven and of the special favour of the Deity: but I think it may be
most clearly accounted for in the admirable discipline and ready
obedience of a large body of industrious and intelligent men, and
in the wise councils of prudent and sagacious leaders, producing a
oneness and concentration of action, the result of which has asto-
nished even those by whom it has been effected. The happy
consequences of this system of united and well-directed action,
under one leading and controlling mind, is most prominently apparent in the erection of public buildings, opening of roads, the
construction of bridges, and the preparation of the country for the
speedy occupation of a large and rapidly growing population,
shortly to be still further augmented by an immigration even now
on their way, from almost every country in Europe.

Upon the personal character of the leader of this singular people,
it may not, perhaps, be proper for me to comment in a communication like the present. I may nevertheless be pardoned for saying,

that to me, President Young appeared to be a man of clear, sound sense, fully alive to the responsibilities of the station he occupies, sincerely devoted to the good name and interests of the people over which he presides, sensitively jealous of the least attempt to undervalue or misrepresent them, and indefatigable in devising ways and means for their moral, mental, and physical elevation. He appeared to possess the unlimited personal and official confidence of his people; while both he and his two counsellors, forming the presidency of the church, seemed to have but one object in view, the prosperity and peace of the society over which they presided.

In their dealings with the crowds of emigrants that passed through their city, the Mormons were ever fair and upright, taking no advantage of the necessitous condition of many, if not most of them. They sold them such provisions as they could spare, at moderate prices, and such as they themselves paid in their dealings with each other. In the whole of our intercourse with them, which lasted rather more than a year, I cannot refer to a single instance of fraud or extortion to which any of the party was subjected; and I strongly incline to the opinion that the charges that have been preferred against them in this respect, arose either from interested misrepresentation or erroneous information. I certainly never experienced any thing like it in my own case, nor did I witness or hear of any instance of it in the case of others, while I resided among them. Too many that passed through their settlement were disposed to disregard their claim to the land they occupied, to ridicule the municipal regulations of their city, and to trespass wantonly upon their rights. Such offenders were promptly arrested by the authorities, made to pay a severe fine, and in some instances were imprisoned or made to labour on the public works; a punishment richly merited, and which would have been inflicted upon them in any civilized community. In short, these people presented the appearance of a quiet, orderly, industrious, and well-organized society, as much so as one would meet with in any city of the Union, having the rights of personal property as perfectly defined and as religiously respected as with ourselves; nothing being farther from their faith or practice than the spirit of *communism*, which has been most erroneously supposed to prevail among them. The main peculiarity of the people consists in their religious tenets, the form and extent of their church government, (which is a theocracy,) and in the nature especially of their domestic relations.

With regard to the first of these, it is not my design to give more than a brief outline, referring the theological student to a treatise on this subject, about, as I understand, to be published by Lieutenant Gunnison, who was attached to the party, and who has paid especial attention to this subject.

The claim of the Mormons is, that they constitute the only true church now upon the earth, that all other denominations of Christians, so called, are out of the true path to heaven, which can only be attained through the administration of the ordinances of their church, by the "Melchisedec priesthood." This, they assert, was removed from the earth some eighteen hundred years ago, since which period, as they insist, no true church has existed, until, in 1826, their founder, Joseph Smith, was visited by an angel from heaven. This favoured man was instructed by the heavenly messenger in the way of truth, and led to a spot where, concealed in a stone box buried in the earth, were a number of records, written upon golden plates, and in a language called by him the "reformed Egyptian." From this box a portion of the records were taken by the angel and given to Joseph, upon whom was also conferred the "power and gift of revelation," by which he was enabled to translate the writing graven upon the plates. This he did, and gave the result to the world, as the "*Book of Mormon.*" Joseph, they say, was also ordained to the "Melchisedec priesthood," with the power of knowledge in all languages, the gifts of the Spirit, and the authority of "binding and loosing." He and an associate were constituted apostles to preach the "gospel," and to establish among the nations the "church of Jesus Christ of the latter-day saints." In 1830, a church was organized, consisting of six members only, which has since grown so as to count its disciples by hundreds of thousands.

The Bible used by the Protestant Christian world is acknowledged by them to be of Divine origin and authority, but they assert that it has been much corrupted and interpolated, so much so as to require in part a new translation, which has been accordingly completed by their prophet Joseph, directly inspired for the purpose, and the book is soon to be published. They claim for the "Book of Mormon" the same Divine origin, and hold it to be equally authoritative with our Scriptures as a rule of faith and practice. In addition, they have the direct revelations which have heretofore been made to the seer, and which are recorded in the "Book of

Doctrines and Covenants;" and they also continue to receive, as intimations of the Divine will, such communications as are now made to his successor from time to time, for their guidance, not only in matters of faith and doctrine, but in those also of worldly policy and the concerns of every-day life. In the gift of miracles, and healing of the sick by the laying on of hands by the elders of the church, they are firm believers; and I have met more than one who has assured me not only that they had been eye-witnesses of the miraculous cures thus performed, but had themselves been the subjects of them.

The mode of worship is, in its general arrangement, the same as that adopted by most Protestant denominations who do not use printed ritual; to wit, singing, prayer, and a sermon or exhortation from the pulpit. A band of music is stationed behind the choir of singers, and not only aids in the devotional services, but regales the audience before and after the close of the exercises.

But it is in their private and domestic relations that this singular people exhibit the widest departure from the habits and practice of all others denominating themselves Christian. I refer to what has been generally termed the "spiritual wife system," the practice of which was charged against them in Illinois, and served greatly to prejudice the public mind in that State. It was then, I believe, most strenuously denied by them that any such practice prevailed, nor is it now openly avowed, either as a matter sanctioned by their doctrine or discipline. But that polygamy does actually exist among them cannot be concealed from any one of the most ordinary observation, who has spent even a short time in this community. I heard it proclaimed from the stand, by the president of the church himself, that he had the right to take a thousand wives, if he thought proper; and he defied any one to prove from the Bible that he had not. At the same time, I have never known any member of the community to avow that he himself had more than one, although that such was the fact was as well known and understood as any fact could be.

If a man, once married, desires to take him a second helpmate, he must first, as with us, obtain the consent of the lady intended, and that of her parents or guardians, and afterward the approval of the seer or president, without which the matter cannot proceed. The woman is then " *sealed*" to him under the solemn sanction of the church, and stands, in all respects, in the same relation to the man, as the wife that was first married. The union thus formed is considered a perfectly virtuous and honourable one, and the lady maintains, without blemish, the same position in society to which she would be entitled were she the sole wife of her husband. Indeed, the connection being under the sanction of the only true priesthood, is deemed infinitely more sacred and binding than any marriage among the gentile world, not only on account of its higher and more sacred authority, but inasmuch as it bears directly upon the future state of existence of both the man and the woman; for it is the doctrine of the church, that no woman can attain to celestial glory *without the husband*, nor can *he* arrive at full perfection in the next world without at least one wife: and the greater the number he is able to take with him, the higher will be his seat in the celestial paradise.

All idea of sensuality, as the motive of such unions, is most indignantly repudiated; the avowed object being to raise up, as rapidly as possible, "a holy generation to the Lord," who shall build up his kingdom on the earth. Purity of life, in all the domestic relations, is strenuously inculcated; and they do not hesitate to declare, that when they shall obtain the uncontrolled power of making their own civil laws, (which will be when they are admitted as one of the States of the Union,) they will punish the departure from chastity in the severest manner, even by death.

As the seer or president alone possesses the power to approve of these unions, so also he alone can absolve the parties from their bonds, should circumstances in his judgment render it at any time either expedient or necessary. It may easily be perceived, then, what a tremendous influence the possession of such a power must give to him who holds it, and how great must be the prudence, firmness, sagacity, and wisdom required in one who thus stands in the relation of confidential adviser, as well as of civil and ecclesiastical ruler, over this singularly constituted community.

Upon the practical working of this system of plurality of wives, I can hardly be expected to express more than a mere opinion. Being myself an "outsider" and a "gentile," it is not to be supposed that I should have been permitted to view more than the surface of what is in fact as yet but an experiment, the details of which are sedulously veiled from public view. So far, however, as my intercourse with the inhabitants afforded me an opportunity of judging, its practical operation was quite different from what I had anticipated. Peace, harmony, and cheerfulness seemed to prevail, where my preconceived notions led me to look for nothing but the exhibition of petty jealousies, envy, bickerings, and strife. Confidence and sisterly affection among the different members of the family seemed pre-eminently conspicuous, and friendly inter-course among neighbours, with balls, parties, and merry-makings at each others' houses, formed a prominent and agreeable feature of the society. In these friendly réunions, the president, with his numerous family, mingled freely, and was ever an honoured and welcome guest, tempering by his presence the exuberant hilarity of the young, and not unfrequently closing with devotional exercises the gayety of a happy evening.

There are many other curious points contained in their religious creed, but it is not my purpose here to write a theological treatise upon their views. The effect of the system, as may be well supposed, is to render the people in a high degree separate and peculiar; and to prevent, not only all amalgamation, but even any intimate association, with other communities.

To this irreconcilable difference, not in speculative opinions only, but in habits, manners, and customs necessarily growing out of them, may, I think, in a great measure, be attributed the bitter hostility of the people among whom they formerly dwelt, and which resulted in their forcible expulsion. The same causes of social incompatibility which existed then, exist now, and in much greater strength—the community being freed from the pressure of public opinion that then surrounded them; and, although the freest toleration is (no doubt sincerely) proclaimed toward any who may choose to settle among them, yet I do not see how it is possible for the members of any other Christian societies, all of which are theoretically and practically opposed to their views, to exist among them, without constant collision, jealousy, and strife. The result, therefore, must be the establishment here of a people of one faith, the fundamental principles of whose civil government will, under the lead of the ecclesiastical hierarchy, be framed to accord with that faith, to build up and support it, and to exclude from all participation in its administration every element that does not fully coincide with its requirements. When what is now but a Territory shall have become a sovereign State, with the uncontrolled power of making its own laws, this will undoubtedly be done; and we shall then see in our midst a State as different from the rest of the Union in faith, manners, and customs, as it is widely separated by the vast plains and inhospitable deserts that surround it. That such a State will soon be formed, no reflecting man can well doubt, who has witnessed the indomitable energy, the unity and concentration of action, together with the enthusiastic spirit of proselytism which seems to possess the entire Mormon community. Their zeal for increasing their sect has already filled the world with their missionaries; and has, within the space of four years, and in defiance of obstacles that would have appalled most ordinary adventurers, collected a population of some twenty thousand souls, all breathing the same spirit, animated by the same hope, bound by the same views, and unitedly engaged, heart and hand, in providing means by which converts to the faith may be transported from all parts of the world to this great head-quarters of the church, "the fountain where truth flows from the lips of the prophet of God, and where true liberty can only be enjoyed by the saints."

A large and constantly increasing fund has been created among them, called "The Perpetual Emigration Fund," which is devoted exclusively to this object, and receives liberal contributions from the "saints," both in this country and in Europe; it being the authorized teaching, all over the world, that it is as much a duty binding on every "saint" "to build up the valleys of the mountains," by assisting forward those brethren who are too poor to provide an outfit for themselves, as it is to be baptized for the remission of sins. The effects of this widely diffused spirit of propagandism are already seen in the number of converts that have been made in most of the countries of Europe, as well as in the Sandwich Islands, and even here in our own country, with all of whom it is made a cardinal point to "gather to the mountains."

Measures are being taken to open a southern route, by which the converts coming from abroad may cross the Isthmus of Panama, and, landing at San Diego, may thence reach the land of promise by a comparatively short and easy transit, without being subjected to the hazard of a sickly voyage up the Mississippi, or to the tedious and expensive journey across the plains. In the mean while, preparations are industriously making in the valley for the reception and immediate accommodation of the coming tide, by the building of houses, sowing large quantities of grain, the erection of mills, the establishment of manufactures, the importation of labour-saving machinery, and the establishment upon a solid basis of the means of education. The manifest object of these harmoniously concerted movements is to concentrate, as speedily as practicable, in "the valley of the mountains," a number sufficiently great to entitle the present Territory of Utah to demand from the General Government admission into the Union as one of the sovereign States of the confederacy, and thus to secure to themselves unmolested the right to carry out in practice the peculiar principles of their creed. That their wishes in this respect will be shortly realized may be considered certain.

Let us now look for a moment at the sources which can be made available for the sustenance of a population so numerous as it is thus confidently anticipated will ere long be congregated within the limits of the "Basin State." Situated so far inland, without water communication with any part of the continent, and isolated by the very nature of the surrounding regions, it will readily be seen that the new State must necessarily depend, in a great measure, for its support, upon means within itself. Agriculture and the raising of stock must therefore be the principal basis of its prosperity. For both these purposes the country which they have settled is, fortunately, well adapted. The land available for the first of these objects, though limited in extent when compared with the vast deserts which intervene, is still ample for the support of a large, though not very dense population. Owing to the almost total absence of rain, from May to October, the dependence of the farmer must be entirely upon irrigation. The means for this are supplied from the reservoirs of snow which accumulate in the gorges of the mountains, furnishing, during the whole of the summer, abundant and never-failing streams, which assume in some instances the character of rivers of considerable magnitude.

The soil, formed chiefly from the disintegration of the feldspathic rock, mixed with detritus of the limestone, of which the mountains are principally composed, is of the most fertile character. Owing to its loose and porous texture, it absorbs water very readily and in large quantities. Consequently, the streams which come rushing down the mountain-sides, when they reach the plain below, begin to dwindle into insignificant rivulets, and soon sink and are entirely lost. Many never reach the base of the mountain at all, being absorbed by the soil; and even in the islands of the lake there are to be found, near the summits, roaring torrents, which, ere making half the descent of the mountain, so completely disappear as to leave not even a dry bed or channel to show they had ever reached the water below. Cultivation is therefore circumscribed within very narrow limits, being generally restricted to a strip of from one to two miles wide, along the base of the mountains, beyond which the water does not reach. The extensive plains between the mountain ranges, although composed of soil nearly equal in fertility, are at present useless for the purposes of agriculture, from the want of water. The smallness of the area suitable for cultivation is, however, compensated by the prodigious productiveness of the soil, which, together with the climate, is peculiarly favourable to the growth of wheat, barley, oats, and all the cereal grains. I brought with me, for distribution, a portion of a crop of wheat, which had produced, upon three and one-half acres of ground, the enormous yield of one hundred and eighty bushels, from a single bushel of seed. In situations peculiarly favourable for watering, the average yield of all lands properly cultivated may be very safely estimated at forty bushels. Maize, or Indian corn, has not as yet proved so successful, owing to the early frosts occasioned by the vicinity of the mountains; but beets, turnips, melons, and especially potatoes, exceed in increase even the most sanguine anticipations. The quality of the latter is fully equal, if not superior, to the best Nova Scotia varieties.

On the eastern side of the Salt Lake Valley, the land susceptible of irrigation stretches along the western base of the Wahsatch Mountains, from about eighty miles north of Salt Lake City to about sixty south of it, the latter portion embracing, toward its terminus, the fertile valley of Lake Utah. This is a beautiful sheet of pure fresh water, thirty miles in length, and about ten in breadth, surrounded on three sides by rugged mountains and lofty hills, with a broad grassy valley sloping to the water's edge, opening to the northward. Through this opening flows the river Jordan, by which its waters are discharged into the Great Salt Lake. The lake abounds in fine fish, principally speckled trout, of great size and exquisite flavour, which afford sustenance to numerous small bands of Utahs.

The Jordan, in its passage, cuts through a cross range of mountains that divides the two valleys, making a deep cañon, in which are rapids. At most seasons of the year a skiff can be safely floated down these boiling waters, if managed with sufficient skill to avoid striking the projecting rocks. The fall continues abrupt for one mile, and the river could here be led along the escarpment of the western hills as far as to a point opposite the mouth of the Little Cotton-wood, and thence on a curve to Spring Point, at the north end of the Oquirrh Mountain, thus probably bringing under irrigation about eighty square miles of fertile land.

Near the eastern shores of Lake Utah, a site for a city has been selected on the left bank of the Provaux or Timpanogas River, an affluent of the lake, which is to be called *Provaux City*. From Ogden City on the north, all the way to this latter "Stake of Zion," the base of the Wahsatch range is studded with flourishing farms, wherever a little stream flows down the mountain-side with water sufficient for irrigating purposes; while in the gorges and cañons of the mountain are erected the saw and grist mills. Of the former, sixteen, and of the latter, eleven have been completed, and others are in the process of erection.

To the south of Lake Utah, on one of its tributaries, another city has been founded, called *Paysan*, and a hundred and thirty miles farther, on the road to California, another, named *Manti*, in what is called San Pete Valley. Still farther south, near Little Salt Lake, two hundred and fifty miles south of the city, a fourth called *Cedar City*, has been laid out, in a spot possessing the advantages of excellent soil and water, plenty of wood, iron ore, and alum, with some prospect of coal. It is the ultimate object of the Mormons, by means of stations, wherever the nature of the country will admit of their settling in numbers sufficient for self-defence, to establish a line of communication with the Pacific, so as to afford aid to their brethren coming from abroad, while on their pilgrimage to the land of promise. These stations will gradually become connected by farms and smaller settlements wherever practicable, until the greater part of the way will exhibit one long line of cultivated fields from the Mormon capital to San Diego.

The mode adopted for the founding of a new town is peculiar and highly characteristic. An expedition is first sent out to explore the country, with a view to the selection of such points as, from their natural advantages, offer facilities for a settlement. These being duly reported to the authorities, an elder of the church is appointed to preside over the little band designated to make the first improvement. This company is composed partly of volunteers and partly of such as are selected by the presidency, due regard being had to a proper intermixture of mechanical artisans, to render the expedition independent of all aid from without. In this way the settlement at San Pete was begun, sixty families leaving in a body, under one of the high officers of the church, and that in the month of October, undergoing all the rigours of cold and snow, to establish another "stake" in the wilderness. In December of the following year, another expedition,

FORT UTAH   VALLEY OF THE GREAT SALT LAKE

similarly composed and commanded, succeeded, with one hundred and thirty men and families, in planting the settlement at *Little Salt Lake*, which is represented as being now in a very flourishing condition. The succeeding March, a third party, with a hundred and fifty wagons, left the capital for the purpose of establishing a settlement in the southern part of California. It was to be situated at no great distance from San Diego, and near Williams's *ranche* and Cahone Pass, between which and Little Salt Lake it is designed to establish other settlements as speedily as possible. By means of these successive places of refreshment, the incoming emigration from the Pacific will be enabled to "go from strength to strength" till they reach the Zion of their hopes.

At Salt Lake City itself, energetic measures are being taken for opening a woollen factory, the raw material being furnished from sheep raised in the valley, to the grazing of which the mountain slopes are admirably adapted, and whose production has already attracted the attention of this energetic and far-seeing people. A pottery for the manufacture of earthenware is completed; and cutlery establishments have been successfully commenced. Extensive arrangements are going forward for raising the sugar-beet, which, under such favourable circumstances, cannot but prove successful; and ere long it is confidently anticipated that a sufficient quantity of sugar will be manufactured from it to meet all their wants. At present they are supplied with this article and other groceries, as well as with dry-goods and clothing, from extensive stocks brought in by enterprising merchants from the States; but the policy of the people is to provide for their own wants by their own skill and industry, and to dispense, as much as possible, with the products of the labour of others.

While all these exertions are making for the physical development of a new empire among the mountains, the mental elevation of the people by education has been by no means lost sight of. Liberal appropriations of land and money have been made for the establishment of an university, the grounds for which are laid out and enclosed, being situated on one of the terraces of the mountain overlooking the city. A normal school, designed for the education of those who desire to become teachers, is already in successful operation. School-houses have been built in most of the districts, both in the city and country, which are attended by old as well as young, and every effort is made to advance the mental improvement of the people.

When it is remembered that within the space of four years this country was but a wild and dreary wilderness, where the howl of the wolf and the yell of the miserable Indian alone awoke the echoes of the mountains, and where the bear, the deer, and the antelope roamed securely over what is now a compact and populous city; that the physical obstacles to the occupation of a region so unpromising were sufficient to discourage the most sanguine imagination and to appal the stoutest heart,—the mind is filled with wonder at witnessing the immense results which have been accomplished in so short a time, and from a beginning apparently so insignificant.

Apprehensions have been entertained as to the expediency of giving any countenance to the founding, in our midst, of an association of men so peculiar in views, and so distinct in principles, manners, and customs, from the rest of the American people. Serious doubts, too, have been expressed in regard to the policy of appointing Mormons to offices of high trust in the administration of the affairs of the newly-erected territory; and direct charges have been widely published, seriously affecting the patriotism and personal reputation of the Mormon leaders, as well as the loyal feelings of the people toward the General Government. Such doubts and apprehensions are,. in my judgment, totally groundless, and the charges I believe to be either based upon prejudice or to have grown out of a want of accurate information. A residence of a year in the midst of the Mormon community, during the greater part of which period I was in constant intercourse with both rulers and people, afforded much opportunity for ascertaining the real facts of the case.

That a deep and abiding resentment of injuries received and wrongs endured in Missouri and Illinois pervades the whole Mormon community, is perfectly true; and that among many of the less informed, and, I regret to add, some even whose intelligence and education ought to have enabled them to form more correct opinions, this exasperation has extended itself to the General Government, because of its refusal to interpose for their protection at the time of these difficulties, is also true; but, from all that I saw and heard, I deem it but simple justice to say, that notwithstanding these causes of irritation, a more loyal and patriotic people cannot be found within the limits of the Union. This, I think, was emphatically shown in the promptitude and cheerfulness with which they responded to the call of the Government to furnish a battalion for service during the Mexican war. While in the heart of an Indian country, and on the eve of a long and uncertain pilgrimage into an unknown wilderness, they were suddenly called upon to surrender five hundred of their best men to the hazards of a hostile campaign, and to the exposure and vicissitudes of a march of two thousand miles across trackless deserts and burning plains, to fight the battles of their country. Their peculiar circumstances presented almost insuperable objections to a compliance with the requisition, yet not the slightest hesitation was evinced. " You shall have your battalion at once," was the reply of President Young, " if it has to be a class of our elders ;" and in three days the force, recruited principally among fathers of families, was raised and ready to march. Here certainly was no evidence of a lack of patriotism.*

---

* The following extract from a sermon of Brigham Young to his people will, I think, confirm the correctness of my views as to the sentiments of the Mormon leaders, at that time, on this subject :—

" I want to say to every man, the constitution of the United States, as formed by our fathers, was dictated, was revealed, was put into their hearts by the Almighty, who sits enthroned in the midst of the heavens; although unknown to them, it was dictated by the revelations of Jesus Christ, and I tell you, in the name of Jesus Christ, it is as good as I could ever ask for." " I say unto you, magnify the laws. There is no law in the United States, or in the constitution, but I am ready to make honourable."

Many more expressions of a like character might be quoted, but the above are sufficient to show what were the opinions of the rulers.

The following language, used by General D. H. Wells, at the celebration of the fourth anniversary of the advent of the Mormons into the Valley, will show, I think, what was the feeling of the people :—

" It has been thought by some, that this people, abused, maltreated, insulted, robbed, plundered, murdered, and finally disfranchised and expatriated, would naturally feel reluctant to again unite their destiny with the American republic." * * * " No wonder that it was thought by some that we would not again submit ourselves (even while we were yet scorned and ridiculed) to return to our allegiance to our native country. Remember, that it was by the act of our country, not ours, that we were expatriated; and then consider the opportunity we had of forming other ties. Let this pass, while we lift the veil and show the policy which dictated us. That country, that constitution, those institutions, were all ours ; they are still ours. Our fathers were heroes of the Revolution. Under the master spirits of an Adams, a Jefferson, and a Washington, they declared and maintained their independence; and, under the guidance of the Spirit of truth, they fulfilled their mission whereunto they were sent from the presence of the Father. Because demagogues have arisen and seized the reins of power, should we relinquish our interest in that country made dear to us by every tie of association and consanguinity ?" * * * " Those who have indulged such sentiments concerning us, have not read Mormonism aright; for never, no never, will we

10

Whether in the pulpit, in public addresses, in official documents, or in private intercourse, the same spirit of lofty patriotism seemed to pervade their whole community. At the same time, it should not be concealed that a stern determination exists among them to submit to no repetition of the outrages to which they were subjected in Illinois and Missouri; but, on the contrary, to resist by force and to the last extremity, from whatever quarter, any such interference with what they consider their civil and religious rights, guarantied to them, as to other citizens, by the constitution of the United States. Vain-glorious vaunts may indeed have been sometimes made by individuals whose knowledge and judgment were not equal to their religious zeal, as to the ability of the community to maintain itself in the fastnesses of the mountains, even against the military forces of the Government; but we know that there are in every society men whose valour is ever great in proportion to the remoteness of the danger. I have no idea that any such collision was ever seriously anticipated.

Upon the action of the Executive in the appointment of the officers within the newly-created Territory, it does not become me to offer other than a very diffident opinion. Yet the opportunities of information to which allusion has already been made, may perhaps justify me in presenting the result of my own observations upon this subject. With all due deference, then, I feel constrained to say, that in my opinion the appointment of the president of the Mormon church, and head of the Mormon community, in preference to any other person, to the high office of Governor of the Territory, independent of its political bearings, with which I have nothing to do, was a measure dictated alike by justice and by sound policy. Intimately connected with them from their exodus from Illinois, this man has been indeed their Moses, leading them through the wilderness to a remote and unknown land, where they have since set up their tabernacle, and where they are now building their temple. Resolute in danger, firm and sagacious in council, prompt and energetic in emergency, and enthusiastically devoted to the honour and interests of his people, he had won their unlimited

---

desert our country's cause; never will we be found arrayed by the side of her enemies, although she herself may cherish them in her own bosom. Although she may launch forth the thunderbolts of war, which may return and spend their fury upon her own head, never, no never, will we permit the weakness of human nature to triumph over our love of country, our devotion to her institutions, handed down to us by our honoured sires, made dear by a thousand tender recollections."

Such, surely, is neither the language nor the spirit of a disloyal people.

confidence, esteem, and veneration, and held an unrivalled place in their hearts. Upon the establishment of the provisional government, he had been unanimously chosen as their highest civil magistrate, and even before his appointment by the President, he combined in his own person the triple character of confidential adviser, temporal ruler, and prophet of God. Intimately acquainted with their character, capacities, wants, and weaknesses; identified now with their prosperity, as he had formerly shared to the full in their adversity and sorrows; honoured, trusted, the whole wealth of the community placed in his hands, for the advancement both of the spiritual and temporal interests of the infant settlement, he was, surely, of all others, the man best fitted to preside, under the auspices of the General Government, over a colony of which he may justly be said to have been the founder. No other man could have so entirely secured the confidence of the people; and this selection by the Executive of the man of their choice, besides being highly gratifying to them, is recognised as an assurance that they shall hereafter receive at the hands of the General Government that justice and consideration to which they are entitled. Their confident hope now is that, no longer fugitives and outlaws, but dwelling beneath the broad shadow of the national ægis, they will be subject no more to the violence and outrage which drove them to seek a secure habitation in this far distant wilderness.

As to the imputations that have been made against the personal character of the governor, I feel confident they are without foundation. Whatever opinion may be entertained of his pretensions to the character of an inspired prophet, or of his views and practice on the subject of polygamy, his personal reputation I believe to be above reproach. Certain it is that the most entire confidence is felt in his integrity, personal, official, and pecuniary, on the part of those to whom a long and intimate association, and in the most trying emergencies, have afforded every possible opportunity of forming a just and accurate judgment of his true character.

From all I saw and heard, I am firmly of opinion that the appointment of any other man to the office of governor would have been regarded by the whole people, not only as a sanction, but as in some sort a renewal, on the part of the General Government, of that series of persecutions to which they had already been subjected, and would have operated to create distrust and suspicion in minds prepared to hail with joy the admission of the new Territory to the protection of the supreme government.

The native tribes with whom we came in contact in the valley were the most degraded and the lowest in the scale of being of any I had ever seen. They consisted of the "root-diggers," a class of Indians which seemed to be composed of outcasts from their respective tribes, subsisting chiefly upon roots dug from the ground, and the seeds of various plants indigenous to the soil, which they grind into a kind of flour between two flat stones. Lizards and crickets also form a portion of their food. At certain seasons of the year they obtain, from the tributaries of both the Salt Lake and Lake Utah, a considerable quantity of fish, which they take in weirs or traps, constructed of willow-bushes. Those that we saw were branches from the Shoshonees or Snakes, and from the large and warlike tribe of Utahs, which latter inhabit a large tract of country to the southward. They are known among the traders by the designation of "snake-diggers," and "Utes;" those of the latter tribe, which inhabit the vicinity of the lakes and streams and live chiefly on fish, being distinguished by the name of "Pah Utahs," or "Pah Utes,"—the word Pah, in their language, signifying water.

While engaged in the survey of the Utah Valley, we were no little annoyed by numbers of the latter tribe, who hung around the camp, crowding around the cook-fires, more like hungry dogs than human beings, eagerly watching for the least scrap that might be thrown away, which they devoured with avidity and without the least preparation. The herdsmen also complained that their cattle were frequently scattered, and that notwithstanding their utmost vigilance, several of them had unaccountably disappeared and were lost. One morning, a fine fat ox came into camp with an arrow buried in his side, which perfectly accounted for the disappearance of the others.

After the party left Lake Utah for winter quarters in Salt Lake City, the Indians became more insolent, boasting of what they had done—driving off the stock of the inhabitants in the southern set-tlements, resisting all attempts to recover them, and finally firing upon the people themselves, as they issued from their little stockade to attend to their ordinary occupations. Under these circum-stances, the settlers in the Utah Valley applied to the supreme government, at Salt Lake City, for counsel as to the proper course of action. The president was at first extremely averse to the adoption of harsh measures; but, after several conciliatory over-tures had been resorted to in vain, he very properly determined to

UTAH INDIAN PRISONERS UNDER THE COMMON PLATFORM IN FORT UTAH

Ackerman Lith 379 Broadway N.Y.

put a stop, by force, to further aggressions, which, if not resisted, could only end in the total destruction of the colony. Before coming to this decision, the authorities called upon me to consult as to the policy of the measure, and to request the expression of my opinion as to what view the Government of the United States might be expected to take of it. Knowing, as I did, most of the circumstances, and feeling convinced that some action of the kind would ultimately have to be resorted to, as the forbearance already shown had been only attributed to weakness and cowardice, and had served but to encourage further and bolder outrages, I did not hesitate to say to them that, in my judgment, the contemplated expedition against these savage marauders was a measure not only of good policy, but one of absolute necessity and self-preservation. I knew the leader of the Indians to be a crafty and blood-thirsty savage, who had been already guilty of several murders, and had openly threatened that he would kill every white man that he found alone upon the prairies. In addition to this, I was convinced that the completion of the yet unfinished survey of the Utah Valley, the coming season, must otherwise be attended with serious difficulty, if not actual hazard, and would involve the necessity of a largely increased and armed escort for its protection. Such being the circumstances, the course proposed could not but meet my entire approval.

A force of one hundred men was accordingly organized, and, upon the application of President Young, leave was given to Lieutenant Howland, of the Mounted Rifles, then on duty with my command, to accompany the expedition as its adjutant: such assistance also was furnished as it was in my power to afford, consisting of arms, tents, camp-equipage, and ammunition.

The expedition was completely successful. The Indians fought very bravely, but were finally routed, some forty of them killed, and as many more taken prisoners; the latter, consisting principally of women and children, were carried to the city and distributed among the inhabitants, for the purpose of weaning them from their savage pursuits, and bringing them up in the habits of civilized and Christian life. The experiment, however, did not succeed as was anticipated, most of the prisoners escaping upon the very first opportunity.

On the 22d of February, about three P. M., a slight shock of an earthquake was felt in the southern part of the city, the vibrations being sufficient to shake plates from the shelves and to disturb milk in the pans.

Advantage was taken of the confinement of the party to winter quarters to observe for the latitude, to arrange and plot the notes of the survey as far as it had advanced, and to collect and prepare specimens of the zoology of the valley. These specimens have since been classified and arranged with characteristic ability by Professor Spencer F. Baird, of the Smithsonian Institution, whose report on that subject is hereto appended. Specimens of the different thermal waters, also, were collected and brought safely as far as Pittsburgh; but, in their transportation thence by the express line, most of the vessels containing them were unfortunately broken, and their contents lost. This was a subject of much regret, as interesting results had been anticipated from the analysis. Such as escaped destruction have been carefully analyzed by Dr. L. D. Gale, of Washington, and the results will be found in Appendix F.

During the winter, a large boat was built for the survey of the Salt Lake. This was an achievement of no little difficulty, as almost every stick of timber used in the construction had to be procured from the cañons of the mountains, piece by piece; and the planking, although of the best material the country afforded, was so "shaky" and liable to split and crack, that it was totally unfit for the purpose. Had time permitted, it had been my purpose to procure, before setting out, a couple of Francis's metallic life-boats for this service, which would have saved much time and labour. The experience of the exploring expedition to the Dead Sea has fully proved the entire fitness of these boats for service of this nature; and the ease with which they can be transported in sections, and be put together for instant use, will doubtless render them hereafter an indispensable part of the equipment for every exploration of a similar character. Where the use of wagons is practicable, these boats can readily be mounted on wheels and made to answer the purposes of a wagon-box; and where this is not the case, their arrangement into sections will allow of their being packed and transported on the backs of mules with but little inconvenience.

CHAPTER VIII.

EARLY KNOWLEDGE OF THE EXISTENCE OF A BODY OF SALT WATER
IN THIS REGION, BY BARON LA HONTAN.—SURVEY OF THE GREAT
SALT LAKE.

THE opening of the spring at length enabling us to prepare
for a renewal of active operations in the field, the opportunity
was eagerly embraced, since upon the completion of the survey
before the setting in of cold weather depended the return of the
party to their homes before the recurrence of winter.

The season was now approaching when it would become our
duty to enter upon a critical examination of this interesting and
hitherto almost unknown region, and the remarkable body of
water to which it is indebted for so much of the interest which
attaches to it. It may not, therefore, be deemed inappropriate to
look back and see what ideas prevailed in regard to it during the
infant period of our national geography.

The existence of a large lake of salt water somewhere amid the
wilds west of the Rocky Mountains seems to have been known
vaguely as long as one hundred and fifty years since. As early as
May, 1689, the Baron La Hontan, "lord-lieutenant of the French
colony at Placentia in New Foundland," wrote an account of discoveries in this region, which was published in the English language in 1735.

In the letter, which is dated at "Missilimakinac," he gives "an
account of the author's departure from and return to Missilimakinac; a description of the Bay of Puants, and its villages; an
ample description of the beavers, followed by the journal of a
remarkable voyage upon the Long River, and a map of the adjacent country."

Leaving Mackinaw, he passed into Green Bay, which he calls
"the Bay of Pouteouotamis," and arrived at the mouth of the
Fox River, which he describes as "a little deep sort of a river
which disembogues at a place where the water of the lake swells
three feet high in twelve hours, and decreases as much in the
same compass of time."

" The village of the Sakis, Pouteouatamis, and some Malominis, are seated on the side of that river, and the Jesuits have a house or college built upon it." Ascending the Fox River, called " the river of Puants," he came to a village of " Kikapous, which stands on the brink of a little lake in which the savages fish great quantities of pikes and gudgeons." (Lake Winnebago?)

Still ascending the river, he passed through the " little lake of the Malominis," the sides of which " are covered with a sort of oats which grow in tufts, with a small stalk, and of which the savages reap plentiful crops," and at length arrived at the land carriage of Ouisconsinc, which we finished in two days; that is, we left the river Puants, and transported our canoes and baggage to the river Ouisconsinc, which is not above three-quarters of a league distant or thereabouts." Descending the Wisconsin, in four days he reached its mouth, and landed on an island in the river Mississippi.

So far the journey of the Baron La Hontan is plain enough ; but beyond this point it is rather apocryphal. He states that he *ascended* the Mississippi for nine days, when he "entered the mouth of the Long River, which looks like a lake full of bulrushes." He sailed up this river for six weeks, passing through various nations of savages, of which a most fanciful description is given. At length, deterred by the advance of the season, he abandoned the intention of reaching the heads of the river, and returned to Canada, having, at the termination of his voyage, first " fixed a great long pole, with the arms of France done upon a plate of lead." The following is his description of " the Long River." "You must know that the stream of the Long River is all along very slack and easy, abating for about three leagues between the fourteenth and fifteenth village; for there, indeed, its current may be called rapid. The channel is so straight that it scarce winds at all from the head to the lake. 'Tis true 'tis not very pleasant, for most of its banks have a dismal prospect, and the water itself has an ugly taste; but then its usefulness atones for such inconveniences, for 'tis navigable with the greatest ease, and will bear barques of fifty tons, till you come to that place that is marked with a *flower-de-luce* in the map, and where I put up the post that my soldiers christened *La Hontan's limit*."

It was at this place that the baron received his information respecting the lake of salt water. He says, " Two days after, the cacick" (of the Gnacsitares) " came to see me, and brought with him four hundred of his own subjects and four Mozeemlek savages, whom I took for Spaniards. My mistake was occasioned by the great difference between these two American nations; for the Mozeemlek savages were clothed, they had a thick bushy beard, and their hair hung down under their ears; their complexion was swarthy, their address was civil and submissive, their mien grave, and their carriage engaging. Upon these considerations I could not imagine that they were savages, though, after all, I found myself mistaken. These four slaves gave me a description of their country, which the Gnacsitares represented by way of a map upon a deer's skin, as you see it drawn in this map. Their villages stand upon a river that springs out of a ridge of mountains, from which the Long River likewise derives its source, there being a great many brooks there, which, by a joint confluence, form the river."

" The Mozeemlek nation is numerous and puissant. The four slaves of that country informed me that at the distance of one hundred and fifty leagues from the place I then was, *their principal river empties itself into a salt lake* of three hundred leagues in circumference, the mouth of which is two leagues broad; that the lower part of that river is adorned with six noble cities, surrounded with stone cemented with fat earth; that the houses of these cities have no roofs, but are open above, like a platform, as you see them drawn in the map; that besides the above-mentioned cities, there are above an hundred towns, great and small, round that sort of sea, upon which they navigate with such boats as you see drawn in the map;* that the people of that country made stuffs, copper axes, and several other manufactures, which the Outagamis and my other interpreters could not give me to understand, as being altogether unacquainted with such things; that their government was despotic, and lodged in the hands of one great head, to whom the rest paid a trembling submission; that the people upon that lake are called Tahuglauk, and are as numerous as the leaves of trees, (such is the expression that the savages use for an hyperbole;) that the Mozeemlek people supply the cities

---

* The boats, with a drawing, are thus described in the map:—" The vessels used by the Tahuglauk, in which two hundred men may row, provided they are such forms as ye Mozeemlek people drew me on ye bark of trees. According to my computation, such a vessel must be one hundred and thirty feet long from the prow to the stern."

or towns of the Tahuglauk with great numbers of little calves, which they take in the above-mentioned mountain; and that the Tahuglauk make use of these calves for several ends; for they not only eat their flesh, but bring 'em up to labour, and make clothes, boots, &c. of their skins. They added, that it was their misfortune to be took prisoners by the Gnacsitares with war, which had lasted for eighteen years; but that they hoped a peace would be speedily concluded, upon which the prisoners would be exchanged, pursuant to the usual custom. I could pump nothing further out of 'em, with relation to the country, commerce, and customs of that remote nation: all they could say was that the great river of that nation runs along westward, and that the *salt lake* into which it falls is three hundred leagues in circumference and thirty in breadth, its mouth stretching a great way to the southward." " I would have fain satisfied my curiosity, in being an eyewitness of the manners and customs of the Tahuglauk, but that being impracticable, I was forced to be instructed at secondhand by these Mozeemlek slaves; who assured me upon the faith of a savage that the Tahuglauk wear their beards two fingers' breadth long; that their garments reach down to their knees; that they cover their heads with a sharp-pointed cap; that they always wear a long stick or cane in their hands, which is tipped, not unlike what we use in Europe; that they wear a sort of boot upon their legs which reach up to their knee; that their women never show themselves, which perhaps proceeds from the same principle that prevails in Italy and Spain; and in fine, that this people are always at war with the puissant nations that are seated in the neighbourhood of the lake, but withal that they never disquiet the strolling nations that fall in their way by reason of their weakness—an admirable lesson for some princes in the world, who are so much intent upon the making use of the strongest hand. This was all I could gather upon that subject. My curiosity prompted me to desire a more particular account;* but unluckily I wanted a good interpreter:

---

* On that part of the map which is confessedly derived from Indian authority is the following note:—"A map drawn upon stag-skins by yᵉ Gnacsitares, who gave me to know yᵉ latitudes of all yᵉ places marked in it, by pointing to yᵉ respective places of yᵉ heavens that one or t'other corresponded to; for by this means I could adjust yᵉ latitude to half a degree or little more; having first received from them a computation of yᵉ distances in fazons, each of which I compute to be three long French leagues."

OLD ELK AND HIS SQUAW — UTAH INDIANS.

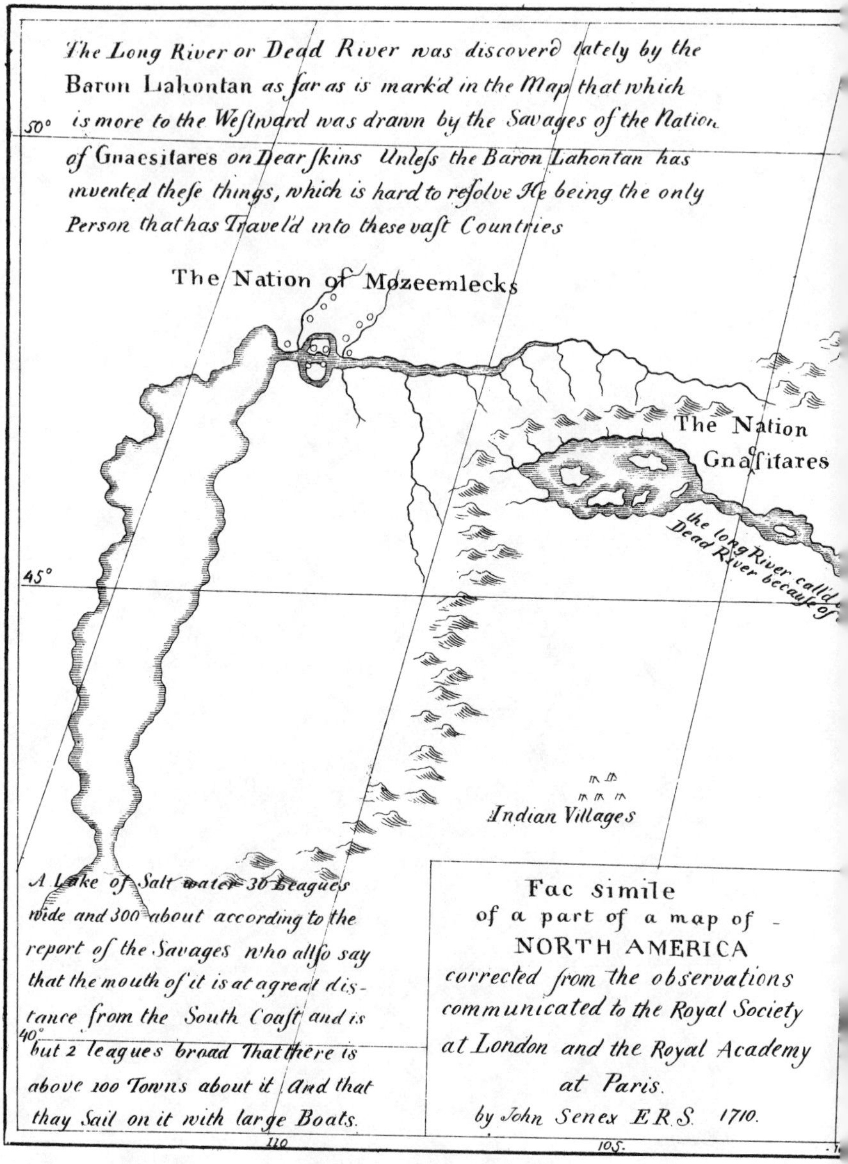

The Long River or Dead River was discover'd lately by the
Baron Lahontan as far as is mark'd in the Map that which
50° is more to the Weſtward was drawn by the Savages of the Nation
of Gnaeſitares on Dear ſkins Unleſs the Baron Lahontan has
invented theſe things, which is hard to reſolve He being the only
Person that has Travel'd into these vaſt Countries

The Nation of Mozeemlecks

The Nation
Gnaſitares

the long River call'd
Dead River becauſe of

45°

Indian Villages

A Lake of Salt water 30 Leagues
wide and 300 about according to the
report of the Savages who allſo say
that the mouth of it is at a great distance from the South Coaſt and is
40°
but 2 leagues broad That there is
above 100 Towns about it And that
thay Sail on it with large Boats.

Fac simile
of a part of a map of
NORTH AMERICA
corrected from the obſervations
communicated to the Royal Society
at London and the Royal Academy
at Paris.
by John Senex E.R.S. 1710.

110   105

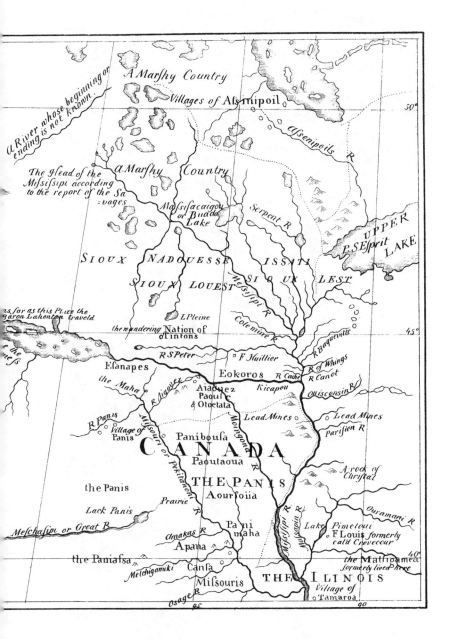

A River whose beginning or ending is not known

A Marshy Country

Villages of Assinipoil

50°

Assenipoils R

The Head of the Mississipi according to the report of the Savages

A Marshy Country

Serpent R.

Massisacaigou or Buade Lake

P. S Esprit

UPPER LAKE

SIOUX NADOUESSE

ISSATI

SIOUX LOUEST

SIOUX LEST

Mississipi R.

as far as this Place the Baron Lahonton traveld

L Pleine

Colenure R

45°

the wandering Nation of Tintons

R Baqueville

R SPeter

F Kuillier

R of Whings

R Canot

Esanapes

Eokoroś

R Cache

the Maha

Aiaouez

Kicapou

Ouisconsin R.

R Aigouez

Paoulé & Otoctata

R Panis

Lead Mines

Lead Mines

Village of Panis

Parisien R

Panibouśa

CANADA

Montonda R

the Panis

Paoutaoua

A rock of Chrystal

THE PANIS

Aourŝoiia

Lack Panis

Prairie

Missouri or Pekitanoui R

Ouramani R

Meschaſipi or Great R

Amakas R

Pa ni maha

Mississipi R.

Missouria R

Lake Pimetoui

F Louis formerly call'd Crevecour

Apana

the Paniaſsa

Canſa R

the Matſioamea formerly lived here

40°

Metchigamuki

Missouris

THE ILINOIS

Osage R

Village of Tamaroa

95

90

TRIANGULATION STATION AND MASS OF MICA SCHIST SUMMIT OF FREMONTS ISLAND

and having to do with several persons that did not well understand themselves, I could make nothing of their incoherent fustian."

A detailed map accompanies this imaginative voyage up this most imaginary river. It is represented as flowing due east through 25 degrees of longitude, numerous streams putting into it on either side, with mountains, islands, villages, and domains of Indian tribes, whose very names have at this day sunk into oblivion. The map was afterward published, in 1710, by John Senex, F. R. S., as a part of "North America, corrected from the observations communicated to the Royal Society at London and the Royal Academy at Paris," and I have annexed it as a specimen of the geographical knowledge of America enjoyed at that period.

This discovery of Baron La Hontan excited, even at that early day, the spirit of enterprise and speculation which has proved so marked a feature in the national character. In a work published in this country in 1772, and entitled "A description of the Province of Carolana, by the Spaniards called Florida, and by the French La Louisiane, by Daniel Cox," the then proprietary, the first part of the fifth chapter is devoted to a "A new and curious discovery and relation of an easy communication between the river Meschacebe (Mississippi) and the South Sea which separates America from China, by means of several large rivers and lakes."

The author says:—"It will be of great conveniency to this country, *if ever it becomes to be settled*, that there is an easy communication therewith and the South Sea, which lies between America and China, and that two ways: by the north branch of the great Yellow River, by the natives called the river of the Massorites," (doubtless the Missouri,) "which hath a course of five hundred miles, navigable to its heads or springs, and which proceeds from a ridge of hills somewhat north of New Mexico, passable by horse, foot, or wagon, in less than half a day. *On the other side are rivers which run into a great lake that empties itself by another great navigable river into the South Sea.* The same may be said of the Meschaouay, up which our people have been, but not so far as the Baron La Hontan, who passed on it above three hundred miles almost due west, and declares it comes from the same ridge of hills above mentioned, and that divers rivers from the other side soon make a large river, which enters into a vast lake, on which inhabit two or three great nations, much more populous and civilized than other Indians; *and out of that lake a great river disem-*

bogues into the South Sea, which is doubtless the same with that before mentioned, the head of the two rivers being little distant from each other.''

In his preface, the writer indulges in the following remarks: "The possibility of a communication by water (except about half a day's land carriage) between the river Meschacebe and the South Sea, stretching from America to Japan, which is represented in the fifth chapter of this treatise, deserves to be well and duly considered." The work contains what is called "a large and accurate map of Carolana, and of the river Meschacebe."

On the third of April, the parties were fully organized; and every preparation being made, teams were despatched to the eastern shore of Antelope Island, with the camp and provisions intended for that division of our force assigned to the survey of the west side of the lake. It was my purpose to form here a small depot, accessible by water, and also to herd the mules and cattle during the summer. Before commencing the actual survey, I designed to make a thorough reconnoissance of the entire lake by water, and to erect stations upon the prominent points of the shores and islands, sufficient to enable me to cover the whole surface with a series of triangles, which would verify the work.

Although it is not my purpose to give a detailed account of every day's operations while engaged upon this duty, I shall make such extracts from the journals as will, perhaps, convey a sufficiently clear idea of this hitherto unknown sea, and of some of the difficulties encountered in its exploration.

After starting the teams, we embarked on board of our new craft, to descend the Jordan to its mouth, where it enters the lake. The stream being much swollen by the melting of the snows, the current was extremely rapid. The dry, leafless willows on the banks were, in some places, black with innumerable birds'-nests, the work of the preceding season, securely built in the midst of impenetrable thickets. The day was bright and warm, and all felt the exhilaration of spirits occasioned by release from a four-months' confinement to weary and monotonous quarters, and were filled with the eager anticipation of ranging over the mysterious waters of this far-famed sea! The grass was becoming green, the waters began to flow in little rills, and the air was vocal with the music of myriads of frogs set free from their icy fetters and exulting beneath the genial rays of an April sun. Every thing betokened the opening of spring, although the surrounding mountains were yet covered with snow, many of them quite down to their bases.

April 4.—After a row of some twenty miles, we reached the mouth of the river, which here spread out into innumerable shallow channels, the intervals between them consisting of soft, shiny mud, nearly level with the surface of the water, and rendering it impossible to find where the mouth actually was. The channels were only a few inches deep, although the current through them was quite rapid, owing to the great body of water coming down from above. The boat soon grounded, and all hands were overboard and commenced dragging her forward by main force. On reaching the broader expanse of water, the channels became less defined and more shallow as we advanced. We were therefore obliged to unload the boat entirely, and to pile up the baggage upon a platform constructed of oars and tent-poles, placed upon camp-stools, buckets and camp-kettles. After six hours of severe labour, we at length succeeded in reaching water that would float our little craft; and, returning to the platform for the baggage, reloaded her, and took once more to the oars, directing our course for Antelope Island, to rejoin the shore party that had approached it by passing over a sand bar which unites it with the mainland. For several miles the water was not more than a foot in depth, but gradually increased to six and eight feet.

After a heavy row of six hours we reached the island, and found the camp already pitched near the beach. Drift-wood was abundant along the shore, and a fire was very grateful, as we had been pulling in the teeth of a raw, cold, west wind, which had sprung up in the afternoon, and which had chilled those not warmed by exercise, to the very bone. A hot stew and plenty of hot coffee soon restored circulation and cheerfulness, and we retired to our blankets and buffalo-skins, spread upon the ground, well prepared by twelve hours of incessant toil for deep and welcome repose. Innumerable flocks of ducks, geese, white swans, and long-legged plover were seen during the day, congregated around the shallows at the mouth of the Jordan.

Friday, April 5.—The water being here very indifferent, we moved about five miles to the northward, and encamped on a rocky point near some large springs of tolerably good water, breaking out from the hills above. It is worthy of remark that the quality of almost all the springs in this region is dependent, in a great degree, upon the season of the year. In the spring and early part of summer, they are supplied by the percolations of the melting snows from the neighbouring hills, which at this season are generally copious, and render the water sweet and palatable. As soon as their supplies from a higher level begin to fail, the soil through which they run, or from the depths of which they rise, being strongly impregnated with minerals, imparts to the water saline or mineral qualities, which in the autumn and winter render them totally unfit for use. Such we found to be the case in the latter part of the succeeding summer.

The rocks among which we had now encamped consisted of granite, or perhaps an altered sedimentary quartz or siliceous sandstone. Drift-wood is scattered along the shores at an elevation of four or five feet above the present level of the lake, which must have maintained that height for a considerable period, since in numerous spots along the drift line unmistakable evidences of a well-defined beach are still to be traced with perfect precision. The wood is small and generally sound, but very dry, and must, from its appearance, have been deposited there for many years. It came, doubtless, from Bear River, the Weber, and the Jordan.

Antelope Island is the largest of the islands in the lake. It is about sixteen miles in length and five miles broad in its widest part. Like all the other islands in the lake, and, indeed, all the prominences observed west of the Wahsatch range and within its valley, it consists of a long rocky eminence, ranging from north to south, rising abruptly from the water, and attaining an elevation of about three thousand feet above the level of the lake. A party was sent up the mountain to erect a triangulation station upon its highest peak. The officer charged with that duty describes the view from this elevation as grand and magnificent, embracing the whole lake, the islands, and the encircling mountains covered with snow—a superb picture set in a framework of silver.

The southern part of the island is connected with the main shore by an extensive sand-flat, which, in the summer, is for the most part dry, but is frequently flooded to the depth of eighteen inches, the water of the lake being driven over it by every gale from the north. Upon the cessation of the wind the water recedes, and then the depressions of the beach are filled with pools of shallow water, which, evaporating under the influence of the sun, leave extensive deposites of salt upon the sand. The beach is at all times sufficiently hard to allow the passage of wagons from the main shore to the island, which is constantly resorted to on account of its affording on the whole of its eastern slope one of the finest ranges for horses and cattle to be found in the whole valley. Being insulated from the main shore, it affords great comparative security from depredations by the Indians. On account of these advantages, and of its being accessible by water, I directed the herd, which had been wintered in Tuilla Valley, to be driven to this island. They were placed under the charge of the herdsman licensed by the Mormon authorities to receive all the cattle which may be committed to his care, he giving bond and security for their safe return, and being held responsible for any loss that may occur. The herd remained here until our departure from the country.

Saturday, April 6.—The night was windy, and the morning cold and raw. Left camp in the boat for an island distant about ten miles to the northward, called by the Mormons, *Castle Island*, for the purpose of erecting a station upon its summit. In crossing from the camp to the island, the lead was kept constantly going. The deepest water found was twelve feet, the depth varying generally from three and a half to six. Doubling the northern cape of the island, we landed upon a narrow beach, west of a projecting little reef consisting principally of green hornblende rock. Mica schist also crops out, at an angle of 70°.

From the drift-wood on the shore, three long poles were selected and carried to the summit of the highest peak of the island, and a station built with them. This was a work of severe labour, as the island was at least eight or nine hundred feet high, the timber heavy, and the ascent, in some places, very steep, exceeding an angle of forty-five degrees. As we rise to the summit, argillaceous schists predominate, filled with cubes of bisulphuret of iron, many of which were found among the detritus of the decomposing rock. Rolled stones and pebbles of quartz and granite, imbedded in a sedimentary rock forming a conglomerate, were also found, with tufa. Upon the side of a large and singular mass of schistose rock, with three large holes worn entirely through it by the disintegration of its softer particles, we found a cross cut into the stone, apparently with a chisel. From the highest table of the island rises an oblong rocky eminence, resembling, from some points of view, ruins of an ancient castle, whence it had received from the Mormons its name of "Castle Island." Frémont called it "Disappointment Island." I deemed it but due, however, to the first

adventurous explorer of'this distant region to name it after him
who first set foot upon its shores, and have therefore called it
Frémont Island. While putting up the station here, search was
made for the cover to the object end of his telescope, which he
states he had left on the summit of the island, but it could not be
found, having probably been buried in the detritus of the rapidly
decomposing rock upon which it had been left.

The island is fourteen miles in circumference, has neither timber nor water upon it, but its sides are covered with luxuriant
grass, and abound in prodigious quantities of the wild onion, wild
parsnip, and *sego,* (*Calochortus luteus.*) The latter is a small
bulbous root, about the size of a walnut, very palatable and
nutritious, and is much used by the Indian tribes as an article of
food. It abounds on hillsides and in stony ground in great
quantities. Near the summit of the island, the sage (*Sarcobatus
vermicularis,* nees,) grew in great profusion, and to an extraordinary size, being frequently eight feet high and six or eight inches
in diameter. Could fresh water be obtained by boring, (and it is
worth the experiment,) a more admirable range than this for
sheep and goats could not be desired. Being surrounded by deep
water, the protection from wild beasts is absolute; an object in
this country of no small importance, where wolves abound in great
numbers. The wild parsnip is already up several inches, and its
vivid green presents a cheerful contrast on the sunny slopes with
the snow-clad mountains which surround us. A single ground-
squirrel was seen; but how he got here, and where he obtained
water to sustain life, is somewhat of a mystery. In all our subsequent examinations not the least indication of a spring was discovered. Our men picked up quite a number of the eggs of the
blue heron, now just beginning to lay, in the tall grass along the
shore.

In approaching the island from the water, it presented the appearance of regular beaches, bounded by what seemed to have
been well-defined and perfectly horizontal water-lines, at different
heights above each other, as if the water had settled at intervals
to a lower level, leaving the marks of its former elevation distinctly traced upon the hillside. This continued nearly to the
summit, and was most apparent on the north-eastern side of the
island.

On our return to camp, we spread our sails merrily to the breeze,
and although our boat was heavy and by no means a clipper, yet

we moved along in all the dignity and complaisance of a first-rate, persuaded that no other craft of equal pretensions had ever floated on the bosom of these solitary waters. After no little consultation, she was finally called " *The Salicornia*," or "*Flower of Salt Lake*," which euphonious appellation the men very soon dispensed with for the more homely but more convenient one of "The Sally." A small skiff had been procured as a consort to our frigate, and after being fitted up and caulked, proved a very valuable addition to our marine.

Tuesday, April 9.—Morning very cool. Heavy blow all last night from the north. Sent a team to the city for an additional supply of provisions and equipage. Started with the boat and nine men to explore and erect stations on the islands in the western portion of the lake, taking two days' provisions and water, and a blanket for each man.

Rounding the northern point of Antelope Island, we came to a small rocky islet, about a mile west of it, which was destitute of vegetation of any kind, not even a blade of grass being found upon it. It was literally covered with wild waterfowl; ducks, white brandt, blue herons, cormorants, and innumerable flocks of gulls, which had congregated here to build their nests. We found great numbers of these, built of sticks and rushes, in the crevices of the rock, and supplied ourselves, without scruple, with as many eggs as we needed, principally those of the herons, it being too early in the season for most of the other waterfowl.

Having erected a station on this island, we started for another, apparently about twenty miles to the westward. The wind was fresh, and we carried away the step of one of our masts in the blow. The crew were all entirely unaccustomed to the water, and were no little alarmed at the heavy swell caused by the gale, which was much greater than I had anticipated, and made most of them quite sea-sick. We arrived at the desired point without accident, and in time to erect a station upon the summit of the island before dark. The island was between six and seven hundred feet high, and six and a-half miles in circumference. As we ascended the slope of the hill, which is much more gentle than that of any other island in the lake, small rolled stones, sand, and gravel are first met with, then slate, covering the ground in broken laminæ; and the summit consisted of ledges of excellent roofing-slate, of which any quantity can be obtained. The latter was filled in places with cubes of bisulphuret of iron, which frequently penetrated several

11

laminæ. I searched diligently, but could find no cubes free, although the rock was full of the small cavities from which they had either been dislodged or had decayed under the influence of the weather. Abundance of the slate can be procured free from this objection; and by trial I ascertained that a nail could be driven through the layers almost as easily as through a shingle. On the shores were large quantities of a deposite resembling hard clay, which had formed when soft upon the rolled stones of the beach, and, when hardened by the sun or other causes, had been broken off, retaining, like a hollow mould, the shape of the stone upon which it had been deposited. The island is surrounded by extensive shoals. The beach is gradually making to the south, and will doubtless join with the wide sand-flats to the south and west before many years.

At sundown we returned to the beach, where we bivouacked on some soft sand, partially protected from the searching wind by a thick growth of grease-wood, which was abundant. Our fires were plentifully supplied from the drift-wood piled up on the shore.

Wednesday, April 10.—Up by sunrise. Breakfast, cold fried bacon, roasted heron's eggs, and cold water. Morning cool—wind from east, afterward shifted to north-east and north. Started for a small island lying about five miles to the northward, to erect a station upon it. We found it be a mere islet, one hundred feet in height, and about a mile in circumference, having a long, narrow sand-spit running off from it in a south-east direction for a mile and a-half. It is merely a pile of granitic conglomerate, with tufa in large masses. Grease-wood seems to be the principal growth, and the whole island abounds in the wild onion, now vividly green, filling the air with its odour. Two species of cactus were also seen. A cliff of slate rock occurred, preserving to a certain extent its laminated structure, but so burned, altered, and filled with pebbles as to be useless. The water, for a long distance around this islet, is shallow, more especially to the westward.

Having completed the station at this point, we returned to Frémont's Island to cover the station there with cloth, so as to render it visible from a distance. After a row of twelve miles we landed on the south-west beach at noon. The water crossed was at first quite shallow, but gradually deepened to eighteen, twenty-four, twenty-seven, and thirty-three feet, and then moderately shoaled to Frémont's Island, being eighteen feet deep within a hundred yards of the shore.

WEST END OF FREMONT'S I, AND PROMONTORY RANGE. LOOKING NORTH. G. S. LAKE.

The west point of the island presents a bold escarpment, one hundred feet in height, of talcose slate, overlaid by granite and gneiss, occasionally traversed by seams of white ferruginous quartz, and containing cubic crystals of iron pyrites. The ascent of the southern slope of the island in this part is much more gradual than from the western point where we first landed, and a beautiful beach, covered with clear, white quartz pebbles, lined the shore of a pretty little bay, now glistening in placid beauty under the rays of the setting sun. The slope on this side presents the same appearance of benches or lines of what must have been water levels or beaches, parallel and horizontal, though apparently not so near to each other as on the north side. Ledges of mica and talcose slate crop out at different heights, with a dip to W. N. W. of about 40°. The slate is soft, slightly unctuous : laminæ regular, parallel, and quite thin.

At some twenty feet above the water, I observed two protruding ledges, in which, lying upon the slate, (which in this case was of a much lighter colour than the rest,) was a dark-brown rock, much vitrified, tinged with iron, and burned so hard that it sounded, when struck, like delf-ware. It had, while in a state of fusion, flowed around the neighbouring rocks, forming a sort of mould or casing over them. These having perished by gradual disintegration, have left the moulds connected, but empty. In this lava, quartz, some white and some tinged with iron, is freely interspered ; in some of the moulds, occasionally seamed with the white quartz veins, was a brown, hard sandstone, which, where exposed, was rapidly disappearing. The vegetation on this side of the island was similar to that on the other : the bunch-grass was especially fine and abundant. After a long and fatiguing row, reached camp at nine o'clock at night.

Thursday, April 11.—Morning bright and warm, with gentle breeze from the south. Got under way early, for the purpose of putting up a station on Mud Island, distant about eight miles. A line of soundings was run until midway, when the boat grounded on a shoal which extends quite to the northern extremity of this part of the lake. The deepest water found on the line was eleven and a-half feet. The skiff was sent ahead with an officer, but it was soon left on the flat, and the party waded through soft mud and water to the shore.

After dragging the large boat half a mile, a sufficiency of water was found to float her, within a hundred and fifty yards of a point of rocks projecting from the mud-plain which surrounds the island. In wading to the shore, we struggled through a deep, soft, dark-coloured mass of what at first appeared to be ooze and slimy mud, but which, upon examination, proved to consist almost solely of the larvæ of insects lying upon the bottom, producing, when disturbed, a most offensive and nauseous odour. The mass was more than a foot in thickness and extended several yards from the shore. A belt of soft, black mud, more than knee-deep, lay between the water and the hard, rocky beach, and seemed to be impregnated with all the villanous smells which nature's laboratory was capable of producing.

The point where we had effected our landing was found to be a protrusion of an isolated pile of metamorphic rock above the vast mud-plain, which latter extended to the northward and eastward, without a shrub or a bush or a blade of grass to be seen upon its surface. This protrusion consisted of various kinds of rock, pushed up from beneath, with a dip to the west from nearly perpendicular to 45°. Slate, almost vertical, was found lying side by side with a dark rock filled with pebbles and stones as large as a man's head, consisting of what appeared to me to be granite altered and burned by intense heat. This dark rock presented some indistinct traces of a laminated structure, and may be slate very much fused. Large boulders of granite and feldspar or quartz, with scales of mica, lay strewn about, and I observed one with several well-defined cubes of iron pyrites imbedded in it. The slate seemed to be completely filled with pebbles and small broken fragments of granite rock, with here and there a cube of iron pyrites. Boulders of feldspathic rock, seamed with white quartz, and containing thin veins of jasper of a brick-red colour, are occasionally found in the slate. Near the western extremity of the point is a different kind of rock—the direction nearly perpendicular. It is of a more sandy structure, but is filled with the same pebbles. The whole has been in a state of fusion.

The mud-flat, where above the level of the water, is thickly covered with round, dark-coloured, circular cakes, precisely resembling, in form, colour, and appearance, the excrement of cattle dried in the sun. Underneath the dry surface of these cakes is a soft, black, and sometimes greenish mud, which, when the cake is moved by the foot, and the dry covering pushed aside, emits a most fetid, sulphurous odour, poisoning all the surrounding air. The substance of which these lumps are formed appears to have

LANDING TO ENCAMP. SHORES OF GREAT SALT LAKE BEAR RIVER BAY.

Ackerman Lith. 379 Broadway N.Y.

boiled up from beneath, through numerous small orifices in the sand, and to have spread itself over the surface of the flat, in a semifluid state, to the thickness of from half an inch to three inches, with various diameters from three inches to a foot. The exposed surface has been indurated slightly by the action of the sun, and has formed a thin, tough, and slightly elastic covering or skin, which retains the substance within in a moist state for a long time. By long exposure, these lumps seem to dry up entirely, although, upon removing them, they are found still to be supplied with moisture from the small orifice or tube in the centre beneath, which latter apparently extends to a considerable depth in the ground.

Having erected the station, we returned to camp, which we did not reach until nearly midnight, all hands being completely worn out by incessant labour of nearly eighteen hours at the oars, and in wading through mud and water. The distance passed over amounted to about thirty miles, and the exposure in the water, at this early season, was peculiarly severe. The team from town, with provisions, &c., returned in the afternoon.

Friday, April 12.—Broke up the camp on Antelope Island, and started for the north end of the lake, to complete that portion of the survey as early in the season as possible. It had already been foreseen that one great obstacle to the rapid prosecution of the work would be the want of fresh water, and means had accordingly been provided for carrying in the boats as much as was possible. Such was the limited means of transportation, that a supply for more than two or three days could not be carried without overloading the boats, already burdened with camp-equipage and provisions. Being uncertain of finding any water at our next contemplated encampment, all the vessels were filled.

After passing Frémont's Island, the water of the lake continued, as on yesterday, very shallow, the deepest being six and a-half feet. We were now in the Bear-River Bay, and the shallowness of the water is no doubt owing to the deposite of immense quantities of alluvion brought down by that river at every freshet, in a state of suspension.

After coasting along the eastern slope of the promontory range, which puts into the lake from the north, and seeking in vain for a point at which to land, we were at length forced to drag the boat to within a mile and a-half of the shore, where we left her stuck fast in the mud. The tents, water, and provisions were placed in the skiff and dragged as far as possible, when the whole had to be packed upon our shoulders and carried to the shore, a distance of rather more than half a mile, through a black, tenacious, and fetid ooze, which rendered wading an excessively fatiguing task.

The camp was pitched in a wide rocky ravine, which had cut entirely through the southern point of a low rocky peninsula, at the foot of and parallel with the main promontory, and we gave it the name of the "Rock Gate" camp.

The formation here was a compact, massive, blue limestone, thickly and irregularly marked with close seams. Numerous brackish and sulphur springs percolate from beneath the foot of the cliffs, forming a black oozy mud, which filled the air with its nauseous odour. Water was found in small quantities at the foot of the mountains to the westward, half a mile distant; and wood for cooking was furnished by the wild sage which grew in scattered patches on the sides of the hills.

Tuesday, April 16.—The survey of Bear-River Bay had been carried on by two parties; that on the eastern side being under the command of Lieutenant Gunnison. In the afternoon a violent storm came up suddenly from the westward, accompanied by thunder, and a gale which instantly prostrated our little encampment. A copious fall of rain, mingled with hail, wetted my party to the skin before reaching camp. The damage was soon repaired, and the tents repitched amid rain, hail, and snow.

As the storm continued with unabated violence, I began to entertain serious apprehensions for the other party, under Lieutenant Gunnison, who were engaged on the flats on the eastern side of the bay; lest, in the darkness, they should miss their way, and be unable to return. At dusk a large signal-fire was built on the hilltop, and guns were fired at intervals to attract their attention. But the night passed without their appearing.

Early the following morning they came into camp, covered from head to foot with salt and mud, cold, wet, hungry, and thoroughly exhausted. A more forlorn-looking group it has seldom been my lot to behold. Anticipating their arrival in some such plight, I had had an early breakfast prepared, with plenty of hot coffee; after partaking of which, they were immediately wrapped in blankets, and a sound sleep restored them to their accustomed strength. The following extract from the journal of Lieutenant Gunnison will give an idea of what they endured in the course of the night. The storm overtook them in the midst of the extensive mud-flats

VALLEY BETWEEN PROMONTORY RANGE AND ROCKY BUTTE – CAMP NO 2. G. S. LAKE.

bordering the eastern side of the lake, without a bush or a shrub to shelter them from its fury. Lieutenant Gunnison says—" The skiff was dragged for half a mile into three inches water, when the wind suddenly shifted to the north, and blew a tremendous gale. Our course was north, and we endeavoured to force our way with four men wading by the sides of the boat, but the gale was too powerful for them, and drove the whole company off the course, so that by the time we were in one foot water, we were obliged to stop ; the spray dashed over the boat in showers ; the rain and hail came down in torrents ; and soon all hands were drenched to the skin. The mist shut down upon us, and we could only see a few steps around. It was nearly sunset, and rapidly growing dark. The men became bewildered, and despaired of reaching camp, declaring that they could not survive till morning. The snow began to fall fast and the air to become more chilly and raw. Our course was now completely lost, and it was rapidly becoming too dark to read the compass much longer. We therefore determined to turn back for the mud-flat from which we had started, so that we might at least have solid ground upon which to pass the night. After wading and dragging our boat for about a mile, we came upon our trail of yesterday. The men becoming too stiff and benumbed to proceed any farther, we managed to turn the skiff up on its side, as a shelter from the piercing wind, and laying down the oars and thwarts to keep us as much as possible out of the mud, (which was about four inches deep,) we huddled together behind it. In a couple of hours the wind lulled, the skiff was turned again upon its bottom, the muddy boards arranged as a sort of platform, and we prepared for our night's lodging. I placed two of the men *edgewise* on the bottom of the boat, and crawled in alongside of them. The two extra men, (there were five of us,) laid themselves down on the lower tier, taking care to break joints. We had a bit of an old sail, which, in turning up the skiff, had been well trampled in the mud, and was in rather a sorry condition. This we dragged over us as a covering from the snow, which was falling fast. Although we were almost freezing, the heat from our bodies was sufficient to melt it and cause it to trickle down upon us, to our great discomfort.

"About eleven o'clock, as nearly as we could judge, the snow ceased to fall, but the piercing wind howled over us till daylight. Nearly frozen to death, we hailed the first streaks of day, and jumped cheerfully into the icy mud, pushed our boat a couple of miles, until the water was deep enough to float her, and in two hours found ourselves once more in camp, where Captain Stansbury anxiously awaited us with dry clothes and a hot breakfast to refresh us after our night's adventure."

Strange to say, no very serious consequences followed this night of severe exposure.

Preparations were now made for removing the camp to the southward. The " Sally," although empty, was found to be nearly high and dry from the effects of last night's norther; and it took all our disposable force to shove her out some half mile into water deep enough to float her. The baggage was then carried out to the skiff, which was hauled and pushed out to the larger boat, then lying nearly two miles off. The water was very cold, and the chilling wind swept down from the Wahsatch Mountains, which were in many places covered with snow nearly to their base.

We coasted along the promontory, as near to the shore as the depth of the water would permit, which was generally within a mile or more, until the afternoon, when we again grounded on an extensive shoal, and were occupied a couple of hours in dragging the boat over it. A small party, in the mean time, waded to the main shore to search for fresh water, evidences of which had been discovered from the boats. After several ineffectual attempts to land, we bore away for Frémont's Island, which we reached about nine o'clock, enlightened by the rays of a young moon. A large fire from drift-wood soon illumined the beach and rocky cliffs. Fried bacon, hard bread, and a single gallon of coffee constituted our supper, no water having been procured during the day, and our supply having been reduced to that quantity. The men being very tired with rowing and wading in the cold wind and water since sunrise, only a single tent was pitched, which was assigned to Lieutenant Gunnison, who had had quite enough of "lying-out" the night previous, and was somewhat unwell in consequence. The rest of us made a spacious and airy bedchamber of the open canopy of heaven. The wind freshened during the night, and rolled in a heavy sea upon the rock-bound shore; and the roar of the waves, as they dashed against it, reverberated among the cliffs like thunder, reminding some of us of scenes far, far away, where more mighty billows paid their unceasing tribute to the strand.

Thursday, April 18.—There not being a drop of water in camp, we got under way without breakfast, and made for a cove just east of the southern extremity of the promontory, where appear-

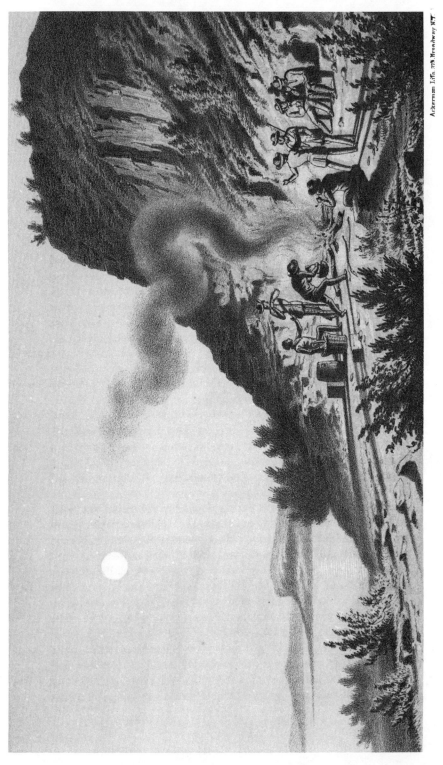

CAMP N.º 4. NEAR PROMONTORY POINT GREAT SALT LAKE.

Ackerman Lith. 379 Broadway N.Y.

ances promised a chance of landing. The water was bold to within three or four boats'-length of the pebbly shore, but the men were obliged to get into the water and carry the baggage to land, and thence nearly a quarter of a mile to the foot of the mountain, before finding ground upon which to encamp. Several of them were quite unwell from previous exposure, and all were jaded, stiff, and sore.

The nearest water was two miles distant, and had to be carried in India-rubber bags and kegs upon the shoulders. No breakfast was to be had until near noon, and the remainder of the day was devoted to rest and to drying our clothing and bedding. The sun was bright for most of the day, but the wind was keen and cold.

The presence or absence of the sun in this climate has a marked influence upon the temperature. The day may be oppressively warm, but as soon as the sun disappears behind the western mountains, a fire is indispensable to comfort. The morning early may be very cold, but soon after the appearance of the sun, cloth coats become uncomfortable. Should the sun become overclouded for any length of time, they are resumed.

Segos are here very abundant, and of a large size, and are found in every tuft of bunch-grass. In the vicinity, a cliff was discovered of alum slate, nearly a mile in length, and about sixty feet in height above the lake. It is traversed by several dikes of trap, with cubical crystals of iron pyrites, and by one dike of quartz rock. The slate contains numerous veins of very pure fibrous alum. Between this cliff and Promontory Point there occur strata of mica slate, fine grindstone-grit, sandstone, and albite.

Friday, April 19.—Rain during the night. Morning wet, cold, and raw. Nevertheless, we started in the boat for a large island west of Antelope Island, which the officers of the party had done me the honour to call by my name. After erecting a station upon its northern point, it was my intention to proceed to *Black Rock*, a large isolated rock on the southern shore of the lake, midway between the two islands, to erect a station upon it: thence I designed to accompany Lieutenant Gunnison to town, and fit out a party, to be placed under his command, for the survey of the eastern shore of the lake, as well as of that part of the valley lying between it and the foot of the Wahsatch range. It rained and snowed several times in the course of the morning, and the day was very cold and unpleasant. We erected the station upon a pro-

minence of the northern extremity of the mountain ridge forming the island, and encamped upon the white-sand beach of a
lovely little bay indenting its eastern shore.

The whole of this part of the ridge consists of large masses of
quartzose and sandstone rock, variously tinged with oxide of iron,
and conglomerates. Heavy squall, with rain and snow, during
the night. Having provided ourselves with only a single keg of
water, in expectation of finding some during the day, we discovered
before night that it was nearly exhausted; so all hands were put
upon short allowance, and a very small cup of coffee was served
out for supper. There was no discontent, however, though all
went to their blankets almost famished for water, and fervently
hoping we might find a supply early in the morning.

Saturday, April 20.—A fresh gale was blowing from the north-
west, which continued to increase during the day. The wind was
excessively cold, and the men were obliged to wrap themselves in
buffalo-skins to keep warm. Setting the foresail, we ran to Black
Rock, a distance of more than twenty miles, in a little more than
three hours. A station was framed from timbers which had been
previously cut in the mountains and hauled to the spot for the
purpose; but the force of the party was not sufficient to raise it.

Orders were sent to the herdsmen in Tuilla Valley, near by, to
bring a team in the morning, to transport Lieutenant Gunnison's
party to the city. A beef was killed and divided between the
companies. The herd was also directed to be removed from
Tuilla Valley to Antelope Island for the season.

The station was raised the following day, and we started for the
city, leaving the boat's crew encamped on the shore of the lake.
The interval, until the 25th, was employed in fitting out the party
destined for the survey of the eastern shore of the lake, which
being completed, I rejoined my people at Black Rock.

Friday, April 26.—A violent blow from the north prevented
our moving before the afternoon; but, just before sundown, the
wind having lulled, we loaded the boat and started for Promontory
Point, where the camp had been left under charge of Mr. Carrington. A southerly breeze struck us about dark, and continued all
night. The weather was clear, but extremely cold. None of my
crew had the least knowledge of managing a boat, and I was
therefore always obliged to take the helm myself whenever the
sails were set. As the wind had now become fair, and there was
no necessity for rowing, each man wrapped himself in his blanket,

Ackerman Lith. 379 Broadway N.Y.

CAVE ON FREMONT'S ISLAND.

and sought repose in the bottom of the boat, while I guided our little craft during the night, until, at the break of day, I sank down, benumbed by the cold and overcome by the fatigues of the preceding day, followed by an incessant watch of more than twelve hours. We were, however, not far from our encampment, having run during the night nearly thirty miles.

The party under Mr. Carrington returned to the camp in the afternoon from Frémont's Island, having completed its detailed survey during my absence. They were almost famished for water, and had "laid out," or bivouacked, for four successive nights. The fresh provisions and vegetables I brought with me were received with much satisfaction.

Before leaving Black Rock, I made an experiment upon the properties of the water of the lake for preserving meat. A large piece of fresh beef was suspended by a cord and immersed in the lake for rather more than twelve hours, when it was found to be tolerably well corned. After this, all the beef we wished to preserve while operating upon the lake, was packed into barrels without any salt whatever, and the vessels were then filled up with the lake-water. No further care or preparation was necessary; and the meat kept perfectly sweet, although constantly exposed to the sun. I have no doubt that meats put up in this water would remain sound and good as long as if prepared after the most approved methods. Indeed, we were obliged to mix fresh water with this natural brine, to prevent our meat from becoming too salt for present use—a very few days' immersion changing its character from corned beef to what the sailors call "salt junk."

Monday, April 29.—Moving camp from Promonotory Point. The morning was bright and clear, but the wind blew a gale from the west, by which the boats, being deeply laden, were so much retarded that with all our exertion we could not get farther than seven miles around the western side of the Promontory, when, to avoid being driven ashore by the violence of the gale, we were obliged to land and encamp for the night. The baggage, as usual, had to be carried about half a mile to obtain ground upon which to pitch the tents. This was found under a high cliff of quartzose rock, with masses among the detritus of nearly pure feldspar.

In the cliff was quite a large cave, which had been used as a shelter by Indians—the marks of their fires being still visible within it. Our men took possession of it, built a large fire, and consoled themselves for the fatigues of the day with a *dance* to the strains of one of the most execrable fiddles I ever listened to anywhere.

The water all the way from Promontory Point is very shallow for a long distance from the shore, which is generally sandy, with pebbles; the detritus from the range being mainly quartzose pudding-stone, hornblende, quartz, and granite.

Tuesday, April 30.—Moved camp again to-day in search of the springs of water I had passed on horseback in October last. The day was calm and warm, and the atmosphere balmy and delightful. In the course of the morning we descried from the boats a patch of reeds on the shore, which our experience had taught us to be an indication of fresh water. We accordingly landed, and found some very indifferent brackish water by digging. Fearful lest we should obtain none better, we filled our vessels and embarked. Crossing a shallow reef of flat rocks, extending from the shore for several miles, we struck at once into deep water— the southern extremity of a large bay with a bold shore, encircled by high and picturesque mountains. The water was twenty feet in depth, and gradually increased to thirty feet, which continued to a projecting rocky point, crossed by a well-defined Indian trail. Near the extremity of the spur is a remarkable cliff, or projection, which towers above the surrounding mountains, forming a prominent and impressive feature in a landscape full of wild and peculiar beauty.

The ridge of which this formed the apex is composed of black, blue, and ash-coloured limestone of a very close texture, seamed in all directions by small veins of white carbonate of lime, producing a very pretty appearance. It would make beautiful mantels and tops for tables, could it be quarried in slabs of sufficient size. Calcareous tufa is forming in large quantities near the base of the mountain. The hillsides contain numerous caves, some of which are of considerable size. Stretching off from the point to the south-west is a ledge of flat sandstone rock, lying in from one to two feet water, which makes a large shoal in that direction. The lower portion of the point itself, extending from the base of the cliff, is also of this rock, lying horizontally about two feet above the level of the water. From the prevalence of this rock here we called it *Flat-rock Point.* Rounding the prominence, the boat was run into a little rocky cove, and the camp pitched in a thicket of grease-wood and artemisia, just above the storm-line of the lake— which is here very determinate.

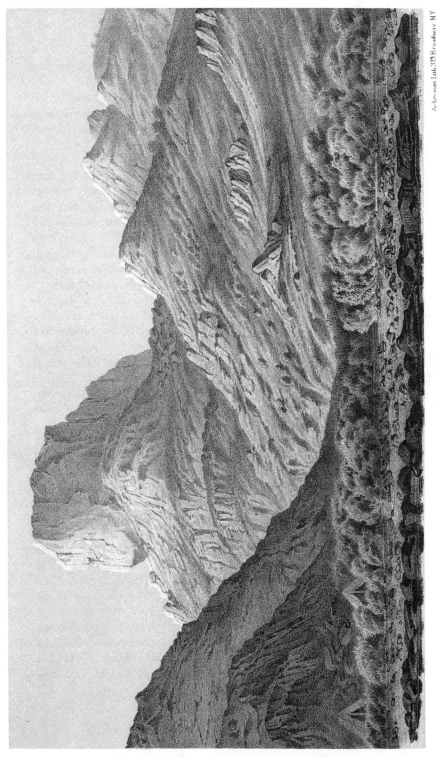

Ackerman Lith.379 Broadway NY

WEST SIDE OF PROMONTORY _ FLAT ROCK POINT

VIEW OF PART OF THE WESTE[R]

LOPE OF PROMONTORY RANGE—GREAT SALT LAKE.

GUNNISON'S ISLAND EASTERN SHORE LOOKING NORTH GREAT SALT LAKE

Ackerman Lith.379 Broadway N.Y.

To the north, the rugged and rocky eminences gradually recede from the shore; to which, a few miles farther on, they again return in a superb semicircular sweep; forming a landscape in the highest degree picturesque and beautiful, to which nothing is wanting but trees. In the centre of the arc a fantastic mass of rock reared its gigantic outline against the sky, presenting from the camp a striking resemblance to an old ruined abbey, glowing and glistening in the rays of the setting sun.

Immediately behind us rose a rounded knob, some two hundred feet in height, composed of one solid limestone rock, in the crevices of which grew, in graceful luxuriance, the everlasting bunchgrass, so characteristic of this region. Upon the shore, among the boulders with which it was thickly strewn, I obtained some fine specimens of dark compact limestone, containing well-defined fossils of *Cyathophyllum* and *Strepletasma*.

The shore party reached camp about dark. They reported finding abundance of the finest water at the head of the bay we had crossed to-day, which was easy of access. This was joyful news, as the water we were using was very brackish and nauseous—so much so as to impart a most disagreeable flavour to the strongest coffee.

Wednesday, May 1.—The survey of the shore-line being in arrears some miles, I availed myself of the opportunity to overhaul the large boat, which was a miserable, lumbering affair, and make such alterations in her as would admit of more convenient and expeditious stowage of the baggage. This having been accomplished, I started in her for the watering-place. After rounding Flat-rock Point, the water was bold and deep to within a boat's length of the shore opposite the springs. I at once recognised the spot as being the same passed by me on horseback during my reconnoissance of the previous October.

Several springs here gush out, fresh, clear, cold, and convenient to the shore. As I anticipated the necessity of frequent visits to this spot, for a supply of water for the party when engaged on the western side of the lake, all hands were at once set to work to run out a pier of stones, alongside of which the boat could lie without danger. This was soon done; some of the springs were cleared out and deepened, and the casks filled, when we returned to camp with a fine fresh breeze. In our progress we passed innumerable flocks of young ducks, which upon our approach dived beneath the surface and disappeared. The gnats have at this camp been almost insufferable during the day, settling on the forehead and ears, getting into the eyes and hair, producing pain and irritation by their bite, and rendering the manipulation of instruments extremely difficult under the tormenting infliction. Fortunately, they always disappear upon the going down of the sun, affording a grateful relief from their annoying attacks.

The following day we attempted to move camp, but after getting under way, the wind blew so hard that we could make but little progress, and were at length obliged to come-to on a sandbar only two miles from our morning encampment, and to carry our camp to land upon our shoulders. Here we met three Shoshonee Indians on horseback, who had been watching our motions for some time. They belonged to a small lodge encamped among the hills a few miles to the northward. They seemed friendly, and expressed much curiosity at the size of the boat, and by signs informed me that they would very much like to borrow it, to pay a visit to the islands in the lake, some of which they gave me to understand they had never reached. Indeed, I doubt if they had ever placed a canoe upon the waters. We saw no sign of any thing of the kind, even upon Utah Lake, although its waters abound with the finest fish. A hearty supper, which they devoured as if they never expected to get another, sent them away delighted with their visit.

In wandering among the artemisia, to-day, I was struck at by a most villanous-looking adder, rather more than two feet in length, and was very near being bitten. It was the first snake I had seen in the country, and I think we only saw one other—a rattle snake —while we were upon the lake.

Friday, May 3.—In about two miles we came upon a number of fine springs, near to which I had encamped last fall. The water then was brackish and bad; but now, owing to the supply from melting snows in the mountains, it was fresh, soft, and delightful. The springs were beautifully clear, and situated amid a large growth of reeds—an invariable indication, here, of fresh water. The one from which we obtained our supply was about fifteen feet long, ten feet wide, and four deep, with overhanging banks of sod. Some curious insects inhabited it, several of which were caught and preserved.

The adjacent hills are composed of gray limestone, overlying the same kind of black marble as that seen at Flatrock Point.

Both are of a very close texture, and would make excellent building-stone.

Around the springs was found, growing in considerable quantity, a plant I had not before seen—called by some of the men *silk-plant*. It somewhat resembles the sumac in appearance, and has at its top a cluster of long slender pods, which, when ripe, split open longitudinally, disclosing a number of seeds, each attached to a fascicle of long silky fibres, resembling very fine threads of spun glass. The bark is tough, strong, and very much like that of flax. The root and the plant, when broken, exudes a milky viscous substance—that from the root is intensely bitter. The Ottoes and Omahas make lariats of the bark, which are said to be stronger and better than those made of hide. It is said to grow abundantly near Council Bluffs, in Missouri. My Frenchman called it *vache à lait*. The Mexican negro cook calls it *capote des acarte*. He says that the Pueblo Indians call it *noche*. They cut it down when ripe, rub it so as to separate the fibres, and make of it beautiful and very strong fishing-lines and fine sewing-thread. They also use a decoction of the root for medicinal purposes—the root itself is put into liquor to make bitters.

Beyond these springs the lake makes a wide, deep bay, stretching far to the northward, near the head of which the promontory range bounding it on the east seems to sink away. On the west, the bay is bounded by a low range of rocky hills, stretching to the north. Between these hills the country is much lower, and ascends northwardly, by a gentle rise, to a belt of low hills far off in the distance; over which, farther to the north-west, is seen a range of snow-capped mountains.

Starting from the springs with the boats, we attempted to make our way to the point where the eastern range seemed to terminate; but found the water so shallow that it was impracticable. After many fruitless attempts, the boat was brought as near the shore as possible, part of the baggage loaded into the skiff, and pushed toward the land. It was impossible, however, to bring even this light barque nearer than within a quarter of a mile of the beach, and the luggage was transported to shore on our shoulders. On landing, we found ourselves on the margin of an immense flat of sand, destitute of the least sign of vegetation, and only a few inches above the level of the water, which covers a large portion of it whenever a fresh wind prevails from the south. It stretches across the head of the bay from near the springs to the southern point of the western promontory, and doubtless at one time formed the northern boundary of the lake in this direction.

At the point where we landed, it was upward of a mile in breadth. There being no wood to be obtained for cooking purposes nearer than the foot of the mountains, all hands were despatched to gather and pack upon their shoulders sufficient for that purpose; and the camp was pitched upon the naked sand. The land party came in at sundown from the line of survey, which had been carried to the point of the mountain at the head of the bay. They reported the discovery there of some springs with a small supply of good fresh water and abundance of excellent grass.

Saturday, May 4.—Morning calm, bright, and balmy. Despatched most of the hands to the springs found yesterday, for water, which they brought on their shoulders to the boat—a distance of over two miles. On their return, we packed the baggage in the skiff, and dragged it about half a mile to the boat. After much difficulty, we extricated ourselves from the shoals, and made for the south point of the range forming the western boundary of the bay. At this point the water is deep, quite to the shore, which is iron-bound by boulders of black rock from the surrounding hills. A small ledge or reef of rock was seen above water some three hundred yards to the south. Rounding the point of this little promontory, we encamped on a small bluff, a short distance from the edge of the water.

The hillsides are covered with broken masses of a very dark-coloured rock, containing much iron, and which, from its peculiar tint, as we approached them from the water, gave the slopes the appearance of being covered with a forest of cedar. These rocks we found, upon landing, to consist of a dark compact limestone, stained, and in many cases apparently vitrified, on the surface by iron. The top of the ridge, which is three or four hundred feet above the water, is crowned by a stratum of light cream-coloured limestone, in a cliff thirty feet in height. All the varieties are of a close texture, and very hard, especially the white, which will, I think, quarry easily. If so, it will be quite valuable, as the shores at this point being accessible for boats, a continuous navigation is practicable to Black Rock, at the southern end of the lake, whence the land-carriage to the city is only twenty miles.

Small quantities of bitumen were found on the shore, in the masses of a substance which lined the beach to the depth of six inches, and resembled in appearance the brown, dried seaweed of the ocean. Under the magnifying glass, these masses were found to consist almost entirely of the larvæ or dried skins of a dipterous insect, adhering together. They had apparently been driven upon the shore at different periods ; some appearing fresher and of a different texture from others, the insects having been of a larger size. The question where these larvæ originated presents a curious · subject of inquiry. Nothing living has as yet been detected in the lake, and only a few large insects in the brackish springs, which do not at all resemble these remains either in shape or size. That they have existed in almost incredible numbers is evident, as the shores are lined with their skins, and the bottom, in many instances, for a long distance out from the shores, is covered with them. This is especially the case in the north-east part of the lake, where they lie on the bottom a foot thick, mingled with the oozy mud, of which they form a large proportion. Yesterday I observed from the shore several dark patches far out in the lake, apparently of dull reddish water, looking very much like large shoals. Upon rowing over some of them, however, I found that this change in the colour of the water, here very shallow, was not occasioned by any marked difference in the depth, but from the bottom being covered with these larvæ, which the oars raised at every stroke, rendering the water turbid and offensive. Some of the deposites were very large, and must have covered many hundred acres.

Monday, May 6.—Morning clear and warm. About a mile to the westward of camp the forces of the land and water party were united, to erect a triangulation station upon a high, rocky knob, near the southern extremity of the range, commanding a view to the south and west. The distance from the water was about a mile, and the elevation of the station about six hundred feet. Some long sticks were selected from a pile of drift-wood on the beach, and transported on the shoulders of the men, over very rocky, ascending ground, covered with large boulders of a close-grained, compact limestone. The labour was very great, and was much enhanced by the annoyance of swarms of gnats. They have become an intolerable nuisance. Our faces and hands are covered with scars and blotches from the incessant irritation occasioned by their bites.

Having erected the station, we proceeded along the shore in search of a camping-place, which was found just south of a little rocky butte, having in front of it the first well-defined reef I had yet seen. Leaving the baggage on the camp-ground, I followed up the shore in search of water, and happily, in little more than a mile, found an abundant supply and very good, in some small ponds, formed by the snow and spring rains, which are, however, dry in the summer. This was a fortunate circumstance, as, otherwise, we should have been obliged to cross the lake during the night to the springs on the western side of the main promontory, as our supply was by this time reduced to half a barrel.

Several horned frogs were found to-day running upon the shores. The sand which forms the beach in this vicinity is worthy of remark. Under a magnifier it is found to consist of rounded globules, chiefly of calcareous rock, worn doubtless by attrition into their present form, not an angular particle being found among them. It is variegated by different and brilliant colours, and reminded me of the sand I had once seen which was brought from the Great Desert of Zahara. Its conformation makes it very fatiguing to walk in, presenting no firm resistance to the foot, but yielding at every step. A piece of bitumen was found buried in the sand, which had adhered to it when softened by the sun, and completely frosted it over, so that it very much resembled one of the small chocolate lozenges of the shops, covered with miniature sugar-plums.

Tuesday, May 7.—After moving camp some few miles above, started for an island in the lake, apparently fifteen or twenty miles to the southward, to place a triangulation station upon it. The wind had been southerly during the night, and had raised such a sea that I found it impossible to force the boat through the water, whose ponderous waves struck upon our bows with a power that was irresistible. After rowing some eight miles, we gave it up and returned to camp.

One of the party, in attempting to cut across the country to-day, got lost, and as he did not return by dark, signal-fires were lighted upon one or two of the neighbouring eminences to guide him to camp. He returned by bedtime, very much exhausted by his wanderings, having been without food or water since sunrise.

Wednesday, May 8.—The day being calm and the water smooth, renewed the attempt made yesterday to reach the island to the southward, taking with us blankets, provisions, and water, prepared to encamp upon it, if necessary. We reached the island after a row of four hours. The water was bold and deep nearly the whole distance—fifteen, seventeen, and twenty feet; and ten feet, within a hundred and fifty feet of the shore.

There are two islands here, one of them quite small, and lying within one hundred yards to the northward of the larger one, of which it has at one time formed a part. We landed at the head of a beautiful little sandy bay, on the eastern side, which has its counterpart on the western, the two being separated by a low, narrow neck of land, forming a delightful little nook, and separating the lofty pile of rock forming the northern part of the island from the rocky cliffs which extend to its southern extremity.

The whole neck and the shores on both of the little bays were occupied by immense flocks of pelicans and gulls, disturbed now for the first time, probably, by the intrusion of man. They literally darkened the air as they rose upon the wing, and, hovering over our heads, caused the surrounding rocks to re-echo with their discordant screams. The ground was thickly strewn with their nests, of which there must have been some thousands. Numerous young, unfledged pelicans, were found in the nests on the ground, and hundreds half-grown, huddled together in groups near the water, while the old ones retired to a long line of sand-beach on the southern side of the bay, where they stood drawn up, like Prussian soldiers, in ranks three or four deep, for hours together, apparently without motion.

A full-grown one was surprised and captured by the men, just as he was rising from the ground, and hurried in triumph to the beach. He was very indignant at the unceremonious manner in which he was treated, and snapped furiously with his long bill to the right and left at everybody that came near him. On the top of his bill, about midway of its length, was a projection about an inch long and half an inch high, resembling the old-fashioned sight of a rifle: in the female this is wanting. We collected as many eggs as we could carry. That of the gull is of the size of a hen's egg, brown and spotted; that of the pelican is white, and about as large as a goose egg. The white of the latter, when cooked, is translucent, and resembles clear *blanc-mange.*

After much searching, we found among the scanty drift-wood along the beach, two indifferent sticks with which to build a station. We set them up on the highest peak of the island, at its northern extremity, where a nearly perpendicular cliff of dark-gray limestone rises from the water to the height of five hundred feet.

It was a work of great fatigue to transport these heavy timbers over a rough, and in many places almost impassable cliff, to the top of this towering peak; and we were no little rejoiced when it was accomplished.

Having built our station, we set out on our return to camp, with a fair wind, which, however, soon died away, and the tired crew were obliged to take to their oars. When within two or three miles of camp, a most furious gale of wind suddenly broke down upon us from the north-west, which soon raised such a sea as rendered the progress of our heavy boat so slow that we did not reach home until ten o'clock, wearied, cold, and hungry. But hot coffee soon restored us, and we enjoyed a deep and most welcome slumber.

Friday, May 10.—Moved again to-day, with the intention of encamping at the head of this arm of the lake, but the water became so shallow that not even the skiff would float, and we had to resort to the usual process of transporting beds and baggage on our backs to the shore. Here we found that we had still half a mile farther to go to reach the nearest artemisia-bushes, which have now become our sole dependence for firewood. The bushes afforded us, it is true, the means of making fire for cooking, but at the same time they gave shelter to shoals of gnats, that drove us almost distracted.

We are now near the head of the northern extremity of the lake, and expect soon to turn our faces to the south, along its western shore. The character of the country has changed somewhat: the hills in the vicinity of the lake have become lower, and abound less in rocks, although the projecting points still consist of that material. Range behind range is seen to the westward across the water, while to the northward the ridges seem to be at first low, but rising in the distance, one above the other, like the seats of an amphitheatre. The following day we erected a large station on a hill south of the camp.

The two last nights we have been regaled by the varied notes of a little brown bird, the only songster I had yet heard in the valley. It sang all night; but I in vain attempted to secure it as a specimen. A couple of blackbirds, also, hung around the camp, and enlivened us with an occasional note. Abundance of a fine small pepper-grass grew in the sandy soil, which, in the absence of other vegetables, was very refreshing.

Monday, May 13.—Finding it impossible for the boats to advance any farther north, on account of the extensive flats occupying the whole of this end of the lake, I determined to cross to the western side, leaving the shore party to follow the old storm-line, or that indicating the ancient limits of the water.

A small station was put up upon a little rocky projection just north of the camp, which had to be constructed of stone, filled in with earth, as no timber of any kind could be procured for the purpose. A few slender poles of drift-wood were gathered, erected into a small lodge on the top of the mound, and covered over with white cloth. The camp was broken up, and every thing being loaded into the boats, the customary process of wading commenced.

This mode of moving was one of the most disagreeable and onerous of our duties. The boat was nearly two miles from the camp, and the men made their way through a soft, tenacious blue clay, ankle deep, and exposed to the insufferable annoyance of myriads of gnats, which the occupation of both hands in grasping the burden did not allow them to repel; and although, after getting out upon the water, we left for a time our inveterate little enemies behind, it was with the knowledge that the same torment must be again encountered on our next approach to land. In crossing we were repeatedly driven to the southward by the shallowness of the water; and, upon at length reaching the shore, we found, to our dismay, that an extensive flat of sand still lay between us and the line of grass and bushes where alone we could obtain fuel for cooking. Over this the camp was carried upon weary shoulders, and pitched among some artemisia, near "Turret Rock," as we named a large pinnacle toward which we had directed our course in the morning, and which had frequently before attracted our notice.

The soil, after passing the flat, is a hard yellow clay, with some pepper-grass—its only production. We here found a large hole that had been dug by the wolves. It was full of brackish water, which, although unfit to drink, was sufficiently good for mixing bread and for cooking generally. We had learned, by dire experience, not to despise any water, however indifferent, as we did not know at what period we might be reduced to its exclusive use.

The place had long been a resort for the few Indians that occasionally pass through this inhospitable region. Remains of old lodges constructed of sage-bush, beds of the same, collected under the cover of projecting ledges of rock and little caves in the cliff, together with a well-defined horse-trail, showed that this had been a favourite camp-ground. The trail came from the south-west, and led to the northward, probably to the more favoured region of the Pan-nack and the Port Neuf.

The shore party did not reach camp until nearly ten o'clock to-night, having been obliged to cross the extensive flat, some six or eight miles wide, after the termination of a day's work of seven miles of chain-line. They describe the country over which they have passed to-day as a mud-flat, studded with slight elevations, like islands, six or eight feet high, and covered with grease-wood and artemisia. One single stream was passed, four feet wide and one in depth, with gravelly bottom, the water of which was drink-able. The rest was one barren, dreary waste, over which the water of the lake had at one time flowed, and its gradual reces-sion had left behind it nothing but solitude and desolation.

Tuesday, May 14.—Engaged all this day in erecting two tri-angulation stations ; one upon a projecting peak west of Turret Rock, and another upon a high rocky cliff, about a mile north of the camp. As no timber could be obtained within twenty miles, both of these stations were constructed wholly of stone, laid up in a conical form, upon the highest point of their respective peaks, and covered with white cotton. This was a work of great labour, as the stone was difficult to be obtained, and had to be laid with great care to enable the station to resist the force of the violent winds to which it would be exposed. I added to-day the accom-plishment of laying stone-wall to my numerous other avocations, and returned to camp thoroughly wearied, and with the skin of my hands nearly worn through.

The rock upon which the higher station was erected is part of a ridge coming from the north, and terminating at this point in a bold, rugged escarpment, commanding an extensive view to the southward and westward. It consisted of a light-gray limestone, very friable, and rapidly disintegrating. The rocks in the vicinity are completely covered over with a casing of tufa, which has formed upon them, adapting itself to all their irregularities. It is very hard, and as the limestone underneath is constantly crumbling away from it, numerous caves are forming, the roof and sides of which consist of the tufa alone. The covering is from four to six inches thick. In one spot I found the rock for a small space thinly veneered with jade. Some broken specimens of Indian pottery were found at this camp, and also some pieces of obsidian. The latter, probably, had been procured elsewhere by the savages, for making arrow-heads.

The pelican captured upon Gunnison's Island was consigned to the kettle to-day, and boiled, for the purpose of preserving his skeleton. We had not been able to induce him to eat or drink a morsel, so that, finding he would starve to death, I had, a few days before, set him at liberty. He followed the boats for a long distance, but we lost sight of him, and the next morning he was found dead upon the shore. I had made some little progress in taming the fierceness of his nature. He would suffer me to assist him in pluming his feathers; but to all others he was sullen and intractable, snapping violently at every one who approached him.

Thursday, May 16.—We are now to turn our faces to the southward, and to explore the western shore of this solitary sea. From the most elevated points the prospect before us was dreary and discouraging. To the south, as far as the eye could reach, lay a plain of arid white sand, stretching many miles westward to a lofty range of mountains, which had, no doubt, ages ago, formed the barrier to the waters in that direction. A high and rocky hill rose occasionally from this level flat, like an island from the sea, while the scene was here and there relieved by patches of green artemisia—which alone flourished in this inhospitable region. The uncertainty of finding water was the only question which caused the least apprehension in encountering this desert of sand. Labour and fatigue all were willing to undergo ; but, without water, it was impossible to live. We, however, determined to venture ; knowing that, at the worst, we could procure a sufficient supply by crossing to the eastern shore of the lake.

The shore party was provided with as many canteens as were to be found, and we commenced to move the camp; previously establishing a system of signals, by which they might be enabled to find our rendezvous at night. The wading operation had to be undergone as usual, and by noon we were fairly under way. Two long sandspits, or bars, had to be doubled before we could hope to reach any point that would be near the shore party at the termination of their day's work. This was finally accomplished by dint of dragging and wading, and we at length turned in to what, from the boat, we supposed to be the shore. But when within something less than a mile of it, the boat again grounded, and the usual consequences followed. When we reached the beach, before us lay a boundless flat of white sand, only a few inches above the water-level of the lake. A line of artemisia-bushes appeared to be about half a mile distant, and we bent our steps toward it for the purpose of encamping. But the mirage was so great that we found ourselves much deceived in the distance. Instead of half a mile, the bushes were more than two miles off; and after travelling upward of a mile, I concluded to encamp where we were, and to go to the fringe of green for wood enough to cook with. This was accordingly done, and in our search we stumbled on two very pretty little streams of fresh, cool water, within a half-mile of the camp, but which, after flowing a short distance, sank in the sand and disappeared. Upon the banks of one of the creeks was a patch of long, dry, matted grass, which had been beaten down by the winter snows. To this I set fire, as a signal to the shore party of our whereabouts. A huge column of smoke immediately rose to the heavens, and completely answered the purpose. The party, nevertheless, did not get into camp before ten o'clock at night, having been perplexed in the dark by salt creeks and marshes. There was but little joking or music in camp to-night, as the unwearied fiddle had been left in the boat, and the men were thoroughly tired out.

The shore party, to-day, in running their line, crossed several quite large streams of good fresh water; and upon the termination of the day's work, came upon one, eighty feet wide and ten feet deep, by measurement, and flowing with a full current. All of these spring-branches burst forth on the old storm-line of the lake, but none of them ever enter it. They doubtless take their rise in the mountains to the north and north-west, and percolating through the sands, or passing in veins underneath the surface, break forth suddenly into bold streams, with abundance of water, which in a short distance fork and spread out into shallow channels, form a sort of marsh, and are finally altogether absorbed by the sand, long before they reach the lake. In the channels, and on the margin of the streams, grow reeds, dagger-grass, and some cat-tail flags. Numerous insects congregate in the brackish waters of the marshes, affording food for plover, gulls, and innumerable waterfowl. These streams afforded the last fresh water that we found on the western shore of the lake.

Friday, May 17.—Moved camp, taking with us in the boats the shore party, who wished to be landed south of the marshes and mud-flats they had waded through yesterday. The flat where we landed was six miles wide, and covered, in many places, with salt. The nearest wood was at a point of bluff which bounded the plain to the westward. Transporting fuel on men's shoulders, this distance, after a hard day's work, was not to be thought of; so we supped on some hard bread and a small piece of dried beef, which fortunately remained, and laid our blankets down on the sand.

The night was fine, notwithstanding a heavy gust in the afternoon from the south-west, accompanied by rain, the principal part of which fell in copious showers upon the mountains around us. The shore party did not arrive until near ten o'clock, being guided to our bivouac by the light of a lantern elevated upon a spade-handle stuck in the sand. They were not a little disappointed at getting no supper, as they were wet, hungry, and tired.

Saturday, May 18.—As it was manifestly impossible for us to remain here any longer without the means of cooking, I determined to move, although the survey was considerably in the rear. The eyes of my assistant, Mr. Carrington, from exposure to the intense glare of the sunlight from the white sands, had become much inflamed, and I was fearful, at one time, that he would be unable to continue the performance of his duties. He was much better to-day, however, and returned to the line of the survey.

The skiff was despatched along the shore to the northward to search for some indication of the large stream of which mention has been made, and which we hoped might, perhaps, approach near enough to the shore to be made available for the purpose of watering. It should be borne in mind that the line of survey, as has been remarked, followed the storm-line of the lake, which (since leaving Turret Rock,) was many miles west of the lake shore.

After getting the camp on board, I determined to go myself in the yawl, and, if water could be found, to fill up every vessel we could spare, as I was entirely ignorant when we could again procure this indispensable article without crossing the lake to the Indian Springs. A scaffold or platform was made of spare oars and tent-poles, elevated upon camp-stools, placed near the boat in a few inches of water, and all the baggage piled upon it, to lighten the boat. We started after the skiff, passed it, and advanced farther to the north, toward a point on the shore where the appearance of some reeds seemed to indicate the presence of water.

Anchoring our boat to keep her from drifting off, we waded some half-mile to the shore, and proceeded nearly three miles inland on our bare feet, over a sandy flat, and plunged through thick, oozy mud nearly knee-deep until we reached the growth of reeds we had seen from the boat. We here found where one of the streams, formerly passed on the survey, had now spread far and wide over the surface of the plain, making a broad marsh with connecting channels, furnishing plenty of water very nearly fresh. Insects of various kinds abounded in great numbers in the shallows, and had attracted vast flocks of wildfowl from the lake, whose waters afforded them literally nothing either to eat or to drink. We filled up our kegs and commenced our return, when a violent gust arose from the north-west. Fearing the consequences, we hastened our steps; but upon arriving in sight of the beach, we found, as we had anticipated, that the water had receded before the wind full half a mile, and our boat, which we left afloat, was now high and dry upon the sand. As she was very heavy and flat-bottomed, we found it beyond our strength to move her, and consequently made up our minds to spend the night where we were, unless the wind should again change and blow from the southward or eastward, and thus cause a reflux of the water, which would set us afloat once more.

The skiff was despatched with some water to the point agreed upon for the night's encampment, and directed to call at the platform for some provisions and blankets for the shore party, while we remained seated in our boat awaiting the movement of the waters. After watching some hours for a change of wind, the men were directed to coil themselves down in the bottom of the boat, and we all tried to get some sleep, which, tired and weary as we were, soon came to our relief. While we were thus unconscious, the wind veered round to the south, and we were driven by the rising waters farther on the shore than ever. It soon ceased, however, and upon rising, at daylight, we were again hard and fast upon the bottom. As the sun rose, a gentle breeze came up from the south, bringing back with it the refluxed waters, which gradually began to deepen around us. It will thus be seen that the rise and fall of the water of any particular locality is dependent in great measure upon the force and direction of the wind, making a difference of nearly a foot in a very short period of time. This of course makes a corresponding difference in the extent of the sand-flats, amounting, in many cases, to miles in width.

The skiff was descried about sunrise coming in search of us; and when she joined us we succeeded, by the united force of both crews, in dragging the boat into deeper water, and set out on our return to camp, little refreshed, as may readily be believed, by a night's repose in the bottom of the boat, without even a blanket to cover us, and a supper and breakfast of raw bacon.

The shore party had shared but little better than ourselves. Having neglected to provide themselves with the means of making a fire when they left camp yesterday morning, they could cook no food, and were consequently restricted to the same delicate fare as that upon which we had so sumptuously regaled.

Owing to the character of the ground, the past week has been one of unusual exposure and fatigue to both parties, while the progress of the survey has been by no means commensurate with our exertions. The difficulty of approaching the shore, the immense extent of the arid sand-plains, together with the distance of water and fuel, and the labour of obtaining them, have made the duties of the boat's crew, who have been constantly wading in the brine of the lake or plunging and floundering through the deep, soft mud of the marshes, extremely arduous and harassing. The task of the shore party has not been less onerous, owing to the great distances between the camp and their work, the glare from the dazzling white sand, the incessant annoyance of the gnats, and the want of proper food and shelter. We console ourselves, however, with the hope that the worst has been overcome, and that the causes of so much vexation and delay will continue to diminish as we advance to the southward.

Our stock of flour being diminished to little more than one sack, the coffee to sufficient for but a few days' consumption, and the fresh beef having entirely disappeared, we were reduced to fat salt pork and fried bread. It became necessary to renew our supply; and preparations were made for a start early in the morning for Antelope Island, sixty miles distant, where the cattle and mules were herded, and whence a team could be despatched to the city for what we needed.

Monday, May 20.—Morning warm and cloudy. The strength of both parties was required to drag the yawl out into water deep enough to float her. After much wading and hauling, this was at length effected, and we set sail. We continued rowing and sailing all the day. At sundown, the wind hauling into the north-west and blowing quite fresh, the crew were sent to their blankets, and I sat at the helm until daylight, occasionally calling the men to the oars when the wind failed.

I shall never forget this night. The silence of the grave was around us, unrelieved by the slightest sound. Not the leaping of a fish nor the solitary cry of a bird was to be heard, as, in profound darkness, the boat moved on, plunging her bows into the black and sullen waters. As we passed within the shadows of the obscure and frowning mountains, the eye was strained in vain to catch some evidence of life. The sense of isolation from every thing living was painfully oppressive. Even the chirp of a cricket would have formed some link with the world of life; but all was stillness and solitary desolation.

At daylight we were still fifteen miles from the island, and the boat was "hove-to" for breakfast, which consisted of bread and cold bacon, without even a drink of water. Before we passed around the point of Antelope Island, we stopped for a few moments at the little islet near it, where the number of gulls and pelicans was, if possible, greater than we had seen on Gunnison's Island. The whole islet was covered with eggs, chiefly those of gulls, and with innumerable young birds, just hatched, the most of which on our appearance instinctively concealed themselves among the crevices of the rocks, while the parent birds, in countless numbers, anxiously hovered over us, filling the air with their discordant cries. Some young herons and cormorants were also found amid this colony of gulls—the former fierce and full of fight, the latter timid and alarmed, running from their nests to the water, where they endeavoured to conceal themselves by persevering but abortive attempts to dive. We filled half a barrel with the eggs, but most of them proved to be bad.

Stopping for a short time to quench our burning thirst, at a spring breaking forth under a ledge of rocks at the foot of a picturesque little bay on the eastern side of Antelope Island, we reached our point of destination at five o'clock in the afternoon, quite worn down by the incessant toil of nearly thirty-six sleepless hours.

I was much gratified to learn from the herdsman the safe arrival of the party I had despatched to the Uintah Mountains last November on a trading expedition, and that they had brought with them nineteen fine horses. As the party on the western shore were nearly out of provisions, a couple of horses were immediately caught, and, accompanied by a single attendant, I started at once for the city, distant twenty-five miles, leaving directions that a team should follow early in the morning, for the purpose of hauling provisions out to the island. We reached our quarters in the city at two in the morning, and retired to rest, thoroughly wearied out.—The Jordan was over its banks from the melting of the snows in the mountains.

Thursday, May 24.—Having laid in all the necessary supplies, we returned to the island to-day, killed a beef, and made all preparations for an early start next day.

The range for cattle on this island is now very fine, and the herd appears in excellent condition. The drove of Indian horses, which had suffered much from the hard winter at Fort Bridger, begins to improve, and many of them are very handsome animals.

Monday, May 28.—Owing to head winds and heavy blows upon the lake, we have been constantly occupied for the last four days in endeavouring to reach our companions on the salt-plains of the western shore—a place which the men had, not inappropriately, distinguished by the title of "Tophet." An hour before sundown we descried the smoke of their camp-fires near a small island on the west coast, called Dolphin Island, and shaped our course accordingly. When it became dark, we made out the camp-fire itself, and hoisted a signal-lantern to let them know that fresh beef, vegetables, and water were near at hand.

At two in the morning we landed, or rather grounded, near what we supposed to be the sand-flat of the main land, north of the island, and apparently some half-mile from the camp. The moon was shining bright and clear, and, anchoring the boat, lest she should drift off before morning, we shouldered our blankets, a keg or two of water, and some pieces of fresh beef, and commenced our tramp for the encampment. Reaching the shore, we trudged on with bare feet for about a mile, over sharp incrustations of salt and sand, when we most unexpectedly came again to water. Judging it to be a mere pool or washing up of the lake, we disregarded so petty an impediment, and continued plodding our weary way through it for about a mile farther, when, finding that it began to grow deeper and deeper, it being then nearly up to the waist, we returned to the flats, and, kindling a fire of sage-brush, lay down upon the sand until daylight. The night was uncomfortably chilly, and a single blanket was but a sorry protection against the cold, damp sand and the searching winds from the neighbouring mountains.

Tuesday, May 28.—A little after sunrise, we perceived some of the shore party approaching in the skiff; and we now found that, instead of landing last night, as we had supposed, on the main, we had struck a wide sand-flat extending northward from the island, had crossed it, and attempted also to cross the channel which separated it from the main shore, when we were driven back by the depth of the water.

After a hearty breakfast on fresh beef-bone soup, which the poor fellows from the region of "Tophet" enjoyed exceedingly, they were despatched after the rest of their company, with directions to join me at once, in order to survey the island upon which we were at present encamped. They were in rather a deplorable condition; their coffee being exhausted—their flour almost gone—and their stock of water reduced to a single five-gallon keg.

The rest of the day was spent in erecting a station upon the highest peaks of the island, and in unloading the yawl upon a platform placed upon kegs and barrels set up in the water, preparatory to hauling her up, she having become so leaky, from thumping on the rocks and being dragged over sand-bars, as to endanger the safety of the provisions. The gnats here were perfectly intolerable, and drove us almost mad.

The character of the country passed over by the line of survey during my absence was much the same as that which had prevailed more to the northward; viz. extended plains, with grease-wood and sage. Water, there was none; and our sole dependence was now upon the supply to be furnished by the boat from the eastern side of the lake.

The detritus from the mountains, whenever encountered, consisted principally of compact sandstone, abundance of calcareous tufa, coarse sandstone, and conglomerate. From the report of Mr. Carrington, of a partial examination made by him of the range west of Dolphin Island, it consists of calcareous tufa and conglomerate, overlying which was argillaceous limestone of various colours and texture, extending to the base of the short spurs of the ridges; above this was found black, bluish, and gray limestone, very compact and fine grained, veined with calc spar; above this again, was an inferior or earthy limestone, overlaid by a brownish-gray fossiliferous limestone, capped by an argillaceous limestone, which extended to the summit of the range. The vegetation was the ever-recurring artemisia, bunch-grass, and a few scattering dwarf cedars not more than ten feet high.

On the flats near the lake, and immediately west of the island, a large field of solid salt occurred, beautifully crystallized upon the sand, about half an inch thick; and the crystals, from one to two inches in diameter, glittered in the bright sunshine like a bed

GUNNISON'S ISLAND AND STATION - FROM THE NORTH.

of diamonds. The evaporation of the shoal water between the island and the main shore has left this beautiful deposite of salt, which must rapidly increase in extent as the season advances.

Wednesday, May 29.—Before breakfast, all hands hauled up the yawl into a few inches of water, and turned her over to dry, preparatory to caulking and pitching. The survey of Dolphin Island was completed to-day. The summit is some seventy feet above the level of the water, and the island consists mainly of conglomerate in horizontal strata, and varying much in the size of the cemented stones.

To day I made my first essay as a caulker :—caulked, payed, and painted the boat; and although it may not have been very artistically done, yet it fully answered the purpose. I found that the brine of the lake had acted very sensibly upon the iron fastenings of the boat, corroding them much more rapidly than ordinary sea-water would have done.

This day one year ago the expedition left Fort Leavenworth. Of the original members of the party only four now remain: the rest having broken their engagements and gone to the gold-mines. Those that left last autumn by the Little Salt Lake route, were, as we heard, stripped by the Indians of all they possessed, and left to find their way to the land of promise as they could.

Friday, May 30.—Morning calm and pleasant, all hands up early to move camp. The yawl was turned over and launched, and found, to our great satisfaction, to leak but little. As we were again short of water, I determined to run over to Gunnison's Island, and make a survey of its shores, while the boat crossed to the eastern side of the lake to obtain a supply. We landed at two P. M. upon the shores of the same beautiful little bay, with its rocky points and white-sand beach, which had so much delighted us when we first visited the island. Our friends, the gulls and pelicans, had by no means decreased in numbers; the former filling the air with their interminable chattering, which continued the whole night, and formed a most striking contrast to the chilling and deathlike silence of the surrounding shores. The little bay is covered with their forms floating lightly and gracefully upon the undulating waters, and unceasingly engaged in earnest conversation ; while flocks of the more dignified pelicans drew off in separate groups, as if in silent contempt of their more garrulous neighbours.

The island is surrounded by bold, clear, and beautifully translucent water, and is, for its size, one of the most pleasant upon which we have landed. Immediately north, and distant but a hundred yards, is a small rocky islet, which has at one time formed a part of the main island, the bar by which they are connected being plainly visible beneath the water. The space between them forms a beautiful and romantic little bay, with deep, blue water, clear as crystal. The northern end of the main island is a nearly perpendicular cliff of black and gray limestone, between five and six hundred feet in height.

Immediately upon landing, the yawl was unloaded upon the beach, as I intended to despatch her for water across the lake to the Indian Springs—the nearest point where it could be obtained without transporting it from the interior to the boat on the men's shoulders. The skiff, which had started with us from Dolphin Island, had not yet arrived, and I only waited her coming up to take from her some empty kegs, which it was desirable to fill. Toward sundown, the wind began to rise from the south-west and to blow very fresh. It gradually hauled into the west and north-west, and blew most furiously, but favourably for the destined point. Desirous of taking advantage of the gale, I directed the boat to put off without waiting any longer for the skiff, and she was soon lost to the view in the mist and gloom to leeward. The distance to the springs was about twenty miles, which may give an idea of some of the difficulties which had to be encountered in prosecuting the examination of these solitary waters.

Soon after the commencement of the gale, it began to hail violently, accompanied by a darkness and mist which made me uneasy for the safety of the skiff, especially as she had been seen a short time previous about two miles to the westward. Having waited until nearly dark, I concluded that she had been blown past the island by the sudden fury of the gust, and must consequently be in great danger of being lost. We were, however, utterly powerless to aid her, and our only hope for her safety was that she might encounter the yawl, which was seen, shortly after leaving the island, to haul up suddenly to the northward. One of the lookouts reported that he thought he had seen them approaching each other far to leeward. A man sent to a commanding peak with a telescope was "almost sure" that he had seen the two boats together before the thickening mist hid every thing from view. This afforded us some relief, although we were filled with deep anxiety for the fate of our companions, all of whom were young men, and inexperienced in the management of boats, although perfectly competent to guide one over the calm and tranquil waters upon which we had put forth in the morning. All the tent-poles and cooking utensils were in the missing skiff; and as the night threatened to be cold and stormy, a temporary shelter from the weather was hastily erected with spare oars and some drift-wood, which, being covered with a couple of tents, proved a very tolerable substitute for our usually more comfortable quarters.

In a ramble around the shores of the island, I came across a venerable-looking old pelican, very large and fat, which allowed me to approach him without attempting to escape. Surprised at his apparent tameness, we examined him more closely, and found that it was owing to his being perfectly blind; for he proved to be very pugnacious, snapping fiercely, but vaguely, on each side, in search of his enemies, whom he could hear, but could not see. As he was totally helpless, he must have subsisted on the charity of his neighbours, and his sleek and comfortable condition showed that, like beggars in more civilized communities, he had "fared sumptuously every day." The food of these birds consists entirely of fish, which they must necessarily obtain either from Bear River, from the Weber, the Jordan, or from the warm springs on the eastern side of Spring Valley, at all of which places they were observed fishing for food. The nearest of these points is more than thirty miles distant, making necessary a flight of at least sixty miles to procure and transport food for the sustenance of their young. Immense numbers of the young birds are huddled together in groups about the islands, under the charge of a grave-looking nurse or keeper, who, all the time that we were there, was relieved from guard at intervals, as regularly as a sentinel. The goslings are an awkward, ungainly mass of fat, covered with a fine and exceedingly thick down of a light colour.

The island, which is an irregular ridge of rock, protruded from beneath, consists of the same compact limestone as that observed at Flat Rock. Between the water and storm line, on the western beach, coarse and fine conglomerate or pudding-stone is found in broad laminæ, very hard, and generally inclined to the slope of the beach. The layers, or slabs, are of various thickness, and would make excellent pavements.

Saturday, June 1.—As the watering party was still absent, I took such force as remained on the island, to the summit of the high peak, to rebuild the station previously erected there, which, from

13

a distance, I had found to be not sufficiently conspicuous. As the morning was exceedingly hot and sultry, and the ascent of the cliff difficult and toilsome, we imprudently left our upper garments in the camp, and continued our labour upon the station until the middle of the afternoon; when a squall, which had been threatening all the day, burst upon us from the north-west, with great fury, accompanied with vivid lightning and heavy thunder. The sky was black as midnight, and the reverberations of the awful peals of thunder from the surrounding mountains was solemn and sublime. Before the storm came up, the boat with water had been descried to the northward, with both sails set, and I had watched her with great anxiety, as I had but little confidence in the skill of those who had her in charge, and was fearful the squall would come upon them unprepared. I bitterly reproached myself for allowing her to go without me; as, in case of her loss, which, at the time, seemed highly probable, not only would the lives of her crew be sacrificed, but we, who remained on this barren rock, without the means of leaving it and destitute of water, must have miserably perished. To my great relief, however, I saw, through the glass, the sails furled, the masts taken down, and the boat brought to anchor just as the gust struck her, burying every thing in mist and darkness. I thought, too, that I made out the skiff in tow, but was not certain, as the distance was too great. The storm lasted more than an hour—the wind blew a hurricane, and it hailed with great violence, covering the ground in a few minutes with hailstones as large as peas. We sheltered ourselves as well as we could behind some rocky cliffs; but, being thinly clad, we became uncomfortably cold; and, as soon as the hail ceased, we hastened, wet to the skin, to descend to our camp, glad to escape from the piercing wind which swept in furious gusts over our elevated pinnacle.

The yawl, soon after, came into the bay, with the missing men on board, but without the skiff, which, though recovered, had broken adrift in the gale, parting an inch cable, doubled, by which she had been fastened. It appeared, as we had hoped, that those in the yawl had seen the skiff yesterday in the storm, and had succeeded in picking her up. The men in her were without their coats, exposed to the peltings of the hail-storm, sea-sick, almost frozen, and nearly scared to death. Had they not been rescued, they must have suffered terribly, if indeed they had not perished, as they had nothing to eat; their boat at the time was half-full of water, and they incapable, from sea-sickness and fright, of making any further exertion for their safety. Had they used ordinary diligence in the morning, they might easily have reached the island before the storm commenced, and saved themselves much suffering and their companions no less anxiety. The loss of the skiff is severely felt—the nature of the shore being such that the large boat, when loaded, cannot, in many places, approach within two or three miles of the land, and the lighter vessel is therefore indispensable. I was rejoiced that no lives were lost, which there was, at one time, serious reason to apprehend.

We found that the hail had killed a large number of the young pelicans, as, upon the approach of the gust, they had been deserted by their parents, who had betaken themselves to the protection of the neighbouring rocks, leaving their tender offspring to " bide the peltings of the pitiless storm." So much for the ancient fable of their feeding their young from their own veins!

Sunday, June 2.—Last night the wind was from the southeast, which induced me to hope that the skiff might have been drifted somewhere into our neighbourhood, and a man was despatched to the top of one of the cliffs, with a glass, to look out for her. He soon returned, and reported that he had made out what he believed to be the boat, four or five miles to the southward. This was joyful intelligence, and we immediately started after her. We found her in the spot indicated, nearly full of water, but with all the baggage undisturbed. After picking her up, we directed our course still farther to the southward, toward a high peak, which appeared to be either an island or a peninsula. We found it to be the latter, connected by a broad sandbar with a broken rocky range, which forms the northern termination of the ridge bounding Spring Valley on the west, and which I had crossed in November last, on my reconnoissance of the western shore of the lake. We gave it the name of " Strong's Knob."

After strolling a couple of miles on the sand-flat of the main shore, beneath high, broken, perpendicular cliffs of black limestone, being desirous of obtaining a view of the south-western portion of the lake, we ascended one of the highest peaks, from the summit of which rose a perpendicular oblong mass of rocks, which, from its singular resemblance to that article of dress, we called " Cloth Cap." The day was warm, and the mountain up which we clambered from eight hundred to a thousand feet in height. With considerable labour we reached the top, and were

richly rewarded for our toil.   Beneath us, to the west, lay an extended plain of bare, arid sand—stretching, apparently, to the
great range of mountains forming the ancient barrier of the lake-
waters in that direction.   The water-line of the lake bounded this
flat on the north.   South-west from the water, and bounded on the
east by the range upon which we stood, an immense flat stretched
far to the southward, until its termination was lost in the haze
which pervaded the atmosphere.   This, doubtless, comprised within
its dreary waste the desert over which we had passed the preceding autumn.

To the east and north-east lay the lake in calm and placid
beauty; while to the south stretched the broken and rugged mountain upon which we were standing, whose fantastic peaks stood out
in bold relief against the pure and azure sky.   But, beautiful and
interesting as was this vast panorama of mountain, plain, and water, the view to the northward and westward was any thing but
encouraging.   In continuation of the survey, the distance from this
point to Dolphin Island *must* be traversed; but *how*, was a question much more easily asked than answered.

The cliff, or conical peak, which we climbed to-day, consists of
black and gray limestones, of various textures, and all of it highly
fossiliferous, its character, in this respect, becoming more marked
as we ascended, until we reached the summit, called the " Cap,"
which is almost entirely formed of a mass of *cyathophyllæ*, imbedded in limestone, constituting a complete conglomerate of these
fossils.   About halfway up the ascent, was a dark, coarsely granular
limestone, crystalline, and filled with minute fossils of *Ortris*.

The cliffs were veined in many places with fine white, fibrous calc
spar, half an inch thick, some of which was beautifully variegated
and stained by iron.   At the western base of the mountain, we
found quite a large cave, the walls of which were incrusted, in
places, with salt, half an inch thick; and *cyathophyllæ* projected
abundantly from its sides.

On our return to camp, a line of soundings was taken from the
knob to the island: the deepest water found was ten feet.

Tuesday, June 4.—The last two days have been occupied in
surveying the island, in finishing the station upon its summit, and
reconstructing that on Dolphin Island, which had been destroyed
by the storm of Saturday.   Our stock of water being reduced to
less than one day's supply, I started at sundown for the eastern
side of the lake, to renew it, determining to run all night, so as to

return to-morrow, if possible. We left but five gallons in the camp, and took the same quantity with us for our voyage.

The water in the lake, from Gunnison's Island to "the springs," is bold and deep, averaging from fifteen to twenty feet, within a hundred yards of the shore, and reaching in some places thirty-six feet. After rowing till midnight, a slight breeze sprang up, which enabled us to set our sails, and advance, though slowly, on our course. The men had been much fatigued before we started, by a hard day's work in climbing the rocks and rebuilding the stations; so they were sent to their blankets in the bottom of the boat, an order which they most promptly obeyed, and were soon buried in profound repose. The stillness of this beautiful night, as I sat at the helm, guiding our little bark over the solitary waters of this mysterious sea, was most impressive.

> "Silence how dead! and darkness how profound!
> Nor eye nor listening ear an object finds."

The moon rose bright and clear over the rugged cliffs of the promontory, as, an hour before daybreak, we landed at our little pier of stones; and ere long the gray tints of dawn began to appear, followed by the blush of a most lovely morning.

A fire was soon kindled, coffee-pots and camp-kettles made their appearance, and in a short time a smoking breakfast was spread upon a little patch of grass, of which all partook with a keenness of appetite little dreamed of by more refined but less favoured mortals. In less than an hour we had filled our vessels, increased the length and stability of our pier, washed our faces and hands— the first time for ten days, (as water was too precious an article to be wasted for any purpose other than drinking and cooking,)—and were on our way back to camp, where, favoured by a noble breeze from the south, we arrived at two o'clock. The station on the summit was entirely completed and covered with cloth; and the survey of the island being finished, every preparation was made for an early start for the main shore on the morrow, there to renew the dismal scenes of salt-plains, mud-flats, gnats, and musquitoes.

I noticed this afternoon that the gulls'-eggs, which, when we arrived upon the island lay so thick upon the ground that we could scarcely avoid treading upon them, had now entirely disappeared from the vicinity of the camp. They had undoubtedly been removed by the gulls themselves to some safer place of deposite, but how or when the removal had been effected it was impossible for us to discover.

Thursday, June 6.—We left this encampment with reluctance, as it was the most pleasant one we had yet made in our peregrinations around the lake, and pitched our tents once more upon the inhospitable flats of the main western shore. As it was necessary to get a full view of our present position, which it was impossible to obtain unless from some elevation, I started on foot, in company with Mr. Carrington, for a peak some seven miles to the southward, crossing a broad mud-plain, bordered on the right by a range of hills running off to the north-west. Upon reaching the eminence, it was found to be part of a ridge or rocky projection putting down to the border of the lake from the north-west. It rose abruptly from an immense flat of sand and mud, extending some ten miles westward to the base of another similar ridge, at the northern termination of which we had halted in October last, the day previous to crossing the field of salt and reaching Pilot Peak. To the southward the flat continued unbroken by the least elevation for an apparently indefinite distance.

The question which now presented itself was in what way this sterile desert was to be surveyed. Apart from the consideration of time and expense, water was only to be procured by crossing the lake, bringing it to the shore, and then packing it on the backs of my crew for the chain party. This was obviously impossible, as they could not carry enough in that way to supply both the shore party and themselves while passing to and fro over the plain. In addition to this difficulty, how were the provisions to be carried and cooked? These considerations induced me to hesitate in risking the lives of my people by attempting to penetrate this desert, where the slightest derangement of the measures by which they were to be supplied with water might prove fatal. The appearance of the plain indicated that the lake had not been over it for very many years, for it was thickly grown up with grease-wood; and the great probability, if not positive certainty was, that, as the waters were evidently in a state of subsidence, they would never again overflow it. As, therefore, my object was to survey the shore of the lake in its present stage, I determined to abandon, in this instance, the storm-line, and to run the line of survey to a point west of the water, as it then was, and thence to strike across the flat to Strong's Knob, triangulating upon the prominent points of the

LIMESTONE CLIFF NORTH END OF GUNNISON'S ISLAND.

Ackerman Lith.379.Broadway N.Y.

different ranges, so as to obtain their general shape and distances, and sketching in the intervening ground. This course would secure all the ends of practical utility, without the hazard and delay to be incurred by penetrating the desert.

The hill from which we made our reconnoissance was about three hundred feet high, and consisted of coarsely granular and earthy limestone, terminating to the northward in a perpendicular cliff of the same formation, in horizontal strata of only a few inches in thickness from top to bottom, the whole of which was in a state of rapid disintegration.

Friday, June 7.—As it was not expected that the line could reach Strong's Knob before the following day, and there was no intervening point that could be reached by the larger boat, provisions ready cooked and the blankets of the shore party were transferred to the skiff, whose crew was directed to coast along the shallow water as far south as they could get, and then to land in the bight of the bay and await the coming up of the line. Some drift-wood was cut up and loaded into their boat, to enable them to boil coffee for supper and breakfast. The main camp was taken to Strong's Knob, and pitched at the base of the lofty rocky peak which composes it, and which is about seven hundred feet high.

Saturday, June 8.—Morning warm and sultry. A station was erected to-day upon the highest peak of this peninsula. A circular stone enclosure was built up about five feet high, within which the feet of a tripod, made of drift-wood poles, were placed, after the area had been filled in with stones and gravel; the wall was then continued, and the feet of the tripod secured by being built therein. The whole was covered with cotton cloth of different colours, and presented an object that could be easily distinguished in clear weather at a distance of twenty miles.

After completing the station, and while taking a series of angles upon the surrounding peaks and stations, a most furious gale, with low muttering thunder, came up suddenly from the south, which made it difficult to stand erect in our exposed position. With the gale came a mist, which shortly enveloped the lake and surrounding mountains, rendering objects a few miles distant so indistinct as at once to put an end to my observations; and the gale at length rose to such a height that the instrument had to be removed to the shelter of a neighbouring cliff to save it from destruction. The skiff, with the camp-equipage of the shore party, came in about noon. The party itself had bivouacked on the sand the night previous, and were seen from the station, just before the storm came up, making good progress across the flat toward the Knob. As they did not make their appearance at dark, a couple of men were sent to the west end of the Knob to make signal-fires to guide them in. These fires were kept up until nearly midnight, and supper postponed in expectation of their arrival. The lookouts, on their return, reported that they had seen fires to the southwest, and that after waiting for the party more than an hour, had concluded that they must have been unable to find their way in, owing to the darkness. I was quite uneasy about them, as I knew they must be suffering for water, having with them only what they could carry in their canteens. There was no help for it, however, and, about midnight, we took our supper and retired to rest. A number of specimens were added to the herbarium to-day.

Sunday, June 9.—Mr. Carrington came in with his party a little after sunrise. They had struck from the flats to the north point of the range, instead of the peninsula to the north of it, which, intervening between them and our camp-fires, had concealed us from their view. Not finding the camp, as they expected, they had followed along the shore (which here turns to the southward) for five miles in search of it, but being disappointed, had returned to the point which they had first reached, kindled a fire, and lain down on the sand for the night, without either blanket or food. They did not see our signal-fires before reaching this point, as their faces were turned to the south, and, when they did descry them, were too much exhausted to come in. They had suffered much from want of water, but were in good spirits.

A heavy thunder-gust came up in the afternoon, with violent wind from south-west, and more rain than we had seen since we left Salt Lake City. Just before dark, the yawl was despatched across the lake to the springs for water, with instructions to cover the station near them with white cloth, and return as speedily as possible. Evening dark and threatening. The gusts here are short, but the wind very violent, driving the sand before it with great force and velocity.

Monday, June 10.—Dark and lowering early in the morning, with some rain, and the prospect of a wet day. But it soon cleared off, with a brisk cool wind from the north, which anywhere else would have given a clear transparent atmosphere. It seems, however, a striking peculiarity of this climate, that no matter from what quarter the wind may come, nor how great its force, the air continues to be hazy, so that it is impossible to see any distant object with distinctness. Whether it be owing to the elevation and consequent rapid evaporation from the lake, I cannot say, but it occasions great vexation and delay in the observations upon distant objects, and renders the work liable to uncertainty and error.

About two P. M. a most furious gust came up from the south-west, with heavy thunder, and a copious shower of rain and hail-stones as large as hazel-nuts. The squall lasted about twenty minutes, forcing the water up over the beach, overthrowing the tents a second time, completely flooding us with brine, and forcing us to re-pitch our camp higher up the beach. In the course of an hour a fresh gust came up from the west, but it soon hauled into the north, and blew with fury all the night. The weather was quite cold, and the wind piercing, so that we were obliged to bank up the bottoms of the tents, inside and out, with large stones and sand, to keep them from being blown away, and to exclude the chilling blast, which rendered great-coats indispensable to comfort. The yawl is doubtless out on the lake to-night, and the crew exposed to all the inclemency of the storm.

Tuesday, June 11.—The gale still continues, the temperature resembles that of an October morning much more than one in June. Closed tents at breakfast, and the survey party running their line buttoned up to the throat. The morning is bright and clear with flying clouds. The haze, however, envelops the sides of the distant mountains in a mist which renders their outlines distorted and indistinct. The yawl arrived in the course of the morning under oars, having dragged her anchor and drifted to leeward. The night upon the lake, in the open boat, was any thing but agreeable: the gale had raised a heavy sea, which frequently broke over the bows, drenching every one to the skin, wetting their blankets, and rendering sleep impossible. They had reached the promontory on Sunday night, but, in the darkness, had struck it too far north. Yesterday they clothed the station, (which is now quite visible,) filled up their water-vessels, and were about leaving the springs when the storm overtook them. They had very little hail, although in camp it fell very abundantly. They represent the lake as being much higher than when we were last there; owing doubtless to the increased melting of the snows in the mountains, consequent upon the advance of the season. The water, under the influence of the northern blast, rose upon the beach crossed by the line a few days since so as to extend some six or seven miles to the south of it; but this morning it had returned to its old boundaries, upon the subsidence of the gale.

The rock composing Strong's Knob is almost entirely block limestone, very hard and close-grained, veined with spar, and very brittle. Tufa occurs near the base of the hill in large masses, several feet thick, some of which, having formed around large rocks, upon which it had deposited itself, had been precipitated with them from the cliffs above. In other cases, it has formed around the masses after they had fallen, encasing them completely with a shell, frequently two feet thick, and had filled up large interstices between them. Frequently the rock itself has disappeared, leaving the tufa behind, somewhat like a hollow mould after the casting has been removed. At the north-west end of the peninsula is an outcrop of compact sandstone and millstone grit, fifty feet thick, capped by black fossiliferous limestone, slightly inclined. All attempts at taking angles from the station to-day were rendered abortive by the haze which filled the atmosphere and obscured and concealed every distant object. In ascending the mountain, quite a large cave was accidently discovered in the hillside, penetrating about sixty feet, with a width of twenty-five feet and height of ten. It had been the resort of deer and antelope. The rock is black and gray limestone, with some calcareous conglomerate.

Wednesday, June 12.—Moved camp about five miles to the southward. The ridge continues parallel with the shore, and descends by a gentle slope nearly to the water. The shore is rocky with scarcely any sand-flat.

As we were rowing along the shore, we espied an old Indian, with his squaw and papoose, running down the mountain to hail us. We landed, to inquire of him as to the prospect for water ahead of us; but he could give us no information on this subject. He was a Utah digger, and proved to be the same old fellow who had come to us last autumn, in Spring Valley, and who had engaged to bring in a "give-out" mule which we had left behind, for the promised reward of a new blanket. I questioned him about the mule, but he only laughed and would give me no satisfaction. The poor donkey had doubtless furnished his lodge with meat for the winter. He was an old man, nearly sixty, quite naked, except an old breech-cloth and a tattered pair of moccasins. His wife

VIEW FROM STRONG'S KNOB, LOOKING

SOUTH. GREAT SALT LAKE.

was in the same condition precisely, minus the moccasins, with a small buckskin strap over her shoulders in the form of a loop, in which, with its little arms clasped around its mother's neck, sat a female child, four or five years old, without any clothing whatever. She was a fine-looking, intelligent little thing, and as plump as a partridge. The mother seemed to evince much affection for it, and was very much pleased when I threw over its shoulders an old piece of scarlet flannel which had been torn from one of the stations by the wind. I noticed, however, that after they left us, and she thought herself out of our sight, the cloth was fluttering from her own person, and the baby was as destitute as ever. I gave them something to eat, and, what I suspect was more welcome, a hearty draught of water. The poor child was almost famished. The old man was armed with a bow and a few arrows, with which he was hunting for ground-squirrels.

June 13–14.—Moved camp yesterday and to-day, aiming to reach what appeared to be the southern extremity of the spur, at the base of which the line is being run, but were much baffled by shallow water in the attempt. After advancing eight or ten miles, we dragged the boat as near as was possible to the edge of a wide sand-flat, lying between us and the ridge, made a scaffold in the water, and upon it deposited all the provisions, and every thing not needed for immediate use, so as to lighten the boat preparatory to a trip to Antelope Island for water and for another beef from the herd.

Sending the surveying party's camp ashore with three men to pitch it and to cook, I started in the yawl, intending to pass between Stansbury's and Carrington's Islands, which would have made the course very direct. The wind was fresh from the west, and we bowled merrily along over the dense and briny waves, until, upon approaching the passage between the islands, we grounded upon a sandbar, which seemed to stretch from one island to the other, forbidding, apparently, all farther progress in that direction. We then tried to pass to the north-west of Carrington's island, and, for a time, with every prospect of success, when we suddenly found ourselves embayed in a *cul de sac* formed by an extensive sand-flat, which stretched from the island an indefinite distance to the westward.

There was nothing to be done now other than to coast along the edge of this bar until we should be able to get around it to the northward. Night was approaching; the wind was ahead, and rising fast; while lowering clouds spread their black and gloomy pall over the dark, tumultuous waters. With our heavy flat-bottomed boat, rowing against a head wind and a very considerable sea was hard work, especially after a day already spent in severe toil; but we had either to continue on, or to anchor, as there was no shore that we could approach in the dark, on account of the shallowness of the water. We accordingly followed around the edge of the bar, being forced thus to make a circuit of some ten miles, when we finally succeeded in getting to the northward of the shoal, and turned our faces in the proper direction. By this time it was ten o'clock at night, and we had been constantly engaged since daylight. The wind now blowing favourably from the north-west, we again set our sails, the crew was sent to rest in the bottom of the boat, and I continued at the helm during the night.

The western and northern part of this extensive flat (for it is all just above the level of the water) forms, as well as I could judge in the darkness, a hard tufaceous reef, against which a north-west wind dashed the heavy water with great violence. Indeed, for a part of the night, I was guided in my course by the roar of the breakers beating against the reef, reminding me forcibly of similar adventures upon the iron-bound coast of New England, or of the heave of the surf upon the coral-reefs of Florida.

Nothing occurred during the night, except grounding upon the tail of a sand-spit making out to the southward from a little island a few miles north of Carrington's, to which the boys had given the name of " Hat Island." This might easily have been avoided had not the night been so very dark and the lofty range of the Wahsatch Mountains ahead enveloped us in a mantle of such profound blackness that it seemed at every heave of the sea as if we were plunging into the very mouth of Avernus. After shoving the boat over the bar with handspikes, we struck immediately into deep water, and as I now knew every inch of the way, the people again retired to their blankets, being very weary. The night soon began to clear away and the stars to appear, their beams reflected brilliantly in the dense water of the lake. Flashes of vivid lightning blazed up occasionally from behind the mountains, and several meteors, some of great size and dazzling brilliancy, shot down the sky to the north-east. This was the third entire night I had thus spent upon the lake, sitting quietly at the helm, guiding my little bark over its solitary waste. Again was I struck with the deep and profound silence that reigned around me. The night was cold, and I found two great-coats exceedingly welcome.

While passing from camp over the sand-flats, this morning, I observed a quantity of translucent, white, pink, and blood-coloured matter, of a gelatinous, or rather mucilaginous character, spread about in coagulated masses upon the sand, whither it had apparently been washed up from the lake by yesterday's gale. The quantity was considerable, and, if the whole shore was similarly lined, must have been very great. An incredible number of small black flies, also, perfectly covered the white sand near the shore, changing its colour completely—a fact only revealed as the swarms rose upon being disturbed by our footsteps. They, too, had apparently been driven in by the storm; for I afterward discovered that they were almost as thick upon the water as upon the land, moving over its surface with great ease and swiftness. In the shallows left by the receding waters, I noticed also quite a number of ants, (the first I had seen,) drowned seemingly by the overflow. Both of these insects doubtless furnish food for the gulls and snipes, which are almost the only birds found along the shores.

Saturday, June 15.—Daylight found the boat at the mouth of the passage between Frémont and Antelope Islands, and, shortly after, we entered the beautiful little cove on the north-east side of the latter, from the banks of which several springs trickle down from the base of a small cliff of protruding rocks.

The scene was calm and lovely in the extreme. The rays of the rising sun, glancing brightly over the eastern mountains, shone upon the tiny ripples of the placid little bay, upon whose bosom a flock of snow-white gulls was calmly floating; while the green and gently sloping shores, covered with a luxuriant growth of rich and waving grass, contrasted strongly in our minds with the dreary and desolate waste of sand over which we had been roaming for the last month. Several little mocking-birds were singing gayly on the shore, and the shrill, cheerful whistle of the curlew resounded along the beach. Four graceful antelopes were quietly grazing on the grassy slope, while the cry of the wild duck, and the trumpet-note of the sandhill crane were heard in the distance. The whole formed a picture which, in this desolate region, was as welcome as it was rare.

I found, this morning, that my conjecture respecting the food of the gulls had been correct. Across the little bay ran a broad streak of froth or foam, formed by the meeting of counter currents,

and driven in by the wind. Passing through it, I found it filled
with the small black flies, such numbers of which I had noticed
yesterday. In the midst of these were flocks of gulls, floating upon
the water and industriously engaged in picking them up, precisely
as a chicken would pick up grains of corn, and with the same rapidity of motion.

We landed at our first camp-ground near the box-elder tree,
about two hours after sunrise, making twenty-four continuous hours
that I had sat at the helm, without a moment's respite. A messenger was despatched to the person in charge of the cattle, with
directions to drive up the herd, out of which one was selected and
killed. The rest of the crew were engaged in filling the water-vessels from an excellent spring near the shore. Here I enjoyed the
exquisite luxury of washing my face and hands, for the first time in
more than two weeks—water being too scarce an article in the camp
to allow that privilege to any other person than the cook.

About eleven o'clock I had the pleasure of meeting my friend
and efficient assistant, Lieutenant Gunnison, whom I found busily
engaged in pushing forward the field-work of his portion of the
survey, with his accustomed industry and energy. He had completed the survey of the eastern side of the lake, and was at the
time engaged in that of Antelope Island. He brought news of the
arrival of the first mail this year, and a large packet of letters from
home. After concerting measures for meeting on the western shore
of the lake, where our surveys were to join, he returned to his camp.
Every preparation being made for an early start in the morning, I
retired to read my letters and to refresh my weary spirits by repose.

Sunday, June 16.—As the party on the flats was nearly out of
water when we left them, and the weather was so uncertain as to
render the time occupied in our return to them equally so, I determined to leave to-day.

Rounding the north point of Antelope Island, we called at the
little islet to which we had given the name of Egg Island, to look
after our old friends, the gulls and pelicans. The former had
hatched out their eggs, and the island was full of little, half-fledged
younglings, who fled at our approach, and hid themselves under the
first stone they could find. We caught several of them, and amused
ourselves by putting them into the water, when they immediately
followed the instinct of their natures, and paddled away with their
little black feet most assiduously. One poor fellow, about four
inches long, driven by the extremity of his fear, took to the water

of his own accord, when he was swept out by the current to the distance of two or three hundred yards, and seemed quite bewildered by the novelty of his situation. As soon as he was discovered by the old birds, who hovered over our heads by thousands, watching our proceedings with great anxiety and noise, one—the parent, we judged, by its greater solicitude—lighted down by his side, and was soon joined by half a dozen others, who began guiding the little navigator to the shore, flying a little way before him, and again alighting, the mother swimming beside him, and evidently encouraging him in this his first adventure upon the water. The little fellow seemed perfectly to understand what was meant, and, when we sailed away, was advancing rapidly under the convoy of his friends, and was within a few yards of the shore, which he doubtless reached in safety.

The young herons had grown, since our last visit, to nearly their full size, although they were not sufficiently feathered to fly. They, too, fled as fast as they could, and "cached" themselves in the recesses of the rocks. When closely pursued, however, they would turn and fight most fiercely—striking furiously with their long sharp bills as well as with their claws—screaming all the while with a shrill, discordant, and angry note. Those that were too small to leave the nest were equally pugnacious—standing on the defensive, with a watchful and determined eye, which evinced any thing but a disposition to succumb, if attacked. A large number of young cormorants (*Phalacrocorax*) were also seen, who exhibited the same combative spirit when hard pressed; but the greater portion of them ran from the nest to the water, where they gave instant evidence of the peculiar instinct belonging to the species, by desperate attempts to dive, and thus conceal themselves beneath the water. This they were unable to do, owing, I suppose, partly to the great density of the water, and partly to their want of strength. The stench was very offensive, from the quantity of fish brought by the parent birds for the support of their very numerous progeny.

We reached camp about ten o'clock at night, after dragging over the shoals and wading about a mile through soft mud, half-leg deep, and filled with little, sharp rocks, which cut our feet until they bled. A rain-storm came on just before our arrival, with violent wind, which lasted all the night.

Monday, June 17.—As it was manifestly impossible to prosecute the survey any farther south by means of the boats, it was determined to complete the examination of the islands, and then to finish

the remainder of this part of the work from the eastward, employing mules, if possible, to furnish the party making it with provisions
and water.

Both parties, therefore, proceeded to Carrington's Island,
which we reached late in the afternoon, effecting a landing on its
southern shore. It rained heavily and was very cold, with a gale
from the northward; and we landed wet and almost frozen, having
spent one of the most disagreeable days we had yet endured upon
the survey. Continually baffled by shoals, which could not be seen
until the boat grounded upon them, the whole day had been consumed in making a distance which, under ordinary circumstances,
might have been accomplished in a few hours.

The two following days were occupied in the survey of this
island, and of a small one about five miles to the northward of it.
The water between them is quite shoal, the deepest being only six
and a-half feet.

The station previously erected upon the summit of Carrington's
Island had been torn down, doubtless by some wandering Indians,
as we saw the remains of their fires in the immediate vicinity.
They were probably attracted by the cloth with which it was
covered, and must have reached it by wading and swimming to the
island from the mainland.

The slate found when we first landed upon this island abounds
also in various localities. Quartzose rock, generally with a dip of
5° to the south-east, was observed in large boulders on the southern
slope, veined with thick seams of white quartz. Limestone was
also found on the south-west portion of the island, near the base of
the hill. On the north-east point was an outcrop of quartzose rock
plentifully seamed with white and ferruginous quartz. Striated
talcose slate, very much contorted, occurred in the centre of the
island, and, to the west, gray granite, with quartzose conglomerate.
The island is about eight miles in circumference, exclusive of the
flats, which stretch out from it to the southward and westward, and
which are more extensive than the island itself, being terminated
on the west by the rocky reef passed on Friday night.

It abounds in the sego, (*Calochortus luteus*,) which is beginning
to seed, and, with its beautiful white, lily-like flowers, whitens
and enlivens the gentle slopes of the island. A large number of
other plants was also collected here, among which *Cleome lutea, Si-
dalcia neo mexicana, Malvastrum coccineum, Stephanomeria minor,*

Ackerman Lith. 379 Broadway N.Y.

CARRINGTON'S ISLAND, FROM STANSBURY'S ISLAND, WEST SIDE.

a new species of *Malacothix*, and *Grayia spinosa* were the most prominent.

Thursday, June 20.—Moved camp to the north point of Stansbury's Island, and commenced the survey of it, which occupied us until the 26th. This is the second island in point of size in the lake, being twelve miles long and twenty-seven in circumference. Like Antelope Island, it is a high rocky ridge, rising abruptly from the plane of the lake, and reaches, in its greatest elevation, the height of nearly three thousand feet. It is, at this time, in fact, a peninsula, the space between it and the mainland, which formerly was covered by the water, being now occupied by a broad, level plain of sand, thickly overgrown in places by artemisia. The scenery, especially on the eastern side, is in many places wild, rugged, and grand. Peak towers above peak, and cliff beyond cliff, in lofty magnificence, while, crowning the summit, the "dome" frowns in gloomy solitude upon the varied scene of bright waters, scattered verdure, and boundless plains of arid desolation below. The eastern shore, in many parts, affords springs of excellent water, and the numerous tracks of wolves, deer, and antelope, added to the frequent remains of Indian fires, indicate that these spots have long been the favourite haunts of both man and beast. In the vicinity of these springs, the grasses are rich and abundant, and the range for cattle the best I have seen in the country. Both this and Antelope Island have been reserved by the sagacious Mormon authorities for grazing purposes.

In skirting the shores, several plants were collected for preservation; among which were the *Comandra umbellata*, a new genus of *Elymus*, *Stipa juncea*, and the *Elymus striatus*. Various seeds were also gathered.

The western shore of the island is, at this season, so far as we could discover, entirely destitute of water, although, while the snows on the summit are melting, some must doubtless reach it. The party, while engaged here, had to be supplied from the opposite side of the island.

According to previous concert with Lieutenant Gunnison, a beacon-fire was lighted on a commanding eminence on the evening of the 22d, which was immediately responded to by a similar signal from Black Rock. I crossed over to his camp on the following day, to borrow some provisions and arrange for the further prosecution of the survey. It was agreed that while I was completing the survey of this island, the line on the flats, which we

14

were obliged to abandon for a time from want of water, should be resumed and completed by Lieutenant Gunnison, his provisions and water being transported upon mules.

On our return from his camp, we had not proceeded more than a mile, before a sudden and violent gust, accompanied with lightning and thunder, drove us to the shore for safety, our little skiff being too small and fragile to withstand the fury of the waves. I have had frequent occasion to remark in what a very short time a gust, sweeping down from the mountains, will lash the heavy water of the lake into waves of very considerable magnitude. The seas are short, and the commotion as suddenly subsides with its exciting cause. The rise and fall of the waters on the shores is thus occasioned, and frequently precedes the current of air by which it is produced.

Wednesday, June 26.—The survey of the island shore being completed, the whole party ascended to the highest peak to erect a triangulation station upon it. The day was intensely hot, and the sun beat down upon the eastern slope, as we climbed up its rugged sides, with a force that was very oppressive. Every man was packed, like a mule, with tools and provisions; but principally with water, in India-rubber bags and canteens.

After a severe climb of some three hours, through rich bunchgrass near the base, artemisia and grease-wood higher up, and, still higher, over rocky projections covered with stunted cedar, we at length reached the summit of the "dome." From this point, the highest within the circuit of the lake, we had expected to enjoy a noble view of both it and the surrounding islands and mountains; but, unfortunately, the atmosphere was filled with so thick a haze that our hopes were wholly disappointed. In our ascent, quite a variety of plants were collected and carefully preserved. Among these, several have been ascertained by Professor Torrey, to whom the whole collection has been submitted for examination, to be new species; among others, a *Heuchera, Peretyle, Cowania,* and *Chenactis.*

After resting under the shadow of some wide-spreading cedartrees, (the first shade we had enjoyed for months,) the summit of the peak was cleared, and a circular wall built, five feet high, of stone, upon the top of which was erected a triangulation station of wood, covered with cloth. An attempt was made to take some observations here with the theodolite, but the atmosphere was so filled with vapour that they were not at all satisfactory.

EAST SIDE OF STANSBURY'S ISLAND.

The island where we descended is a ridge composed of a stratum of white siliceous sandstone, two hundred feet thick, underlying one of black and gray limestone, which latter constituted its summit, and was filled with fossils of *Cystiphyllnm, Syringipora, Favosites, Fenestella, Streptilasma,* and *crinoidal joints, lima* in crystalline limestone, and *cyathophyllæ.* In our return from the top of the mountain, we followed the narrow, dry bed of a ravine or cañon that had been formed by the rush of a torrent of melting snows in the spring of the year. It was amazing to see what huge masses of rock had been moved by this agency—many of several tons weight having been carried far into the plain below. As we descended, the gorge, which had at first been almost shut up between perpendicular cliffs of white sandstone, opened out into a superb, wide, and gently sloping valley, sheltered on each side by beetling cliffs to the very water's edge, effectually protected from all winds, except on the east, and covered with a most luxuriant growth of rich and nutritious bunch-grass.

Near the shore of the lake, abundant springs of pure, soft water gush forth, amply sufficient for the consumption of all the stock the valley could supply with food. As a range for cattle, it was all that could be desired; and is superior to either Tuilla Valley or Antelope Island, on account of the complete protection it affords from the storms of winter, here both long and severe.

To-day has been one of severe suffering, from the insufficient supply of water we were able to carry with us, every drop of which was consumed long before we commenced our descent from the mountain.

Thursday, June 27.—The survey of the lake was finished yesterday, having occupied the incessant labour of nearly three months. Nothing now remained but to complete the observations upon the different triangulation stations that had been erected in the course of the examination. The camp was broken up, and we returned to our depôt on Antelope Island; discharged such of the hands as were no longer required, procured a fresh supply of provisions from the city, and, on *Wednesday, July 3d,* started on our tour around the lake, leaving three men upon the island, to take charge of the herd and to prepare the pack-saddles required for our return to the States.

The triangulation of this part of the survey occupied us until the 16th, during which time the lake was again traversed in every direction, and observations were taken from the various stations that had been erected upon prominent headlands on the shore and on the summits of the several islands.

While engaged upon this duty, we frequently enjoyed the luxury of bathing in the water of the lake. No one, without witnessing it, can form any idea of the buoyant properties of this singular water. A man may float, stretched at full length, upon his back, having his head and neck, both his legs to the knee, and both arms to the elbow, entirely out of water. If a sitting position be assumed, with the arms extended to preserve the equilibrium, the shoulders will remain above the surface. The water is nevertheless extremely difficult to swim in, on account of the constant tendency of the lower extremities to rise above it. The brine, too, is so strong, that the least particle of it getting into the eyes produces the most acute pain; and if accidentally swallowed, rapid strangulation must ensue. I doubt whether the most expert swimmer could long preserve himself from drowning, if exposed to the action of a rough sea.

Upon one occasion a man of our party fell overboard, and, although a good swimmer, the sudden immersion caused him to take in some mouthfuls of water before rising to the surface. The effect was a most violent paroxysm of strangling and vomiting, and the man was unfit for duty for a day or two afterward. He would inevitably have been drowned had he not received immediate assistance. After bathing, it is necessary to wash the skin with fresh water, to prevent the deposite of salt arising from evaporation of the brine. Yet a bath in this water is delightfully refreshing and invigorating.

The analysis of this water by Dr. Gale has shown that it contains rather more than 20 per cent. of pure chloride of sodium, and not more than 2 per cent. of other salts, forming "one of the purest and most concentrated brines known in the world." Its specific gravity was 1.17, but this will slightly vary with the seasons, being doubtless affected by the immense floods of fresh water which come rushing down into it from the mountains, in the spring, caused by the melting of the snows in the gorges.

Thursday, July 16.—To-day we took a final leave of this singular lake. The difficulty of finding water fit for the ordinary purposes of life—the necessity of transporting, by means totally inadequate, every pound of provisions and every drop of water needed for the daily consumption of a large party of men—the unavoidable distance of our depôt, and the barren, savage inhospi-

PEAK ON EAST SIDE OF STANSBURY'S ISLAND—ANTELOPE I IN THE DISTANCE.

Ackerman Lith.r 379 Broadway NY.

tality of the region we were obliged to traverse, have made this survey one of unusually arduous and protracted toil. But the salubrity of the climate is such that, notwithstanding our constant exposure to the vicissitudes of the elements, a large portion of the time without the protection of tents, not a man was seriously unwell, and most of the party were in the uninterrupted enjoyment of robust health.

The survey of the eastern side of the lake had, in the mean time, been completed by the party under Lieutenant Gunnison. The following extract from his report to me, will sufficiently exhibit the character of this portion of the valley :—

"To recapitulate and give the result of the field-notes. Two lines have been located, the shore of the lake and base of the hills, in order to give the flat occupied by the farmers. These lines are determined by the three-point problem, as numerous points of the triangulation afforded facilities, and we had no boat on the lake.

"The land on the north of Bear-river Bay, ten miles wide to the base of the hills, is a clay barren. Numerous springs issue from the hills, which soon sink. They are all more or less brackish, but seem to answer well for cattle. There is fine pasturage in the high grounds. The clay-flat has numerous buttes about six feet above the lower plain : these are islands left by the washing down of the original level, and have nearly perpendicular sides. The lake waters are driven by storms over the flat and wash off from the buttes, which will soon disappear. Drift-wood is found some miles from the present shore. Light carriages can be taken over the flat near the Bear River outlet and along the shore : the shore intervening, to the hills, is soft and impracticable. In the Salt Lake Valley, on the Bear and Malade rivers, is some excellent soil for grain. Fifty miles could be irrigated, but the expense would be heavy in constructing a dam at the " gates"—that is, where Bear River breaks through the Wahsatch range. The river at the ferry was two hundred feet wide and twelve deep."

" Near the river, and twelve miles below the " gates," are the hot and cold springs. They issue at the foot of the flanking terrace of hills, and have excavated for themselves a circular hole, fifteen feet deep, with sloping sides and a deep channel leading into the meadow. There are currents issuing between different strata of conglomerate and limestone, within a few feet of each other, of which one is a hot sulphur, a second warm and salt, and the third cool, drinkable water. At numerous places fine salt is brought up and jets of gas emitted: the salt forms an incrustation around the hole, and is pure enough for table use. Some small rivulets descend from the mountains as you proceed south; two of which, fed by springs, could be used for irrigation and enrich farms of one hundred acres each."

" Box-elder is a beautiful stream of clear, sparkling water, except when swollen in the spring by the rapidly melting snow. It was swelled into a large river during the survey, and overflowed all its banks. This stream, and the two south, to Bright Creek, can be carried over some excellent land, and made to water ground enough for five thousand people."

" Red Springs are hot waters, impregnated with iron, which is deposited and colours the ground crimson red: hence the name. The salt-flats extend from the lake to this point, and a low flat sweeps round to Weber River, of the clay barren character, between the north branch of the river and Mud Island. The river was now swollen, and filled several channels over this flat, entering the lake to the northward; and many were ten feet deep, with a swift current. At the mouths they shoal, but were very uncomfortable to ford, as we did, by wading, as the water was of the temperature of melting ice and snow."

" In the angles of Red-spur and Main range are small streams for farming purposes; but the Ogden river, as it bursts out of a narrow cañon, furnishes an opportunity for mill privileges and irrigating canals seldom equalled. On its bank is the site of Ogden City. Beautiful meadows, the river-level of which is subject to overflow, are below the junction with the Weber; and I estimate forty square miles on these streams as capable of cultivation."

" The freshets had swept off all the bridges, and embarrassed us much. To survey the delta of Weber and cross the rivers required boats. We obtained hides, and, by the aid of some Flathead Indians, constructed a "bull-boat," by taking willow rods and laying a keel and longitudinal ribs between two stakes driven into the ground, marking the length, and then cross-sticks, tied with thongs, making the skeleton of a canoe. Three hides were sewed together; the sides of the centre one and one end of each of the others being joined and then softened in water: they were now stretched over the willow-work, and the seams made tight by a composition of melted tallow and ashes. Our wagons were taken into parts, a rope was stretched over a foaming, tossing, boiling

ENTRANCE TO THE VALLEY OF THE WEBER RIVER.

Ackerman Lith 379 Broadway N.Y.

torrent, at a narrow chasm, where the banks were high enough for landing, and then the frail, bending boat, by repeated journeys, carried us all over safe, with our baggage and instruments. It was a severe day's work, however, and the risk of life and property very great; but the only insurance to be had was in the company of prudence, skill, and perseverance."

"Between Weber and Ogden the land is too high for irrigation, except by some rivulets which afford but a small supply. Along the Weber, below the cañon, is a narrow meadow strip, and to the south a flanking spur from the mountains, of six successive terraces, ten miles broad, and sloping to the lake. These are grazing lands for Weber settlement. South of the terrace pastures commences a series of creeks of bright, sparkling water, that irrigate a strip of land averaging two miles in width, and extending to the vicinity of Hot Spring, three miles from Salt Lake City. This includes Miller's and Session's settlements, and is covered with lovely fields and gardens. From the hot spring to the city are numerous warm fountains that deposite gypsum and other sulphates. These waters give delightful baths, but destroy the fertility of the soil. The south shore-line of the lake, from the mouth of Jordan River, was measured by the chain on the soft, sandy beach and barrens. The line of the Jordan river was previously chained, and I passed over the traverse range with the triangulation in the valley of Lake Utah. From the Jordan cañon to Dry Cotton-wood is a grazing range. At the outlet of the lake there is a reed marsh which, by early cutting the dense growth, a pretty hay can be made. It will be difficult to obtain irrigable land until we reach the Spring creek, and we have to rely on the American Fork for water to irrigate with. A beautiful and wide bottom land lies along the lake shore, for some miles under the control of this stream; and from the crossing to the heads of Pomont-quint is a rich alluvial soil, mixed with vegetable mould. A series of rolling, round hills now occur between the Pomont creek and Timpanogas, well grassed for cattle ranges. On the Timpanogas bottoms wheat grows most luxuriantly, and root-crops are seldom excelled. A continuous field can be made thence to the Wa-ke-te-ke creek, and the lovely Utah valley made to sustain a population of more than a hundred thousand inhabitants. The west of the lake is grazing land, and a road on this side to the southern settlements is the natural line of travel from the capital city below. Warm springs issue near the outlet, and the mists from the cooling waters give at all seasons the appearance of rising smoke and steam from a manufacturing hamlet. A limestone quarry is located here. The water on the west side of the lake is bold, and much of the way a towline might be used to propel boats. The Jordan is too crooked and shallow in places for boating. A magnificent water-power exists at the cañon, very accessible for teams; and here the river could be led out along the western or eastern base of the hills, for either manufacturing or irrigating purposes."

The following summary exhibits the amount of work done in prosecuting this examination:

1. The selection and measurement of a base line, six miles in length.
2. The erection of twenty-four principal triangulation stations, the lumber for many of which was hauled a distance of upward of thirty miles. Many of these, put up in the fall of 1849, had to be renewed in the summer of 1850, having been torn down and used for fuel by the Indians during the winter, as well as by some of the inhabitants, who probably supposed they had already fulfilled the purpose for which they were erected.

	Miles.
3. The survey of the Great Salt Lake, the shore line of which, exclusive of offsets, extends to	291
4. The survey of the islands in the lake	96
5. The survey of Utah lake	76
6. The survey of the River Jordan connecting the two lakes and some tributaries	50
Making in all	513

7. The observations from different triangular stations, extending from the northern extremity of the Salt Lake to the southern boundary of the valley of Lake Utah, comprising an area of more than five thousand square miles, and involving the necessity of traversing a large extent of country, both by land and by water.

The triangulation of the valley south of the Salt Lake and the observations for the azimuth of the base line were finished on the 12th of August, and the time until the 28th busily occupied in preparations for our return.

I had determined, if possible, to find a practicable route to the

Ackerman, Lith. 379 Broadway, N.Y.

VALLEY OF THE JORDAN, FROM THE MOUTH OF THE SHE—RENTE.

southward of that now crossing the mountains by the South Pass. I therefore disposed of all my wagons, and such instruments and public property as were no longer necessary, by selling them to the Mormon authorities; and arranged for the transportation of the baggage of the party entirely by pack-mules. The horses purchased from the Uintah Indians the past winter enabled me to mount a force sufficiently numerous for self-protection upon the projected route—part of which lay through the common battle-ground of the Sioux, Snakes, Utahs, Blackfeet, and Crow Indians.

Before taking leave of the Mormon community, whose history has been the subject of no little interest in the country, I cannot but avail myself of the opportunity again to acknowledge the constant kindness and generous hospitality which was ever extended to the party during a sojourn of rather more than a year among them. The most disinterested efforts were made to afford us, both personally and officially, all the aids and facilities within the power of the people, as well to forward our labours as to contribute to our comfort and enjoyment. Official invitations were sent by the authorities to the officers of the party, while engaged in distant duty on the lake, to participate in the celebration of their annual jubilee, on the 24th of July, and an honourable position assigned them in the procession on that occasion. Upon our final departure, we were followed with the kindest expressions of regard, and of anxious hopes for the safety and welfare of the party upon its homeward journey.

CHAPTER IX.

HOMEWARD JOURNEY.—EXPLORATION OF A NEW PASS THROUGH THE
ROCKY MOUNTAINS.

Wednesday, August 28.—Having completed our arrangements, we left the city of the Great Salt Lake for home, and encamped at the mouth of the "Big Kanyon," which affords a pass through the Wahsatch range of mountains to the plains beyond.

Thursday, August 29.—Morning fine and cool. A train of Mormon wagons, just arrived from the States, is encamped near us. Our road to-day is up the Golden Pass, through a cañon formed by Big Kanyon Creek, and which has lately been opened and worked by the Mormons, who demand a small toll on each animal, to be devoted to its improvement. The ascent is not so abrupt as I had anticipated. The valley is very narrow, with bold escarpments on either side, scarcely affording space between them for the passage of the turbulent little mountain-stream, which, with its bright, flashing waters, comes tumbling down the pass with a cheerful, murmuring sound, producing, after the dead silence of the barren plains and dreary sand-flats of the lake, a sensation peculiarly pleasant and refreshing.

The road, which is very crooked, and in many places even dangerous, passes over a friable sandstone, underlying a heavy stratum of limestone. Cedar, oak, maple, service-berry, aspen, bitter cotton-wood, and willows are found in the pass; and I observed several fine vines of the wild hop, loaded with fruit. Much heavy grading, expensive side-cutting and walling, besides inclined planes, would be required to render this pass at all eligible for the passage of a railway. A good wagon-road, however, can here be made, and at a moderate expense. The great obstacle to the use of all these mountain passes is the vast accumulation during the winter of snow, which, drifting over from the bordering heights, effectually blocks up the valleys, not unfrequently to the depth of thirty feet; thus rendering them impassable from five to six months in the year.

As the sun went down, the temperature became sensibly lower, and at nine o'clock the thermometer stood at 46°. Observations of Polaris gave for latitude 40° 45′ 40″.5. Day's march up the pass, seven miles.

Friday, August 30.—Morning clear and cool. Thermometer at sunrise, 52°. Our road continued up the Big Kanyon Creek, (crossing its south fork) for five miles, when we reached the summit of the range, and struck upon Bauchmin's Creek, a branch of East Kanyon Creek, which latter is a tributary of the Weber. Latitude by meridian observation at summit, 40° 44′ 48″. The valley is here from two to three miles broad, and near the summit several large pines are growing, as yet undisturbed by the emigration. Scrub-oak and aspen constitute the predominant growth.

The road continues up the valley of Bauchmin's Creek, crossing several small affluents, until reaching a main fork coming in from the right. This stream, which is six feet wide and two feet deep, heads in a range of hills three miles to the south-west, whence it issues with a beautifully clear and rapid current, and, crossing the valley, joins the main stream and flows west and north-west into the Weber. Where it issues from the hills, it enters a lovely and fertile circular meadow, about three miles in diameter and skirted with trees. A couple of miles north-east, a trail passes over the hills to the Provaux, a tributary of Lake Utah, six or eight miles distant. Crossing this beautiful little prairie, which is called Parley's Park, and passing around the head of a noble spring on our left, we crossed Bauchmin's Creek, here about twenty feet wide and two deep, with a rapid current and clear, cold water. Following up a dry channel for two miles, we encamped upon a little spring branch with plenty of fine grass.

The country is becoming more level and the valley much wider. The ascent for the last two miles is quite gentle, and the land excellent. Wheat could be raised in large quantities on the prairie land which lies on our left, all the way from Bauchmin's Creek. Distance from Salt Lake city, thirty miles, Latitude, 40° 43′ 04″.8.

Saturday, August 31.—Starting the train on the road, with directions to encamp at the ford of the Weber, I made a detour to the right, with a small escort, to examine a prairie called Camass Prairie, through which a level and practicable route was said to exist between the heads of the Weber and the Timpanogas.

Following for about five miles a south-easterly course up the valley of Silver Creek, a tributary of the Weber, we left it at a land where it comes from the south-west, and ascended a ridge, or *divide,* and descending it on the opposite side, through a ravine on its eastern slope, about a mile in length, we came into the wide valley of a small stream flowing into the Timpanogas toward the south-east. Crossing this, we ascended a long slope to the top of a broad level ridge, on the eastern side of which the Timpanogas itself flows southwardly, and finally discharges itself into the Utah Lake. From this point, Timpanogas Peak, in the vicinity of the lake, bears south, 10° west. At the head of a dry ravine putting into the Timpanogas, a meridian observation was taken for the latitude. Duchesne's Pass bears south, 70° east, and the heads of Timpanogas and Weber rivers, north, 70° east.

Leaving this summit, we struck north-east about four miles, and descended the bluffs bordering the south-western side of Camass Prairie until we reached the plain, which we found to be a most lovely, fertile, level prairie, ten or twelve miles long, and six or seven wide, and extending north-west and south-east from the Timpanogas to the Weber. At the south-eastern end of the prairie, the Timpanogas breaks forth from a range of lofty mountains, and skirts the edge of it, passing near the base of some high hills on the south-east; while from near the same point, the most southerly branch of the Weber issues also and crossing to the western end of the same prairie, discharges its waters into the main stream. This latter, coming through a deep cañon from the north-east, bounds the prairie on the north-west, and winding its sinuous course through a wilderness of willow and cotton-wood thickets, pursues a north-western direction for about fifteen miles to the point where it is crossed by the road.

The pass made by the Weber through the mountain, although narrow, is said to be practicable by one of the guides, who passed through it in former years with a train of pack-mules.

Several little streams of pure, clear water wind through this fertile prairie, cutting small, deep channels for themselves in the rich alluvial soil; their existence being only discernible from the increased height and luxuriance of the grass upon their borders, and occasional clumps of willows flourishing along their edges. The prairie, from one end to the other, from the Weber to the Timpanogas, is one level plain, covered with a heavy growth of rich grasses, and affords a passage from one stream to the other as perfect as could be desired. Bear River is said by our guides to take its rise in the same mountain with the Weber and the Timpanogas. Should such be the case, (and there is no reason to doubt it,) an easy communication can be obtained by means of the valley of that stream into this prairie, and thence down the valley of the Timpanogas into that of the Utah Lake.

The grade down the Timpanogas is described to be easy, and the cañon through which it descends to the level of the Salt Lake basin to be sufficiently wide for the construction of a road. Such a route would obviate many difficulties which must be encountered in descending either of the only other two practicable cañons through the mountain in the vicinity of Salt Lake City, or in going through that of the Weber River. When once the level of the basin is attained, the way from Utah Lake, either north or south, appears to be open.

In the event of any exploration for a railroad to California or Oregon, upon a route so far north, a careful examination of the country from the point where the main emigration-road strikes

Bear River, up that stream to its source, or at least to a point where a crossing could be obtained over to the heads of the Weber, thence down that stream into the Camass Prairie, and thence, crossing the prairie, down the Timpanogas to the Utah Valley, offers, I think, the most feasible mode of crossing the formidable obstruction presented by the Wahsatch range of mountains.

Fording the Weber at the north-west end of the prairie, we followed down its right bank, recrossed, and struck once more into the beaten track, which we followed in pursuit of the train.

The weather had been very threatening during the afternoon, and the lurid clouds and muttering thunder gave token of the approach of a heavy storm. About dark the tempest burst upon us. Rain fell in torrents, intermingled with hail; and, as it increased in violence, was accompanied by a darkness so profound that it became impossible to distinguish the road, or even the horses upon which we were riding. The lightning blazed with such intense brightness around us that we became completely blinded, and the storm driving furiously in our faces, it was with the greatest difficulty we could keep the track for a few yards at a time. We were ten miles from camp, and felt ourselves in a rather uncomfortable situation. The guide, who had preceded us, and had arrived at the encampment before the storm began, surmising what must be our condition, with commendable foresight despatched a couple of men to meet us with a lantern, by the aid of which we succeeded in reaching the tents about ten o'clock, thoroughly drenched, cold, and exhausted, having been in the saddle, without food, for more than fifteen hours. A basin of hot soup and a cup of strong coffee soon revived us, and, wrapped in our blankets, we slept soundly, regardless of the tempest, which flashed and raged around us the whole night.

It may be remarked here, that the Camass Prairie consists of most, excellent land, and can be irrigated over its whole extent with comparatively little labour. Water for stock is abundant, and timber for ordinary farming purposes is plentiful and convenient. The broad-leafed dock of the eastern prairies abounds here, and it is the only spot where I have observed it since leaving the Missouri. A species of geranium was very abundant, and also a great variety of asters. The surrounding hills are full of rolled stones or very coarse gravel, principally of sandstone, much stained by iron.

After leaving the prairie, and crossing the Weber, several vertical trap dikes were observed on the hillsides; and one, in particular, consisted of what resembled a gigantic stone fence, half a mile in length, regularly laid up, the stones composing it being entirely separate from each other, and from six to eight feet cube, the whole presenting the appearance of a fine specimen of Cyclopean masonry.

The road pursued by the train crossed Silver Creek, and continued down the right bank of the Weber for seventeen miles, where it was forded, and the camp made for the night. Grass and fuel plentiful. The Weber bottom, as far as the mouth of Red Fork, five miles beyond, presents many beautiful little prairies on either side of the stream, fringed with belts of large cottonwoods, affording good locations for many small grain and stock farms. The rock observed from the road was principally a light-gray, fine-grit sandstone, with a dip of 30° to the north-west and west north-west, some pudding-stone, and earthy red sandstone. Day's march, nineteen miles. Lat. 40° 53' 41".3 Lon. 111° 36' 26".

Sunday, September 1.—Engaged in *drying up* after last night's rain, which had thoroughly soaked a portion of the baggage. In the afternoon the arms were cleaned and inspected, and the men engaged in firing at a mark.

Monday, September 2.—Last night was quite cold, and at sunrise the thermometer stood at 33°, with a heavy frost covering the ground. The horses took a stampede during the night, being frightened probably by a bear or a wolf, and this morning were very wild and difficult to catch. The cattle evince an obstinate determination to run back on the road, and require a constant and strick guard to prevent them.

The road continued down the valley of the Weber, now reduced to about a mile in width, being confined on the right by high rounded hills, with gray sandstone cropping out, with a dip of 30° N. N. W. Crossing a small affluent, called Morin's Creek, and a short distance farther on another, for which the mountaineers have no name, it not being deemed worthy of notice by them, as no beaver had ever been found in its waters, at five miles we crossed Red Fork, at its junction with the Weber, which is here a clear, rapid stream, one hundred and twenty feet wide, and two and a-half deep in the channel. At the junction, meridian observations gave for the latitude 40° 57' 41". Distance from Salt Lake City, fifty-four and a-half miles.

At this point the old road turns off to the right in nearly a north-easterly course, and follows up the valley of Red Fork: the ascent, except for the first three miles, in which the rise is tolerably rapid, is moderate, enough so for a railroad, and the valley sufficiently wide and direct for such a purpose, without the necessity of resorting to curves of a small radius.

The valley of this stream seems to have been the result of some convulsion forming an anticlinal axis, the strata on either side of the cañon dipping in opposite directions; that on the left to the north-west, and the other to the south-east, with an elevation gradually increasing as we ascend until it reaches 45°. High, perpendicular cliffs of red sandstone conglomerate, intermingled with lime and quartzose pebbles, and occasionally fine-grit sandstone, were continuous on the north side of the cañon the remainder of the day's travel. These strata varied from one to thirty feet in thickness, and near the mouth of the fork the cliffs were from one hundred and fifty to two hundred feet in height, with lofty peaks of the more indurated portions of the rock towering toward the sky in a wild and picturesque manner.

As we advanced up the valley, several unconformable strata of horizontal sand and pudding stone were observed overlying the dipping rock, the red sandstone intermingled occasionally with the yellowish-gray, yellowish, and white varieties. To the right the hills are rounded at their summits, and their sides for the most part are covered with soil, through which the rock occasionally appears. Water, grass, and wood are sufficiently abundant for camping purposes. Toward the lower end of the valley, wild cherries and wild hops of the best quality abound in great profusion.

Ninety-five wagons were met to-day, containing the advance of the Mormon emigration to the valley of the Salt Lake. Two large flocks of sheep were driven before the train, and geese and turkeys had been conveyed in coops, the whole distance, without apparent damage. One old gander poked his head out of his box and hissed most energetically at every passer-by, as if to show that his spirit was still unbroken, notwithstanding his long and uncomfortable confinement. The appearance of this train was good, most of the wagons having from three to five yoke of cattle, and all in fine condition. The wagons swarmed with women and children, and I estimated the train at one thousand head of cattle, one hundred head of sheep, and five hundred human souls.

Our day's march was only sixteen and a-half miles. Several

circum-meridian observations of Altair, gave for latitude of the camp 41° 2′ 27″.26 ; long. 111° 30′ 34″.

Tuesday, September 3.—Ther. at sunrise, 31°. The road continues to follow up the valley of Red Fork. In about six miles we came in view of a remarkable little eminence in a bluff of red sandstone, which almost perfectly resembled a rustic cottage, with a deep-arched doorway and gently sloping roof, covered with scattering cedars. The illusion was very strong, and became more and more perfect as we approached, until we almost expected to see some one issuing from the portal to gaze upon the passing train. The valley of Red Fork to this point is very beautiful, beginning to widen considerably, and becoming more level.

For about a mile from camp, gray sandstone takes the place of the red, after which the latter predominates, but not in such continuous ledges as heretofore. Opposite "the Cottage," a broad, level ravine comes in from the S. S. E., which apparently heads somewhere near the sources of Morin's Creek, and, from the trending of the hills, may connect with those of the Weber itself. If this should prove to be the case, the circuitous route by the mouth of Red Fork may be entirely avoided, as well as the descent to the Weber, and the rise from it, both which are unavoidable by the route now pursued. A short distance beyond the Cottage, a broad ravine comes in from the N. N. E., which is, in fact, the main Red Fork—the eastern branch, along which the road passes, being called Echo Creek.

In the forks of the two streams, at the foot of a bluff of horizontal red and gray sandstone, observed for time and latitude. We called the bluff "Chicken-cock Bluff," from the strong resemblance to that bird of a large cedar on its summit. Ascending this elevation, I obtained a view of the valley of Red Fork, of Echo Creek, and also of the ravines coming into the former from the S. S. E. It is highly probable that a pass may be obtained by means of one of these valleys over to some of the head branches of the Weber, or to the river itself, before it enters the Camass Prairie. It is worth a careful examination, as success would insure an almost level and very direct route through the Timpanogas Valley to that of the Great Salt Lake at Utah.

On the right bank of Red Fork, just above the junction of Echo Creek, in a cliff of horizontal red sandstone, the escarpments were much worn and rounded, as if by the action of water, and wrought into strange and fantastic shapes, many of them resembling turrets, bastions, &c. Yesterday numerous places were observed in the high cliffs below, where a black and apparently viscid substance, resembling mineral tar, had oozed out between the strata and trickled down the face of the cliffs. This would seem to indicate the vicinity of coal, although no other evidence of its presence was discovered.

From the mouth of Echo Creek to Cache Cave, a distance of five and a-half miles, the cliffs begin to disappear, the rocks cropping out only occasionally through the soil, and the hills gradually diminishing in height. From Cache Cave, (which is merely a small hole or grotto in a large gray-sandstone rock appearing in a low bluff on the left,) the route winds up the valley of Echo Creek, and ascends a pretty steep hill to the dividing ridge between the waters of the Weber and Yellow Creek, a tributary of Bear River, into which it discharges its waters about six miles below.

Here it was evident that the road should not have followed the valley of Echo Creek at all, but should have continued up the valley of Red Fork, from "Chicken-cock Bluff" to a depression in the hills to the northward, leading over into Yellow Creek, by which the route would have been shortened as well as much improved. From this ridge the Weber Mountains can be seen through the Red Fork Kanyon, distant about twenty miles, and also the mountains beyond Camass Prairie.

From the observations taken from this elevation, there is every indication that by following up the valley of Yellow Creek to its head, a good route may be obtained over to the waters of the Weber before it enters Camass Prairie, by which the whole descent of Red Fork can be avoided, and also the consequent necessity of the ascent of the Weber for twenty miles to that beautiful meadow, whence, as before remarked, the route to the Timpanogas is as level as a floor. Here the roads might fork, one leading to Utah Lake, by the Timpanogas, and the other, by Silver Creek, Bauchmin's and Golden Pass Creeks, to Great Salt Lake City. Any exploration, for either a railroad or a permanent mail route through this region, should embrace a careful examination of the country in this vicinity.

Encamped on the banks of Yellow Creek, which is about three feet wide, with steep banks, and fringed with willows, but no timber. Day's march, seventeen miles. Distance from Salt Lake City eighty-two miles. Lat. 41° 09′ 00″.2; long. 111° 14′ 13″.

Wednesday, September 4.—Morning quite cool. Ther. at sun-
15

rise, 31°. In a quarter of a mile the road turns abruptly to the right and follows up Needle Creek, (a branch of Yellow Creek,) with a gentle ascent, passing a ridge crowned with broken pointed crags of conglomerate, which, from the acicular form of the projections, has gained for it the name of "The Needles." Ascending to the head of this stream, we descend into the valley of Bear River, the low bottom of which is here about a mile and a-half wide, and thickly covered with clumps of cotton-wood. The river is about four hundred feet in width, two and a-half in depth, flowing with a strong current over a bed of large pebbles. Crossing this stream the road keeps the valley of Sulphur Creek for about two miles, where we halted to noon, near an excellent spring of good cold water. A meridian observation gave for latitude 41° 08′ 08″.28.

A short distance north of the road, and on the north bank of the creek, a bed of bituminous coal was discovered, between two nearly vertical dikes of light-gray coarse-grit sandstone, one hundred and fifty feet apart, the course of which is north, 30° east. The outcrop was about eight feet wide by four feet thick, and was only visible against the south side of the north dike. It appeared to be quite an extensive deposite, but its depth and width can only be ascertained by further examination. Specimens of it, although much weathered, burned in the camp-fire with a clear, bright flame. The seam had a direction apparently the same as that of the dikes, with a dip of 70° S., 70° E. From the base of the bluff issued several sulphur springs, and south about a mile and a-half, a spring of Petrolium, or mineral tar, oozes from the low bank of a little rivulet flowing into the valley of Sulphur Creek from the south-west. The emigrants collect it for medicinal purposes and for greasing their wagon-wheels. The bank from which it issues is full of rolled pebbles, but no ledge is visible.

From this point to the southward lay a broad expanse of country, considerably lower than our level, stretching away toward the heads of Bear River. To the south-east a little park of timber grew near the bluffs which form what is termed the "Rim of the Basin," and from which flow the heads of Sulphur Creek : to the eastward a low table extended toward the heads of the Muddy, a tributary of the Colorado of the Gulf of California.

Returning to our place of nooning, we again struck into the road, and, passing over a level country for two or three miles, we at length ascended the ridge dividing the waters which discharge themselves within the Great Basin, from those which flow into the Pacific.

The ascent is gentle and winding.   Numerous springs burst out on either side, near the summit of the ridge, amid groves of aspen, which cover the sides of the surrounding hills.

It was with no little exultation that we reached this eastern barrier of the Great Basin, in which we had been floundering amid dreary deserts and barren mud-plains for the last thirteen months, and to which we now bade adieu with feelings of unfeigned satisfaction.   Directly upon the summit, by the side of the road, was the fresh grave of some poor fellow who had come thus far on his journey to the land of promise—a land he was destined never to behold.

From the top of the pass, it was evident that a much better location for the road could have been made from the head of Muddy to that of Sulphur Creek, by which the route would have been rendered much more direct, and at least two formidable elevations avoided.

From conversations with several individuals well acquainted with the country in this vicinity, especially with Major Bridger, who has traversed this whole region for the last thirty years, as well as from my own observations, which go in a great measure to confirm their statements, I feel convinced that the best route for a road into the Salt Lake Valley would be obtained by ascending Black's Fork to Fort Bridger; passing thence to Bear River, distant twenty-five miles; then crossing Bear River and ascending its valley until we strike upon the heads of a branch of the Weber; following down which for fifteen miles, the main stream is reached about two miles north of Camass Prairie.   Into the latter, access through the upper cañon is not difficult.   This, so far as can be judged from the information obtained, and from the partial observations we had ourselves the opportunity of making, would afford a route entirely practicable for a railroad, the chief obstacle presenting itself being the liability to obstruction from the snows that would be likely to accumulate in the cañon of the Weber.   From the Camass Prairie, as before observed, the road might fork, the branch which leads to the city descending the Wahsatch range by the Golden Pass as at present, while the other, following down the Timpanogas, would enter the Salt Lake basin near to Lake Utah.

Following a ridge for about eight miles from "the Rim of the Basin," we encamped at Red or Copperas Spring, a tributary of the Muddy, (an affluent of Green River,) after a march of twenty-six and a-half miles.   The road to-day has been hilly, but good;

fuel, grass, and water abundant, and at convenient points. Lat. 41° 13′ 46″; long. 110° 48′ 00″.

Thursday, September 5.—Morning cool and slightly cloudy. Ther. at sunrise, 37°. A march of sixteen miles brought us to Fort Bridger, on Black's Fork of Green River. This is a trading-post much frequented by the Shoshonees, Utahs, and Uintah Indians, and is owned and conducted by Messrs. Vasquez and Bridger, from both of whom we received the kindest attention and every assistance which it was in their power to render.

Black's Fork, upon which the fort is situated, is a considerable stream of excellent, clear, sweet water, which rises in the Bear River mountains, and discharges its waters into Green River, or the Rio Colorado of the Gulf of California. A mile and a-half above the fort, it divides into four streams, which reunite two miles below, forming several islands, upon the westernmost of which the fort is beautifully located, in the midst of a level, fertile plain, covered with a luxuriant growth of excellent grass. Numerous groves of willows and cotton-wood, with thickets of hawthorn, fringe the margins of the streams, and afford fuel and timber for the necessities of man, and shelter for cattle from the inclemency of the winter. Black and white currants are tolerably abundant, and are now ripening upon the banks of the rivulets. The emigrant road forks here, one branch leading to Fort Hall, by the Soda Springs, and the other, pursuing a more southerly course, leads to the City of the Salt Lake, the distance to which by the travelled road is one hundred and twenty-four and a-half miles: this, may be materially shortened by a judicious location of the route.

From its position with regard to several powerful Indian tribes which inhabit this region, Fort Bridger offers many advantages for the establishment in its vicinity of a military post. It occupies the neutral ground between the Shoshonees and the Crows on the north; the Ogallalahs and Sioux on the east; the Cheyennes on the south-east; and the warlike tribe of the Utahs on the south. A competent force established at this point would have great influence in preventing the bloody collisions which frequently occur between these hostile tribes, and would afford protection and aid to the great tide of emigration which, for years to come, must continue to flow in one ceaseless current to Oregon and California.

The party remained here several days, to readjust the packs, and to complete the final arrangements for crossing the plains. The trunks and heavy baggage were left in charge of Major Bridger, to be forwarded by a Mormon train from the city; Governor Young having kindly engaged to see that they were safely transported to St. Louis.   Carrying with us, therefore, only such articles as were absolutely indispensable, we prepared for our departure.   During our stay, daily observations were taken, the results of which gave for the lat. 41° 18′ 12″.8; and long. 110° 32′ 23″.

On the 7th the mail arrived, bringing the unlooked-for intelligence of the death of the President of the United States.

Before leaving Salt Lake Valley, it had been determined not to return by the beaten track, but to endeavour to ascertain the practicability of some more direct route than that now travelled to the waters of the Atlantic.   If it should prove to be practicable to carry a road across the north fork of the Platte, near the Medicine Bow Butte, and, skirting the southern limit of the Laramie Plains, to cross the Black Hills in the vicinity of the heads of Lodge-pole Creek, and to descend that stream to its junction with the South Fork of the Platte, nearly a straight line would thus be accomplished from Fort Bridger, and the detour through the South Pass and the valley of the Sweetwater, as well as all the ruggedness of the Black Hills, upon that line, be entirely avoided.   The country through which the proposed line would pass was represented as entirely.practicable and as affording every probability of success.

Major Bridger, although at considerable sacrifice of his own interest, with great spirit offered his services as guide, he being well acquainted with the ground over which it was my desire to pass. The offer was most cheerfully accepted; and as our route would lay directly through the war-ground of several powerful Indian tribes, care was had fully to equip the party with arms and ammunition necessary for our defence.

Tuesday, September 10.—We left Fort Bridger in the afternoon, and proceeding about five miles down Black's Fork, encamped in a small meadow upon the right bank, with good grass for the animals.   A merchant-train for Salt Lake passed us during the day, from which I procured some sugar and coffee, of which articles we were nearly destitute, the supply of Salt Lake City having been exhausted long before our departure.

Wednesday, September 11.—Ther. at sunrise, 23°.   Our route to-day follows the emigration road down Black's Fork, which is twice crossed.   In eight miles from camp we crossed Smith's Fork, a pretty little stream of good water, which also takes its rise in the Bear-river Mountains, near the heads of Black's Fork, into which it falls about twelve miles below Fort Bridger.   Continuing in the valley of Black's Fork, after a march of nearly eighteen miles en-camped on its right bank, about half a mile above the mouth of the Muddy, another affluent coming in from the left.   Lat. 41° 28′ 56″.38; long. 110° 18′ 50″.

Since leaving the basin and entering the valley of Green River, a remarkable change in the face of the country is apparent.   In-stead of the disturbed and upheaved rocks which characterize that region, flat tables or terraces of horizontal strata of green and blue sand and clay, and sandy conglomerate, or agglutinated sand, now form the principal feature of the country, standing alone, like island buttes, amid the barren plains, or forming escarpments which alternately impinge upon the banks of the winding streams. These tables, which extend from the rim of the basin to the South Pass, and thence to Brown's Hole on Green River, are apparently the result of a deposite in still water.   The layers are of various thicknesses, from one foot to that of a knife-blade, and the hills are fast wearing away under the influence of the wind and rain.

The whole country looks as if it had, at one time, been the bot-tom of a vast lake, which, bursting its barrier at Brown's Hole, had been suddenly drained of a portion of its waters, leaving well-defined marks of the extent of the recession upon the sides of these isolated buttes.   As the channels became worn by the passage of the water through the outlet into Green River, another sudden de-pression followed, and the same operation was repeated at still a lower level.   There are three well-defined levels, and the same ap-pearances of horizontal water-lines occur here as were noticed upon the hillsides of the islands in the Great Salt Lake; save that in the latter case they are more numerous and closer together, and the subsidence of the waters appears to have been more gradual.   The surface of the ground was strewn with fragments of obsidian, black, shiny pebbles, flints, and white, yellow, and smoky quartz.

A high wind from the W. S. W. blew up clouds of dust, and, at every turn of the road, announced the approach of crowds of emigrant-wagons, wending their way to the Mormon valley, with droves of cattle and sheep, whose fat and thriving condition, after so long a journey, was the subject of general remark, and excited universal admiration.

Thursday, September 12.—Last night was very cold, and at sunrise the thermometer stood at 22°. Shortly after leaving camp we ascended a hill opposite the mouth of the Muddy, and reached a remarkable isolated butte, to which the traders have given the name of "The Church." It is composed of green and brown indurated clay and brown sandstone, seamed and furrowed by the elements into fantastic and picturesque forms, resembling somewhat the ruins of a huge antiquated castle. Following the old road for a couple of miles farther, over a level country of sand and clay, almost denuded of vegetation, except occasional patches of artemisia, which seems to claim as its peculiar property soil where nothing else will grow, we came in sight of a high butte, situated on the eastern side of the Green River Valley, some forty miles distant: a landmark well known to the traders, and called by them Pilot Butte.

Leaving the emigrant road here, we struck for this prominent elevation, passing, on our way to it, over a barren plain formed by the washings from the hills, which had covered up every vestige of vegetation, and presented an aspect of dreary desolation saddening to the heart. Passing a small brackish spring, which issues from the base of some coarse brown sandstone rocks, rising abruptly from the level plain to the height of twenty feet, we halted to take a meridian observation, which gave for latitude 41° 31' 08".5. The mouth of Ham's Fork bears north 20° west, distant four miles, the mouth of Black's Fork being about thirty miles below. From this point the land descends gently for twelve miles to Black's Fork, which we crossed at an excellent ford, and encamped on its left bank, amid thickets of willows, and fine grass for our animals. The stream was about a hundred and forty feet wide, and easily forded. In times of high water it is probably from two hundred to two hundred and fifty feet wide, with a depth of from six to eight feet.

The vegetation, to-day, has been very sparse, and consists principally of dwarf sage and grease-wood bushes, with low bunch-grass. Black currants abound on the banks of the stream. In many places the ground has been thickly strewn with gravel and pebbles, mostly siliceous, with occasional appearance of argillaceous limestone. Day's travel, twenty-five and a-half miles; total from Fort Bridger, forty-seven and a-half miles.

Friday, September 13.—Morning overcast, and threatening rain. Ther. 47°. As we were in the act of leaving the camp-ground, an alarm was given that a body of armed men on horseback was charging down upon us at full speed. The pack-mules and loose animals were immediately driven back into the bushes, where they could be more easily defended, while, accompanied by Major Bridger, I advanced to the bank of the stream to reconnoitre. We soon ascertained that the party consisted of a band of some twenty Shoshonees, who were out upon a hostile expedition against the Utahs, and that, mistaking, as they said, the smoke of our fires for that of their enemies, they had charged down upon us, in full expectation of effecting a surprise. As soon as they discovered their mistake, they crossed the creek in compliance with our invitation, and greeted us in the most friendly manner. The party was armed in a most heterogeneous way, some having rifles, others old bayonets fastened upon the extremities of long poles, and the rest bearing only bows and arrows, with a little round shield suspended from their necks. They were, for the most part, well-mounted upon small, but apparently excellent horses.

There being no longer any occasion for alarm, the animals were driven from their cover, and leaving our red friends to pursue their own course to the southward, we resumed our march, although it had commenced to rain quite heavily, with every prospect of a stormy day. Recrossing Black's Fork, we followed up a small depression, and in about a mile reached by a gentle ascent the summit of a long ridge, stretching eastwardly toward the valley of Green River. Crossing this ridge we struck upon the broad valley of another affluent of Black's Fork, which we pursued for about six miles to its head, when we reached the "divide" between that stream and the waters of Green River. From the "divide" we descended a long and winding ravine, called Rabbit Hollow, which joins the valley of Green River two miles above the mouth of Bitter Creek, a considerable stream flowing into that river from the eastward. The lower part of Rabbit Hollow will require to be partially worked, to avoid the bends of the dry bed of a stream which winds from side to side of the narrow bottom; but, with this trifling exception, an excellent wagon-road can be traced from Green River at this point to Fort Bridger, and by a very direct route. The north side of this ravine, near its mouth, is flanked by lofty vertical cliffs of indurated green clay and shales, overlaid by horizontal strata of a soft, yellowish sandstone. The same formation occurred on the eastern side of Green River; and the turreted appearance of the crumbling sandstone cliffs, four hundred feet in height, was in a high degree imposing and picturesque.

At this point we crossed the river, between banks some thirty feet high and eight hundred feet apart. The deepest water found in crossing was three feet, but in high stages it is a formidable stream, and will require to be ferried. The bottom is about a mile in width, and is covered with thickets of willows and abundance of grass. Following down the left bank of the river, we encamped in a clump of bitter cotton-woods, where, owing to the suspicious vicinity of our Indian acquaintances of the morning, the animals were securely picketed and the guard doubled for the night. Two or three Indians had followed us all day, and, after partaking of a hearty supper, left us just before dark—as they said, to rejoin their companions. We did not, however, feel called upon to place the most implicit confidence in their statements, and the necessity of increased vigilance during the night was impressed upon the guard, lest, upon waking in the morning, we should find that our animals had disappeared. The weather began to clear before night, and enabled us to obtain an observation of Altair, which gave for latitude 41° 30′ 44″.5, longitude 109° 38′ 40″. Day's march, thirteen and a half miles; and sixty-one miles from Fort Bridger, by the route we have pursued, which, with a little care, can be much improved and shortened.

Saturday, September 14.—Ther. at sunrise, 46°. A dense fog concealed every thing from view. The night had passed without disturbance, which led me to suppose that the Indians yesterday had really no design upon our horses, as I had suspected. As it was impossible to move while the fog continued, the men were occupied in cleaning their arms, wetted by yesterday's rain. Black currants and buffalo-berries abound upon the banks of the river. The latter grow in great profusion upon a shrub about fifteen feet high. The berry is about the size of a pea, of a bright scarlet colour, and contains but one seed. It has a pleasant acid flavour, and would make an excellent jelly. The Indians are said to be extravagantly fond of it.

Before noon the fog lifted, with the promise of a fair day; we saddled up and started on our journey, directing our course up the valley of Bitter Creek, which enters Green River about a mile below. Crossing the bottom of Green River Valley, we passed the mouth of Bitter Creek, and ascended it the whole day's march. For the first half-dozen miles, the valley is much cut up by deep gullies, worn by the water from the rapidly decomposing hills on each side of the stream. These, however, present no serious obstacle to the easy construction of a good road: the soil being porous, and mixed with a large proportion of gravel, can be readily graded. So rapid is the disintegration of the sandstone bluffs, and so constant the wash of the soil, that the valley, so far, is almost entirely destitute of even a spear of grass, and presents a most desolate appearance.

After passing this *mauvaise terre* the route is quite level, presenting no obstruction of consequence, except the necessity of occasionally crossing the creek, which will be somewhat difficult, as the bed of the stream is not unfrequently at a depth of twenty feet below the level of the bottom, with perpendicular banks on each side. But the earth is easily removed, and very little labour will render these crossings by no means formidable. At a point thirteen miles from the mouth of Bitter Creek, we found a bed of bituminous coal cropping out of the north bluff of the valley, with every indication of its being quite abundant.

For the first seven or eight miles after entering the valley, the formation was similar to that of Rabbit Hollow and Green River, and the strata horizontal: they then began to dip gradually to the west and north-west, until, at this point, the elevation had reached 20°. The coal was of the same character as that found on Sulphur Creek, near the crossing of Bear River, alternated in beds of various thickness, from a few inches to several feet, with yellowish and light-gray sandstones. Major Bridger informed me that, about a mile from the mouth of the creek, a large bed existed, which, from his description, resembled lignite, but which, owing to other occupations, I had passed without observing. One of the men reported to me that he had noticed it, and had seen a piece of coal lying in the bed of the creek as long and as thick as a man's body. This had apparently fallen from an outcrop in the south bank, which was about four feet in thickness. Major Bridger also stated that a similar bed is to be found to the south of the mouth of Black's Fork, that he had used it for years, and that it burned freely, with a clear, white blaze, leaving little residuum, except a small white ash. From this outcrop, as we ascended the valley, the strata became more nearly horizontal; and at the termination of the day's march, some four miles beyond, had nearly recovered its level position.

The valley of Bitter Creek generally has but little snow in it during the winter, and was formerly a rendezvous for the trappers and traders, on account of the abundance of buffalo. None of these animals are now to be seen in the region. The only vegetation, to-day, has been a little dwarf artemisia, grease-bush, rabbit-bush, salt-grass in the narrow strips of bottom-land, and an occasional dwarf cedar on the bluffs. Appearances indicate that the bed of the stream, which has no banks above the general level of the bottom, has been completely filled by the spring rains, overflowing the low grounds and carrying down immense quantities of soil, which has been deposited below, upon the broad flats of Green River. The ridges on each side of us to-day have been principally composed of horizontal gray limestone and disintegrating agglutinated sand; the escarpments, rounded into fantastic forms of bastions, buttresses, and turrets, by the action of the winds and the rains, were in many cases quite beautiful. Day's march, seventeen miles. Lat. 40° 34′ 41″.8; long. 109° 23′ 9″.

Sunday, September 15.—Morning slightly cloudy. Ther. at sunrise, 44°. The water being very indifferent, and wood difficult to be obtained, it was determined to make a march to-day to a spring supposed to be about ten miles up the valley. Bitter Creek, at this camp, flows in a bed twelve feet below the plain of the bottom, and the water in its present stage is about sixty feet wide by six inches in depth. But the accumulation of large piles of flood-wood shows that during the spring freshets, the whole valley, here about one thousand feet wide, is completely covered with water. The general course of the valley for ten miles was north, 74° east, over a very level flat. About halfway of this distance the sand-cliffs disappear, and the valley opens wide, with rounded hills on each side, much less elevated than the bluffs below. At this point the stream forks, one branch coming in from the south, with a wide level valley. About thirteen miles above, it forks again, both branches heading within two miles of each other, in a small mountain, in which Red Fork, another affluent of Green River, flowing into it below Brown's Hole, also has its sources. One of the guides says that there is a good route by Red Fork to Green River, and thence to the heads of Bear River.

A short distance on our left lay a small, shallow lake, some six miles in circumference, formed by the drainage from the hills on the north and east, and very probably by some springs in the vicinity, as the waters appeared clear and fresh.

After passing that point, the hills began to approach each other more closely, and the ascent became rather more abrupt, with numerous gullies, or drains, crossing it at right angles, rendering the trace, heretofore unexceptionable, rather more unfavourable. From the lake we followed the right bank of the east fork of the creek for six miles, when we again crossed it, and one mile beyond we broke out, from a bed twelve feet thick, some beautiful specimens of excellent bituminous coal, which burned in our camp-fires with a clear yellow flame. In the sides of the ravines putting into the valley are abundant beds of this mineral.

The rock is very much of the same character as that observed below—red, white, and yellow sandstone, with a slight dip to the east and north-east. In some places, nodules of rock, deeply tinged with oxide of iron, were frequent. The rock is very porous, and rapidly disintegrating under the action of snow and frost, and is washed down into the valley by the spring rains in great quantities, so that vegetation, except grease-wood and salt-grass, is very sparse.

Continuing up the left bank seven miles farther, we encamped in the forks, after a journey of twenty-five miles, near two cold sulphur springs which issue from the base of a cliff of light-gray coarse-grit sandstone, having fragments of coal interspersed, so as to form something like a pudding-stone of coal and cemented sand.

Near the northern spring some beautiful white lichens were growing on the rocks over which it flows; and under the projecting cliff, some highly coloured ones, with variegated hues, like the neck of a mallard. Currant-bushes were quite plentiful, and the plain near the springs has a dense growth of broad-leafed blue-joint and wire-grass, among which I observed some purple asters. A mile and a-half north of the camp, on the North, or Evans's Fork, is an outcrop of coal, ten feet thick; but most of that in sight appeared to be but imperfectly mineralized. Indications were also observed of the presence of iron-ore near the camp. Lat. of the camp, 41° 30′ 51″.4. Long. 108. 50′ 34″.

Monday, September 16.—Our route to-day continues up the east or left fork of Bitter Creek. Sandstone cliffs bound the valley on the north side, in which I observed a stratum of coal, which was exposed for a hundred yards, and was at least ten feet in thickness. During the whole day's march this mineral was met with in every favourable locality, and in quantities apparently without limit. The formation was the same as lower down the stream, except that the dip was north-easterly, at an angle of from 5° to 10°.

Several bands of antelope were seen, and one of the hunters brought in a noble buck. Grouse, also, were abundant, and very fat. A bear, too, was seen taking a good look at us, but, not liking our appearance, he made off with all haste before we could get a shot at him.

The trace for a road has been good, and the distance travelled in nearly an eastern direction was twenty-two miles. Our observations gave for latitude 41° 28' 9''; longitude 108° 41' 9''.

Tuesday, September 17.—Our course to-day was up the east fork of Bitter Creek, about south 70° east, for eighteen miles, when we reached its head, ascending very gently to the dividing ground between it and the waters of Muddy Creek, an affluent of Little Snake River, which flows into the Yampah, about twenty miles above the entrance of the latter into Green River. Here we leave the valley of Bitter Creek altogether, having followed it from its mouth for seventy miles. On the level table forming the "divide" is a butte composed of sand and clay, a hundred and fifty or two hundred feet high, standing isolated and detached from the range of bluffs to the south and east of it, and to which, from its shape, we gave the name of "The Haystack." From this landmark we travelled in nearly an eastern direction, gradually descending, for six miles, to the valley of a small branch of the Muddy, to which we gave the name of "Bridger's Fork of Muddy," and encamped in its valley, although the water was so strongly impregnated with alkali that the animals drank it with evident reluctance and disgust.

The valley is here much cut off by abrupt gullies and ravines, formed by the wash from the hills, and in many places the ground is covered with a crust of impure soda to the depth of half an inch. The grass, since our noon halt, has been very scarce, and our poor mules have fared rather badly. Several buffalo were seen to-day, and one antelope killed. Our hunters are calculating largely upon the sport before us as we approach the buffalo range, and are much excited at the prospect of once more revelling in their favourite fare. Day's travel, twenty-six miles. Lat. 41° 28' 39''; long. 108° 14' 24''.

Wednesday, September 18.—Ther. at sunrise, 44°. A slight "stampede" occurred among the horses last night, owing to the blundering of an old buffalo bull into the camp. Several of the animals broke from their fastenings and fled in dismay, but were all ultimately recovered.

Our course lay down the valley of Bridger's Fork for three and a-half miles, when it opens suddenly between two high cliffs of red and green indurated clay, and strata of coarse-grit brown sandstone, upon a vast rolling prairie, extending from the Platte to Snake River. To this opening we gave the name of "Red Gate." The general direction of the low range bounding the western side of this prairie is about north-east and south-west. Upon entering the plain, a magnificent view opened before us. On our right, to the south and the east, extended the Elk Mountains, with their blue peaks, in which the Elk River takes its rise; to the left of these rose a high square butte, marking where the three branches of St. Vrain's Fork enter the Snake River. On our left stretched far off to the northward the ascending ridge of prairie forming the "divide" between us and the waters of the Sweetwater and the North Fork of the Platte, while before us, and at right angles with our course, ran four rolling prairie ridges, the farthest of which, about forty miles distant, formed the western boundary of the Park Mountains. Bridger's Fork, the little stream whose valley we had followed to the Gate, pursued a wandering course to the southeast through the prairie, its existence marked only by an occasional clump of willows. A few buffalo bulls were quietly grazing upon the plain, and now and then a small herd of antelope, bounding away over the hills, gave life and spirit to the picture.

The soil from this point to Muddy Creek is for the most part of an excellent quality, but, from want of moisture, can never be appropriated to any other purpose than grazing. The grass, though thin, is very nutritious. Small sage, salt grass, greasewood, a purple aster, together with bunch-grass, and, in the more sandy portions, small cacti, were the principal plants. The tops of the ridges were strewn with a flat, black gravel, with pebbles of yellow and white quartz. An occasional drain was crossed, which gave indications of having contained water quite recently; but all of these were now dry. As long as the water lasted, the whole plain must have been covered with buffaloe and antelope, as the profusion of "sign" abundantly proved; but as this indispensable article was absorbed by the sandy soil, they seemed, from the direction of their trails, to have struck a course for the Vermilion. Many large bear-tracks were also seen, making in the same direction.

After travelling six miles across this undulating prairie, we reached the right bank of the valley of Muddy Creek, twenty-five miles above its confluence with Little Snake River.   This stream, which rises in the Park Mountains, here makes a valley of four miles wide, and the descent to the bottom of the creek is from a hundred to a hundred and fifty feet down a washed and broken bluff of sand and clay, much worn into gullies and ravines.   The descent is too steep, where we struck the bluff, for a good wagon-road; but, by a detour from the " Gate" of two miles to the south, the descent will be very much more gradual, and the greater part of the high, broad ridge over which we passed will be avoided.

Upon the top of this ridge I found, scattered over the surface, a large number of silicefied petrifications of shells.   Passing two remarkable little sandstone buttes, on our right, one of which was covered with cedars, (the first trees we had seen since leaving Green River,) and on our left two flat-topped whitish clay or marly mounds, connected by an escarpment, we encamped in a deep bend of the Muddy, which was fringed with willows, having selected the spot with the view of more securely guarding our animals from the nocturnal attacks of any wandering bands of Indians.

We are now upon the war-ground of several hostile tribes, who make this region the field of mutual encounter, and increased vigilance is consequently necessary to guard against a surprise—an occurrence which, as one of its least unpleasant consequences, might leave us on foot in the midst of the wilderness.   All firing of guns, without express permission, except in case of the most urgent necessity, has been strictly forbidden, and every man slept with his arms by his side.

As we were reposing our weary limbs before the camp-fire, regaling ourselves with a pipe, now our only luxury, Major Bridger entertained us with one of those trappers' legends which abound as much among these adventurous men as the " yarns" so long famous among their counterpart, the sailors, on a rival element. A partner of his, Mr. Henry Frappe, had a party of what, in the language of the country, are called "free men," that is, independent traders, who, some nine years before, were encamped about two miles from where we then were, with their squaw partners and a party of Indians.   Most of the men being absent hunting buffalo, a band of five hundred Sioux, Cheyennes, and Arapahoes suddenly charged upon their camp, killed a white man, an Indian, and two women, drove off a hundred and sixty head of cattle, and, chasing the hunters, killed several of them in their flight, the residue escaping only by abandoning their horses and hiding in the bushes. Intelligence of this onslaught reached Major Bridger, then occupied in erecting a trading-post on Green River; he sent Frappe advice to abandon his post at once, for fear of worse consequences. The advice, however, was neglected, when, about ten days after, as his party was on their way to join his partner, they were again suddenly attacked by another large party of the savage allies. He had but forty men; but they instantly "forted" in the corral attached to the trading-post, and stood on their defence. The assault lasted from noon until sundown, the Indians charging the pickets several times with great bravery; but they were finally repulsed with the loss of forty men. Frappe himself was killed, with seven or eight of his people.

I give this as a sample of the perilous adventures in which these rude and daring men, almost as wild as their savage foes, were engaged, as things of course, and which they related around their camp-fires with a relish quite professional.

The only vegetation at this camp was a few scattering clumps of small willows and some black currant-bushes: the supply of grass was scanty. Muddy Creek runs between perpendicular cut clay-banks, forty feet apart; the water at the present stage being only four feet wide and four inches deep. Day's travel, very direct as to course, twenty and a-half miles. Lat. 41° 27' 06".1; long. 107° 52' 41".

Thursday, September 19.—Slight frost in the night. Ther. at sunrise, 35°. The night passed without alarm; and, crossing the creek, we continued up its left bank, and soon reached a point where it made a long cañon through the hills. The ground was rough and filled with gullies made by the rush of the spring freshets. The soil was loose and sandy, and the waters had cut numerous deep and narrow channels across the valley, whose perpendicular banks obliged us to pass along the base of the bluffs, in order to head, and thus avoid them. The creek had to be crossed some six or eight times, and, upon the whole, this has been the roughest and most difficult part of the route. Before noon we passed a spot where a party of fourteen fur-traders, under Mr. Vasquez, had "forted" and fought forty Ogallalah Sioux for four hours, successfully defending themselves and repulsing the Indians. One of our men, a half-breed hunter, had himself been in the fight, and pointed out to me the localities with the most minute particularity of bloody detail.

A meridian observation gave for latitude 41° 28′ 28″. A few aspens occur in the bottom, with abundance of artemisia, some of which were six and eight feet in height. An occasional outcrop of coal was also observed; the argillaceous shale, some three hundred feet in height, through which the creek cuts a channel, dipping north-westerly at an angle of 20°.

Beyond this point the creek makes another cañon, which, requiring some reconnoissance, we turned down into a pretty little bottom, fringed with willows, currant-bushes, and birch, and encamped, having made only fourteen miles. We found the creek filled, at short intervals, with beaver-dams, some of which had been but recently constructed, the chips made by cutting down the bushes, and the paths made through the grass and brush by dragging them into the water, being still plainly discernible. The stream furnishes some small fish, among which were speckled trout.

Friday, September 20.—Morning clear and bright. Ther. at sunrise, 31°. Clouds however soon began to gather, and finally covered the whole sky. It had been determined to go on until ten or eleven o'clock, and then to make a halt of part of two days to rate our chronometers, and to obtain, if practicable, a series of satisfactory observations for longitude. But the sun being entirely obscured, and it coming on to rain, the march was continued during the day. It unexpectedly cleared in time to obtain a meridian observation for the latitude.

Leaving the camp-ground early, we continued up the right bank of the Muddy, over rather rough ground, covered with sage, for a couple of miles, to within one mile of the point where the main fork comes in from the Park Mountains on the south-east, where it heads. Here we turned to the left up a beautiful pass, about a mile and a-half in length, with a uniform gentle ascent to its summit. From the top of this pass we continued for four miles over a gently undulating country, sloping to the right into the drainage of the Muddy. Here we reached *the dividing height between the waters of the Pacific and those of the Atlantic.*

One universal shout arose at the announcement of this fact; and visions of home and all its joys floated before the imagination in vivid brightness. That to which we had so long been looking forward, as a thing that might one day be, now seemed almost within our grasp; for we knew that the waters which we had at length reached, flowed, in one unbroken stream, almost to the very

16

feet of those who were dearest to our hearts. Often have I experienced the same feeling, when, in the dark and solemn forest, I have sat by my solitary camp-fire on the bank of some murmuring stream. The waters seemed a connecting link with human beings, however distant; and as I thought whither they would flow, I felt myself not so utterly alone. None but those who have experienced it, know how much companionship there is in the gentle murmur of a flowing stream. Such were now our sensations as with light hearts and buoyants spirits we galloped down the grassy slope.

Before us lay an undulating country, descending gently toward the east; beyond, in the distance, frowned the Medicine-bow Butte, at the foot of which flowed the waters of the Platte, while to the southward of this famous headland stretched far away the Park Mountains, whence issue so many tributaries to the Pacific. From this important summit we commenced a scarcely perceptible descent into a wide grassy hollow, forming the valley of a now dry rivulet, which, in the spring, discharges its waters into Sage Creek, an affluent of the North Fork of the Platte. Two miles east of the "divide," we halted to take a noon observation for latitude, which placed us in 41° 33' 22''.3, the computed longitude being 107° 30' 48''. Grass and water were scarce, and the growth of artemisia very thick, making it somewhat difficult to pass our little wagon over it. Near the mouth of this little stream we crossed over to another, heading near to· it, and running parallel with it, upon the banks of which we encamped, after a deeply interesting march of nearly twenty-two miles.

From what has been seen since crossing the summit, I am satisfied that it would have been better had we kept more to the southward before crossing it. If, leaving the ridge forming the southern boundary of the valley, we had followed either the stream upon which we are now encamped, or even the valley of another, some miles still farther south, we would not only have somewhat shortened our route, but obtained a greater abundance of grass, wood, and water, from a high ridge which bounds all these little streams on the south. Observations gave for latitude of the camp 41° 35' 41''; longitude 107° 21' 52''. Distance from Fort Bridger, two hundred and seven miles.

With the exception of the rough ground near the head of the Muddy, which offers no obstruction of consequence, a perfectly feasible, and indeed a most excellent route, whether for a

wagon or railroad, has thus been traced, presenting fewer obstacles to the construction of either than almost any tract of the
same length in the country.   The grades will be easy, the bridg-
ing comparatively light; and, with the exception of the crossing
of the valley of the Muddy, where a long and heavy embankment
may be required, the cuttings and fillings will be entirely within
moderate limits. In no case will an inclined plane be required ; and
the route is more than usually free from the objection of high and
narrow cañons, liable to be filled up or obstructed by snow during
the winter.

Saturday, September 21.—Morning clear and bright.   Ther.
at sunrise, 35°.   Ice formed in the buckets during the night.
Passing down the right bank of the little drain upon which we had
encamped, we encountered the usual impediments from thick artemisia, and numerous little gullies, many of which were deep and
difficult to cross.   To avoid them, we turned more to the south, and
crossed Sage Creek, an affluent of the Platte, about four miles
above its mouth.   The water was eight feet wide, and three or
four inches deep, with a free current, and vertical clay banks.
This part of the route was over a sand and clay soil, denuded of
vegetation, and strewn over with black schorl gravel, and an immense quantity of white quartz pebbles, in angular fragments,
that did not seem to have been water-worn.

After the crossing of Sage Creek, upon approaching the Platte,
we encountered many ravines coming down from a ridge on our
right, the intervening ground being washed almost entirely bare of
grass or vegetation of any kind.   In many places the surface of
the ground was covered with small broken fragments of crystallized
sulphate of lime, of a rich brown colour, mostly as clear as mica,
(for which, indeed, it was at first mistaken,) and many specimens
were perfectly transparent.   Large quantities of pure white quartz
gravel, also, were brought down from the hills, and lay mingled
with the gypsum.

After a march of sixteen miles, we encamped on the left bank
of the North Fork of the Platte, in a lovely bottom, amid picturesque
groves and clumps of gigantic cotton-woods.   The ground was
covered with a luxuriant growth of nutritious grasses, among which
buffalo-grass was quite abundant.

In this region the bottom land is principally confined to the left
bank, and is from a quarter to half a mile in width.   On the right
bank are escarpments of rock a hundred and fifty or two hundred

feet in height—the cliffs rising abruptly from the water's edge. The formation consists of horizontal strata of a soft, coarse, brown sandstone, overlaid by bituminous shales, above which are clay and earthy marl, the whole capped with a heavy stratum of sandstone. The river in its present stage is one hundred and sixty feet wide and two feet deep; the bed consisting of gravel, rolled pebbles, and boulders, among which a red feldspathic granite, gneiss, granite, quartz, and a very compact, firm-grained, ferruginous limestone are the most prevalent.

The cotton-woods round our camp are the first trees, worthy of the name, that have greeted our eyes for more than a year. They seemed to us like old friends, and, as they waved in the fresh breeze over our heads, reminded us of those beloved woodlands from which we have been so long separated. Oh! with what longing desire had we looked forward to such a sight; while our souls, sick of rolling prairies, barren plains, bald and rocky ridges, muddy flats, and sandy wastes, sought in vain for the forest shade and those hills of living verdure which give the charm to every landscape. Day after day, week after week, had we journeyed over that desolate basin, without a tree to be seen in the whole horizon. But now the rustling sound of embowering leaves assured us that we had once more reached a spot fitted by nature for the habitation of man.

The place we now occupy has long been a favourite camp-ground for the numerous war-parties which annually meet in this region to hunt buffalo and one another. Remains of old Indian stockades are met with scattered about among the thickets; and the guide informed us, that four years since there were at one and the same time, upon this one bottom, fifteen or twenty of these forts, constructed by different tribes. Most of them have since been destroyed by fire. As this was the season of the year when we might expect to find them upon their expeditions, we were on the *qui vive*, lest we should be surprised. Arms were inspected and put in order and a vigilant guard kept during the night.

It had been intended to reach this camp by ten in the morning, so as to rate the chronometers and take lunar observations for the longitude. We arrived, however, barely in time to obtain a meridional observation, which gave our latitude 41° 32′ 49″.2. Computed longitude, 107° 6′ 11″.

One of the pack-mules, having for his burden all the flour belonging to the officers' mess, had, by some oversight, been left behind at the morning's encampment, nor was the incident discovered until near the end of the day's march. Two men were immediately sent back to recover him, but returned unsuccessful. They declared that the creature must have hidden himself purposely in the thicket near the camp—a trick to which it is said some of these animals are addicted. A detail of six men was ordered to start back for him early in the morning.

Archambault killed a remarkably fat buffalo cow to-day, which gave us plenty of the finest beef. Side and hump ribs, and buffalo hump—that precious morsel of all mountain connoisseurs—graced our humble board, (or rather the top of our mess-chest,) and we only needed the presence of dear but absent friends to render our dainty repast all that an epicure could desire. Another cow was also killed, which contained a dead and thoroughly dried fœtus, about one-third grown, which had apparently been enclosed in the uterus and preserved for a long time. The hunters say that such is not an unfrequent occurrence.

Sunday, September 22.—We remained at this pleasant camp all the day, being Sunday. The detail sent after the missing pack-horse returned about one o'clock, having discovered him, with his pack undisturbed, hidden in the brush in the vicinity of the camp of yesterday morning.

The day was warm and balmy, with fresh breezes from the north-west. The evening closed with heavy gusts of wind from the south-west, with appearance of rain. Several herds of buffalo were seen during the day.

Monday, September 23.—Morning warm and cloudy. High wind during the night, with a slight sprinkle of rain. We followed up the left bank of the Platte, in an eastern direction, when we crossed it on a ripple, with a depth of eighteen inches. Swift current, clear, transparent water, rolled stones and pebbly bottom.

A large portion of the way from camp was through a natural park of noble cotton-wood trees, sixty feet high, and two and three feet in diameter, and over a rich level bottom, covered with a luxuriant growth of grass. Major Bridger informs me that, for twenty miles above, the river presents the same beautiful appearance, every little bottom formed by the windings of the stream being covered by a growth similar to that through which we had just passed.

Immediately above where we crossed, were about twenty Indian forts, or lodges constructed of logs set up endwise, somewhat in the form of an ordinary skin lodge, which had been erected among the timber by different war-parties: they appeared to be very strong, and were ball-proof.

From the river we turned more to the northward, in order to pass around the northern end of Medicine-bow Butte, a small isolated mountain, detached from the main range immediately south of it. The ground rose gently for nine miles, when we reached the bank of a small stream issuing from the pass between the butte and the range just referred to.

It was through this gorge that Frémont passed in 1842; but as he had represented it as very rough, and our guides declared it to be wholly unfit for the passage of wagons, it was determined to look for a route farther to the northward. We halted to noon on this little stream, to which we gave the name of "Pass Creek," and to take a meridian observation, which gave the latitude 41° 37' 15".8. Crossing this creek and passing over a pretty little prairie, covered with grass, now cropped close by herds of buffalo and antelope, we continued our journey near the northern base of the butte for about ten miles. At night, we encamped upon a branch of Rattlesnake Creek, at the foot of a spur, the sides of which were covered with a heavy growth of pine. The route travelled from the Platte has been too far to the right for a good wagon-road. By following up a wide, smooth valley running parallel with our route, and about a quarter of a mile to the left, an excellent road may be obtained, with a regular ascent, until reaching the south branch of Rattlesnake Creek, where some uneven ground, but presenting no material obstruction, will have to be encountered.

Numerous bands of buffalo and antelope were seen during the day, and in the afternoon, a monstrous bull was killed; but the hunters took only a piece of hide from the back, to make lash-ropes for the packs, the marrow-bones from the hindlegs, and the tongue, leaving at the very least six hundred weight of good beef on the ground for the wolves and the ravens. In several places along the route to-day, I noticed fragments of white crystallized sulphate of lime, bituminous shale, clay-slate, and marble; and after striking the valley of Rattlesnake Creek, indications of coal. Latitude of camp by observation, 41° 40' 45".2. Longitude, 106° 43' 37". Day's march, twenty-three miles.

Tuesday, September 24.—Ther. at sunrise, 51°. Last night was cloudy, and we lost an observation of Altair. A good one of

Polaris was however obtained, about midnight, which gave the latitude.

Early in the morning, a large herd of buffalo was seen quietly feeding on the side of a high hill, about a mile to the southward. Archambault was soon in the saddle, and, approaching through a ravine, which concealed him from their sight, he reached the top of the hill immediately above them undiscovered. The whole herd was in full view of the camp, then busily engaged in packing the mules for the day's march. Soon the crack of a rifle and the sudden fall of one of the dark objects on the hillside gave notice that the work of destruction had commenced. Keeping himself concealed behind a large rock, the hunter very leisurely shot down four of these monsters, although one was much more than we could carry with us. When, satisfied with his morning's success, he showed himself from behind his breastwork, the whole band scoured off as fast as they could "tumble ahead." I rode up to the scene of this wanton butchery, and, for the first time, witnessed the operation of cutting up a buffalo.

Contrary to the custom among us, the skinning process commences by making an incision along the top of the backbone, and separating the hide downward, so as to get the more quickly at what are considered the choice parts of the animal. These are the "bass," a hump projecting from the back of the neck just before the shoulders, and which is generally removed with the skin attached: it is about the size of a man's head, and, when boiled, resembles marrow, being exceedingly tender, rich, and nutritious. Next comes the "hump," and the "hump ribs," projections of the vertebræ just behind the shoulders, some of which are a foot in length. These are generally broken off by a mallet made of the lower joint of one of the forelegs, cut off for the purpose. After these come the "fleece," the portion of flesh covering the ribs; the "depuis," a broad, fat part extending from the shoulders to the tail; the "belly fleece;" some of the ribs, called "side ribs," to distinguish them from the hump ribs; the thigh or marrow-bones, and the tongue. Generally the animal is opened and the tenderloin and tallow secured. All the rest, including the hams and shoulders—indeed, by far the greater portion of the animal—is left on the ground. When buffalo are plenty, the hump, bass, and tongue—very frequently only the latter—are taken, and occasionally a marrow-bone for a tit-bit.

This is called butchering "mountain fashion," and a most bar-

barous fashion it is.   The bulls are never killed for food except in case of necessity, their flesh being very inferior to that of the cows; but an old mountaineer cannot resist the temptation of a fair shot at one when it offers.

It is vain to remonstrate against this wholesale destruction. The hunter, this morning, rather plumed himself on his great moderation in only killing four, when it was wholly within his power to kill as many as he pleased: at the same time he knew that one would have amply supplied all our wants.   Indeed, of the four killed, but three were butchered, (that is, the choice parts only taken away,) and we left the ground, having two pack-mules and all the riding-horses loaded down with meat, the fourth animal being wholly untouched; thus abandoning to beasts of prey enough of the richest and sweetest beef to supply a very respectable market for a week.   All intercession in favour of the poor buffalo is looked upon by these old mountain-men with a strange mixture of wonder and contempt, which strongly reminded me of the expression of honest Dandie Dinmont, in Scott's admirable tale of Guy Mannering: "Weel, that's queer aneugh! Lord save us! to care about a brock!"

The train, in the mean time, had moved forward, ascending a dry branch of Rattlesnake Creek, running E. N. E., with a gradual rise.   Reaching its head, in a low gap, we attained the summit, and struck upon a hollow or depression leading down to a small branch, which, rising near the northern end of Medicine-bow Butte, winds its way through a broad and lovely valley, and discharges its waters into the Medicine-bow River.

The route led us over some swelling ridges making toward this branch from the mountains on our right, and, crossing three other little streams, tributary to it, we reached in ten and a-half miles the banks of the Medicine-bow River.   Here we encamped in a thicket of tall timber and underbrush, on an old Indian camp-ground; the remains of several old forts, now decayed and in ruins, being still visible.

On its north-western, northern, and north-eastern sides, the Medicine-bow Butte is surrounded by a well-defined ridge, from which it is separated by a broad intervening valley, the ridge appearing to be concentric with this part of the butte, and three or four miles distant from it.   Through this the Medicine-bow River breaks, passing for twenty miles between vertical walls of rock with wide alternate bottoms on either side.

The scenery from the "divide" was in beautiful contrast with that of the country left behind us. Broad and grassy valleys were spread out before us, bounded by low rounded hills covered with verdure, over which ranged bands of buffalo, while little flocks of antelope bounded gracefully around us. The low bottom of the Medicine-bow, upon which we are encamped, is thickly covered with excellent grass, and the stream has an extensive fringe of willows and rose-bushes, with occasional groves of cotton-wood and aspens. The night was too cloudy to admit of an observation; but a meridian altitude of the sun gave for latitude 41° 41′ 50″.9.

Wednesday, September 25.—The wind blew furiously all night; and as we had for so long a time been unaccustomed to the sound of the blast rushing through a forest, our slumbers were frequently broken by the apprehension lest the tall trees, beneath whose spreading branches we had encamped, should be blown down upon our heads. Immediately upon leaving camp, we crossed the Medicine-bow, and ascended a high bluff, whence Laramie's Peak was distinctly visible, bearing north, 45° east. The route continued over a rolling country, crossing several small streams heading in the Medicine-bow Mountains on our right. Game was seen during the day, in greater abundance than we had yet met with it; and, from the fact of our being off the great line of emigration, the buffalo were quite tame, some of the old bulls allowing us to approach very near to them and moving off quite lazily. The antelope, too, seemed to regard us with more curiosity than fear, and repeatedly stopped within shot to take a good look at us, and then trotted off entirely at their leisure. Being already supplied with meat from yesterday's slaughter, we suffered them to frisk around us unmolested; scorning to touch venison when buffalo-meat was so abundant.

An incident occurred in the course of the morning which came near proving fatal to my friend, Lieutenant Gunnison. Seeing a small band of buffalo near at hand, he started on his horse to run one of them down, as the creature's hide was wanted for the repair of our little wagon. The train had passed on for about a mile, when one of the men galloped up and reported that Lieutenant Gunnison's horse had thrown him, and that he was fearful something serious had happened. I instantly rode rapidly to the point indicated; and found my excellent officer partially delirious, reclining on the ground, his face and hands covered with blood, and

his horse, a fine roan, lying dead by his side. The scene was soon
explained. When starting after the buffalo, Mr. G. had handed
his gun to one of the party, and, drawing a revolver from his
holster, set off in pursuit. In crossing a narrow ravine his horse
had stumbled and nearly fallen : the nervous contraction of the fingers caused by the endeavour to save himself had occasioned the
discharge of the pistol, the ball of which, passing directly through
the neck of the horse, had killed him instantly; and his rider was
hurled with great violence to the ground. I was much relieved to
find that no bones were broken, and that, with the exception of
some severe scratches, and a violent jar of the system, nothing
very serious had happened. It was a narrow escape, however;
for a broken bone, so far from surgical aid, would have proved no
light matter. After the detention of an hour, Lieutenant G. was
mounted upon another horse, and accompanied the train as usual,
his ambition for running buffaloes entirely satisfied.

A meridian altitude of the sun gave for latitude 41° 38′ 38′′.6.
Laramie Peak bearing north 29° 30′ east, mag. The afternoon's
march was over a beautiful rolling country, lying at the foot of
the Medicine-bow Mountains, whence issued several small streams,
emerging from narrow cañons, their sides clothed with cotton-
wood, aspen, and cedars—their windings through the plains to the
northward being distinctly traceable by the rich belts of green
that clothed their banks. The soil was sandy, and profusely
covered with small fragments of white, smoky, and rose quartz,
very pure, and in many cases nearly translucent, which had been
washed down from the mountains. We made but one march to-
day, and, crossing the east fork of the Medicine Bow, encamped
three miles below, upon the banks of Frappe's Creek, one of its
tributaries. The east fork, where we crossed it, is about forty
feet wide and one foot deep, flowing with a rapid current and pure
limpid water over a pebbly bed. The bottom of this pretty little
stream is about a mile wide, well covered with grass, and tolerably
wooded with cotton-woods and aspens. The mountain-sides on our
right have been well clothed with fir and pine. Frappe's Creek is
so called from the fact of Mr. Frappe having been some years
since robbed, at the mouth of this stream, of a band of sixty
horses, by a party of Aricarrees. Day's march, seventeen miles.
Lat. 41° 33′ 6′′. Long. 106° 15′ 58′′.

Thursday, September 26.—Morning clear. Ther. at sunrise,
48°. A high wind from the south-west. To-day we entered the

Laramie Plains, and travelled over a beautiful rolling country, covered with grass, with here and there a small lake or pond, formed in the low grounds by the drainage from the neighbouring hills. A meridian observation gave the latitude 41° 28′ 16″. From this point we took a course a little to the south of east, for a prominent landmark which rises near the heads of Lodge-pole Creek, an affluent of the South Fork of the Platte, and in ten miles reached the western fork of the Laramie River, upon the left bank of which we encamped. The river is twenty feet wide and eight or ten inches deep, flowing with a rapid current over a bed of pebbles. The bottom is about four miles wide, with abundance of fuel and grass. The trace to-day has been rather undulating; but an excellent road can be located without difficulty. Buffalo have been very numerous and tame. Day's march, twenty-one miles. Latitude, by observation, 41° 19′ 43″.4. Long. 105° 57′ 12″.

Friday, September 27.—Clear and calm. Ther. at sunrise 41°. Slight frost on the grass in the low grounds. Crossing the west fork of the Laramie River, our course was nearly due east, over a gently rolling prairie. The trace is smooth, and had we crossed the Laramie Fork about a mile to the northward, it would have been as level as could possibly be desired, with not a bush or ravine to obstruct the passage. The timber which clothes the hills on the south ceases at their base. Artemisia has entirely disappeared.

About eleven o'clock, two of the scouts who had kept on the left flank of our little party were descried descending from the hills at full gallop, waving their hats, and giving the alarm of Indians. We were at the time in the midst of a broad prairie, toward which rolling ridges sloped gently on either hand, and at a considerable distance before us rose a bold prairie ridge: not a bush or a tree was to be seen which could be converted into a covert for defence. The train was immediately halted, the pack-mules and loose animals caught up and led by their halters to prevent them straying from the band, and the men were formed into two lines behind our little wagon, between which the led animals were driven, the whole being closed up by a guard in the rear. In a few minutes our simple arrangements were completed, and we moved forward over the plain, prepared to make as stout a resistance as circumstances would permit.

In a hollow on our right lay two lakes, or ponds, and some three miles ahead ran the main fork of the Laramie. Herds of buffalo were seen rapidly emerging from the little hollows on our left and spreading in great confusion over the plain—a sure indication that they had been disturbed by some cause behind the hills. At length scattered bands of mounted Indians were discovered moving rapidly at a considerable distance before us; and occasionally a look-out could be seen motionless upon the summit of some elevated mound, apparently watching our movements. At noon a short halt was ordered near some ponds of water, and a meridian altitude of the sun taken, which gave the latitude 41° 15′ 41″.4. We then moved forward, and, in three miles, reached the main fork of the Laramie, a beautiful little stream of pure, cold water, about fifty feet wide, and eighteen inches deep, flowing with a free current to the northward, between low grassy banks, over a bed of pebbles and gravel. It had been intended simply to make a short nooning here, and then to push forward toward the heads of the Lodge-pole Creek with all possible speed. This intention was frustrated, however, by the appearance of the Indians, who were discovered moving toward us from various points and in considerable numbers. Uncertain of their intentions, or of the amount of their force, I deemed it prudent to prepare for their reception.

About a quarter of a mile above us, on the right bank of the stream, was an isolated little grove of cotton-woods, of which I determined to take possession, and there to await the approach of our red brethren: this was accordingly done; the animals were taken into the grove and picketed. In a short time, by felling a few trees and piling up such as were found lying upon the ground, an enclosure was constructed, which a strong force of Indians would have found it somewhat difficult to carry in the face of thirty rifles. In the mean time, Indian scouts made their appearance upon the surrounding hills, reconnoitring us, and seemed to be as uncertain of our character and intentions as we were of theirs. Having completed our little field-work, the United States flag was displayed, and we sat down to lunch, having eaten nothing since sunrise. Finding the Indians only hovered around at a distance, Major Bridger, shouldering his rifle, walked out toward them, and made various signs to an advance party that came out to meet him. We soon perceived that they had recognised him; when, finding that we were white men, and not a hostile band of Indians as they had supposed, they commenced a perfect race for our camp, and in a few minutes a stream of Indians galloped up, holding out their hands to shake with any and every body they met. They proved to be a large band of Ogallalahs, (one of the numerous bands of Sioux,) who had discovered us early in the morning, and had been anxiously watching our movements all the day, having mistaken us for a war-party of Crows. As soon as they saw the flag displayed, they knew at once that we were whites, but had hesitated to approach us, through fear of the small-pox, which they represented as raging below and in the neighbourhood of Fort Laramie. They had fled hither to avoid it, and were much alarmed lest we should have it among us. Being assured to the contrary, they poured in upon us from all quarters, and our camp was soon crowded with them. Several of the chiefs and head men had certificates from the commanding officer at Fort Laramie, and from different emigrant companies, as to their friendly character, which they handed to me with an *empressement* which showed the great importance they attached to them. Some coffee, flour, and sugar were served out to them, together with all the tobacco I could spare; and after a plentiful repast, they departed for their village on the Laramie, about two miles below, with every demonstration of good-will. The head chief, who rejoiced in the very original title of "Buffalo Dung," gave me a warm invitation to pay him a visit in the morning; which I promised to do.

The band consisted of several hundred: they were, for the most part, fine-looking men, straight, tall, and athletic, and generally well mounted. I afterward learned that as soon as they recognised our flag, and became satisfied as to our character, they had sent word to the spot selected for their temporary camping-ground, whereupon the squaws, reassured, immediately commenced putting up the lodges; and before sundown the plain was white with them.

Among the Sioux was one solitary, dignified old Cheyenne chief, who figured in the undress frock of a major of artillery, buttoned closely up to his throat, and of which he seemed not a little vain. To my surprise, I found that he did not understand the Sioux tongue at all, and communicated with those of that tribe wholly by signs. The Sioux chief with the unpronounceable name, the translation of which has already been given, was a noble-looking old man, and very much disposed to be sociable. He explained to me that he was greatly afflicted with sore eyes, and begged for something to cure them. I had nothing but an old pair of goggles, with very dark green glasses, which I gave him, and with which he was very much delighted, mounting them with great complacency, although it was then very nearly dark. With a spy-glass, also, they were very much pleased, and through it watched the erection of their lodges with great wonder and interest. A Colt's revolver, when explained to them, excited many remarks, and evidently increased their respect for the strength of our little party.

There was one circumstance, however, that attracted my attention in this interview with these untutored sons of the forest more than any other; and that was the perfection and precision to which they appear to have reduced a system of purely arbitrary and conventional signs, by which, all over this vast region, intercourse, though of a limited character, may be held between tribes who are perfect strangers to each other's tongue. After partaking of such food as could be hastily prepared for them, the principal men seated themselves on the ground, in a circle around the camp-fire in front of the tent, and the pipe of peace was filled and duly circulated in regular succession. Our esteemed friend and experienced mountaineer, Major Bridger, who was personally known to many of our visitors, and to all of them by the repute of his numerous exploits, was seated among us. Although intimately acquainted with the languages of the Crows, Blackfeet, and most of the tribes west and north-west of the Rocky Mountain chain, he was unable to speak to either the Sioux or Cheyennes in their own tongue, or that of any tribe which they could understand. Notwithstanding this, he held the whole circle, for more than an hour, perfectly enchained and evidently most deeply interested in a conversation and narrative, the whole of which was carried on without the utterance of a single word. The simultaneous exclamations of surprise or interest, and the occasional bursts of hearty laughter, showed that the whole party perfectly understood not only the theme, but the minutiæ of the pantomime exhibited before them. I looked on with close attention, but the signs to me were for the most part altogether unintelligible. Upon after inquiry, I found that this language of signs is universally understood by all the tribes.

At sundown the whole band left for their village; previous to which, a venerable old Indian traversed the camp, haranguing the young men in an elevated and monotonous tone, the purport of his exhortation being, as I was told, a warning to them not to touch or meddle with any of our property. But the old man's advice was of little avail; for we ascertained, soon after their departure, that a couple of axes, a blanket, and an excellent rifle had mysteriously disappeared.

Saturday, September 28.—Morning clear and bright. At an early hour several of our yesterday's visitors were on the ground, in the hope of securing a good breakfast. We mentioned to them our loss of the previous evening, and they promised to do what they could to recover our property. The train was directed to move forward under the charge of Major Bridger; while, accompanied by a whole troop of Indians, I rode over to the village to pay my respects to the chief, according to promise. This village was the largest and by far the best-looking of any I had ever seen. It consisted of nearly one hundred lodges, most of which were entirely new, pitched upon the level prairie which borders on the verdant banks of the Laramie. No regular order seemed to be observed in their position, but each builder appeared to have selected the site for his habitation according to his own fancy.

We rode at once to the lodge of the chief, which was painted in broad horizontal stripes of alternate black and white, and, on the side opposite to the entrance, was ornamented with large black crosses on a white ground. We found the old fellow sitting on the floor of his lodge, and his squaw busily engaged over a few coals, endeavouring to fry, or rather to boil, in a pan nearly filled with grease, some very suspicious-looking lumps of dough, made doubtless from the flour they had received from us yesterday. The chief courteously invited us to take something to eat, which, having the fear of the very questionable lumps aforesaid before our eyes, we modestly declined. By the aid of one of my men who had been among these tribes for two years, I made out to inform him that some of his young men had, when on a visit to our camp yesterday, stolen some of our property, and requested him to take measures for its restoration. He at once said that there were in the company of visitors a number of Cheyenne Indians, and that *they*, and not the Siouxs, (or "Dahcotahs," as they all called themselves,) must have been the depredators. He promised, however, to send out the crier, and try to ascertain whether the things could not be recovered. I soon recognised the cry of the old Indian of yesterday, who went around the village making proclamation of the loss. After some further conversation, another chief, named the "Iron Heart," rose up and invited us to a feast at his lodge: we accordingly accompanied him, and found him occupying the largest and most complete structure in the village, although I was assured that the Sioux frequently make them much larger. It was intended to be used whenever required, for the accommodation of any casual trader that might come among them for the purpose of traffic, and was accordingly called "The Trader's Lodge." It was made of twenty-six buffalo-hides, perfectly new, and white as snow, which, being sewed together without a wrinkle, were stretched over twenty-four new poles, and formed a conical tent of thirty feet diameter upon the ground, and thirty-five feet in height.

After we had seated ourselves upon the skins provided for our accommodation, the pipe was duly passed around, and the *feast* was introduced. It consisted of a tin pan containing a parcel of dried buffalo-meat, which had been boiled in simple water, without salt, and suffered to get cold. This was brought in by an old squaw, and placed upon the ground before us, with a basin of water. Although we had not long before breakfasted heartily upon roasted rib and tender-loin, we were in courtesy obliged to partake of this rather lean fare with apparent satisfaction, notwithstanding that the pan containing it looked as if a thorough cleansing would most materially have improved its appearance. We accordingly ate a morsel or two, when, most fortunately, an old Indian came in, who, after taking a few whiffs of the pipe which was passing round, reached out his hand for the pan, and very soon discussed the whole of its contents without the slightest scruple.

The feast being finished, we rose to take our leave; when the chief courteously motioned us to remain, saying that they were haranguing the village in hopes of recovering our lost property. Although I had not the least idea that we should ever see any of the stolen articles again, yet we continued to sit, listening to the bellman-like proclamation going on outside, until at length I explained to the chief that I could wait no longer; that my young men had gone forward, and that it was necessary I should overtake them; whereupon we shook hands and parted. He was a remarkably fine-looking man, of about forty-five, with a face denoting strong character, great firmness, and yet, as I thought, a kind heart. His influence with his people was said to be very great. One thing in his manner struck me with surprise: I observed, during our interview, that he always passed the pipe without smoking; and upon afterward inquiring the reason of an omission so unusual, found that it was "against his medicine" to smoke in the presence of others, and that whenever he indulged in this Indian luxury, it was when alone. Returning to the lodge of the fat old chief, whose merry laugh and cheerful physiognomy denoted a great love of fun, and not a little of good eating, we soon found that all hopes of the lost rifle were vain, and immediately left the village.

This band of Ogallalah Sioux was about a hundred lodges strong, and seemed to possess a large number of fine horses, as well as a good many excellent mules; the latter procured, no doubt, by trading with the emigrants along the road to California and Oregon.

From the village we pursued a south-east course to overtake the train, which, after passing in an easterly direction over a level grassy prairie, with plenty of fine water, had ascended the western slope of the Black Hills. Having ridden a mile or two, we enjoyed an opportunity of witnessing what is technically called a "surround" of buffalo, by a band of about fifty Indians on horseback. The poor animals were in great confusion and terror, the Indians being in full pursuit. We did not halt to see the end of the hunt. During the chase a small band was driven near us, and a fine fat cow was secured by a shot from one of my revolvers. A mile or two farther on, we found a couple of our hunters very amicably engaged in dividing the carcass of another buffalo with half a dozen Indians, who laid claim to a share of the prey, on the ground, that although the buffalo was actually killed by the white men, one of their own number had first wounded it; in proof of which they pointed to an arrow deeply buried in its side. The claim was cheerfully admitted, and the game in consequence equally shared. The Indians told us that to the eastward of this point we would see no more buffalo; in this, however, they proved to be mistaken. At the western base of the ridge we passed through another village of fifty lodges of the same tribe, who were moving to the southward.

For the last seven or eight miles, the prairie has been strewn with the carcasses of buffalo, from which the choice pieces only had been selected by these untutored epicures, leaving the remainder, from which they had not taken the trouble even to remove the skin. Carcasses thus left on the open prairie are not unfrequently completely cured, or rather "mummified," in the sun, so that they seldom exhibit any sign of decay.

Ascending the western slope of the Black Hills by a very gentle rise, we followed the trail of our party, passing between low cliffs and detached masses of red and gray sandstone, worn into isolated pillars, hillocks, and other forms by the action of the elements. The beds appeared to be thick and extensive, but the strata were

17

thin, varying from half an inch to six inches, between which an occasional layer of brown and reddish argillaceous limestone was found interposed.

Passing over an undulating and gradually rising country, for seven or eight miles, we at length overtook the train, which had halted to noon on a small tributary of the Laramie River. Aspen, fir, pine, and cedar here occurred in scattering clumps, and the grass has been abundant. From this point we continued our course more to the north-east for four or five miles, over ground considerably cut up by ravines, when we reached the summit of the ridge, which gives rise to the head of Lodge-pole Creek, an affluent of the South Fork of the Platte, into which it discharges its waters nearly south of Ash Hollow, and about seventy miles above the junction of the two great branches which form that well-known stream. Lodge-pole Creek here takes its rise in a high ridge, and falling with a rapid and sudden descent, forms a deep and precipitous cañon, at the bottom of which it continues to wind its way until it reaches the plain at the foot of the eastern slope of the Black Hills. It is represented as having a width between the cliffs which enclose its valley, sufficient for a road, by crossing the stream from side to side; but I was deterred from attempting the passage, not only by the rugged descent from the ridge, but by the quantity of timber growing in the cañon, through which it would have been necessary to cut our way the whole distance. In addition to this, the ridge appeared to be much lower to the southward, in the direction of the heads of Box-elder River and *Fontaine qui bouit*, while, toward the northward, it appeared to become higher and still more rugged. This induced me to believe that we had crossed the ridge too far to the northward, and that a more feasible route could be traced south of our line of travel, by which much of the elevation we had attained (which amounted to about a thousand feet) might be avoided.

We accordingly followed down the ridge in a S. S. E. direction for six miles, when we struck upon a little stream, which we supposed to be a branch of Lodge-pole, but which, as we afterward ascertained from some Cheyenne Indians, was a branch of Crow Creek, another affluent of the South Fork, and which flows into it from this point in a north-easterly direction. Here we encamped for the night, with good grass and water, after a very interesting, though somewhat fatiguing journey of twenty-two miles. Immense droves of buffalo were seen in every direction during the day. An

observation of Altair gave for the latitude of the camp, 41° 8′ 2″;
long. 105° 24′ 11.″

Sunday, September 29.—Ther. at sunrise, 28°.   After passing
through about two miles of pine and aspen woods, the country became a rolling prairie, which obliged us to wind about considerably
among the hills to avoid the undulations of the ground.   Our general course was east for eleven miles, when, descending the eastern
slope of the ridge, we struck upon the heads of a little stream
issuing from a rugged cañon of red feldspathic granite, at the base
of the hills, and flowing into the plain below.   We learned from a
band of Cheyennes, who paid us a visit about sundown, that this
was another branch of Crow Creek.   Here the main ridge of the
Black Hills suddenly falls off into a range of lower elevation,
which again slopes to a plateau of clayey and earthy marl.   The
timber which had clothed the ridge ceases upon reaching the plain,
but the stream is fringed with willows.   Where the creek issued
from the cañon, wild cherries, and yellow, red, and black currants
occurred in great profusion and fully ripe.   The yellow variety
was particularly good, resembling in flavour a mellow sour apple.

From our noon halt of yesterday, the formation has consisted
chiefly of massive red feldspathic granite, with an occasional heavy
out-crop of ferruginous quartz.   Following down this branch for
four miles, we encamped on its left bank, with good grass and water.
A village of Cheyennes was encamped a short distance to the north
of us, who, as soon as they descried our party, immediately paid
us a visit.   They hung around the cook-fires till the guard was set
for the night, when I notified the chief of the fact, and desired
him to send his people away, at the same time informing him that
should any attempt be made during the night to disturb our animals, the guard had positive directions to fire upon the marauders.
He made them an harangue to this effect, and they immediately
left us, some for a ride of ten miles back to the vicinity of our
morning encampment, vhence they had followed and accompanied
us during the day, partly from curiosity, and partly from the hopes
of a plentiful meal.   Day's march fourteen and a-half miles.   Latitude by observation 41° 9′ 3″.5; longitude 105° 8′ 24″.

Monday, September 30.—The camp was up long before daylight,
and we were on the road by sunrise.   Finding that the branch of
Crow Creek, upon which we had encamped, passed too much to the
southward for our purposes, we turned our faces to the north, and
followed along the base of the Black Hills, about four miles distant,

crossing the hills and hollows formed by the drains coming from them, the undulations, however, being quite gentle. On our right, about two miles distant, stretched a high table ridge, or plateau, rising one hundred and fifty or two hundred feet, its western escarpments abrupt, nearly vertical, and capped in this vicinity by argillaceous limestone and sandstones, with occasional strata of pudding-stone. Between this plateau on our right and the Black Hills on our left, there is a marked depression or valley, averaging about four miles in width, and which appears to have been cut out by the violent action of an immense body of water flowing in a northern direction. The valley extends along the base of the Black Hills, from where we first descended their eastern slope, to the Chugwater; the range of marly hills reaching, as our guides told us, to the Platte, in the vicinity of Scott's Bluffs, and thence to "Chimney Rock" and "The Court-house." The formation appeared to be the same as that observed at those localities. The depression thus formed is called the "Cheyenne Pass," from the constant use made of it by that tribe in their migrations to and from the Platte. From the red cañon of Crow Creek to some distance down the Chugwater, a range of lower hills, apparently of lime and sandstone of different colours and qualities, occurs, flanking and following the general direction of the main back-bone of the Black Hills. Through these, the numerous streams which take their rise in the ridge beyond have forced a passage in deep, narrow, and rugged cañons, and, after crossing the Cheyenne Pass, have broken through the marly plateau on our right, in their passage through the plains to the eastward into the North and South Forks of the Platte.

Following the Cheyenne Pass nine miles from our morning's camp, after crossing the north or main fork of Crow Creek, some two miles below its cañon, we struck upon the southern branch of Lodge-pole Creek, and, five miles beyond, halted to noon upon Bear Creek, one of its tributaries, where a meridian observation gave for the latitude 41° 21′ 45″.7.

We had now reached the heads of the stream, which I had previously determined to follow to its confluence with the South Fork of the Platte. As we could expect to receive no addition to our supplies before reaching Fort Kearny, I despatched an express to Fort Laramie for such articles of food as were required, and occupied the interval until their return in making an examination of the eastern base of the Black Hills to the northward.

Having now brought our reconnoissance for a new route from the waters of the Pacific to a point where its results can be at least approximately ascertained, it is very gratifying to be able to state that these results are, in a high degree, satisfactory; more so, indeed, than I had anticipated.

It has been ascertained that a practicable route exists through the chain of the Rocky Mountains, at a point sixty miles south of that now generally pursued, and in a course as much more direct as the chord of an arc is than the arc itself. A glance at the map, and a little attention to the table of latitudes, will show that from Great Salt Lake City to the head of Lodge-pole Creek, a distance of four hundred and eighty-four miles, the difference of latitude is but 35′ 42″; and that while the greatest northing made by the proposed line is but little more than 20′ north of Lodge-pole Creek, the greatest deviation to the south is but little more than three miles: so that the entire route through that long distance *varies but a trifle from a straight line.* When extended to the junction of Lodge-pole with the South Fork of the Platte, it will appear to be the chord of an arc formed by the present course of emigration. The distance from Fort Bridger to Fort Laramie, by the present route, is four hundred and eight miles; while, by the new route from Fort Bridger to the eastern base of the Black Hills, (a point equidistant with Laramie from the forks of the Platte,) it is but three hundred and forty-seven miles: so that a saving is effected, in the total distance, of just *sixty-one miles.* It must be kept in mind, too, that the distance thus ascertained was measured by an odometer, following all the undulations of the natural surface, in the course of a very rapid reconnoissance, without any minute knowledge of the localities, or any endeavour whatever to make even an approximate location for a road. When these localities come to be minutely examined, and the comparative advantages of different courses ascertained and duly weighed, there can be no doubt that even this large saving in distance may be still further increased, by shortening the route wherever it shall be found practicable. The examination of the country proved it be more favourable than we had at first supposed. For even after so successfully crossing the summit dividing the Pacific from the Atlantic waters, serious fears were still entertained lest some formidable, if not insurmountable obstruction, should be encountered in the character of the ridge of the Black Hills, intervening as it does between the Laramie Plains on the west and the great slope to the Atlantic which commences at their eastern base. All apprehensions on this head were, however, set entirely at rest by the reconnoissance, which fully demonstrated the existence of a route through these hills, not only practicable, but free from any obstructions involving in their removal great or unusual expenditure.

It was a subject of deep regret that our only remaining barometer (a cistern barometer) had been broken by the warping and cracking of its wooden frame in the dry and rarefied atmosphere of these elevated regions; as it would have been in the highest degree satisfactory to have made a precise comparison of the relative elevations of the ground on the line of this reconnoissance with those already ascertained by previous explorations upon the old route by the South Pass, the Sweetwater, and North Fork of the Platte. Although this was unfortunately impracticable, yet a careful observation of the ground on both routes has enabled me to form a general comparison between them; and has led to the unhesitating conclusion that, in point of diminished distance, easy grades, freedom from serious obstacles, and convenience and abundant supply of materials for construction, the line of this reconnoissance presents a trace for a road that is not only perfectly feasible, but decidedly preferable to the other.

From the head of Crow Creek, the way to the eastward lies open in various directions. By striking over to the Lodge-pole, and pursuing the valley of that stream to its junction with the South Fork of the Platte, an almost straight line will be secured from Fort Bridger to the Forks of the latter. Thence the Missouri can be reached either by the north bank of the river, on the route at present travelled by the Mormons, or by following its south bank, and crossing over to the Blue, below Fort Kearny: the valley of the latter stream can thence be pursued to its junction with the Kansas, and thence along that river to its confluence with the Missouri. Should a route still farther south be deemed desirable, the features of the country show, that by adopting the valley of a stream flowing between the Lodge-pole and the Crow, it would not be difficult to strike the South Fork of the Platte in the direction of the heads of the Republican Fork of the Kansas, and by means of this latter stream either to reach the Missouri at the mouth of the former, or, by a slight divergence, at some lower point, as might be thought most expedient.

It had been my intention to continue the reconnoissance from the head of the Lodge-pole to its junction with the Platte, and thence either on the dividing ground between that river and the Republican, or (had that proved unfavourable or impracticable) by the valley of the latter stream; either of which lines would have led us over ground as yet unexplored. Circumstances unfortunately prevented this design from being carried into execution.

As any examination of the country over which we passed, other than a very general one, was foreign to the objects contemplated by my instructions, I have contented myself with simply adverting to such prominent geographical features of the country as came under my observation; being satisfied that so weighty an enterprise as the selection and construction of a great line of communication with the Pacific waters will not be entered upon without previously well-considered and connected explorations. These, of course, will be of a character much more minute and elaborate than could be possibly made in the progress of a rapid reconnoissance, the results of which must necessarily be of a character too general to form the basis of other than a conjectural estimate as to comparative merits of different and conflicting routes.

The valley of the Salt Lake being the only point between the Missouri and the Pacific whence supplies of provisions can be procured, it must become an object of no little importance to embrace it in any scheme for a road across the continent.

I have already, in a previous portion of this report, suggested the route which I considered the best between Fort Bridger and that point, and which, taken in connection with the line to the head of Crow Creek, will give an excellent trace for a wagon-road all the way to the city. As to a railroad, the route is good as far as Camass Prairie; but the trace thence by either of the cañons at present travelled through the Wahsatch range to the city, will, I think, be impracticable, or at least enormously expensive. From the Camass Prairie, however, it is proposed to descend the Timpanogas, which reaches the upper level of the Salt Lake Valley at Lake Utah, some fifty miles south of the city. This part of the route I have not personally examined, but from descriptions given of it by the guides and others, I have little doubt that it will prove entirely practicable.

After reaching the Salt Lake Valley, the road, as I have heretofore suggested, might fork, one branch leading to Oregon, and the other to the Pacific within the limits of California. The former would descend the valley of the Jordan, to Salt Lake City, whence it would traverse a perfectly level country, along the eastern shore of the Salt Lake, to the ford of Bear River; crossing which, it would proceed in a north-west course, following the present emigration road until it would intersect that from the Soda Springs to the Humboldt, or Mary's River. The route to California would pursue a south course at the western base of the Wahsatch range of mountains, on the line now occupied by the Mormon settlements, and would either strike the Pacific at San Diego, or, by doubling the southern extremity of the Sierra Nevada, should that be found practicable, reach San Francisco by the Tulare Lakes and the valley of the San Joachin. As to the character of this latter route I have no precise information; but it has been frequently traversed by various companies of Mormon explorers, who declare it to be perfectly practicable; and the Mormons themselves are seriously contemplating the construction of a railroad over it, by which to secure an outlet to the ocean for the products of their territory.

Most of the projects for a railroad across the continent, as far north as 40° and 41°, look to the valley of the Humboldt as a point whence, by the branching of the road, the Pacific coast both of Oregon and California may be reached: the former by the valley of the Wallamutte, and the latter by the Salmon-trout Pass, or some other, through the Sierra Nevada. The mode that has been proposed for reaching this valley, is from the South Pass, by Sublette's Cut-off, to the Soda Springs, and thence in a south-western direction to the valley of the Humboldt. This part of the route, (from the Soda Springs to the Humboldt,) I apprehend, from the formation of the country over which it must necessarily pass, will be extremely difficult and expensive.

The northern rim of the Great Basin, or the elevated ground which divides it from the valley of the Columbia, does not consist, as has been supposed, of one continuous mountain range which may be flanked, but of a number of long, abrupt, detached, parallel ridges, extending in a north and south direction, and separated by intervening valleys, which constitute, as it were, so many summit levels, whence the waters flow north on the one side into the Columbia, and south on the other into the Great Basin. Any line, therefore, from the Soda Springs to the valley of the Humboldt, will necessarily be obliged to encounter these ridges at nearly a right angle, and will subject any trace for a road across them to variations of level, which cannot but prove obstacles of a most serious character. The route by the Salt Lake City, and thence around the northern shore of the lake, would intersect that from the Soda Springs before reaching Goose Creek, and would, from all the information I have been able to collect, pass over much more eligible ground.   From the city to the crossing of Bear River and the Malade, (a distance of eighty miles,) I know the ground, from personal observation, to be unexceptionable.   Thence, since the trace pursues a course as far south of the breaks of the northern rim of the basin as it is possible, on account of the lake, it is fair to presume that the inequalities of the ground will be much less than by the proposed route from the Soda Springs.

Any line from the Wahsatch Mountains to the valley of the Humboldt, north of the Salt Lake, cannot but prove exceedingly expensive, for the reasons just given.

But by passing south of it, a line can, I think, be found which would be comparatively free from· this objection.   After reaching the Utah Valley by the Timpanogas cañon, the road might either be carried to Salt Lake City on the eastern side of the Jordan Valley, and thence to the south shore of the lake at Black Rock; or it might cross the Jordan at the traverse range near its cañon, follow down the western side of· the same valley, and doubling the south extremity of the Oquirrh Mountain, reach the south shore of the lake at the same point, viz. Black Rock. From Black Rock the route would follow near to the shore of the lake as far as Strong's Knob, unless further examination should discover a practicable passage through the range of which it is the northern extremity, and which forms the western boundary of Spring Valley.   The route thus far from Salt Lake City would be over an absolutely horizontal plain.   From Strong's Knob, the same level desert plain extends westward for seventy or eighty miles, to the Pilot Peak range of hills, which, following the general law of the great mountain ranges in this region, extends from north to south. Having myself traversed this desert from the northern end of the Lake to Pilot Peak, and thence to Black Rock on its extreme southern shore, I can speak with confidence as to its character. It is one uniform, level plain, without verdure, and presents ground for a road that is absolutely faultless.

Westward of the range referred to I have not penetrated; but, reasoning from the structure of similar ridges in this part of the basin,—which are generally short, abrupt, and disconnected protrusions above the general level of the country, having broad level plains between them,—little doubt is entertained that a passage can, without much difficulty, be traced through to the heads of the

Humboldt.   The distance will not exceed one hundred miles; and the object to be attained renders it certainly well worthy of a careful examination.   Should the result prove favourable, we have then a perfectly practicable trace from the forks of the Platte to the valley of the Humboldt, preferable in many respects to that presented by the Sweetwater, the South Pass, and the Soda Springs.

With these general observations upon a route hitherto untraversed, I leave the subject, and return once more to our encampment at the head of the Lodge-pole.

The interval until the 6th of October was occupied in making an examination of the country to the northward of the heads of Lodge-pole; in the course of which we crossed the several sources of Horse Creek, and entered the picturesque valley of the Chugwater.   The character of the country did not vary materially from that farther south.   In several localities the ground was strewn with fragments of white quartz, and jasper of a blood-red colour. In the bed of the Chugwater, and on the sides of the adjacent hills were found immense numbers of rounded black nodules of magnetic iron-ore, which seemed of unusual richness.   The Chugwater winds from side to side of a level, well-sheltered valley, clothed with abundance of grass, and is handsomely timbered with box-elder and willow thickets, affording covert for great numbers of deer, which were more plentiful here than anywhere upon the route.   The valley is a favourite wintering spot for the Cheyenne Indians.

While encamped on the Chugwater, I sustained a severe injury by a fall, which not only incapacitated me from mounting my horse, but confined me altogether to my bed until our arrival at Fort Leavenworth.   This unfortunate accident obliged me, although with the greatest reluctance, to forego the projected reconnoissance of the valley of the Lodge-pole and of the Republican Fork, to which I had looked forward with the most sanguine anticipations. It was a source of much satisfaction, under this severe disappointment, that the great object with which we left Fort Bridger had been successfully attained.

An express was sent to Fort Laramie for surgical aid, and for an ambulance, which arrived on the 9th, and on the 12th we reached the fort.   Here every kindness was extended to us by the officers of the post; and on the 16th we left our hospitable friends, the train being in charge of Lieutenant Gunnison.   Taking the usual emigration road, we arrived at Fort Leavenworth on the 6th of November. On the 6th of December, I arrived in Washington, and had the honour to report to yourself in person.

I am, Sir,

Very respectfully,

Your obedient servant,

HOWARD STANSBURY,

Capt. Corps Topographical Engineers,

U. S. Army.

COL. JOHN JAMES ABERT,

Chief of the Corps of Topographical Engineers,

Washington.

APPENDIX A.

TABLE OF DISTANCES MEASURED ALONG THE ROUTE TRAVELLED BY THE EXPEDITION IN 1849.

OUTWARD JOURNEY.

From Fort Leavenworth, on the Missouri River, to the City of the Great Salt Lake: forming a Traveller's Guide to the several Watering and Encamping Places on the Route across the Plains, by which each Day's March may be regulated.

HOMEWARD JOURNEY.

A similar Table from Great Salt Lake City, showing the distances along the New Route explored in 1850, from Fort Bridger, across the Laramie Plains, to the heads of Lodge-Pole Creek, and thence, by Fort Laramie, to the Missouri River, at Fort Leavenworth.

ALSO,

The Measured Distances on a Route from Great Salt Lake City to Fort Hall in Oregon.

APPENDIX A.

TABLE OF DISTANCES MEASURED ALONG THE ROUTE TRAVELLED BY THE EXPEDITION IN 1849.

OUTWARD JOURNEY *from Fort Leavenworth, on the Missouri River, to the City of the Great Salt Lake.*

DATE. 1849.	PROMINENT POINTS AND REMARKS.	Inter-mediate Distance.	Day's March.	Total from Fort Leavenworth.
May 31	FORT LEAVENWORTH—Latitude, N. 39° 21' 14", according to Lt. Col. Emory; Longitude, W. 94° 44', according to Nicollet.			
	SPRING CAMP—Good cool water, and fine grass for the cattle.	6.480	6.480	6.480
June 1	NOON HALT—Near this point the road has since been abandoned for the ridge between the Missouri and Kansas Rivers; the directions are therefore made succinct until reaching the Big Blue.	7.443	......	13.923
	BRANCH—Fuel and water plenty........	4.742	12.185	18.665
" 2	SMALL CREEK—Road difficult on account of deep gullies.	7.383	7.383	25.048
" 4	INDIAN CREEK—Cross three small creeks in the first 12 miles.	18.437	18.437	43.485
" 5	INDEPENDENCE ROAD—Crossing of the St. Joseph's and Independence Road.	3.000	......	46.485
	KANSAS BRANCH—Travelling over the ridge; rising ground 6 miles, then descending, to branch creek.	9.500	......	55.985
	CREEK................................	6.858	19.358	62.843
	CREEK................................	5.335	......	68.178
	CREEK CAMP—Here we defiled to the left, leaving the road almost half a mile, for fuel and water.	14.900	20.235	83.078
" 7	THE GROVES—Fuel and water; small creek, running north.	10.790	......	93.868
" 8	NEEMAHA—Tributary of the Missouri..	6.984	17.774	100.852
	NEEMAHA BRANCH—Road has wound along the ridge between two branches of this creek. Noon halt.	8.870	......	109.722

270

OUTWARD JOURNEY—*Continued.*

DATE. 1849.	PROMINENT POINTS AND REMARKS.	Intermediate Distance.	Day's March.	Total from Fort Leavenworth.
June 8	CAMP CREEK—Fine timber and grass. Creek runs south.	7.692	16.562	117.414
" 9	VERMILION—This creek heads about 1 mile to the north-east; the ford is miry. It enters the Big Blue 20 miles above its mouth.	12.680	......	130.094
	BIG BLUE RIVER—Bank steep, bottom hard, and water 2½ feet deep. River 120 feet wide, with a brisk current.	13.863	26.543	143.957
" 11	KETCHAM'S CREEK—This is sometimes called Ten-mile Branch. Enters Big Blue below. Good grass, and some wood. Road excellent, on rolling prairie after ascending from the Blue River. The Independence Road joins it 8 miles from the Blue.	12.031	......	155.988
	TURKEY CREEK—Plenty of wood, and good grazing.	5.205	17.236	161.193
" 12	WEST TURKEY CREEK—A branch of Big Blue River.	10.588	......	171.781
	WYETH'S CREEK — Tributary of Big Blue. Good grazing, and fuel in abundance.	6.355	......	178.136
	EMIGRANTS', or WALNUT CREEK—Encampment to south of the road, in order to obtain water, wood, &c. This is a tributary of the Little Blue River.	9.915	26.858	188.051
" 13	SANDY CREEK—Camp. In about 1 mile from the last creek is a small branch; then rise considerably to a ridge; then descend to Sandy Creek, where we find feed for the cattle.	4.901	4.901	192.952
" 14	BIG SANDY CREEK—Bed is 200 feet wide, and heavy for teams.	12.918	......	205.870
	AFFLUENT—Stream small, and flows into Little Blue. The road lies on the ridge between the Sandy and Little Blue, and touches ravines in which water may be had in several places. Cross some small creeks, branches of Little Blue.	8.230	21.148	214.100
" 15	LITTLE BLUE RIVER—Left bank, up which the road lies. The road passes over some spurs from the plains, into the valley-bed, to avoid gullies. The valley is two miles wide, well wooded, and grass excellent.	8.003	......	222.103
	CAMP..	17.500	25.503	239.603
" 16	LITTLE BLUE VALLEY—The road crosses some sharp gullies, and the wheels require to be locked frequently. Camp.	24.540	24.540	264.143
" 18	LITTLE BLUE—Point of leaving the stream.	12.165	......	276.308

OUTWARD JOURNEY—*Continued.*

DATE. 1849.	PROMINENT POINTS AND REMARKS.	Inter-mediate Distance.	Day's March.	Total from Fort Leavenworth.
June 18	THIRTY-TWO MILE CREEK—A small, winding stream, with scattering trees.	7.430	......	283.738
	PLATTE RIVER—Strike the Platte in a broad valley. This road has since been abandoned for one on the left, more direct to Fort Kearny.	12.355	31.950	296.093
" 19	FORT KEARNY—Passing up the valley of the Platte, fuel difficult to be had in high water, and mostly on the islands. The fort consists of several adobe buildings for offices, stables, and two wooden structures for quarters. Emigrants and travellers obtain various supplies at the Sutler's.	14.920	14.920	311.013
" 21	CAMP 18—On the Platte....................	10.392	10.392	321.405
" 22	CAMP 19—On the Platte. Fuel along the river.	22.832	22.832	344.237
" 23	CAMP 20—On the Platte....................	23.469	23.469	367.706
" 25	CAMP 21—On right bank of Platte River; the road level and good, but fuel scarce.	24.222	24.222	391.928
" 26	CAMP 22—On South Fork of Platte, 6 miles above the junction of the Forks.	20.818	20.818	412.746
" 27	CAMP 23—On South Fork. Water, timber, and grass plenty.	11.338	11.338	424.084
" 28	CAMP 24—On South Fork.................	13.906	13.906	437.990
" 30	CAMP 25—On South Fork.................	26.787	26.787	464.777
July 2	FORD OF SOUTH FORK—This is the upper ford, and easily crossed in low stages of the river. Width 700 yards.	14.602	14.602	479.379
" 3	ASH HOLLOW—At the outlet of small creek into the valley of North Fork. The ascent for one mile on a hard road, to the rolling prairie; continue on this to within one half mile of North Fork; then descend pretty steep hills, and wind down Ash Hollow to the North Fork. Fuel in the hollow.	18.551	18.551	497.930
" 5	CAMP 28—Along the North Fork; road, most of the way heavy sand. Cedars in the gullies on the left.	22.895	22.895	520.825
" 6	CAMP 29—On North Fork. Sandy, and over spur of the table land on the left or south side. Court-house 12 miles ahead.	19.324	19.324	540.149
" 7	CAMP 30—At a cool spring, 10 miles from *Chimney Rock.* Water cool and abundant, but fuel must be brought from the bluff, two miles.	25.040	25.040	565.189
" 9	SCOTT'S BLUFF—These bluffs are about 5 miles south of the river. The road up the bluffs steep, but on good, hard, gravelly ground. A small spring at	31.017	31.017	596.206

OUTWARD JOURNEY—*Continued.*

DATE. 1849.	PROMINENT POINTS AND REMARKS.	Intermediate Distance.	Day's March.	Total from Fort Leavenworth.
July 9	the top of the first hill. Robideau has a trading post and blacksmith's-shop here, but the post is to be removed to a creek south, and over the bluffs.			
" 10	CREEK—Affluent to Horse Creek. No timber, good grass.	13.062	13.062	609.268
" 11	HORSE CREEK—No wood on this creek below the hills. The road now passes over rolling ground, leaving the Platte some distance to the right. Much of the way but few scattering trees to be seen.	1.504	......	610.772
" 11	CAMP—On the Platte	19.970	21.474	630.742
" 12	FORT LARAMIE—Camp half a mile above the fort. Cross the Laramie Fork below the fort about one mile.	16.264	16.264	647.006
" 18	WARM SPRING—The road taken leads over the Black Hills some distance south of the river; it avoids the Kanyon passes, and usually has better feed for cattle, except when it is consumed by the multitude of travellers.	13.423	13.423	660.429
" 19	BITTER CREEK BRANCH; COLD SPRING —Leaving the Warm Spring Valley, ascend a pretty steep hill, and pass over ridges to Bitter Creek.	10.469	......	670.898
	BITTER CREEK—Main branch, up which the road lies; fuel and grass abundant; stream 10 feet wide and 6 inches deep.	5.720	16.189	676.618
" 21	HORSE-SHOE CREEK—The road follows up a dry branch; no water until arriving at Horse-shoe Creek. Timber, grass, &c. Cross at the forks, and rising, pass over two ridges, with dry beds of streams.	13.490	......	690.108
	SPRING—A spring and bed of creek, the water in pools.	7.059	20.549	697.167
" 23	LA BONTÉ RIVER—From the spring rise to a high, undulating ridge, the road very crooked. Descending for 1½ miles to dry bed of creek, follow this half a mile.	10.085	......	707.252
	BRANCH	6.000	......	713.252
	CAMP—At the head of a spring branch. Road over hills, the wheels require frequent locking. Cross branches now dry. But few good situations for camping.	8.284	24.369	721.536
" 24	LA PRÉLE RIVER—Stream 16 ft. wide. We have crossed two dry beds of creeks, and a spring containing wa-	7.250	......	728.786

18

Outward Journey—*Continued.*

DATE. 1849.	PROMINENT POINTS AND REMARKS.	Inter- mediate Distance.	Day's March.	Total from Fort Leavenworth
July 24	ter from the melting of the snow. This occurs occasionally in pools, at this season.			
	CHERRY CREEK—A small stream; not to be depended on for water. Grass very scarce.	4.250	......	733.036
	ELDER CREEK—Small stream, good water, and scattering timber.	1.020	......	734.056
	FOURCHE BOISE RIVER—Good grass and fuel; stream 30 feet wide.	3.228	......	737.284
	NORTH FORK OF THE PLATTE—Camp on right bank. Grass scarce.	4.275	20.023	741.559
" 25	DEER CREEK—Clear, good water, with abundance of fuel, and coal found on the east side of the stream, a little above the crossing. Also a coal-mine in the hills.	5.000	......	746.559
	PLATTE FERRY—Lower ferry, established by emigrants. River rapid, muddy, and deep.	.760	......	747.319
	CAMP—After crossing, the road is through heavy sand most of the way, and the sand-hills often touch the banks, and must be ascended. The south bank is preferable, as far as the upper ferry.	9.820	15.580	757.139
" 26	SPRING CAMP—Brackish water in some ponds. The road has risen upon the undulating table-land above the river-level. Road heavy.	12.222	12.222	769.361
" 27	UPPER FERRY—Opposite upper ferry.	5.200	......	774.561
	RED SPRING—Near the Red Buttes. Road to-day hilly, and through heavy sand most of the way. There are mineral springs and alkaline lakes along this part of the route, dangerous for cattle. Water good in some places along the road.	18.871	24.071	793.432
" 28	SPRING AND RIVULET—Grass not plenty. Sage the only fuel.	16.821	16.821	810.253
" 30	GREASEWOOD CREEK—Six feet wide; road sandy.	6.100	......	816.353
	SALÆRATUS LAKE—Lake west of the road. Water poisonous to cattle. The salt used for bread-making.	6.214	......	822.567
	SWEETWATER RIVER—River crooked, 150 feet wide, 2 feet deep. At this season, the current is gentle. Grass plentiful, fuel scarce.	6.464	18.778	829.031
" 31	ROCK INDEPENDENCE—A granite rock, oval or egg-shaped.	.750	......	829.781
	DEVIL'S GATE—A kanyon of steep rocks, 400 feet high; the river runs through the chasm.	5.270	......	835.051

OUTWARD JOURNEY—*Continued.*

DATE. 1849.	PROMINENT POINTS AND REMARKS.	Intermediate Distance.	Day's March.	Total from Fort Leavenworth.
July 31	CREEK—Bad crossing, from the steep banks.	.480	......	835.531
	CREEK — Tributary of Sweetwater, 5 feet wide.	.500	......	836.031
	CAMP—On Sweetwater, in a bend, on the south side.	2.361	9.361	838.392
Aug. 1	SWEETWATER—Road leaves the river, and passes over hills.	7.639	......	846.031
	ALKALI LAKE—The efflorescence on the shores is like snow.	.500	......	846.531
	CAMP—On Sweetwater. Grass good...	13.500	21.639	860.031
" 2	PLATEAU—Cross the river four times this day. Camp on a plateau, after leaving river, some miles back. The water with a sulphurous smell. Sage for fuel.	19.977	19.977	880.008
" 3	ICE SPRING—Ice found by digging in the ground.	.250	......	880.258
	STEEP HILL — Descending from the bluffs.	10.000	......	890.258
	RIVER—The road joins the river, which is crossed frequently.	3.113	......	893.371
	CAMP—On south bank, having forded four times. Good place to encamp.	6.830	20.193	900.201
" 4	ROAD—Leaves the river, and passes over hills to avoid kanyons. Water in small streams every two or three miles; greasewood and sage for fuel. Some of the hills are steep, and require the wheels to be locked to descend safely.	0.750	......	900.951
	CAMP — On the Sweetwater. There are alkaline springs in the vicinity, poisonous to cattle.	22.537	23.287	923.488
" 6	SOUTH PASS — Summit of the ridge which divides the waters of the Atlantic from those of the Pacific.	9.000	......	932.488
	PACIFIC SPRINGS—Fine grass, good water, and sage plenty, for fuel.	4.531	......	937.019
	PACIFIC CREEK—Crossing miry.........	1.500	......	938.519
	CAMP—On Dry Sandy. The water is brackish; fuel scarce, and little grass.	10.239	25.270	948.758
" 7	JUNCTION—The Oregon road over the "Dry Drive," or Sublettes' Cut-off, branches here. Take the left hand.	5.500	......	954.258
	LITTLE SANDY—20 feet wide. Water good, and fuel plenty.	8.205	......	962.463
	BIG SANDY—Barren, sandy land. Road good. Stream 110 feet wide by 2 feet deep.	6.201	19.906	968.664
" 8	BIG SANDY—Cutting off bends of the river, no grass or water on this drive, after leaving the river two miles from the last camp.	19.045	19.045	987.709

Outward Journey—*Continued.*

Date. 1849.	Prominent Points and Remarks.	Inter-mediate Distance.	Day's March.	Total from Fort Leavenworth.
Aug. 9	Ford of Green River—Good camp grounds on this river. Ford crosses diagonally. A ferry is kept near the ford at high water.	11.778	......	999.487
	Camp—On right bank of Green River..	1.000	12.778	1000.487
" 10	Green River—Road leaves river, and crosses to Black's Fork. No water for 15 miles.	2.250	......	1002.737
	Black's Fork—100 feet wide, 2 feet deep. Grass and fuel.	15.500	......	1018.237
	Camp—On Ham's Fork......................	3.875	21.625	1022.112
" 11	Ham's Fork—Cross the stream, which is 50 feet wide near camp; good bottom.			
	Black's Fork—Strike Black's Fork again; cross the stream three times. Grass and water, for camping purposes, along its entire bed.	2.000	......	1024.112
	Smith's Fork—Tributary of Black's Fork.	12.125	......	1036.237
	Fort Bridger—Camp, one quarter of a mile east of fort. The road, for several miles, leaves the fork to the right, but it can easily be reached for making camps. There is a road from Ham's Fork, on the west side, to be used when the creek is swollen.	18.727	32.852	1054.964
" 16	Muddy Creek—Empties into Black's Fork below Fort Bridger. The road is the same as is described in the homeward journey of 1850, as far as the mouth of the Red Fork of Weber River.	14.830	14.830	1069.794
" 17	Bear River—The road winds up a ridge, and crosses a mountain. This can be avoided by striking up Muddy Creek a few miles, and crossing over to Sulphur Creek.	19.032	19.032	1088.826
" 18	Red Fork—In Red Kanyon, below Cache Cave.	18.754	18.754	1107.580
" 20	Weber River—At junction of Red Fork.	16.540	......	1124.120
	Camp—On right bank of Weber, at "The Obelisks."	2.000	18.540	1126.120
" 21	Weber Ford—Ford good, but current swift, over pebbles. Good timber, and feed. Leave the river here, to avoid kanyon.	2.000	......	1128.120
	Long Hill—Here you ascend a hill, winding along a rivulet of good water.	1.500	......	1129.620
	Summit—The descent from this to Bauchmin's Creek is on a side hill, and dangerous.	4.750	......	1134.370
	Bauchmin's Creek—18 feet wide, clear water; fuel and grass plenty. The	4.500	12.750	1138.870

OUTWARD JOURNEY—*Continued.*

DATE. 1849.	PROMINENT POINTS AND REMARKS.	Inter-mediate Distance.	Day's March.	Total from Fort Leavenworth.
Aug. 21	measurements are taken, to-day, from Clayton's guide-book—the Odometer being disarranged.			
" 22	BIG KANYON CREEK—Cross Bauchmin's Creek thirteen times; then, at 8 miles, begin the ascent of the mountain along a small creek, well wooded, and grass good on the ascent. The summit, at 12 miles distance, gives a view of the Great Salt Lake Valley. Hill steep to descend.	13.500	13.500	1152.370
" 23	BIG KANYON CREEK—Leave this creek and turn to the right. You can pass down on the left through the Golden Pass, and avoid this mountain.	4.500	......	1156.870
	EMIGRATION CREEK—You ascend a long hill, and then descend a steep one, to this creek.	1.750	......	1158.620
	CAMP—On Emigration Creek............	3.000	9.250	1161.620
	MOUTH OF KANYON—Opening to the valley.	2.000	......	1163.620
	CITY OF THE GREAT SALT LAKE........	5.000	7.000	1168.620

Homeward Journey from Great Salt Lake City to Fort Leavenworth, on the Missouri.

Date. 1850.	Prominent Points and Remarks.	Intermediate Distance.	Day's March.	Total from Salt Lake City.	Latitude.	Longitude.
Aug. 27	GREAT SALT LAKE CITY—In the valley of the Great Salt Lake, four miles square, extending east from the bank of Jordan river, ten miles above its mouth, along the base of a spur from the Wahsatch mountains—laid out in squares, with the Temple-block in the centre: streets 132 feet wide; lots 132 by 264 feet: Capital of Utah Territory, and contains 5000 inhabitants, a Mint, Court-house, and Tithe Store-houses. Founded in 1846, by the Presidency of Latter-day Saints.				40° 46′ 08″	112° 06′ 08″
" 28	GOLDEN PASS KANYON—Camp No. 1. Base of mountain on *Obit-to-kee-chee*, or Big Kanyon Creek. The road passes through a part of the "Big Field," six miles square, south of the city: laid off in five-acre lots, with lanes and streets between them.	8.59	8.59	8.59		
" 29	FORKS OF KANYON CREEK—Camp No. 2. Enter Kanyon, and pass the toll-house. The road is cut, in many places, around points of perpendicular rocks, and some of the curves are so abrupt that the forward cattle must be detached. Cross the stream several times—great care required. The road is being improved by labor. The scenery is grand.	7.05	7.05	15.64	40° 45′ 40″.5	111° 53′ 14″
" 30	FORD OF THE SOUTH FORK OF KANYON CREEK—Road lies on the table land, near the creek, with plenty of grass, fuel, and water. Creek 6 feet wide.	2.05	.....	17.69		
	SUMMIT OF WAHSATCH RANGE.—Ascent has been gentle, and across several small tributaries of the South Fork of Kanyon Creek.	3.43	.....	21.12	40° 44′ 48″	111° 46′ 55′.5
	TRIBUTARY BRANCH TO BAUCHMIN'S CREEK—Having crossed a rivulet previous—descent gentle and grassy.	3.64	.....	24.76		
	BRANCH—As above, at west side of Parley's Park. This is a	2.18	.....	26.94		

Date	Description	Dist.	Dist.	Total	Latitude	Longitude
	beautiful meadow, with streams fringed with willow, running through it—a fine cattle range.	.98	14.24	27.92	40° 43' 05"	111° 38' 46".8
	BAUCHMIN'S CREEK—A branch of Weber river; entering below the lower ford; drains the Park; stream 50 feet wide, and ½ deep.	1.96	......	29.88		
"31	COLD SPRING—Camp No. 3—On east part of Park: there are several fine cool springs in the vicinity, but no wood. Artemisia on the hills near by.	.95	......	30.83		
	SILVER CREEK—In East Park; creek 30 by 2 feet, well grassed; and willows, as in west, or Parley's Park. Good ford.	1.67	......	32.50		
	SUMMIT OF RIDGE between Weber river and Silver Creek—Ascent and descent gentle.	2.22	......	34.72		
	SPRING—This spring is on the east side of the ridge. Aspens and grass abundant.	6.01	......	40.73		
	SILVER CREEK—At the ford, near its entrance to Weber river. The road has been in the level of the bottom land of Weber river for 4 miles; river densely fringed with poplar.	8.25	19.10	48.98	40° 53' 41".3	111° 36' 26"
	FORD—Camp No. 4—Weber ford, upper, or Golden Pass ford. This is an excellent crossing, and fordable during the whole season of travelling.	.85	......	49.83		
Sept. 2	MORIN'S FORK—Tributary of the Weber; 30 by ½ feet. A trail leads off from this creek to a crossing of Bear River.	4.77	......	54.60	40° 57' 41".07	111° 40' 46"
	RED FORK—Near its junction with Weber River—join the old road 300 yards beyond, and turn up the valley of Red Fork.	10.73	16.35	65.33	41° 02' 27".2	111° 30' 34"
	CAMP No. 5—Road crosses Red Fork several times; the banks are steep, and careful driving is required. The sandstone and conglomerate bluffs are 150 feet high, cut into saw-teeth points, and are exceedingly picturesque. On the south side the hills are steep, with rounded summits.	5.82	......	71.15		
"3	RAVINE—Dry at this season; banks steep..............	2.40	......	73.55		
	CHICKEN-COCK BLUFF—Noon—A small stream enters Red Kanyon from the north, called "Echo Creek," from the reverberations in Red Kanyon.	......	......		41° 06' 26".1	111° 22' 06"
	THE SPRINGS—Issuing from the rocks on the north side. A grassy valley spreading out here, and at the rise on the Cache hills.	1.25	......	74.80		

HOMEWARD JOURNEY—*Continued.*

Date. 1850.	Prominent Points and Remarks.	Intermediate Distance.	Day's March.	Total from Salt Lake City.	Latitude.	Longitude.
Sept. 3	CACHE CAVE and a tributary—The Cave is in the bluffs, half a mile north of the road. Grass and sage plenty, and cedars on the bluffs.	2.24	......	77.04		
	SPRING—Base of the hill before ascent to the summit..........	3.16	......	80.20		
	SUMMIT—The hill is long, and in some places pretty steep; road smooth.	.55	......	80.75		
	YELLOW CREEK—Camp No. 6.—Half a mile below forks. A fine meadow on this creek, which is fringed with willows; no timber; stream 3 feet wide, and sharp banks—hill, to descend to this camp, steep, but smooth, and firm ground.	1.45	16.87	82.20	41° 09' 00".2	111° 14' 18"
" 4	THE NEEDLES—High pointed rocks: basaltic masses of conglomerate; cemented pebbles. Needle Creek, a small rivulet that joins Yellow Creek, is to be crossed near this point.	.88	......	83.08		
	SUMMIT between Yellow Creek and Bear River—The ascent and descent gentle and easy. The road should be carried to the south a half mile, through a lower level.	6.36	......	89.44		
	BOTTOM OF BEAR RIVER............................	1.85	......	91.29		
	BEAR RIVER—Right bank ; ford on large pebbles ; current swift, and river 400 feet wide—depth variable. The bottom land is here half a mile wide, and the river banks covered with cotton wood.	.94	......	92.23		
	SULPHUR CREEK—Near the crossing; creek 10 feet wide. An excellent spring of good water on the south; and a short distance east, several strong sulphur springs. A bed of coal crops out in the bluff on the north side. About one mile south, there are the tar springs, where this substance can be gathered for greasing wagons, and is said to be beneficial for galled horses, &c.	1.93	......	94.16	41° 08' 08".2	111° 01' 22"
	RIM BASE—At the foot of the hill, called the "Rim of the	4.29	......	98.45		

Camp	Description				Latitude	Longitude
	Basin." The road should have followed up Sulphur Creek a short distance farther, and crossed the ridge on a lower level.					
	ASPEN SPRING—Cool and delicious water; plenty of wood......	.84	......	99.29		
	SUMMIT—The ascent has been easy, gentle, and winding......	.56	......	99.85		
	COPPERAS SPRINGS—Camp No. 7—In a broad grassy ravine: several springs issue here, and some give a deposit tinged red by iron. The road has descended gently on the backbone of a spur from the Rim Mountain.	8.95	26.60	108.80	41° 13′ 46″	110° 48′ 00″
" 5	MUDDY CREEK—Tributary of Black's Fork: stream 20 feet wide; good ford.	3.97	......	112.77		
	HILL CREEK—Which joins the Muddy below: at base of steep hill which you ascend, and on the table, there is usually water to be had, from springs, one and a half miles from this creek, with good grass and sage for fuel. Descending thence a long and gentle slope.	1.53	......	114.30		
	FORT BRIDGER—On Black's Fork of Green River; built by Jas. Bridger, for a trading post; admirably situated between several tribes of Indians, and commands their trade; a good position for a military post. Timber in abundance for fuel, and fine grazing. The creek divides above the fort, and forms several islands, and drains the lake country at the foot of the Bear River Mountains.	10.15	15.65	124.45	41° 18′ 12″.8	110° 32′ 23″
" 10	BLACK'S FORK—Road cuts off the turns of the Creek, and often leaves it far to the left. There is a track also on the left bank, to the mouth of Harris's Fork, but it is longer.	4.25	4.25	128.70		
" 11	SMITH'S FORK—Branch of Black's Fork—Rises near the same, at foot of Bear Mountains; 30 feet wide; shallow; willows and sage for fuel.	15.52	......	144.22		
	BLACK'S FORK—Camp on right bank, nearly opposite the mouth of the Muddy. Groves of cotton-wood, black and yellow currant bushes, and good grass.	2.25	17.77	146.47	41° 28′ 56″.6	110° 18′ 50″
" 12	SOUTH PASS ROAD—Here we leave the old road through the South Pass, and turning to the right, commence the exploration of a new route, farther to the south.	2.49	......	148.96		
	SPRING—Under a point of ragged sandstone bluff; water a little brackish, and scanty; sage plenty.	8.52	......	157.48		

HOMEWARD JOURNEY—*Continued.*

Date. 1850.	Prominent Points and Remarks.	Intermediate Distance.	Day's March.	Total from Salt Lake City.	Latitude.	Longitude.
Sept. 12	PLAIN—Meridional observation gives the latitude. The route lies across the great bend of Black's Fork.	2.42	......	159.90	41° 31′ 08″.3	110° 04′ 15″
	BLACK'S FORK—A gentle slope, for six miles, on the eastern side of the table land; no water at this season; road good; ford easy; creek 150 feet wide; buffalo-berry and currant-bushes for fuel.	12.01	25.44	171.91		
" 13	SUMMIT of ridge between Black's Fork and Green River—Road good, and ascent gentle; thence down Rabbit Hollow.	7.44	......	179.35		
	GREEN RIVER—Right bank; river 800 feet wide; ford good at this stage of the water; cross diagonally. The road descends into Rabbit Hollow, and winds along the dry channel of a creek in the bottom.	4.46	......	183.81		
	CAMP No. 12—Following down left bank to near the outlet of Bitter Creek; fuel abundant.	1.47	13.37	185.28	41° 30′ 44″.5	109° 38′ 40″
" 14	BITTER CREEK COAL-BED—Strike Bitter Creek in one mile from Camp. There is coal on the left bank, under a high bluff, two miles from the mouth.	13.59	......	198.87		
	EVANS'S TRACE—Camp No. 13—This is a trace made by a party of emigrants from Arkansas, in 1849, which continues north of Bitter Creek to Bridger's Fort. The grass on this part of the route is very limited, and sage the only fuel. Water slightly brackish and sulphurous.	3.44	17.03	202.31	41° 34′ 40″.8	109° 28′ 09″
" 15	POND—Half a mile to the north-east is a small pond.....	10.60	......	212.91		
	FORD—Cross to the left bank; Evans's Trace on the right; creek 80 feet wide, and 6 feet deep; banks steep.	5.92	......	218.83		
	SULPHUR SPRINGS—Camp No. 14—Several beds of coal crop out in the bluffs along the creek, and are easily crumbled down for fuel. The springs are on the right bank, and issue from the base of high bluff rocks of gray sandstone. Evans's	8.34	24.86	227.17		

No.	Remarks	Dist.		Total	Latitude	Longitude
	Trace takes the north-east branch, and joins, near the Platte River.	6.80	......	233.97		
16	COAL RIDGE—Up the left bank, and across a ridge, with coal cropping out. The road can follow the level ground. To follow the creek from this hill, prolongs the distance, but the crossing is very difficult on account of steep clay-banks.	5.45	......	239.42	41° 30' 51"	108° 50' 34"
	NOON—The meridian observation gives position in latitude......	10.06	22.31	249.48	41° 28' 09"	108° 41' 09"
	EAST FORK—Camp No. 15.—Grass good, and large sage for fuel. Sage hens abundant, and antelope plenty.					
17	SPRING BLUFF—Noon halt—Small streams from springs on south-east enter the main branch in this vicinity.	9.63	......	259.11	41° 24' 12"	108° 31' 00"
	SUMMIT—Leaving Bitter Creek waters, pass up a gentle slope to summit.	9.85	......	268.96		
	HAY-STACK—A beacon 120 feet high, of clay, standing apart from larger plateaus on the south and east.	.58	......	269.54		
	SPRINGS—Camp No. 16.—Alkaline water; head of Bridger's Fork. This water is barely drinkable for man or beast. Sage-brush furnishes the fuel, and grass very thin.	6.01	26.07	275.55	41° 28' 39"	108° 14' 24"
18	PLAINS—At west side of the plains of Muddy Creek.............	3.69	......	279.24		
	RIDGE—Noon halt—On a low ridge from the north. The road is very good, over grassy plains and buffalo ranges.	7.89	......	287.13	41° 28' 14"	108° 02' 11"
	MUDDY CREEK—Camp No. 17.—A branch of Little Snake River. The road should pass to the south, around a ridge which has a steep descent on the east side. Two sandstone buttes north of the road, covered with cedars.	8.87	20.45	296.00	41° 27' 06".1	107° 52' 41"
19	NORTH BEND OF MUDDY CREEK—On right bank, near Vasques' battle-ground. Very soon we enter the kanyon, where the road is on narrow table-land, at the foot of steep hills and rocks.	10.39	......	306.39	41° 28' 28".5	107° 41' 21"
	KANYON OF MUDDY CREEK—Road easily made practicable. Cherries and currants abundant in the fruit season.	2.67	......	309.06		
	BEAVER DAMS—Camp No. 18.—Small prairie with good grass. Fresh dams seen here in considerable numbers. Cattle can be easily guarded. Several gullies to cross to-day. Aspen, service-berry, cherry, and on the escarpment, cedar trees and bushes.	1.08	14.14	310.14	41° 27' 41"	107° 38' 48"

HOMEWARD JOURNEY—*Continued.*

Date. 1850.	Prominent Points and Remarks.	Intermediate Distance.	Day's March.	Total from Salt Lake City.	Latitude.	Longitude.
Sept. 20	Muddy Creek—Leave this creek one mile below its forks. It rises in the Park Mountains.	2.27	......	312.41		
	Summit between the Pacific and Atlantic Waters—Ascent very gentle; pass several small springs. The champagne country continues to the Wind River Mountains, and can be crossed in many places, the choice being determined by considerations of fuel and water.	6.38	......	318.79		
	Spring—Noon halt—Aspen grove spring, head of a branch to Sage Creek. The route to the south of this, along the base of Aspen Mountain, would be shorter and better.	2.22	......	321.01	41° 33′ 22″.3	107° 30′ 48″
	West Branch—Leave this branch, and pass over a low swell to the east.	6.23	......	327.24		
	Middle Branch—Camp No. 20—On right bank of a small stream from the south. Sage abundant; grass rather poor.	4.65	21.75	331.89	41° 35′ 21″	107° 21′ 52″
" 21	Evans' Trace—Direction from the camp is toward the Medicine-bow Mountains. Evans' Trace from Bitter Creek here crosses Sage Creek valley.	1.90	......	333.79		
	Sage Creek—From south; 40 feet wide; a brisk shallow stream; then ascend and pass over a gullied ridge.	6.47	......	340.26		
	North Fork of the Platte River—Left bank: a beautiful poplar grove and park; remains of old Indian forts: warground of neighbouring tribes; fine grazing; buffalo herds are frequently met with here. The measured distances to this point are checked by the longitude given by Col. Frémont.	7.92	16.29	348.18	41° 32′ 49″.2	107° 06′ 11″
" 23	Platte Ford—The road along the left bank in cotton-wood groves; hills and valley well grassed; ford over a ripple; deepest water at present stage, 2½ feet, and banks easy. Thence rise gradually to the plain.	2.98	......	351.16		

Date	Stations and Remarks				Latitude	Longitude
	Noon on Plain—Extending to the base of the hills west of Medicine-bow Butte. Meridian observation.	9.09	......	360.25	41° 37' 15".8	106° 53' 31"
	Pass Creek—Descends from the Medicine-bow Pass; plain destitute of wood, except sage-bushes.	1.06	......	361.31		
	Branch—From foot of buttes on the west side of Medicine-bow Butte.	2.00	......	363.31		
	Rattlesnake Creek—This creek heads in Medicine-bow Butte, and the hills on the west of it; is 5 feet wide, by 4 inches, at lowest stage; brisk current; many gullies in the argillaceous deposite, and road winding for two miles.	3.09	......	366.40		
	Camp No. 21—On south branch of Rattlesnake Creek, between West and Medicine-bow Butte; haw, willows, and birch for fuel, and good bunch-grass for cattle.	4.99	28.21	371.39	41° 40' 45".2	106° 48' 37"
" 24	Summit—Ascend to gap on a gentle slope; good road; then a slight descent to Laramie Plains, crossing several small spring creeks, tributary to Butte Creek.	1.24	......	372.63		
	Butte Creek—Small creek of pure water. Latitude by noon observation......	3.67	......	376.30	41° 41' 50".9	106° 36' 57"
	observation......	1.80	......	378.10		
	Creek—Clear water spring, 6 feet wide and 3 inches deep, lowest stage; willow-clumps.	2.08	......	380.18		
" 25	Medicine-bow River—Camp No. 22.—The banks are low, wooded, and firm. Water at present low stage, 25 feet wide and 6 inches deep; rapid current.	1.84	10.66	382.02		
	Aspen Creek—*This part of the plain dangerous to run buffalo, on account of large sage and frequent gullies!*	4.38	......	386.40		
	Birch Creek—Small birch and other trees; grass in patches, good.	1.52	......	387.92		
	Meridian Observation—Noon halt......	2.35	......	390.27	41° 38' 38".6	106° 24' 47"
	Alder Creek—Tributary to East Fork of Medicine-bow River; good grass.	3.58	......	393.85		
	East Fork Medicine-bow River—Near the kanyon; creek 20 feet wide, and 1 foot deep; rapid current, pebbly bed, and runs through beautiful bottom land.	2.14	......	395.99		
	Frappe's Creek—Camp No. 23.—A branch of Medicine-bow River; 6 feet wide, ½ foot deep; about a half-mile from the kanyon.	2.97	16.94	398.96	41° 33' 06"	106° 15' 58"

Homeward Journey—*Continued.*

Date. 1850.	Prominent Points and Remarks.	Intermediate Distance.	Day's March.	Total from Salt Lake City.	Latitude.	Longitude.
Sept. 26	LAKE FORK—Small stream running north into small lake. The plain covered with grass, and delightful road. Some poplar-trees on the Fork. Second lake stream 1 mile from the first.	6.16	.....	405.12		
	PLAINS—Meridian observations for latitude	4.48	.....	409.60	41° 28′ 16″	106° 06′ 35″
	POND—Rolling country for a few miles	2.53	.....	412.13		
	STREAM—Small stream, branch of Laramie River	5.02	.....	417.15		
	LARAMIE FORK—Camp No. 24—25 feet wide, by 8 inches deep, low stage; banks low and firm; easily forded; grass inexhaustible, and fuel pretty abundant; West Fork.	2.72	20.91	419.87	41° 19′ 48″.4	105° 57′ 12″
" 27	PONDS—Two small ponds; miserable water. Meridian observations for latitude.	11.78	.....	431.65	41° 15′ 41″.4	105° 45′ 39″
	LARAMIE MAIN FORK—Right bank at Poplar Fork. Excellent grass and good ford at this place. Sioux and Cheyenne hunting-grounds. A road to Fort Laramie, along this river, used by the traders.	3.08	14.86	434.73		
" 28	SPRING BRANCH—Fine level road; good water and fuel. Here the road should keep more southerly, crossing the Black Hills over a lower ridge, and crossing Crow Creek, deflect northerly, to Lodge Pole Creek; thence down its valley to its junction with the South Fork of the Platte.	7.59	.....	442.32		
	TETON—Opposite a lone peak called "The Teton," on the Black Hills slope. . The rise is quite gradual.	6.17	.....	448.49		
	SPRING, and small branch, in ravine	1.80	.....	450.29		
	SUMMIT—Between Laramie River and Crow Branch	2.75	.....	453.04		
	CROW BRANCH—The route was changed from the timbered heads of Lodge Pole Creek, to turn southerly to Crow Creek. This crook in the trace can be avoided by keeping to the south.	3.54	21.85	456.58	41° 08′ 02″	105° 24′ 11″
" 29	CROW CREEK—At the kanyon opening; the road is on the ridge,	10.93	.....	467.51		

Date	Description				Latitude	Longitude
	at the heads of ravines and spring-branches of Crow Creek. Pines, fir, cotton-wood, for timber; currants and hawthorn bushes, and low bush, black cherries.					
	CAMP No. 27—Down left bank; trees ended; willows for fuel; the creek sinks into the sand just below. The road from this point should strike eastwardly, crossing several small branches, and finally follow down Lodge Pole Creek, to the South Fork of the Platte River.	3.72	14.65	471.23	41° 09' 03".5	105° 08' 24"
30	CROW BRANCH—Passing north, into the Cheyenne Pass, along the foot of the Black Hills on the west, and a table-land, two hundred feet above the level of the road, two miles to the right.	3.43	......	474.66		
	LODGE POLE BRANCH—Supposed branch of Lodge Pole Creek; 3 feet wide; no fuel in the pass; but at the kanyon, abundant.	5.77	......	480.43		
	LODGE POLE CREEK—About two miles below Kanyon Creek; 3 feet wide.	3.00	......	483.44		
	NOON HALT—Bear Creek, a branch of Lodge Pole Creek; water in pools.	2.14	......	485.58	41° 21' 45".7	105° 12' 21"
	HORSE CREEK—Supposed south branch.	4.01	......	489.59		
	HORSE CREEK—Main branch; 4 feet wide.	1.20	......	490.79		
	NORTH BRANCH—Having crossed a marsh rivulet.	1.67	......	492.46		
	CHUGWATER RIVER—Camp No. 28—From the north branch, you soon pass over a low "divide," to a dry branch of Chug-water; thence, down this, to the Chug gates, where there is plenty of box-elder, willows, &c. Here the river breaks through a plateau that joins the table on the east side of the Cheyenne Pass.	8.99	30.23	501.45	41° 45' 35".8	104° 59' 25"
Oct. 1	CHUGWATER RIVER—Pass down bank, crossing the creek at four and three-fourth miles; cross the main stream twice; fuel and grass abundant; high land on each side of the stream.	4.75	......	506.20		
	NOON HALT—Bottom-land one-fourth mile wide. Observation for latitude.	9.68	......	515.88	41° 39' 58".4	104° 56' 45"
	CAMP No. 29—On the bottom-land, which is here half a mile wide. A reconnoissance made from this point, among the Black Hills, is not here inserted.	3.98	17.71	519.16		

HOMEWARD JOURNEY—*Continued.*

Date. 1850.	Prominent Points and Remarks.	Intermediate Distance.	Day's March.	Total from Fort Laramie.	Total from Salt Lake City.	Latitude.	Longitude.
Oct. 10	Camp No. 33—Along the bottom land; good road........	12.65	12.65	......	531.81		
" 11	Fort Laramie—Rising to the rolling table-land, and turning toward the west to avoid the gullies of "Goshen's Hole," prolongs the road three miles. It is better to keep down the Chugwater, passing the "Chimney," to Hunter's Spring, and thence to the fort.	34.03	34.03	......	565.84	42° 12′ 38″.2	104° 31′ 26″
" 16	Ford of Laramie River—Ford the stream just below the fort. Pass Bissonette's trading-post, five miles from Laramie.	......	......	......	......	42° 12′ 22″	104° 31′ 26″
"	Camp No. 35—On the right bank of the North Platte; good timber and grass for camping purposes.	6.80	6.80	6.80	572.64		
" 17	Badeau's—A trading house, without pickets. Below this, pass over a ridge to avoid the river, which impinges on the clay banks; then along Platte bottom.	2.00	......	8.80	574.64		
"	Richard's—Trading-post belonging to the American Fur Company. Average width of bottom 3 miles, having grass and timber abundant.	10.76	......	19.56	585.40		
"	Horse Creek—Timber has become scarce along the river—here there is none.	16.69	......	36.25	602.09		
" 18	Camp No. 36—Turning down Horse Creek a short distance; then towards Platte, obliquely, to a small creek.	1.59	31.04	37.84	603.68	41° 55′ 36″.7	103° 58′ 28″
"	Old Track—A road lies along the river, but it is not worn; said to be shorter than that by Scott's Bluffs. We ascend gently to the old track, which leaves the river at Horse Creek.	5.90	......	48.74	609.58		
"	Scott's Bluffs—At a small rivulet, row of old, deserted houses. A spring at the foot of Sandstone Bluffs, where the road crosses the ridge. Cedars on the Bluffs, and good grass on the plain.	7.62	......	51.86	617.20	41° 48′ 25″.7	103° 45′ 02″

Date	No.	Remarks					Latitude	Longitude
Oct. 18	18	CAMP No. 37—Bottom widens to eight miles. Good grass, but no fuel. Some drift-wood on the islands, and cedars on the hills to the south.	20.83	34.35	72.19	638.03	41° 45' 39"	103° 21' 44"
"	19	NOON HALT—About two miles below the "Court House," in the hills. Road has departed, most of the way, from the river banks from one to three miles, but here touches the right bank.	22.19	......	94.38	660.22		
		ELK CREEK—Bed 20 feet by ½ foot. Flows from the south-west. Rises in a valley behind Chimney-rock bluffs and ridge.	1.00	......	95.38	661.22		
"	20	PLATTE—Camp No. 38—Good grass along this part of the bottom; fuel scarce.	11.46	34.65	106.84	672.68	41° 33' 22"	102° 45' 10"
		CREEK—Coming from S. S. E. 20 feet wide, 5 inches deep.	1.50	......	108.34	674.18		
		RIDGE—Sandy ridge, to avoid the Steep Bluff; north bank.	10.00	......	118.34	684.18		
		DRY CREEK—A sandy bed. Water flows from melting snow. Water a short distance to south, in pools.	8.20	......	126.54	692.38		
		BLUFFS—Ascend about 60 feet above the river, and keep at this elevation for two miles.	8.00	......	134.54	700.38		
"	21	CAMP No. 39—On bank of Platte. Fuel difficult to find...	2.48	30.18	137.02	702.86		
		ASH HOLLOW—The road continues at foot of bluffs; heavy sand. Cedars, in the hills, for camping purposes. Ash Hollow has abundance of ash and poplar wood; a small stream in the bottom. This is a deep chasm, made by the washing-out from the dividing ridge between the Platte Forks. Here the road leaves for the South Fork, and the ridge is crossed by several tracks; one leads to the junction of the two forks, ours to the upper crossing of the South Fork.	12.18	......	149.20	715.04		
"	22	MERIDIAN—At the last point, for water, at this season.....	1.19	......	150.39	716.23	41° 17' 18".7	102° 02' 28"
		FORD—Camp No. 40—Upper ford. For one and a half miles gentle ascent, in hollow; then a long, steep hill to ascend; thence fine road to the ford, last mile descending.	17.57	30.98	167.96	733.80		
		FORD OF SOUTH FORK OF THE PLATTE—Width of ford 2045 feet; deepest water in channel 18 inches, where, in July, 1849, we found 3½ feet.						

HOMEWARD JOURNEY—*Continued.*

Date. 1850.	Prominent Points and Remarks.	Intermediate Distance.	Day's March.	Total from Fort Laramie.	Total from Salt Lake City.	Latitude.	Longitude.
Oct. 22	Spring—Near the river bank a fine, large, cool spring.....	13.40	......	181.36	747.20		
	Camp No. 41—Along the level bottom, good road. Here the plain, three miles wide, could be irrigated. Willows and small cottonwood on the islands.	17.94	31.34	199.30	765.14		
" 23	Camp Ground—About a mile above the junction of the forks of the Platte. Here is plenty of wood and fine grass. The road rises to the table-land at this place, and occasionally descends to the bottom.	11.70	......	211.00	776.84		
	Spring Creek—Camp No. 42—Leaving the road track at the foot of the table-land, pass down toward the Platte one mile, and encamp on a small creek, which rises from springs above.	23.58	35.28	234.58	800.42		
" 24	First Creek—Continuing down the Valley of the Platte; islands in the river covered with trees, but wood difficult to obtain. The table is broken, as it approaches the bottom on the south, into bluffs and hills, with occasional cedars.	11.20	......	245.78	811.62		
	Fourth Creek—Two small streams intermediate. Timber on the south bank.	5.15	......	250.93	816.77		
	Camp No. 43—At the "Two Trees," two large cottonwoods, which serve as beacons, but will probably be felled by travellers.	18.94	35.28	269.87	835.71		
" 25	Plumb Creek—The bottom has widened to about fifteen miles, is well grassed; fuel can be obtained here.	30.52	......	300.39	866.23		
	Camp No. 44—A small branch of the river can here be crossed, and fuel brought from the island. The soil is marly sand, with some loam, and easily irrigated from the river.	3.82	34.34	304.21	870.05		
" 26	Eighteen-mile Point—Along the bank; road good........	15.41	......	319.62	885.46		

Date	Localities and Remarks						
Oct. 26	FORT KEARNY—Opposite Grand Island, in the level plain, about three quarters of a mile from the Platte River. The sutler's store will supply travellers with groceries, cloths, and many useful articles.	15.95	31.36	335.57	901.41	40° 38' 45"	98° 58' 11"
" 28	PLATTE—Leave the Platte. The course is south-easterly, across the bottom, and, passing to the table-land, between bluffs of sand and sandstone. Cross the divide on an undulating prairie. Hills not steep.	10.23	......	345.80	911.64		
	THIRTY-TWO MILE CREEK—A tributary of Little Blue. Very little water, and that in pools. Scattering cottonwood trees.	22.38	32.61	368.18	934.02		
" 29	LITTLE BLUE—Cross a gully, and descend gently...........	7.40	......	375.58	941.42		
	NOON HALT—A branch from the south-west here joins......	6.05	......	381.63	947.47		
	DRY SANDY CREEK—The road occasionally rises to the higher ground, where the river impinges upon the banks.	15.95	29.40	397.58	963.42		
" 30	OAK GROVE—The road here strikes the river, having been on the upland for ten miles from Dry Sandy.	13.50	......	411.08	976.92	40° 13' 41"	97° 54' 36"
	TURN CREEK—We leave Little Blue at this place. The route from Oak Grove often interrupted by gullies, along which oaks, elms, and ash are found.	12.00	25.50	423.08	988.92	40° 11' 16"	97° 39' 02"
" 31	CREEK—Branch of Turn Creek. Scattering trees, and good grass.	3.00	......	426.08	991.92		
	CREEK—At two miles, thence four and a half miles to wood, on dry bed of creek.						
	OX-BOW CREEK—Little water at this season; wood and water for camping in early summer.	15.00	......	441.08	1006.92		
	BIG SANDY—Fuel and water good. Grass on the hills.....	7.99	25.98	449.07	1014.91		
Nov. 1	BRANCH—At twelve miles, with wood. A branch of Turkey Creek.	13.77	......	462.84	1028.68		
	TURKEY CREEK—The road has been winding and hilly, but on firm ground.						
	TEN MILE BRANCH—Tributary of the Big Blue. Fuel, water, and grass.	19.83	33.60	482.67	1048.51		
" 2	BIG BLUE—Rolling country. Stream at low stage; 160 feet wide by 2½ feet deep. Thence a long ascent.	12.04	......	494.71	1060.55		

HOMEWARD JOURNEY—*Continued.*

Date. 1850.	Prominent Points and Remarks.	Intermediate Distance.	Day's March.	Total from Fort Laramie.	Total from Salt Lake City.	Latitude.	Longitude.
Nov. 2	VERMILION—Cross a small branch half a mile from Big Blue.	19.49	31.52	514.20	1180.04		
" 3	JUNCTION—The old road, to the north, is near the Vermilion; the new track keeps on the ridge, having the heads of streams frequent, with timber on either hand, at a short distance from the road.						
	BRANCH—Supposed tributary to the Big Nemaha, 10½ feet wide by 2 inches deep.	24.05	......	538.25	1204.03		
	CREEK—Runs south, into the Nemaha; the road passing between branches.	12.08	36.13	550.33	1216.17		
" 4	NEMAHA BRANCH—We ascend, from the tributary, to high ground; good road.	19.57	19.57	569.90	1235.74		
" 5	CREEK—Runs south.................	7.60	......	577.50	1243.34		
	CREEK—Runs south; has fine timber and grass in vicinity.	4.66	......	582.16	1248.00		
	CREEK—Rising a long slope, and then descending from the ridge.	5.46	......	587.62	1253.46		
	INDEPENDENCE CREEK—Road sinuous; on the dividing ridge between affluents of Kansas and Missouri Rivers.	14.89	32.61	602.51	1268.35		
" 6	FORT LEAVENWORTH—The road winds on the "divide" till within fourteen miles from the fort, and then descends and crosses several small streams, affluents of the Missouri.	22.74	22.74	625.25	1291.09	39° 21' 14"	94° 44' 00"

DISTANCES *measured by the Odometer, from the North Line of the City of the Great Salt Lake to Cantonment Loring, in Oregon.*

	Miles.
Weber River, near Brown's	37.05
Ogden's Pass, opposite the Pass into	43.68
Maple Creek, tributary to Bright Creek	53.29
Box Elder Creek	61.19
Small Lake	64.97
Hot Springs—Fresh, Cold Springs 25 feet off	71.96
Bear River—Ford	79.10
First Spring	91.96
Second Spring—4 fine springs, ⅓ mile further	97.11
Spring Branch	103.39
Large Spring	107.43
Creek	111.40
Camp on Malade	114.33
Small Stream	118.22
Hedspeth's Cut-off—road from Bear River	125.46
End of Pass, in Hedspeth's Cut-off	129.84
East Fork of Malade	132.07
Summit of Ridge	134.78
Foot of divide of Malade and Pannack Rivers	140.42
Kanyon of Pannack	145.07
Branch of Pannack—after 3 small branches have been crossed.	155.59
Forks of Pannack	159.12
Windmill Rock	164.09
Leave the Pannack	171.97
Port Neuf River	177.00
Crossing of Stream	179.81
Cantonment Loring, 5 miles beyond Fort Hall	187.75

DISTANCES FROM THE STATE-HOUSE, *City of the Great Salt Lake, to the Settlement in the San Pete Valley, on a branch of Sevier River. Communicated from the San Pete Company's Journal.*

PROMINENT POINTS AND CAMPING DISTANCES.	Miles.	Totals.
To Kanyon Creek Bridge	4¼	
" Mill Creek	2½	6¾
" First Cotton-wood Creek	2	8¾
" Bishop Crosly's	3	11¾
" Second Cotton-wood Creek	1	12¾
" Forks of Road	1¼	14
" Dry Creek	3½	17¼
" Willow Creek	2¾	20¼
" Hot Springs	2¾	23
" Summit of Hill at Jordan Kanyon	2	25
" Dry (Utah) Creek	6¼	31¼
" American Spring	1¾	33
" American Creek	1¼	34½
" Marsh Creek	3¾	38¼
" Cedar Grove	5¼	43½
" Timpanogas River	2½	46
" Spring Base of the Mountains	5¾	51¾
" Spring Creek	¾	52½
" Pimquan Creek	1	53½
" Pequinnetty (Spanish Fork) Creek	6	59½
" Clear Creek	3	62½
" Petenete Creek	2¼	64¾
" Aph "	3¼	68
" Wa-ka-tiky (Summit Creek)	2¾	70¾
" Pungun—Ghost Spring	7¼	78
" Warm Spring Creek	¾	78¾
" Watage " At 3¾ miles take left-hand road	3¼	82
" Ona-pah (Salt) Creek at kanyon	8¾	90¾
" Kanyon Forks	2	92¾
" Third Crossing of Ona-pah	2½	95¼
" Summit leaving Ona-pah Valley	3	98¼
" Pleasant Creek, in San Pete Valley	5¾	104
" Springs in Slough	6¾	110¾
" San Pete Creek	1¾	112¼
" San Pete Crossing	1¾	114¼
" Timpa Creek	9¼	123½
" Mouna Creek	2	125½
" City Creek, 12 feet wide	5¼	130¾

NOTE.—The San Pete Settlement was began in 1849, and in 1850 a city was laid out by the Presidency. The distances measured by an Odometer, attached to a wagon. This is on the road to Iron City, in the Little Salt Lake Valley, and the southern road to California.

APPENDIX B.

LATITUDES AND LONGITUDES OF THE PRINCIPAL
TRIANGULATION STATIONS;

TABULATION OF THE TRIANGLES DEVELOPED IN THE SURVEY
OF THE GREAT SALT LAKE;

AND TABLE OF GEOGRAPHICAL POSITIONS.

NOTE.

THE Angles of the Triangulation were measured with a seven-inch theodolite, by Draper. The instrument was scarcely competent to the work, from the low power of its telescope, the great distance between most of the stations, the mirage, and the almost constant haze that pervaded the atmosphere. Many repetitions of the readings were consequently necessary to secure the requisite accuracy in the results. This was peculiarly the case in obtaining the Azimuth of the Base Line, which was fixed by observations of the Polar Star. The work is believed to be sufficiently accurate to correct the detailed measurements, as well as to form a basis upon which a triangulation may hereafter be extended over this great internal basin, should such a work ever be contemplated by the Government. The natural features of this desolate region, abounding as it does in lofty eminences, widely separated by intervening level plains, is admirably adapted to such an operation; although its execution could not but be attended with great labour and privation. Many of the deserts would furnish extended plains, absolutely level, upon which a degree of the Meridian could be measured to great advantage.

APPENDIX B.

GREAT SALT LAKE VALLEY.

Latitudes and Longitudes of the Principal Triangulation Points and Stations.

No.	LOCALITIES.	Latitude.	Longitude.
No. 1	Near Adobe Hall, in the city. Long. from Frémont.	40° 46′ 04″	112° 06′ 08″
" 2	East end of base-line........................	40° 53′ 15″.6	112° 11′ 17″.8
" 3	West end of base line........................	40° 51′ 28″	112° 17′ 45″.8
" 4	Constitution Hill, north of city...........	40° 48′ 03″.6	112° 06′ 51″
" 5	Rose Spring, west side of Great Salt Lake valley.	40° 38′ 30″.9	112° 16′ 00″
" 6	On mound near mouth of Dry Cotton-wood.	40° 34′ 24″.3	112° 07′ 12″.7
" 7	On the table east side of Jordan Kanyon.	40° 26′ 51″.3	112° 06′ 40″.5
" 8	North-east shore of Utah Lake............	40° 21′ 24″.9	112° 04′ 38″.1
" 9	Near Timpanogos Kanyon, east side of Utah Lake.	40° 19′ 47″.9	111° 53′ 37″.9
" 10	West side of mountain, at Jordan Kan-yon.	40° 26′ 49″.7	112° 09′ 05″.2
" 11	Young's Peak, highest Point on Ante-lope Island.	40° 57′ 20″.5	112° 25′ 20″.3
" 12	Black Rock; south shore Great Salt Lake: salt-works.	40° 43′ 08″	112° 26′ 02″.4
" 13	Carrington Island............................	41° 00′ 06″.6	112° 46′ 26″
" 14	Frémont Island	41° 10′ 04″.6	112° 32′ 47″
" 15	Strong's Knob, west side of Great Salt Lake.	41° 14′ 28″.2	113° 05′ 08″.8
" 16	Promontory Point............................	41° 11′ 54″.3	112° 38′ 02″
" 17	Gunnison Island..............................	41° 20′ 23″.9	113° 03′ 23″.8
" 18	Dolphin Island.	41° 27′ 38″.7	113° 11′ 52″.5
" 19	Horned Frog, on east side of north-west branch of Lake.	41° 27′ 55″.5	112° 54′ 44″.7
" 20	Saturday, on mound, north-east side of Spring Bay.	41° 33′ 06″.2	112° 59′ 42″.4
" 21	Lighthouse, north end of Lake, west shore.	41° 42′ 22″.6	113° 02′ 29″.7
" 22	Mud Island, near mouth of Bear River.	41° 14′ 53″.8	112° 26′ 29″.8
" 23	Dome on Stansbury's Island	40° 51′ 18″	112° 42′ 31″.3
" 24	Head Peak, north of Bear River Bay...	41° 35′ 46″.6	112° 27′ 07″.3

TABULATION OF TRIANGLES.

No.	Station.	Ang.	Log.	Side opposite.	Length. Feet.	Length. Miles.	Logarithms.
1. { A.	East Base.............	102° 49′ 49″.4	9.9890187	B. C.	54,299.5	10.2840	1.0121502
{ B.	West Base.............	42° 29′ 51″.2	9.8296627	A. C.	37,620.5	7.1251	0.8527942
{ C.	Constitution Hill.....	34° 40′ 19″.4	9.7550198	A. B.	31,680	6.0000	0.7781513
	Base Line.............	......	......	......	31,680	6.0000	0.7781513
2. { B.	West Base.............	61° 43′ 37″	9.9448281	D. C.	71,630	13.5663	1.1324610
{ C.	Constitution Hill.....	76° 23′ 27″	9.9876321	D. B.	79,028.4	14.9713	1.1752650
{ D.	Rose Spring..........	41° 52′ 56″	9.8245173	B. C.	54,299.5	10.2840	1.0121502
3. { C.	Constitution Hill.....	34° 50′ 25″	9.7568571	E. D.	47,507.8	8.9977	0.9541817
{ D.	Rose Spring..........	85° 41′ 23″	9.9987699	E. C.	82,923.4	15.7052	1.1960445
{ E.	Dry Cotton-wood......	59° 28′ 12″	9.9351864	C. D.	71,630	13.5663	1.1324610
4. { D.	Rose Spring..........	27° 06′ 00″.6	9.6585337	E. F.	45,901.4	8.69345	0.9391922
{ E.	Dry Cotton-wood......	124° 46′ 07″.4	9.9145867	F. D.	82,771.3	15.67640	1.1952452
{ F.	East Utah Kanyon.....	28° 07′ 52″	9.6734732	D. E.	47,507.8	8.99770	0.9541817
5. { E.	Dry Cotton-wood......	13° 42′ 25″	9.3746675	F. G.	11,099.7	2.10222	0.3226563
{ F.	East Utah Kanyon.....	87° 47′ 10″	9.9996757	E. G.	46,805.6	8.86471	0.9476645
{ G.	West Utah Kanyon.....	78° 30′ 25″	9.9912034	E. F.	45,901.4	8.69345	0.9391922
6. { F.	East Utah Kanyon.....	104° 59′ 03″	9.9849759	G. H.	38,715.4	7.33248	0.8652507
{ G.	West Utah Kanyon.....	58° 56′ 18″	9.9327844	F. H.	34,331.5	6.50218	0.8130592
{ H.	Near Outlet of Dry Creek.....	16° 04′ 39″	9.4423815	F. G.	11,099.7	2.10222	0.3226563
7. { F.	East Utah Kanyon.....	37° 59′ 00″	9.7891802	H. I.	51,762.6	9.80354	0.9913830
{ H.	Near Outlet of Dry Creek.....	117° 55′ 33″	9.9462334	F. I.	74.313	1.40746	1.1483362
{ I.	Timpanogas...........	24° 05′ 27″	9.6108564	F. H.	34,431.5	6.50218	0.8130592

		Station	Angle	Log	Initials	Distance		
8.	H.	Near Outlet of Dry Creek	66° 20' 41"	9.9618841	I.J.	49,534	9.38145	0.9722701
	I.	Timpanogas	40° 28' 54"	9.8123817	H.J.	35,107.6	6.64918	0.8227682
	J.	Long Point on Utah Lake	73° 10' 25"	9.9809965	H.L	51,762.6	9.80354	0.9913830
9.	I.	Timpanogas	37° 12' 30"	9.7973123	J.L.	47,768.5	9.04708	0.9565085
	J.	Long Point	103° 57' 28"	9.9869838	I.L.	76,660.8	14.51910	1.1619416
	L.	Table Point	38° 50' 02"	9.7815507	I.J.	49,534	9.38145	0.9722701
10.	I.	Timpanogas	22° 37' 37"	9.5851554	L.M.	29,855.6	5.65448	0.7523930
	L.	Table Point	76° 18' 10"	9.9874699	I.M.	75,394.7	14.27930	1.1547075
	M.	Tongue Point	81° 04' 13"	9.9947040	I.L.	76,660.8	14.51910	1.1619416
11.	C.	Constitution Hill	87° 32' 12".5	9.9995985	D.Y.	122,129	28.1305	1.3641858
	D.	Rose Spring	56° 35' 30".5	9.9215664	C.Y.	102,043.9	19.3265	1.2861537
	Y.	Young's Peak	35° 52' 17"	9.7678737	C.D.	71,630	13.5663	1.1324610
12.	C.	Constitution Hill	52° 15' 52"	9.8980908	Bk. Rock Y.	86,367.6	16.3575	1.2187190
	Y.	Young's Peak	58° 36' 24"	9.9312602	Bk. Rock C.	93,221.5	17.6556	1.2468884
		Black Rock	69° 07' 44"	9.9705255	Y. C.	102,043.9	19.3265	1.1324610
13.		Black Rock	44° 40' 32"	9.8470118	Y. Car. Id.	99,237.6	18.7950	1.2740420
	Y.	Carrington's Island	37° 43' 40"	9.7866880	Y. Bk. Rk.	86,367.6	16.3575	1.2187190
		Young's Peak	97° 35' 48"	9.9961715	Car.I.Bk.Rk.	139,905.7	26.4973	1.4232017
14.		Carrington's Island	53° 40' 34"	9.9061633	Y. Ft. Id.	84,855.4	16.0711	1.2060448
	Y.	Young's Peak	55° 53' 35"	9.9180263	Car. I.Ft.Id.	87,205.0	16.5161	1.2179078
		Frémont Island	70° 25' 51"	9.9741605	Y. Car. Id.	99,237.6	18.7950	1.2740420
15.		Carrington's Island	90° 41' 28"	9.9999684	Ft. I.Strong.	151,245	28.6449	1.4570473
		Strong's Knob	35° 12' 27"	9.7608289	Ft. Car. I.	87,005	16.5161	1.2179078
		Frémont Island	54° 06' 05"	9.9085150	Car.I.Strong	122,526	23.2057	1.3655939
16.		Frémont Island	111° 11' 24"	9.9695962	Y. Mud I.	106,809.6	20.22910	1.3059774
		Young's Peak	21° 00' 57"	9.5546417	Ft. I Mud I.	41,082.4	7.78077	0.8910229
		Mud Island	47° 47' 39"	9.8696636	Ft. I. Y.	84,855.4	16.07110	1.2060448

TABLE OF GEOGRAPHICAL POSITIONS.

1850.	LOCALITIES.	Latitude.	Longitude west of Greenwich.
No. 1	Adobe Hall, Great Salt Lake City. The longitude from Col. Frémont.	40° 46′ 08″.3	112° 06′ 08″
" 2	Junction of Forks of Golden Pass Creek; near point of union of old and new roads.	40° 45′ 40″.5	111° 53′ 14″
" 3	Dividing ridge, Wahsatch chain..........	40° 44′ 48″	111° 46′ 55″.5
" 4	Parley's Park; spring east of Bauch- min's Creek.	40° 43′ 04″.8	111° 38′ 46″.2
" 5	Weber River; upper ford....................	40° 53′ 41″.3	111° 36′ 26″
" 6	Junction of Red Fork and Weber River.	40° 57′ 41″.07	111° 40′ 46″
" 7	Spring in Red Kanyon.	41° 02′ 27″.26	111° 30′ 34″
" 8	Red Kanyon at Chicken-cock Bluff; junction of Echo Creek.	41° 06′ 26″.1	111° 22′ 06″
" 9	At Yellow Creek, tributary of Bear River.	41° 09′ 00″.2	111° 14′ 13″
" 10	Sulphur Creek: one mile east of Bear River Ford, and north of Tar Springs.	41° 08′ 08″.18	111° 01′ 22″
" 11	Copperas Spring, in Great Coal Basin...	41° 13′ 45″.7	110° 48′ 00″
" 12	Fort Bridger.	41° 18′ 12″.8	110° 32′ 23″
" 13	Black's Fork, near Muddy Creek........	41° 28′ 56″.38	110° 18′ 50″
" 14	Near Spring on the plain, in the bend of Black's Fork.	41° 31′ 08″.5	110° 04′ 15″
" 15	East bank of Green River....................	41° 30′ 44″.5	109° 38′ 40″
" 16	Bitter Creek....................	41° 34′ 40″.8	109° 23′ 09″
" 17	Bitter Creek, at the Sandstone Bluffs...	41° 30′ 51″.4	108° 50′ 34″
" 18	Bitter Creek Prairie....................	41° 28′ 09″.2	108° 41′ 09″
" 19	Bitter Creek; head spring branches....	41° 24′ 12″	108° 31′ 00″
" 20	Bridger's Fork of Little Snake River...	41° 28′ 39″	108° 14′ 24″
" 21	On the plains of Muddy....................	41° 28′ 14″.1	108° 02′ 11″
" 22	On the west bank of Muddy Fork, a branch of Little Snake River.	41° 27′ 06″.13	107° 52′ 41″
" 23	North bank of the Muddy, near Vas- ques' battle-ground.	41° 28′ 28″.49	107° 41′ 21″
" 24	In the Kanyon of Muddy Fork............	41° 27′ 41″	107° 38′ 48″
" 25	On a rivulet near Bridger's Pass.........	41° 33′ 22″.3	107° 30′ 48″
" 26	Branch of Sage Creek....................	41° 35′ 21″	107° 21′ 52″
" 27	On North Platte. The longitude taken from Col. Frémont's maps, 1848.	41° 32′ 49″.2	107° 06′ 11″
" 28	On the plain west of Medicine-bow Mountain.	41° 37′ 15″.8	106° 53′ 31″
" 29	Rattlesnake Creek, near Medicine-bow Butte.	41° 40′ 45″.2	106° 43′ 37″
" 30	Laramie Plains....................	41° 41′ 50″.9	106° 36′ 57″
" 31	Laramie Plains....................	41° 38′ 38″.6	106° 24′ 47″
" 32	Frappe's Creek....................	41° 33′ 06″	106° 15′ 58″
" 33	On route across Laramie Plains..........	41° 28′ 16″	106° 06′ 35″
" 34	West Fork of Laramie River.............	41° 19′ 43″.4	105° 57′ 12″
" 35	2.72 miles west of Laramie River; Main Fork.	41° 15′ 41″.4	105° 45′ 39″
" 36	In Black Hills; on a branch of Crow Creek.	41° 08′ 02″	105° 24′ 11″

GEOGRAPHICAL POSITIONS—*Continued.*

1850.	LOCALITIES.	Latitude.	Longitude west of Greenwich.
No. 37	Crow Creek, one and a half miles below the kanyon.	41° 09′ 03″.5	105° 08′ 24″
" 38	Branch of Lodge Pole Creek, in Cheyenne Pass.	41° 21′ 45″.7	105° 12′ 21″
" 39	Branch of Chug-water River...............	41° 45′ 35″.8	104° 59′ 25″
" 40	Chug-water River; Bridger's ravine....	41° 39′ 58″.4	104° 56′ 45″
" 41	Fort Laramie..............................	42° 12′ 38″.2	104° 31′ 26″
" 42	North Platte River; left bank, below mouth of Horse Creek.	41° 55′ 36″.7	103° 58′ 23″
" 43	Scott's Bluffs..............................	41° 48′ 25″.7	103° 45′ 02″
" 44	Left bank of Platte River..................	41° 45′ 39″	103° 21′ 44″
" 45	Left bank of Platte River..................	41° 33′ 22″	102° 45′ 10″
" 46	Ash Hollow; one mile from river........	41° 17′ 18″.7	102° 02′ 28″
" 47	Fort Kearny................................	40° 38′ 45″	98° 58′ 11″
" 48	Oak Grove; Little Blue River.............	40° 13′ 41″.2	97° 54′ 36″
" 49	Road at leaving Little Blue River........	40° 11′ 16″	97° 39′ 02″
" 50	Fort Leavenworth, according to the determinations of Major Emory and M. Nicollet.	39° 21′ 14″	94° 44′ 00″

REMARKS.

The longitudes given in the table depend upon those assumed for Fort Leavenworth, and a point in Great Salt Lake Valley, taken from Nicollet and Frémont. Their means for fixing these points were so superior to ours that they are necessarily adopted; our sextants being imperfect, and the mode of transporting chronometers, of the kind furnished, interfering with their regularity. On leaving Fort Leavenworth, the two chronometers differed but 8.5 seconds; they were put into leather boxes, carefully adjusted upon two mounted men, and at the end of the first six miles differed 11 minutes and 11 seconds. From subsequent observations the loss was attributed to No. 1961. They were then carried in a spring-wagon with the other instruments. The average daily difference for the entire route was a little above one second. The relative rate was, for sixteen days, a losing one of half a second; then, to Laramie, one and a half second's gain. Thence they were carried in another light wagon, and the rate was about one second. Whatever important changes one received, was therefore partaken by the other.

Allowing the entire change of the first day to be due to No. 1961, and taking the longitudes of the termini as stated above,

	sec.
The average rate of gain for chronometer No. 1631, daily, is	8.031
Average rate at beginning and end of journey	7.010
At Fort Leavenworth	10.000
At Great Salt Lake City	4.020

	h. m. s.
Time by sextant observations at Great Salt Lake City	7 49 43
" " " Fort Leavenworth	6 28 31
Difference chronometer time	1 21 12
" in mean time by assumed longitudes	1 09 17.1
Chronometric gain	11 54.9
Time by sextant observations at Fort Laramie	7 17 29

The number of days between the respective observations, was, from Leavenworth to Laramie, fifty days; thence to Great Salt Lake City, thirty-nine days. The proportion of gain is therefore 6 min. 41.6 sec., and 5 min. 13.3 sec. Making these corrections, and converting into siderial time, the longitude of Laramie will be given at 105° 19′ 50″.

But taking the rate at the termination of the journey, and applying it to the time given at Laramie, we have,

Longitude, Great Salt Lake	112° 06′ 08″
" Laramie	104° 40′ 35″

This would agree better with that of Frémont in 1842; but he observes in his book of 1843, that the longitudes of that year are thrown too far west collectively, and proposes to correct, at *Fontaine qui Bouit:* taking the amount of correction given at that station in 1845, at 15′ 49″, his observations place Laramie in 104° 31′ 54″, which is nearly that adopted in the accompanying map, resulting from measured distances and observations, on the homeward journey. Relying upon the accuracy of the map of 1845, we have checked the work made up from course and distance, measured by an odometer, at the crossing of the North Fork of the Platte, and reduced the longitude of Camp 32 on Chugwater, at 104° 56′ 45″. The chronometric difference of this camp and Laramie is taken, on account of the good apparent work of the time-keepers and the winding of the road, at 25′ 19″, which gives the longitude of Fort Laramie at 104° 31′ 26″. Thence to Fort Leavenworth the intermediate points where latitudes were taken, we make up from course and distance as before.

The lunars taken at Laramie and in the Salt Lake Valley, are disregarded, the instruments used being too imperfect for such work. On the return journey the chronometers were carried in panniers on the most gentle mules. Their comparison exhibits "jumps and stops" so great as to forbid this mode of conveyance. Between Salt Lake City and Bridger's Fort, the loss of 1631 upon its companion was 52, and 29.5 sec. on two respective days; on the last day's travel 1961 stopped entirely, and at the arrival at Fort Laramie, 1631 was 23 minutes in advance of the time of starting.

There can be no doubt that light balanced pocket chronometers are best suited to this method of determining difference of longitude. They can be put on spiral springs with suitable packing, in boxes, and strapped so as to ride horizontally on the body of the mounted man. The chronometer should be put into its place after the carrier has mounted, (if on horseback,) and taken out by the astronomer at the halting, before alighting. But what is of great importance, the *travelling rate* of the instrument should be found previous to commencing the journey. This could be done by having it transported, in the manner intended on the route, the average daily number of hours, at the place of fitting out. With three well-tested chronometers, much confidence might be placed in their work, and if either one varied the others would detect it. Three persons should carry them.

A remarkable fact is shown by those chronometers in our journey. Their rates were given at Philadelphia. At Fort Leavenworth they both had the same *relative* rate, but had increased from less than one to ten seconds gain, having been transported in stages over the mountains. After being some months stationary, in the winter at the Salt Lake, they together returned to nearly the rates at Philadelphia. It would appear, therefore, that such derangements do not obtain and affect these instruments merely while moving, but that it is gradually recovered from when returned to permanent rest.

J. W. GUNNISON, *Lieut. Top. Eng's.*
In charge of Astronomical Department.

CAPT. H. STANSBURY, *Top. Eng's.*
Commanding Expedition to Great Salt Lake.

APPENDIX C.

ZOOLOGY.

QUADRUPEDS AND BIRDS, BY PROF. SPENCER F. BAIRD.

REPTILES, BY PROF. BAIRD AND CHAS. GIRARD.

INSECTS, BY PROF. HALDEMAN.

APPENDIX C.

ZOOLOGY.

It is much to be regretted that the circumstances of the Salt Lake Expedition were such as to prevent as much being done in the way of collections in Natural History as the accomplished head, Captain Stansbury, and his assistant, Lieutenant Gunnison, had intended. Called upon to start almost at a day's notice, they found it utterly impracticable to obtain the proper preservative materials, apparatus, and other necessary outfit for making collections, in the limited time allotted to them. Nevertheless, it will not be a matter of surprise to those who are acquainted with the gentlemen concerned, to learn how much was actually accomplished, as will be shown by the published results. In fact, no Government expedition, since the days of Major Long's visit to the Missouri, has ever presented such important additions to Natural History. Of the great advancement of geographical knowledge, the reports of the officers will speak for themselves.

The mammals observed, as might be supposed, belong mainly to the Rocky Mountain series. The most interesting fact in their history is the determination of the existence in Utah of the great-tailed fox, now for the first time described, although mentioned by various travellers.

The birds brought in by the expedition, belong chiefly to the waders and swimmers. The number is not sufficient to draw any general conclusion as to the ornithological fauna of Salt Lake Valley; although the indications are that this forms a meeting point for the species of the Saskatchewan, the Pacific, the Missouri, and of New Mexico.

A South American duck was obtained for the second time in North America, (*Pterocyanea rafflesii*,) the single specimen previously found in the country having been shot in Louisiana. A new bluebird, (*Sialia macroptera*,) appears to be abundant. An exceedingly interesting fact is found in the determination of the

307

winter quarters and range of *Leucosticte tephrocotis*. The only specimen previously seen of this bird was obtained by Dr. Richardson on the Saskatchewan.

The reptiles procured are all new, excepting two: of these, one, *Holbrookia maculata*, was recently described by Mr. Girard, from the Platte, and the other, *Phrynosoma douglasii*, from Oregon, by Bell. None of the new species have ever been found elsewhere. Among these is the finest species of *Cnemidophorus* in North America. To Mr. Girard, equally with ourselves, is due the credit of the article on the reptiles, especially for the monograph of *Phrynosoma*, which is entirely from his pen.

Many specimens of insects were procured, but unfortunately injured or lost on the return. The few preserved have been ably determined by Professor Haldeman, as will be seen by his report. The principal entomological result is the precise determination of the destructive grasshopper, which, but for the interposition of a species of tern, at one period was near turning the "Garden of the Mountains" into a desert.

Of shells and other invertebrate forms, no specimens were brought in, excepting in too fragmentary a state to admit of determination.

By the kind permission of Colonel J. J. Abert, Chief of the Topographical Bureau, so well known for his liberality and love of science, we have been permitted to examine a small but exceedingly interesting collection of birds and mammals, procured by his son, Lieutenant J. W. Abert, in New Mexico. Among them we found a new species of bird and one new mammal, descriptions of which, with lists of the other species, we have subjoined. We have also ventured to include, in the article on reptiles, descriptions of some new species from Oregon, Texas, and New Mexico, collected by officers of the army. With the cheerful acquiescence of Captain Stansbury, we have likewise appended to the article on birds a complete list of all the trans-Mississippi species not included in Audubon's American Ornithology, adding the few found since his time east of this great natural boundary. For assistance in correcting and extending this list, we are under great obligations to Mr. John Cassin, of Philadelphia, who is now engaged in publishing a continuation of Audubon's Ornithology, to include all the species mentioned in it.

S. F. BAIRD.

MAMMALS.

BY S. F. BAIRD.

1. VULPES MACROURUS, Baird.—Great-tailed Fox.

WE greatly regret that the specimens of this, the most important addition to our fauna made by Captain Stansbury, should be of such character as not to admit of a description based upon the skull. None were found by the party, all brought in being cased skins purchased of hunters in Salt Lake Valley, and, as usual, without the skull.

In general appearance, this species resembles the red fox, *Vulpes fulvus*, in its different varieties. From these, however, it may be at once distinguished by the great length of the tail, which exceeds that of the latter species by six inches, and more. In the best specimen procured, the back is of mixed grizzled gray colour as in the gray fox or badger, the hairs being dark brown at the base, then yellowish white, and finally, tipped with black. These hairs are interspersed in a very abundant soft fur, of uniform colour, varying in tint with the region of body. A decided black colour prevails on the muzzle, sides of face, top of head, and upper part of neck, separated from that of the back by a rather uniform ferruginous in front of the shoulder. On the shoulders, the gray exhibits a slight tendency to a cross, and widens posteriorly, including the outside of thighs, and extending a short distance on the tail. There is a considerable admixture of black around the eyes. The sides of the neck and body, concavity of the ear, basal anterior portion of the convexity, and space across lower neck, are light ferruginous; the remaining portion of the convexity of the ear black; chin, throat, legs, belly, top, and sides of the tail, black. The tip of the tail is dirty white; beneath, with region about the arms and posterior edge of thighs, light ferruginous; whiskers, black.

Length (approximate) from snout to base of tail 33 inches.
Tail to end of vertebræ.................................. 18 "
" " tip of hair.................................. 22 "
Breadth of tail, flattened.............................. 9 "

Hairs on sides of tail.................................... 4½ inches.
"   " tip 4   "
Forearm.. 10   "
Height of ears............. 3   "

Another specimen, much like the last from Fort Laramie, has the top of the head and posterior half of the back grizzled yellow, gray, and black, anterior half of back and across shoulders nearly to elbow with a much greater predominance of black; basal half of the convexity of the ears and the entire concavity, with the edges, sides of neck and of body behind the forelegs, light-yellowish. Legs and beneath black, as also muzzle and ears, with the exception just stated. The fur is very full and soft, and the feet densely clothed with long, crimped, soft hair.

Another specimen indicates quite a different variety, with a much closer resemblance to the red fox. The colour above is light ferruginous, deeper toward the dorsal line; beneath, white. The hairs at the base are, as usual, lead colour. The fur, however, along and toward the dorsal line is terminated for the greater part of its length by a rich chestnut, rather darker behind. The long scattered hairs on the back are mostly black, tipped with light yellow; laterally, this fur is light ferruginous, fading off into white toward the belly. This ferruginous is more distinct immediately over the back. Inner sides of legs, sides of head, and concavity of ears, likewise yellowish white. Upper part of muzzle, around the eye, and on top of head, grizzled chestnut, like the back. Convexity of posterior surface of ear, black. The sides of the soles also indicate black, although the legs are too much mutilated to show distinctly the colour. The general colour of the tail is yellowish white, deeper above: the long hairs of top and sides tipped with black. Tip of the tail, white. The feet in all the varieties are densely covered with hair on the under surface.

In this species we find all the varieties of the common red fox, *Vulpes fulvus*, as the chestnut, the black, the silver gray, cross, &c. How far its range extends we are at present unable to state. It probably, however, reaches the Pacific coast, and far to the north in the Rocky Mountains. Indeed, we consider it very improbable that the ordinary red fox extends west of the Missouri. As regards the eastern range, we have seen specimens from Fort Laramie, and Audubon and Bachman refer to a skin from Fort Union, at the mouth of the Yellowstone, which may possibly belong to the same species.

2. Putorius vison, Lin.—Mink.

Putorius vison, Dekay, N. Y. Zool. pl. 1, p. 37;—Aud. & Bach. **Quadrupeds, I.** 250, pl. 33.

The well-known and destructive mink appears to be common in the valley of Salt Lake, several specimens having been procured. The colour is more uniform than common in Eastern specimens, there being no trace of the yellow spot on the chin. In one individual, however, the edge of the lower lips is white.

3. Putorius erminea, Lin.—Ermine.

Putorius noveboracensis, Dekay, N. Y. Zool. pl. 1, p. 36.
Putorius erminea, Aud. & Bach. II. 36, pl. 59.

This species occurs abundantly throughout the northern and temperate parts of the whole northern hemisphere.

4. Meles labradoria, Sabine.—Badger.

Meles labradoria, Sabine. Captain Franklin's Narrative, p. 649;—Richardson, F. B. A. L. p. 37;—Aud. & Bach. Quad. I. 360, pl. 47.

The American badger is found in the interior of North America, especially in the regions bordering on the Rocky Mountain ranges.

5. Gulo luscus, L.—Wolverene.

Ursus luscus, L. Syst. Nat.
Gulo luscus, Rich. F. B. A. I., 41;—Aud. & Bach. Quad. I. 202, pl. 26.

The wolverene, known also as carcajou and glutton, is an inhabitant of the arctic regions of the northern hemisphere, extending as far north as lat. 75. In North America, it is an inhabitant of the whole of the British and Russian possessions. It is found sparingly in Maine, Massachusetts, and Northern New York, although exceedingly rare. Farther west it is more abundant, particularly along the upper Missouri and the Rocky Mountain ranges. The locality here assigned, of Salt Lake, is the most southern limit yet given.

To the traveller and trapper on the prairies or among the mountains, the wolverene is the greatest nuisance imaginable.

It ferrets out the caches of provisions and skins, and devours their contents greedily, its enormous strength being such as to enable it to remove almost every weight which may be placed upon the articles concealed. It destroys the traps set for other animals, and tears to pieces their contents. Indeed, in the·Northern United States, this animal is dreaded more than the panther or bear, being invested with fabulous attributes of ferocity and danger. This is, to a much less degree, the case in the Rocky Mountains; but everywhere the wolverene is attacked with caution.

6. FIBER ZIBETHICUS, L.—Muskrat.

Fiber zibethicus, Aud. & Bach. Quad. I. 108, pl. 13.

The muskrat abounds over the greater part of the American continent, extending from the Atlantic to the Pacific. Its northern and southern limits are not well ascertained: those assigned to it by Audubon and Bachman are lat. 69° to lat. 30°.

7. SPERMOPHILUS 13-LINEATUS, Mitchill.

Sciurus 13-*lineatus,* Mitchill's Medical Repository for 1821.
Spermophilus hoodi, Sabine.
S. tridecem-lineatus, Aud. & Bach. I. 224, pl. 39.

The little prairie squirrel, so common in Wisconsin, Michigan, and Minnesota, would seem to have a very extensive range, in being found by the expedition on the Platte beyond Fort Laramie. The specimen is, however, immature, and it is quite possible that further investigation may show this to be a species distinct from the St. Peter's specimen described by Dr. Mitchill.

8. OVIS MONTANA, Desm.—Bighorn.

Ovis montana. Rich. F. B. A. I. p. 271;—Aud. & Bach. Quad. II. 164, pl. 73.

The specimen of bighorn, or Rocky Mountain Sheep, brought home by Captain Stansbury, was shot on Chug-Water. It is the largest individual we have ever seen, although itself possibly not of maximum size. It differs somewhat from the description in Audubon and Bachman, in having the posterior line of all the legs yellowish white, this colour extending to the axillæ in front, and confluent behind with the white of buttocks, scrotum, and thighs. The dorsal line is inconspicuous, except on the darker tips of the short mane.

> Circumference of horn at the base.......17 inches.
> Length of horn along the convexity.....36½ "
> Distance between the tips of horns.....18 "

The bighorn, at one time erroneously supposed to be the same as the old-world argali, is common in the ranges and hills' belonging to the Rocky Mountain system.

COLLECTED BY LIEUTENANT ABERT.

1. Pseudostoma castanops, Baird.

This beautiful species was collected by Lieutenant Abert along the prairie road to Bent's Fort. In general colour it is of a pale yellowish-brown, with an ample patch of light chestnut on the side of the head and face, deepest above. The dorsal line is not darker than the rest of the fur. In size it is intermediate between *P. borealis* and *bursarius*.

The colour of the fur above is slightly grizzled, and much lighter than in *P. bursarius*; beneath, paler. Throat, space between the forelegs and sides of arms, pale rusty. The chestnut marking, on the side of the head, is very strongly defined, occupying on each side a nearly circular space of about one and three-quarter inches in diameter, with the nearly obsolete ear as a centre. These chestnut spaces do not quite meet on the crown and occiput, but leave a rectilinear interval, coloured like the rest of the back, of about one-eighth of an inch in width. On the muzzle, however, from above the eyes, the colour of opposite sides is confluent.

The hind feet and toes are thinly covered with whitish hairs, which on the fore feet appear more ferruginous. The claws are white, but sufficiently transparent to allow the coagulated blood in the phalanges to show through them.

> Length to base of tail (approximate)............... 8 inches.
> Tail... 2⅝ "
> Hand (along the palm)................................... 1 3/12 "
> Length of exposed part of middle anterior claw. ½ "
> Hind feet (along sole) from heel..................... 1 4/12 "
> Middle claw... 19/60 "

BIRDS.

By SPENCER F. BAIRD.

1. BUTEO BOREALIS, Bp.—Red-tailed Hawk.

Falco borealis, Wils. VI. 72, pl. 52.—Aud. Biog. I. 265, pl. 51.

Salt Lake. Found by Gambel in California.

2. ACCIPITER FUSCUS, Bp.—Sharp-shinned Hawk.

Falco velox, Wils. VII. 110, pl. 45, fig. 1 (young female).
Falco pennsylvanicus, Wils. VI. 13, pl. 16, fig. 1 (adult male).
Falco fuscus, Aud. Biog. IV. 522, pl. 374.

Salt Lake.

3. ATHENE HYPUGAEA, Cassin.—Burrowing Owl.

Strix hypugæa, Bp. Am. Orn. I. 72, pl. 7.
Strix cunicularia, Aud. Biog. V. 264, pl. 432, f. 2.
Athene socialis, Gambel, Pr. A. N. S. III. 47.

Abundant in the valley of Salt Lake and on the plains east and west of the mountains.

4. SIALIA MACROPTERA, Baird.—Long-winged Bluebird.

MALE.—Salt Lake City, March 18, 1850.

A specimen of *Sialia* was procured by Captain Stansbury, which, at first sight, was referred to *S. arctica* of Swainson. On comparing it with others from Fort Union, the differences were found to be sufficiently great to constitute a distinct species. The Fort Union specimen was clearly referable to *S. arctica* of Swainson shot at Fort Franklin, Great Bear Lake, so that it becomes necessary to impose a new name upon the one from Utah. Not having at hand specimens from the Pacific coast, it is impossible to say to which species the birds described by Audubon as *S. arctica* belong, (probably *arctica.*)

The principal difference between the two allied species is to be found in the longer wings, and much smaller and weaker claws, with rather longer toes, of the *S. macroptera,* as will be sufficiently evident from the table of comparative measurements. The bill, too, of the latter, although of much the same proportions, is decidedly smaller.

As in *S. arctica*, the upper parts are a bright azure blue, more lustrous and deeper on the wings, rump, and tail-coverts. The lower parts are of a light greenish blue, excepting the lower belly and sides, abdomen, and tail-coverts, which are white.

The white of the lower parts is clearer and extends higher up on the belly than in *S. arctica*, and the quills and tail-feathers are much bluer, this colour greatly predominating over the brown on the inner webs and inner faces of the feathers. The clove-brown shows somewhat conspicuously as a broad tip to the quills, which, besides, are very narrowly margined, terminally and internally, with whitish. The outer margins of the primaries, towards the tips, shade into greenish blue. Owing, perhaps, to the plumage not being quite full, many of the feathers of the back and breast have grayish tips.

DIMENSIONS.

	Sialia macroptera, (Salt Lake, Male.)	*S. arctica*, (Fort Union, Male.)
Total length	$7\frac{1}{4}$ inches.	(Skin contracted) $6\frac{1}{4}$ inches.
Extent	$14\frac{3}{10}$ "	"
Wing folded	$4\frac{10}{12}$ "	" $4\frac{4\frac{1}{2}}{12}$ "
Tail to insertion of middle feathers	$3\frac{2}{12}$ "	" $2\frac{3}{4}$ "
Depth of fork	$\frac{5\frac{1}{2}}{12}$ "	(Tail worn) $\frac{4\frac{1}{2}}{12}$ "
Projection of longest primary beyond longest secondary or tertiary, (wing not shut close)	$1\frac{11\frac{1}{2}}{12}$ "	
Do. wing shut close	$1\frac{3}{4}$	$1\frac{7}{12}$ "
Longest primary beyond shortest, (9th)	$1\frac{10}{12}$ "	$1\frac{5}{12}$ "
Second primary longer than first, (spurious)	$3\frac{11\frac{1}{2}}{12}$ "	$2\frac{8\frac{1}{2}}{12}$ "
Bill along ridge	$\frac{5\frac{2}{3}}{12}$ "	$\frac{6\frac{2}{3}}{12}$ "
Bill, gape	$\frac{9\frac{1}{2}}{12}$ "	$\frac{10}{12}$ "
Tarsus	$\frac{10}{12}$ "	$\frac{10\frac{1}{2}}{12}$ "
Middle toe	$\frac{8}{12}$ "	$\frac{7\frac{1}{2}}{12}$ "
" " with claw	$\frac{10}{12}$ "	$\frac{10\frac{1}{2}}{12}$ "
Lateral toes, (equal)	$\frac{5\frac{2}{3}}{12}$ "	$\frac{4\frac{1}{2}}{12}$ "
" " with claw	$\frac{7}{12}$ "	$\frac{7}{12}$ "
Hind toe	$\frac{4\frac{1}{2}}{12}$ "	$\frac{3}{12}$ "
" " with claw	$\frac{6}{12}$ "	$\frac{6}{12}$ "

(In *S. macroptera*.)
1st quill spurious; 3d, longest; 2d, little shorter; 4th, rather less than 2d.

5. PARUS SEPTENTRIONALIS, Harris.--Black-head Titmouse.

Parus septentrionalis, Harris. Proceed. Acad. Nat. Sc. Phil. II. 300 (Dec. 1845).

A single individual of this rare species was procured by Captain Stansbury. This bird was first described by Edward Harris, Esq., from a specimen shot on the Yellow Stone River in July, 1843, and is the largest of the American species of true Black-cap Titmice, three in number. It is not improbable that two species may be confounded under the name of *septentrionalis*, as this specimen is quite different from one collected by R. H. Kern, in New Mexico. The latter is, however, too much mutilated and faded to serve as a proper standard of comparison, for which we must wait to get better specimens.

6. STURNELLA NEGLECTA, Audubon.—Western Lark.

Sturnella neglecta, Aud. Biog. 2d ed. VII. 340 (1843).

The distinctions between the old *Sturnella ludoviciana* and the present species are quite obscure. A specimen from Fort Union, presented to us by Mr. Audubon, agrees with the published characters in nothing but the bands on the middle tail-feathers, which replace the scolloping seen in *S. ludoviciana*. The tail is quite as much rounded, and the bill of the same size. The Salt Lake bird has the tail more square, and the bands on the middle tail-feathers still more distinct than in the one from Fort Union. The size is fully as large as that of the common species. The specimen was shot March 18, 1850, in the cañons between Salt Lake City and the Hot Springs. This lark utters a single rough note like that of the European starling.

Length... 10¼ inches.
Extent .... 16½ "

7. NIPHŒA OREGONA, Audubon.—Oregon Snowbird.

Fringilla oregona, Towns. Journ. Acad. Nat. Sc. Phil. VII. 188 (1837).—Aud. Biog. V. 68, pl. 298, fig. 3, 4.
Fringilla hudsonica, Var. Licht. Abh. Ac. Wiss. Berl. for 1838, 424.
Fringilla nortonensis, Gm. I. 922, 87.

This interesting species, so similar to *N. hyemalis*, or common snowbird of the Atlantic region, replaces it in the Pacific. It

occurs abundantly in Oregon and California, as well as in New
Mexico and Utah.

Length of specimen shot March 21st............... 5¾ inches.
Extent... 9¾ "

8. Peucæa lincolnii, Audubon.—Lincoln's Finch.

Fringilla lincolnii, Aud. Biog. II. 539 pl. 193 (1834).
Peucæa lincolnii, Aud. Syn. 113 (1839).

A specimen of this bird was shot at Salt Lake, March 21, 1850.
The species was first described from individuals killed in Maine,
since which it has been found in very small number—more abundantly about Carlisle, Pa., than anywhere else. The Salt Lake
specimen agrees with one brought from the upper Missouri by Mr.
Audubon, in having a more grayish tinge than that usually seen
in individuals from the Atlantic coast. The black marks on the
dorsal feathers are also larger and more decided. The bill, too,
appears a little smaller. These differences, however, are hardly
specific.

Length of Salt Lake specimen........................ 5¾ inches.
Extent.. 8 "

9. Leucosticte tephrocotis, Swainson.—Gray-crowned Finch.

Linaria (Leucosticte) tephrocotis, Sw. Fauna Bor. Amer. II. 265, pl. 50 (1831).
Erythrospiza tephrocotis, Aud. Synopsis, 125.—Nuttall's Manual, 2d. ed. I. 632.
Fringilla tephrocotis, Aud. Biog. V. 232, pl. 424, fig. 3.
Leucosticte tephrocotis, Bp. & Schl. Monog. des Loxiens, pl. 42.—Gray's Genera
    Avium, 536.

This exceedingly interesting bird was first described by Swainson and Richardson, from a specimen procured by the latter,
May, 1827, on the Saskatchewan River, in lat. 54°. But a single
individual was obtained, which was subsequently presented to the
Museum of the Zoological Society of London. From this, all the
published descriptions have been made, even that by Mr. Audubon,
who was unable himself to procure a specimen. For the sake,
therefore, of multiplying comparisons, we shall present an original
description taken from the bird brought home by Captain Stansbury. This was procured on the 21st of March, 1850, in Salt
Lake City.

MALE. General colour of back, scapulars, hind neck, belly,

breast, and indeed of the entire foreparts, (excepting the crown,) of a dull chestnut-brown, darkest on the chin, throat, and cheeks. Feathers of the back and breast with light margins. Upper part and sides of the head, including the lores, lower eyelid, and occiput, (excluding ear-coverts,) ash gray, lighter behind. A patch of dull black on the crown and forehead. Lesser wing-coverts, rump, under and upper tail-coverts, sides of body, abdomen, and thighs, having the feathers tipped with a beautiful purplish pink, giving to the rump the appearance of transverse bands. Tail-feathers dark-brown, narrowly margined externally with rose; inner secondaries and primary coverts more broadly with dull white, all the quills being faintly tipped with brown. Nostrils covered by a tuft of whitish recumbent feathers; a similar tuft at the side of the mouth. Bill, feet, and wings as described by Richardson.

Length	$7\frac{1}{2}$	inches.
Extent	12	"
Folded wing	$4\frac{1}{4}$	"
Tail to rump	$2\frac{3}{4}$	"
Tarsus	$\frac{3}{4}$	"

This species comes nearest to *Leucosticte griseinucha* of Brandt, 1842; *L. griseigenys*, Gould, an inhabitant of Russian America and the Aleutian Islands. This latter species may, however, be at once distinguished by the possession of gray cheeks and ear coverts.

10. Otocoris occidentalis, McCall.

Otocoris occidentalis, McCall, Pr. A. N. S. Phil. V. 118 (June, 1850).

This species of sky lark is founded by Colonel McCall upon an immature bird, shot near Santa Fé in July. Captain Stansbury's specimen was killed near Salt Lake City, March 18, 1850, and is, consequently, an adult, in winter plumage. It differs from winter specimens of *Otocoris alpestris*, in having no yellow on the throat and superciliary stripe, more black on the cheeks, and less on the breast, and a very slight ferruginous tinge of the upper parts and sides of the body. The white across the forehead is more distinct. The bill is shorter, more slender, and more curved.

Length	$6\frac{1}{2}$	inches.
Wing	$4\frac{1}{12}$	"
Tail	$2\frac{3}{4}$	"

From *Alauda flava* of Audubon it differs in the larger size, and in having the middle tail-feathers like the upper coverts, instead of being black.

11. PICUS TORQUATUS, Wils.—Lewis's Woodpecker.

Picus torquatus, Wils. III. 31, pl. 20, fig. 3 (1811).—Aud. Biog. V. 176, pl. 416, fig. 7, 8.

This beautiful woodpecker belongs to the Pacific fauna, not having been observed east of the mountains. It occurs abundantly along the western coast.

12. TETRAO UROPHASIANUS, Bp.—Cock of the Plains, or Prairie Cock ; Sage Cock.

Tetrao urophasianus, Bp. Zool. Journal, III. 214 (1827).—Aud. Biog. IV. 503, pl. 37 ; Syn. 205.

A single specimen of this magnificent bird was shot near the mouth of Bear River, on the eastern side of the Lake, May 8th. It is found on the plains skirting the Rocky Mountains, seldom coming down to the Missouri, except far to the north. It is not yet recorded as being found on the coast of California, although abundant along the Columbia River. Its flesh is not usually considered edible, from feeding so much upon the artemisia or sage.

Length.. 28 inches.
Extent.. 38 "

13. CHARADRIUS VOCIFERUS, L.—Killdeer.

Charadius vociferus, L. 253, 3;—Aud. Biog. IV. 191, pl. 225.

Common across the continent.

14. GRUS CANADENSIS, Temm.—Brown Crane.

Ardea canadensis, L. Syst. Nat. 234, 3.
Grus canadensis, Aud. Biog. III. 441, pl. 61.

The brown cranes were found during fall and winter in immense flocks in the marshes along Salt Lake. They presented their usual watchfulness and difficulty of approach. No white ones were seen. Occurs in large flocks throughout the whole interior of North America.

> Length of a female..45 inches.
> Extent..75½ "
> Legs, bill, and feet, black; eyes, orange. Male, 41 by 69.

15. Botaurus lentiginosus, Montagu.—Bittern.

Ardea lentiginosa, Mont. Orn. Dict. Suppl. 1813.—Rich. F. B. A. II. 374.—Nutt.
    Man. II. 60;—Aud. Syn. 263.
Ardea minor, Wils. Am. Orn. VIII. 35, pl. 65, fig. 2 (1814).—Aud. Biog. IV. 296,
    pl. 337.

This bird appears to be a great wanderer. Although an exceedingly rare visitant in Europe, the species was first described from a specimen shot in Ireland. It occurs throughout the United States, West Indies, California, and the fur countries up to lat. 58°.

16. Numenius longirostris, Wils.—Long-billed Curlew.

Numenius longirostris, Wils. Am. Orn. VIII. 23, pl. 64, fig. 4 (1824).—Aud.
    Biog. 240, pl. 231.

A specimen was shot on Antelope Island. The species occurs abundantly throughout the interior of this country, along the Missouri, and on the prairies. Common also in New Mexico and California.

17. Symphemia semipalmata, Hart.—Willet.

Scolopax semipalmata, Gm. I. 659, 33.—Wils. Am. Orn. VIII. 27, pl. 56.
Totanus semipalmatus, Rich. F. B. A. II. 388, pl. 67.—Aud. Biog. IV. 510, pl. 274.
Catoptrophorus semipalmatus, Bp. Syn. 323 (1828).
Symphemia atlantica, Raf. Jour. de Phys. vol. 88, p. 417 (1819).

Shot on Salt Lake. Common both on the Atlantic and Pacific coasts.

18. Recurvirostra americana, Gm.—Avoset.

Recurvirostra americana, Gm. 693, 2.—Aud. Biog. IV. 168, pl. 318.

Salt Lake, March, 1850. Not noticed on the coast of the Pacific.

19. Cygnus americanus, Sharpless.—Swan.

Cygnus americanus, Sharpless, Silliman's Journal XXII. 83 (1831).—Aud.
Biog. V. 133, pl. 411; Synopsis, 274.
Cygnus bewicki, Richardson, Fauna Bor. Am. II. No. 224.

Of two specimens shot March 10, 1850, in Jordan River, one was in full plumage. The other, a male, not quite mature, had the space in front of the eyes and the flattened space at the base of the bill above, covered with scattered, minute feathers. The orange spot is indicated through the feathers. The bill is black at the tip, base, and along the commissure, and of a dull yellowish in the intermediate area. Feet mottled. The older one measured 51 inches in length and 76 in extent. Weight, 15¼ pounds. The young one, 47 by 71; weight, 9¼ pounds.

The range of this species is quite extensive. Inhabiting the Atlantic in winter, especially Chesapeake Bay, it was found on the Saskatchewan, in lat. 64°, by Sir John Richardson, and on the Columbia River by Dr. Townsend, thus extending across the continent.

20. Anser erythropus, L.—White-fronted Goose.

Anas erythropus, L. I. 197, 11.
Anas albifrons, Gm. 509, 64.
Anser albifrons, Nutt. II. 346.—Aud. Biog. III. 568, pl. 280; Syn. 270.

Jordan River, Salt Lake, in March. Found in California, Oregon, and east of the Rocky Mountains generally.

21. Anser canadensis, Vieill.—Wild Goose.

Anas canadensis, L. Syst. Nat. I. 198, 14.—Wils. Am. Orn. VIII. 52, pl. 67, fig. 4.
Anser canadensis, Rich. F. B. A. II. 468.—Nutt. Man. II. 349.—Aud. Biog. III. 6,
pl. 201; Syn. 270.

This common bird occurs entirely across the continent, being found abundantly in California, Oregon, the Atlantic States, and the intermediate country. In summer it goes northward to breed, extending almost to the shores of the Arctic seas. This goose constitutes the principal summer food of the inhabitants of the fur countries, large numbers being salted down for winter use.

The specimens procured were shot on Salt Lake.

22. ANAS BOSCHAS, L.—Mallard; Green-head.

Anas boschas, L. I. 205, 40.—Wils. Am. Orn. VIII. 112.—Nutt. Man. II.—Aud.
  Biog. 164, pl. 221; Syn. p. 276.

Abundant on Jordan River. Found throughout the United
States, California, Oregon, and fur countries.

23. MARECA AMERICANA, Steph.—Bald-pate.

Anas americana, Gm. Syst. Nat. I. 526, 97.—Wils. Am. Orn. VIII. 86, pl. 69, fig. 4.—
  Aud. Biog. IV. 337, pl. 335.
Mareca americana, Steph. Shaw. Zool. XII. 135.—Rich. F. B. A. II. 445.

The bald-pate, so well known in the Chesapeake Bay region,
for the impudence with which it robs the canvass-back of its
favourite food, the celery grass, was found in considerable number on the Jordan River. It is abundant in California and Oregon, as well as the country east of the mountains.

24. QUERQUEDULA CAROLINENSIS, Bp.—Green-wing Teal.

Anas carolinensis, Gm. I. 533, 103.—Aud. Syn. 28.
Anas crecca, Wils. VIII. 101, pl. 70, fig. 4.—Aud. Biog. III. 218, pl. 228.

Jordan River, March 26, 1850. This species appears to be
very abundant about Salt Lake. It is equally common in California, as well as east of the mountains.

25. PTEROCYANEA RAFFLESII, King.—Red-breasted Teal.

Anas rafflesii, King. Zool. Jour. IV. 87, Suppl. pl. 29 (1828).—Jard. and Selby's
  Illust. N. S. pl. 23.—Cassin, J. A. N. S. IV. 195 (1841).
"*Anas cæruleata,* Licht."
"*Anas cyanopterus,* Vieill."

This beautiful species is now for the second time presented as
an inhabitant of North America. In 1849, Dr. Pilate, of Ope-
lousas, Louisiana, sent a specimen, shot in his vicinity, to the
Philadelphia Academy of Natural Sciences, which was announced
by Mr. Cassin as new to our fauna. The species was first founded
on specimens obtained by King, in the Straits of Magellan. It
frequents the coast of Chili, whence specimens have been sent by
Lieutenant J. M. Gilliss.

The Red-breasted Teal appears to be a common bird in Utah, three having been shot in Jordan River. As the species has never been described from a North American specimen, we subjoin the following, taken from those brought by the expedition.

MALE.—Head, neck, anterior part of body, sides, flanks, bar across the vent, rich purplish chestnut, deepest and most lustrous across the breast, faintest across the vent. Upper part of the head to occiput, the chin, and lower tail-coverts, dull-brownish black. Lower part of breast, belly, and abdomen, (encircled by the chestnut just mentioned,) obscure brown, and faintly glossed with grayish and chestnut. Lower wing-coverts, subscapulars, and tips of primary coverts, white, showing on the latter as a conspicuous white patch. Shoulders, lesser coverts, and greater part of two of the longest scapulars on each side, bright blue, (darkest on the latter.) Speculum, grass green. Longest scapulars with a central streak of yellowish white, and variously margined and mottled with chestnut. Back, rump, and upper tail-coverts, margined with dull chestnut. Bill black, feet yellow. Bill long, narrow, somewhat wider towards the tip; nostrils oval, lamellar, rather long. Tarsi short, and feet small. Outer toe, without its claw, about equal to the inner with claw. Tail rather long, wedge-shaped, of fourteen feathers.

Total length (skin much stretched)............................ 20 inches.
Bill above .... 2 "
From rictus.. $2\frac{1}{12}$ "
Tarsi... $1\frac{2}{12}$ "
Middle toe and claw... $1\frac{1}{12}$ "
Wing, from flexure.. 8 "
Tail.. $3\frac{1}{4}$ "

FEMALE.—Similar in general pattern of colouration, the chestnut, however, replaced by the mottled yellowish and brown characterizing the female ducks. This pervades the whole inferior portions, not excepting the tail coverts. The black of the head, and the blue on the shoulders, (not on the scapulars,) are retained.

26. DAFILA ACUTA, Bp.—Sprig-tail Duck.

Anas acuta, L. I. 202, 28.—Aud. Biog. III. 214, pl. —

Salt Lake. Found across the continent.

27. FULIGULA AFFINIS, Eyton.—Little Black-head; Shuffler.

Fuligula affinis, Eyton, Mon. Anatidæ (1838).
Fuligula mariloides, Vig. Zoology of Beechy's Voyage (1839).
Fuligula marila, Aud. Biog. III. 226, pl. 229.
Fuligula minor, Giraud, Birds of Long Island, p. 323 (1844).

Salt Lake, March 21, 1850. Found across the continent; very common throughout the interior.

28. CLANGULA ALBEOLA, Bp.—Butter-ball.

Anas albeola, L. Syst. Nat. I. 199, 18.—Wils. VIII. 51, pl. 67, f. 2, 3.
Fuligula albeola, Aud. Biog. IV. 217, pl. 325.

Provost Fork, February 22, 1850. Occurs from the Atlantic to the Pacific.

29. PELECANUS TRACHYRRHYNCHUS, Lath.—White Pelican.

Pelecanus Americanus, Aud. Biog. IV. 38, pl. 311; Syn. p. 309.

The only specimen in the collection is in the form of a skeleton. This wants the peculiar vertical lamina of the bill, but in all probability belongs to the above species, the female of which is usually without this appendage.

It is mentioned by Gambel as common on the coast of California In winter it is found in the Southern Atlantic and Gulf States, and to some distance up the Mississippi Valley. Exceedingly abundant about Salt Lake.

30. PHALACROCORAX DILOPHUS, Sw.—Cormorant.

Pelecanus (Carbo) dilophus, Sw. F. B. A. II. 473 (1831).
Phalacrocorax dilophus et *floriduus*, Aud.

Salt Lake.

31. COLYMBUS GLACIALIS, L.—Loon.

Colymbus glacialis, L. Syst. Nat. I. 221, 5.—Sw. Faun. Bor. Amer. II. 474.—Nutt. Man. II. 573.—Aud. Biog. IV. 43, pl. 306; Syn. 353.

This species of loon, shot on Salt Lake and brought in by Captain Stansbury, enables us to give to it a locality more western than any yet recorded. It is abundant throughout the United States, where the difficulty of shooting it has passed into a proverb.

BIRDS COLLECTED IN NEW MEXICO BY LIEUT. ABERT.

1. FALCO SPARVERIUS, L.—Sparrow-hawk.
2. PIPILO ABERTI, Baird.

This species at first sight exhibits a strong resemblance to *Pipilo fusca* from Monterey, from which, however, it differs in many characteristic features. The colour above is of a nearly uniform rusty-brown, or olive, no material difference in tint being descernible on the head and rump, as in *P. fusca*. Beneath, and on the sides of the neck, the colour is much like that of the back, with a stronger tinge of ferruginous, however, which becomes very decided about the lower tail-coverts. The markings around the bill are not very distinct, owing to the mutilated state of the specimen; there appears, however, to be a tendency to black on the loral feathers; the bristles also are black. The throat seems to be uniform in colour with the neck and breast, and unspotted. The tail is uniformly coloured, and is destitute of the light tip of *P. fusca*.

The bill is much stouter than in *P. fusca*, as well as more curved. The claws also are much stronger and larger, the tip of the outer reaching to the middle of the middle one; while in *P. fusca* it only extends to the base.

The general tint of plumage in *P. aberti* has decidedly more of ferruginous than in *P. fusca*. The throat is uniform with the breast, and unspotted; the rump too is uniform with the back; in both these particulars differing from *P. fusca*.

The following table exhibits the relative dimensions of the two species:—

	P. aberti.	*P. fusca.* (Male.)
Length (approximate)	9 inches.	
Wing folded and slightly curved	$3\frac{7}{12}$ "	$3\frac{7}{12}$ inches.
Tail to base of quills	$4\frac{1}{2}$ "	4 "
Bill along the ridge	$\frac{34}{60}$ "	$\frac{34}{60}$ "
Greatest depth of bill	$\frac{22}{60}$ "	$\frac{19}{60}$ "
Middle tail-feather beyond outer,	$1\frac{9}{60}$ "	$1\frac{1}{4}$ "
Tarsus	$1\frac{3}{12}$ "	$1\frac{1}{12}\frac{1}{4}$ "
Claw	$\frac{28}{60}$ "	$\frac{23}{60}$ "
Rest of hind toe	$\frac{20}{60}$ "	$\frac{17}{60}$ "
Middle claw	$\frac{23}{60}$ "	$\frac{17}{60}$ "
Rest of middle toe	$\frac{41}{60}$ "	$\frac{43}{60}$ "

We have dedicated this species to its accomplished discoverer, Lieutenant Jas. W. Abert.

3. AGELAIUS XANTHOCEPHALUS, L.—Yellow-headed Blackbird.

4. PICUS VARIUS, L.—Yellow-bellied Woodpecker.

5. COLUMBA LEUCOPTERA, L.—White-winged Dove.

6. CALLIPEPLA SQUAMATA, Vig.—Blue Partridge.

7. CALLIPEPLA GAMBELI, Nutt.—Gambel's Partridge.

> *Callipepla gambeli*, Nutt. Pr. A. N. S. Phila. 1843.
> *Callipepla venusta*, Gould, Pr. Zool. Soc. Lond. 1846.

Upper parts and breast, lead colour; crown and occiput, chestnut. Base of bill, lore, chin, throat and sides of the neck, black, bounded by a white band, broader on the sides. The eyes are included in this black hood. The chestnut of the crown is margined with white, bordered on each side with black. The lead-coloured feathers of the sides and back of the neck are streaked with black along the shafts. Sides, deep chestnut, broadly lineated with yellowish white. Lower breast, whitish yellow. Indications of a black patch on the belly. Under tail-coverts dull white and black. A long recurved crest of six (remaining?) keeled black feathers, the longest measuring $1\frac{3}{4}$ inches in length. Inner webs of scapulars margined with reddish. Tail much rounded, of twelve feathers; outer $1\frac{1}{4}$ inches shorter than the central. Wing, $4\frac{3}{4}$ inches; tail, 4; tarsus, 1.

8. ACTITURUS BARTRAMIUS, Wils.—Field Plover.

9. RECURVIROSTRA OCCIDENTALIS, VIG.—White-headed Avoset.

This species resembles *R. americana* in the general pattern of its markings, but differs in having a pale-grayish white to replace the buff of the head and neck. It is also decidedly larger, the uncovered part of the tibia measuring $2\frac{3}{4}$ inches instead of 2 inches; and the tarsus 4 instead of $3\frac{1}{2}$ inches. The hind claw is nearly obselete. Bill $3\frac{3}{4}$ inches long.

Found abundantly in New Mexico and California.

LIST OF BIRDS

INHABITING AMERICA, WEST OF THE MISSISSIPPI, NOT DESCRIBED IN
AUDUBON'S ORNITHOLOGY.*

ARCHIBUTEO FERRUGINEUS, Licht. Abh. Ac. Wiss. Berlin for
1838. California.

ROSTHRAMUS SOCIABILIS, Vieill. Nouv. Dict., vol. 18, p. 318.
Miami River; Cape Florida.

STRIX FRONTALIS, Licht. Abh. Ac. Wiss. Berlin. 1838. California.

ACANTHYLIS VAUXII, Towns. Jour. Acad. Nat. Sc., Phila., III. 1,
p. 148. 1839. Columbia River.

CHORDEILES BRASILIANUS, (Gm.)—Lawr. Ann. N. Y. Lyc. April,
1851. Rio Grande, Texas.

ANTROSTOMUS NUTTALLI, Aud. Biog. Birds, 2d ed. VII. 351,
pl. 495. 1847. Fort Union; California.

CERYLE AMERICANA, Boie.—Lawr. Ann. N. Y. Lyc. April,
1851. Texas, Rio Grande.

ORNISMYA COSTÆ, Bourcier, Rev. Zool., 1839, p. 294. California.

CONIROSTRUM ORNATUM, Lawr. Ann. N. Y. Lyc., April, 1851,
pl. 4. Rio Grande, Texas.

PICOLAPTES BRUNNEICAPILLUS, Laf.—Lawr. Ann. N. Y. Lyc.,
April, 1851. Rio Grande, Texas.

TROGLODYTES ALBIFRONS, Giraud. Texas Birds. 1841. *T.
mexicanus*, Sw. Texas.

---

* The list includes a few specimens recently described from the region east of
the Mississippi. As already stated, the birds mentioned here will all be described
and figured by Mr. Cassin of Philadelphia, in his forthcoming work on the Birds of
North America, entitled, "Illustrations of the Birds of California, Texas," &c.,
in continuation of Audubon.

VIREO HUTTONI, Cassin, Pr. A. N. S. Phila. V. 150. Feb. 1851. Monterey.

VIREO BELLI, Aud. Orn. Biog. 2d ed., VII., 333, pl. 485. 1843. Fort Union; California.

VIREO ATRICAPILLA, Woodhouse, Pr. A. N. S. Phila. VI. April, 1852.

VIREOSYLVA PHILADELPHICA, Cassin, Pr. A. N. S., V. 153., Feb. 1851. Philadelphia.

VIREOSYLVA ALTILOQUA, Vieill. Ois. Am. Sept. 1. Pl. 38. 1807. Florida.

SIALIA MACROPTERA, Baird, Stansbury's Report. 1852.

LANIUS ELEGANS, Sw. F. B. A. 1831. Oregon; Fur countries.

LANIUS EXCUBITOROIDES, Sw. F. B. A. 1831. Oregon; Fur countries.

HYPOCOLIUS AMPELINUS, Bp. Con. Gen. Av. I. 336. 1850. California.

ICTERIA VALASQUEZII, Bp. Proc. Zool. Soc. London. 1837. California.

CULICIVORA ATRICAPILLA, Sw. Zool. Ill.—Lawr. Ann. N. Y. Lyc. Sept. 1851. Texas.

SYLVICOLA OLIVACEA, Giraud, Texas Birds, pl. 7. 1841. Texas.

VERMIVORA BREVIPENNIS, Giraud, Ann. N. Y. Lyc. Texas.

TURDUS RUFOPALLIATUS, Lafresn., Rev. Zool. 1840, p. 259. Monterey.

MERULA OLIVACEA, Brewer, Proc. Boston Soc. Nat. Hist. I. p. 191.

MIMUS LEUCOPTERUS, Vig. Zool. of Blossom, 18. 1839. Western N. America.

MIMUS LONGIROSTRIS, Lafresn., Rev. Zool. 105, 1838. California and Mexico.

TOXOSTOMA REDIVIVA, Gambel, Pr. A. N. S. Phila., II. 264, Aug. 1845. Monterey.

Toxostoma curvirostris, Swainson, Matamoras.

Toxostoma lecontei, Lawr.   Ann. N. Y. Lyc., Sept. 1851.
Gila River.

Motacilla leucoptera, Vig. Zool. of Blossom, 1839.   Western
N. America.

Agrodoma spraguei, Aud.   Orn. Biog. 2d ed., VII. 335, pl.
486, 1843.   Fort Union.

Saxicola œnanthoides, Vig. Zool. Beechey's Voyage, 1839·
N. W. Coast of America; Labrador?

Saurophagus sulphuratus, Swainson.—Gambel, in J. A. N.
S. Phila., I. 39.   Gulf of California.

Saurophagus bairdii, Gambel, J. A. N. S. Phila. I. 40, 1847.
California.

Tyrannus cassinii, Lawrence, Ann. N. Y. Lyc. June, 1850.
Texas.

Tyrannula cayanensis, Gm.   Texas.

Tyrannula lawrenceii, Giraud, Texas Birds, pl. 2, 1841.
Texas.

Tyrannula cinerascens, Lawrence, Ann. N. Y. Lyc. Sept.
1851.   Texas and California.

Tyrannula flaviventris, Baird, Pr. A. N. S. Phila., I. 283,
July, 1843.   Carlisle, Pa.

Tyrannula minima, Baird, Pr. A. N. S. Phila., I. 284, July,
1843.   Carlisle, Pa.

Pyrocephalus rubineus, Bodd, (*P. coronata*, Gould)—Lawrence, Ann. N. Y. Lyc. April, 1851.   Rio Grande, Texas.

Setophaga vulnerata, Wagler.   Texas.

Setophaga belli, Giraud, Texas Birds, Pl. 4, fig. 2, 1841.
Texas.

Setophaga rubra, Swainson, Phil. Mag. 1830.   Texas.

Setophaga picta, Swainson, Phil. Mag. 1830.   Texas.

Setaphaga rubrifrons, Giraud, Texas Birds. pl, 7. fig. 1,
1841.   Texas.

EMBERNAGRA RUFIVIRGATA, Lawrence, Ann. N. Y. Lyc., pl. V. fig. 2, April, 1851. Rio Grande, Texas.

EMBERNAGRA BLANDINGIANA, Gambel, Pr. A. N. S. Phila., I. p. 260. Rocky Mountains.

SALTATOR RUFIVENTRIS, Vig. Zool. Blossom, 19, 1839. Western N. America.

EUPHONIA ELEGANTISSIMA, Bp. Proc. Zool. Soc. Lond., 1837. Texas.

SPERMOPHILA ALBOGULARIS, Swainson.—Lawrence, Ann. N. Y. Lyceum, Sept. 1851. Texas.

RHAMPHOPIS FLAMMIGERUS, Jard. Ill. III. pl. 131. Columbia River, Oregon?

CHRYSOPOGA TYPICA, Bp. Con. Gen. Av. I. 480, 1850. California.

FRINGILLA MERULOIDES, Vig. Zool. Blossom. Monterey.

ZONOTRICHIA QUERULA, Nutt. Man. I. 555, 2d ed., 1840. Z. comata, De Wied. Missouri River.

ZONOTRICHIA GAMBELI, Nutt. Orn. I. 557, 2d ed., 1840. Columbia River.

ZONOTRICHIA CASSINII, Woodhouse, Proc. A. N. S. Phila., VI. April, 1852. Texas.

CHRYSOMITRIS LAWRENCEII, Cassin, Pr. A. N. S. Phila., V. 105, pl. 5, Oct. 1850. San Diego, California.

PIPILO FUSCA, Sw. Phil. Mag. 1827. California.

PIPILO OREGONA, Bell, Ann. N. Y. Lyc. 1848. Oregon.

PIPILO ABERTI, Baird, Stansbury's Report. 1852. New Mexico.

EMBERIZA LECONTEI, Aud. Biog. Birds, 2d ed., VII. 338, pl. 488. 1843. Fort Union.

EMBERIZA BAIRDII, Aud. Biog. 2d ed., VII. 359, pl. 500. 1843. Fort Union.

EMBERIZA BILINEATA, Cassin, Pr. A. N. S., Phila. V. 104, pl. — Oct. 1850. Rio Grande, Texas.

EMBERIZA BELLI, Cassin, Pr. A. N. S. Phila., V. 104, pl. 4. Oct. 1850. San Diego, California.

CARPODACUS OBSCURUS, McCall, Pr. A. N. S. Phila., V. 220. June, 1850. Santa Fe.

CARPODACUS FAMILIARIS, McCall, Pr. A. N. S. Phila., VI., April, 1852. New Mexico.

COCCOTHRAUSTES FERREO-ROSTRIS, Vig. Zool. Jour. IV. p. 352. 1828-9. N. W. coast America; California.

CARDINALIS SINUATUS, Bp.—Lawrence, Ann. N. Y. Lyc. April, 1851. Rio Grande, Texas.

PYRRHULA INORNATA, Vig. Zool. of Blossom, 20. 1837. Western N. America.

LEUCOSTICTE GRISEINUCHA, Brandt, Orn. Ross. 1842. Aleutian Islands. (*L. griseogenys*, Gould.)

PLECTROPHANES MACCOWNII, Lawrence. Ann. N. Y. Lyc. Sept. 1851. Western Texas.

PASSERELLA UNALASCHENSIS, Bp. Con. Gen. Av. 477. 1850. Unalascha.

PASSERELLA RUFINA, Brandt, Orn. Ros. Sitka.

EUSPIZA ARCTICA, Bp. Con. Gen. Av. 469. 1850. (*Emberiza chrysops*, Pall.) N. W. Coast.

ALAUDA RUFA, Lath.—Aud. Orn. Biog. 2d ed., VII. 353, pl. 497. 1843. Texas.

OTOCORIS OCCIDENTALIS, McCall, Pr. A., N. S. Phila., V. 218. June, 1851. Santa Fé. Salt Lake City.

STURNELLA NEGLECTA, Aud. Biog. 2d ed. VII. 339, pl. 489. 1843. Upper Missouri; Utah; New Mexico; California.

QUISCALUS MACROURUS, Sw.—Lawrence, Ann. N. Y. Lyc. April, 1851. Rio Grande, Texas.

SCOLECOPHAGUS MEXICANUS, Sw. 2¼ Cent. Birds, No. 66. 1838. (*Quiscalus brewerii*). Fort Union, Missouri; California.

PENDULINUS CALIFORNIANUS, Less. Rev. Zool., 1844, p. 436. California.

PSAROCOLIUS AURICOLLIS, De Wied., Reise, 367. Missouri River.

XANTHORNUS MEXICANUS, Briss.—Vigors, Zool. Blossom. Pacific Coast N. America.

XANTHORNUS AFFINIS, Lawrence, Ann. N. Y. Lyc. April, 1851. Rio Grande, Texas.

ICTERUS CUCULLATUS, Sw.—Lawrence, Ann. N. Y. Lyc. April, 1851. Rio Grande, Texas.

ICTERUS MELANOCEPHALUS, Wagler, Isis, 1829, p. 756. Texas.

ICTERUS VULGARIS, Daud.—Aud. Orn. Biog., 2d ed., VII. pl. 499. 1843. South Carolina.

ICTERUS FRENATUS, Licht. Isis, 1843, p. 59. Greenland? Mexico.

CHAMEA FASCIATA, Gambel, Pr. A. N. S., Phila., II. 265. Aug. 1845. California.

LOPHOPHANES SEPTENRIONALIS, Harris, Pr. A. N. S., II. 300. Dec., 1845. Upper Missouri; Rocky Mountains; Salt Lake.

LOPHOPHANES INORNATUS, Gambel, Pr. A. N. S. Phila., II. 265. California.

LOPHOPHANES WOLLWEBERI, Bp. Comptes Rendus. Sept. 1850. (*P. annexus.*) Cassin, Oct. 1850, Rio Grande, Texas.

LOPHOPHANES ATRICRISTATUS, Cassin, Pr. A. N. S. Phila., V. 103, pl. 2. Oct. 1850. Rio Grande, Texas.

PARUS MONTANUS, Gambel, Pr. A. N. S. Phila., I. p. 259. New Mexico.

GYMNOKITTA CYANOCEPHALA, De Wied., Reise. Upper Missouri; Rocky Mountains.

CYANOCORAX CORONATUS, Sw. Phil. Mag. 1827. Texas.

CYANOCORAX LUXUOSUS, Lesson.—Lawrence, Ann. N. Y. Lyc. April, 1851. Rio Grande, Texas.

CYANOCORAX CASSINII, McCall, Pr. A. N. S. Phila, V. 216. June, 1851. Santa Fé.

GARRULUS CALIFORNICUS, Vig. Zool. Blossom, pl. 5. 1839. Monterey, California.

PICA BEECHEYII, Vig. Zool. Jour. IV. 353. 1828–9. Monterey,

CROTOPHAGA ———? New Orleans. Mr. Audubon's collection.

PIAYA CAYANENSIS, Gambel, J. A. N. S. Phila., I. 25. Gulf of California.

GEOCOCCYX AFFINIS, Hartlaub, Rev. Zool., 1844, p. 215. California.

GEOCOCCYX VIATICUS, Wagler—McCall, Pr. A. N. S. Phila., V. 220. June, 1851. Texas and New Mexico.

MELANERPES ALBOLARVATUS, Cassin, Pr. A. N. S. Phila., V. 106. October, 1850. Sutter's Mill, California.

MELANERPES FORMICIVORUS, Swainson.—Nuttall's Man., I. 166. Santa Barbara, California.

CENTURUS SANTACRUZII, Bp. Pr. Zool. Soc. Lond. 1837, p. 16. Western Texas.

CENTURUS FLAVIVENTRIS, Swainson, $2\frac{1}{4}$ cent., Lardner, Cab. Cyclopædia. Texas.

CENTURUS ELEGANS, Sw.—Lawrence, Ann. N. Y. Lyc. April, 1851. $2\frac{1}{4}$ cent. Rio Grande, Texas.

COLAPTES MEXICANOIDES, Lafres. Rev. Zool., 1844. California.

COLAPTES AYRESII, Aud. Biog. Birds, 2d ed., VII. 348, pl. 494. 1843. Fort Union.

COLAPTES COLLARIS, Vig. Zool. Blossom, p. 24, pl. 9.; Zool. Jour. IV. 354, 1828–9. Monterey.

PICUS SCAPULARIS, Vig. Zool. Jour. IV. 353, 1828–9. San Blas, California.

PICUS NUTTALLII, Gambel, Proc. A. N. S., Phila., I. 259. (*P. wilsonii*, Malherbe.) California.

PICUS SCALARIS, Wagler, Isis, 1829. California and New Mexico.

PICUS LECONTEI, Jones, Ann. N. Y. Lyceum, IV. 489. Georgia.

COLUMBA SOLITARIA, McCall, Pr. A. N. S. Phila., II. 233, July, 1847. Matamoras.

COLUMBA FLAVIROSTRIS, Wagler.—Lawr. Ann. N. Y. Lyceum. April, 1851. Texas, Rio Grande.

PENELOPE POLIOCEPHALA, Wagler.—McCall in Pr. A. N. S. Phila., V. 222. Matamoras and Rio Grande.

ORTALIDA VETULA, Wagler.—Lawr. Ann. N. Y. Lyceum. April, 1851. Texas, Rio Grande.

CYRTONYX MASSENA, Gould.—McCall, Pr. A. N. S. Phila., V. 221. San Pedro and Rio Pecos, New Mexico.

CALLIPEPLA GAMBELI, Nutt. Pr. A. N. S. Phila, I. 260. April, 1843.—*Callipepla venusta*, Gould, Pr. Zool. Soc. Lond., 1846, p. 71. New Mexico and California.

CALLIPEPLA PICTA, Dougl. Linn. Trans. Lond. California.

CALLIPEPLA ELEGANS, Less. Cent. Zool., pl. 61. California.

CALLIPEPLA DOUGLASSII, Vig. Zool. Jour., IV. 353. 1828–9. Monterey, California.

CALLIPEPLA SQUAMATA, Vig. Zool. Jour., V. 275. 1830. New Mexico.

STREPSILAS MELANOCEPHALUS, Vig. Zool. Jour., IV. 353. 1828–9. Monterey.

NUMENIUS RUFIVENTRIS, Vig. Zool. Jour., IV. 356. 1828–9. Pacific coast of N. America.

MACRORHAMPHUS SCOLOPACEUS, Lawrence, Ann. N. Y. Lyc. Mississippi Valley. (*Limosa sbolopacea*, Say).

RECURVIROSTRA OCCIDENTALIS, Vig. Zool. Jour., IV. 356. San Francisco. New Mexico.

ANSER NIGRICANS, Lawr. Ann. N. Y. Lyc., 1846. Atlantic coast.

ANAS UROPHASIANUS, Vig. Zool. Jour., IV. 353. 1828–9. N. W. coast N. America.

DENDROCYGNA ARBOREA? Penn. Mexico. South Carolina?

DENDROCYGNA AUTUMNALIS, Eyton.—Lawr., Ann. N. Y. Lyc. April, 1851. Rio Grande, Texas.

CYANOPTERUS RAFFLESII, King. Salt Lake, Utah. Louisiana.

OIDEMIA VELVETINA, Cassin, Pr. A. N. S. Phila, V. 126. December, 1850. Atlantic coast. (*O. fusca* of former authors).

LARUS BRACHYRHYNCHUS, Gould, Pr. Zool. Soc. Lond., 1841, pl. 106. July, 1843. Zoology of the Sulphur, pl. 34. Western N. America.

LARUS BELCHERI, Vig. Zool. Jour., IV. 358. 1828–9. Pacific coast of North America.

STERNA ELEGANS, Gambel, Pr. A. N. S. Phila., IV. 129. December, 1848. Mazatlan.

STERNA CASPIA, L.—Lawrence, Ann. N. Y. Lyc. May, 1850. Atlantic coast, U. S.

PROCELLARIA MERIDIONALIS, Lawrence, Ann. N. Y. Lyc. February, 1847. Indian River, Florida.

THALASSIDROMA FURCATA, Lath.—Gould, Zool. Sulphur. Russian America.

THALASSIDROMA FREGETTA, Kuhl.—Lawrence, Ann. N. Y. Lyc. April, 1851. Florida.

PHALACROCORAX PERSPICILLATUS, Pall. Zool. Ros. As., II. 303. Gould, Zool. Sulphur, pl. 32. Russian America.

PHALACROCORAX PENICILLATUS, Brandt. Monterey.

URIA BREVIROSTRIS, Vig. Zool. Jour., IV. 357. 1828–9. Pacific coast of N. America.

MERGULUS CIRROCEPHALUS, Vig. Zool. Blossom. 1839. Pacific coast of N. America.

MERGULUS CASSINII, Gambel, Pr. A. N. S. Phila., II. 266. August, 1845. Coast of California.

PTYCHORHAMPHUS ALEUTICUS, Brandt, Bull. Sc. St. Petersburg, II. 1837. Aleutian Islands.

BRACHYRHAMPHUS WRANGELI, Brandt, Bull. Sc. St. Petersburg, II. No. 20. Aleutian Islands.

BRACHYRHAMPHUS BRACHYPTERUS, Brandt, Bull. St. Petersburg. Unalaschka.

REPTILES.

By SPENCER F. BAIRD and CHARLES GIRARD.

Siredon lichenoides, Baird.

Pl. I.

Spec. char.—Body uniform blackish brown, covered all over with licheniform patches of grayish yellow; snout rounded; tail compressed and lanceolated; toes broad and short.

The addition of an authentic new species to the genus *Siredon* will justly be considered as of great interest to herpetologists. Two species are now clearly ascertained to exist; perhaps a third, if the one mentioned by Prof. Owen* be really such. It is not improbable that many more exist, as we have accounts of many localities of "fish with legs," in various parts of Mexico, New Mexico, and Texas, although, as yet, we have been able to procure only these two species. The possession of these, however, allows a comparison of characters by which the absolute generic features of the group can be better ascertained.

The figures hitherto published of *S. mexicanus*, and the imperfect sketch of *S. maculatus*, are far from being satisfactory, and do not allow any accurate comparison to be made of their specific features. As these will have to be critically redrawn in order to meet the wants of science, we have endeavoured to obtain, and we hope with success, figures of *S. lichenoides* that will enable future comparisons to be satisfactorily made. Our specimen is a little more than six inches and a-half in length, the figures being all of natural size. Whether this be the absolute size of the species which it represents, we are unprepared to state. If such was the case, it is considerably smaller than *S. mexicanus*. The tail forms nearly the half of the entire length, and the head a little less than the fifth of the same.

The head is ovoidal, much broader than deep, and the snout rounded, a character which at once will distinguish our species

---

* Annals and Magazine of Natural History, xiv: 1844, 23.

Pl. 1.

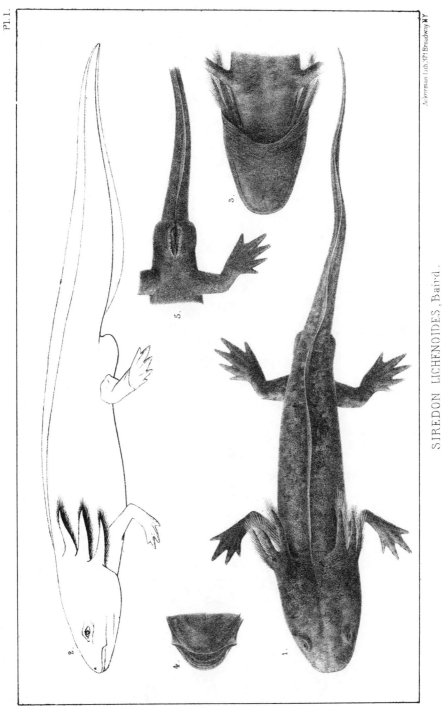

SIREDON LICHENOIDES, Baird.

Ackerman lith. 379 Broadway N Y

from *S. maculatus*, the chief character of which consists in the truncated snout. The eyes are of medium size, situated behind the angle of the mouth. Their position and size in *S. maculatus* we do not know accurately, but in *S. mexicanus* these organs would be considerably smaller and more approximated to the end of the snout, judging of these peculiarities from the various sketches given of that species, and proportionally much smaller than in a specimen of *Siredon* in our possession from the city of Mexico, and of about the same size as our *S. lichenoides*. If these proportions are correct in the drawings of *S. mexicanus*, we would undoubtedly have a species which could not be accurately characterized until further information should be obtained. The nostrils are very small and near the end of the snout. The body is subcylindrical, subfusiform, broader and deeper at its origin than on any point backward. The tail is very much compressed, elongated, and tapering into a point. The dorsal membrane commences at the occiput, rising gradually until the middle of the tail, whence it diminishes again toward its pointed tip. The membrane under the tail is lower than that above, extending from behind the vent to the tip of the tail, and reaching its greatest height on its anterior third, but diminishing more rapidly forward than backward. The anal opening is very large, elongated, and rendered very conspicuous by the great development of the fleshy masses which constitute its margin.

The presence of four external flaps, provided with respiratory fringes, is a generic character, belonging to all the species hitherto known. Their real appearance has been misrepresented in many sketches, as we could satisfy ourselves by the examination of two species preserved in alcohol. The branchial fringes do not extend all along the upper edge of the branchial flap. They occupy densely the lower edge of that cutaneous appendage from its origin to its tip, and thence for a short space above, but much less developed here than below, as we have endeavoured to show in the profile of fig. 2. The fringes themselves are very much flattened, tapering, and disposed upon a double row, so that each of them appears as if double; but it is easy to ascertain that the row on either side does not combine with the other.

The fore and hind legs have nearly the same length when measured from their bases to their extremities; the hind ones, however, are much thicker, and the toes of both pairs are neither so slender nor so elongated as in *S. mexicanus* and *S. maculatus*.

The ground colour is blackish brown; there are irregular patches

22

of grayish yellow spread all over the body, head, and tail, reminding us of surfaces over which lichens grow, whence the specific name by which we designate this species.

It was caught by R. H. Kern, Esq., in Spring Lake, at the head of Santa Fé Creek, in New Mexico, accordingly a member of the fauna of the basin of the Rio Grande del Norte.

In a revision of the *North American Tailed Batrachia*, published in the Journal of the Academy of Natural Sciences, 2d series, vol. i., p. 281, (1849,) we intimated a doubt as to whether *Siredon* or the axolotls were adult animals. Their wonderful resemblance to the larvæ of *Ambystoma punctata* was our chief ground for this belief. Since then, however, we have seen the description and figures by Sir Everard Home of *S. mexicanus*, in which he clearly indicates, in one individual at least, ovaries distended with eggs. We have also seen specimens with the genital apparatus presenting the tumid and highly developed appearance of salamanders in general, when in the breeding season.

CNEMIDOPHORUS TIGRIS, Baird and Girard.

Pl. II.

SPEC. CHAR.—Scales on the subguttural fold small in size; four yellowish, indistinct stripes along the dorsal region.

This species, one of the most elegant of its genus, is the third hitherto described as found in the United States, for we have no doubt that the lizard referred to in Long's expedition, under the name of *Ameiva tesselata*, will come under this genus, and be closely allied to our species. No specimen of this being extant at the present time in any known collection, a direct comparison with the other species of *Cnemidophorus* was not possible. That *A. tesselata*, however, although closely allied to, is not identical with our species, we think that any one will be convinced on comparing Say's description with the figures in pl. II. These are of natural size, and exhibit most admirably the structure of the regions in their most minute details. The plates of the head above (fig. 3), below (fig. 2), and on the sides (fig. 1), need no further description. The minute scales of the back and upper portion of the legs contrast strikingly with the eight rows of large scales of the belly and those of the lower part of the hind legs, as well as with those of the inferior surface of the head and throat. On the tail again, the scales assume another character, well opposed too; they are longer than

CNEMIDOPHORUS TIGRIS, Baird & Girard.

Ackerman Lith,379 Broadway NY

Pl.II.

broad, arranged in annular rows, or else verticillated and slightly carinated. The tail is cylindrical, and two and a-half times the length of the body and head together: it tapers gradually and terminates in a point.

The ground colour appears to have been bluish yellow, marked with irregular patches of black. In some specimens, four longitudinal yellow stripes may be seen extending from the occiput to the base of the tail, and occasionally to a little distance on the latter. In the young state, the black patches predominate, unite, and form, as it were, the ground colour, and the yellow constitutes irregular small spots.

A series of individuals of different sizes were collected by Capt. Stansbury in the valley of the Great Salt Lake.

Genus CROTAPHYTUS, Holbrook.

GEN. CHAR.—Head covered with small and polygonal plates. The occipital proper, minute. Teeth on the jaws, pterygoids and palatines, rudimentary on the latter. Broad auditory aperture. Femoral pores present; no anal ones. Tail very long.

Of the genus *Crotaphytus*, a typical form peculiar to North America, but one single species has hitherto been discovered, the *C. collaris*, observed for the first time by Major Long's party, on their expedition to the Rocky Mountains. The discovery of a second species of this genus within the limits of the United States will be received with interest: both of these have a very close generic relationship, the differences being found in some minor details of their structure.

The generic characters are the following:—The occipital region, vertex, and front are covered with small and polygonal plates. On the superciliary region and around the nostrils the plates are scarcely larger than the scales of the back. The odd occipital plates are inconspicuous, being but very little larger than the surrounding ones. The auditory apertures are broadly open. Teeth exist on the maxillaries, palatines, and pterygoids; conical, acute, and slightly curved on the anterior part of the jaws, they are compressed and tricuspid on the posterior. The palatine teeth are rudimentary. The skin is folded under the throat. The scales of the upper part of the body are polygonal, and smaller than those of the lower part, or belly, and tail; those under the head have nearly the size of those of the back. The femoral pores are very distinct; the anal ones are wanting. The tail is **cylindrical**, longer than the body and head together.

The genus *Crotaphytus* differs from *Holbrookia* in having external auditory apertures, teeth on the pterygoids, and but a minute occipital plate. The shape of the head is likewise more elongated and pointed in front.

CROTAPHYTUS WISLIZENII, Baird and Girard.

PLATE III.

SPEC. CHAR.—Head proportionally narrow and elongated. Cephalic plates and scales on the back very small. Yellowish brown, spotted all over with small patches of deeper brown or black.

C. wislizenii has the same general form and appearance as *C. collaris*, exhibiting the same contracted neck and fold under the throat, the same compact body, the same cylindrical and elongated tail, and the same shape and proportions of locomotive members and terminating toes. The differences by which the two are distinguished, although of a comparatively minor character, are readily appreciable when both are directly compared. Thus the head of *C. wislizenii* is proportionally more elongated and narrower than that of *C. collaris*. The small and polygonal plates which cover its upper surface and sides are smaller, as well as those of the lip of the lower jaw. The scales of the back are likewise smaller, and those of the belly larger. The tail is somewhat longer, and its scales larger in *C. collaris*; these are subverticillated in both species, and subcarinated from the middle of the back toward its extremity. The pores of the lower surface of the thighs are more conspicuous in *C. collaris*, independently of the fact that they are generally less so in the female than in the male of the same species. Immediately behind the vent, at the origin of the tail, there exists, in the male, a row of large scales more uniform in *C. collaris* than in *C. wislizenii*. The specimen figured on our plate III. being a female, these anal plates are not to be seen in fig. 4.

In the colours of the body distinctive marks will at once be found. *C. collaris* possesses on the sides of the neck a double band of black bordered with white, which does not exist in *C. wislizenii*. The upper surface of the body of the former is scattered all over with small yellow dots, which indeed are found in the latter, but are much smaller and more numerous, having in addition, intermixed with them, irregular roundish brown spots, extending

CROTAPHYTUS WISLIZENII, Baird & Girard.

Ackerman Lith,379 Broadway N.Y.

PL III

even to the head. The tail is irregularly annulated with brown and yellow.

Nothing is known of the habits of the crotaphyti. We found in the stomach of one specimen of the *C. wislizenii* the remains of a species of *Cnemidophorus* allied to *C. sexlineatus*.

The specimen which we have had figured was caught near Santa Fé, by Dr. Wislizenus, during the Mexican war. To him we take great pleasure in dedicating it, in testimonial of his zeal for science, during the arduous duties of an army surgeon, while attached to Colonel Doniphan's command. On his return, the specimen was sent to Dr. Le Conte, and by him kindly transmitted to the Smithsonian Institution. The same species was obtained by Colonel J. D. Graham, between San Antonio and El Paso del Norte, while on his journey to the boundary-line, in May last.

Genus HOLBROOKIA, Girard.

Syn. *Cophosaurus*, TROSCH. Arch. f. Naturg. (1850, I.) 1852.

GEN. CHAR.—Head covered with small and polygonal plates. No auditory aperture. No teeth on the palatine bones. A fold of the skin on the breast. Femoral pores present, but no anal ones.

This genus was established in 1850, upon a small lizard, much less remarkable in its general aspect than in its structure. In its appearance it is so similar to certain species of the Chilian proctotreti, that at first glance no one could suppose it to be different from the latter genus. But in examining it more attentively, we find no external opening to the ears, a fact that cannot but strike the observer. There are no teeth on the palatines—another character which distinguishes *Holbrookia* from *Proctotretus*. Both of these genera have a fold under the throat, but the former has femoral pores, which are wanting in the latter. The anal pores are absent in *Holbrookia*, while they exist in *Proctrotretus*.

The genus *Holbrookia* will, no doubt, prove somewhat related to *Crotaphytus*, having, like the latter, the upper surface of the head covered with small and polygonal plates, and well-developed femoral pores. The elongated tail of the crotaphyti, although so disproportionate when compared to *Holbrookia maculata*, will no longer appear as a feature peculiar to the genus, so soon as we shall have an opportunity to give a description and a figure of another species of the same genus, and which was lately collected by Mr. John H. Clark, zoologist to Colonel J. D. Graham, while in charge of the survey of the United States and Mexican boundary.

As these pages were passing through the press, we received the numbers iv. and v. for 1850, and ii. and iii. for 1851, of the "Archiv für Naturgeschichte." The present editor of that periodical, Dr. Troschel, describes, in the fourth number for 1850, a new saurian genus, under the name of *Cophosaurus*, a species of which was brought to Germany by the geologist, Ferd. Rœmer, who visited Texas some years ago. Having the same saurian in our possession, collected in the same locality, as a second but undescribed species of our genus *Holbrookia*, we could readily identify the genus *Cophosaurus*. It is to be regretted that the description of our genus *Holbrookia* which reached Germany in the summer of 1851, that is before the publication of the number iv. of the Archiv. für Naturgeschichte for 1850, has been overlooked by this able German zoologist. The absence of auditory apertures, "aures externæ nullæ," which is the most striking character of our genus, would have struck Dr. Troschel, had he been aware of our description in the Proceedings of the American Association for the Advance of Science, fourth meeting, held at New·Haven, in August, 1850.

As it may hereafter be questioned which of these generic names has the priority, inasmuch as the volume in which *Cophosaurus* is published bears the date of 1850, we deem it proper to call attention to the fact that its publication took place in 1852. Even at the date at which we write these lines, (April, 1852), the year 1850 of the Archiv. für Naturgeschichte has not been completed. This fact shows how an author may be deprived of the fruit of his labours by an anachronism of this kind.

HOLBROOKIA MACULATA, Girard.

PL. VI. FIG. 1–3.

Syn. *Holbrookia maculata*, GIRARD, Proc. Amer. Assoc. Adv. Sc., IV. (1850), 1851, 201.

SPEC. CHAR.—Tail about the length of the trunk. Head subcircular, slightly conical in front. Pectoral fold bordered with large scales.

The general form of this species is rather thick and short than elongated, especially in the female: the young and the males are more slender. The body is subcylindrical, the tail conical and very stout at its origin, tapering however suddenly away. The entire length is between three and four inches, as shown by the

Pl. VI.

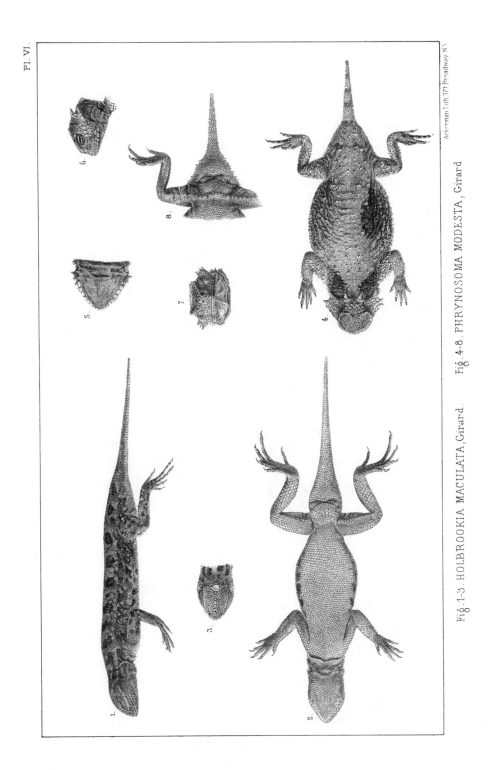

Ackerman lith 379 Broadway N Y

Fig. 1-3. HOLBROOKIA MACULATA, Girard.　　　　Fig. 4-8. PHRYNOSOMA MODESTA, Girard

figures, all of which are drawn of natural size. The tail is of the length of the body, the head excluded. The latter is oval, broader than high; its summit being convex, and its snout truncated. It is covered with small, irregular, and polygonal plates, larger on the middle line of the skull than above the eye, the nose, and the nape. There is a supraorbital carina, with small elongated plates, scarcely to be seen with the naked eye. The infraorbital plates are less numerous, but longer. The eyes occupy the middle of the length of the head. The eyelids are bordered by a row of minute and pointed plates, forming a serrated edge. The nostrils are nearer the end of the snout than the eye. The angle of the mouth extends to the posterior rim of the orbit. The upper jaw is bordered with a row of small, very elongated plates, obliquely imbricated. Margining the lower jaw there are two rows of small angular plates, the larger ones being at the angle of the mouth. There is a single row of small conical teeth on both jaws; those in front are acute and slightly recurved; those behind stouter and erect, with a carina separating the rounded crown from the body of the tooth. The posterior extremity of the tongue has a semilunar notch. As observed in the generic paragraph, there are no external auditory apertures; the tympanum is covered by scales altogether similar to those of the neck. On both sides of the neck and immediately behind the angle of the mouth, is a fold of the skin, which vanishes in a depression under the head. Farther backward, and on the breast, is situated another fold, constituting an elegant neck ring, which, however, does not extend higher than the shoulders.

The anterior legs are shorter and more slender than the posterior. There are five toes, similar in each pair of limbs, elongated, slender, terminated by a compressed and recurved nail. The toes and nails of the posterior limb, however, are a little longer in proportion to the limbs themselves. The fourth toe is the longest, the two external ones the shortest, the second and third nearly equal. There are eleven femoral pores on each thigh.

The scales are slighty imbricated, subcarinated on the back and sides, smooth underneath. They are smaller on the neck and at the base of the limbs than on the sides and back. Those on the tail are indistinctly verticillated. The smallest ones are found under the head, in the region of the groins and behind the vent; they are larger on the abdomen than under the tail. The toes are entirely covered with scales.

The colour, according to a drawing made from life by an artist of great merit, Mr. William H. Tappan, while on the River Platte in 1848, is olivaceous brown, slightly violaceous on the sides of the head. On each side of the body there are two, sometimes three oblong spots, of a deep black; and on the body two rows of quite large, irregular blackish-brown patches, with a band of a lighter colour between each row. There is an indication of a third row of these patches, less apparent, however, in the male, in which again we find two orange-red lines, the uppermost extending to the end of the snout in passing over the eye; the other follows the lower jaw. In advance of the eyes the orange hue of these lines passes into brighter yellow.

This species inhabits the valley of the Platte River, as collected there by W. H. Tappan. We have received several specimens from Texas, collected by General Churchill, one of which is the original from which the accompanying drawings have been made. The individual represented is a female.

Genus UTA, Baird and Girard.

GEN. CHAR.—Upper part of body covered with minute scales; a pectoral fold; auditory apertures; femoral pores, but no anal ones.

The genus which we now establish will not fail to attract the attention of herpetologists, having a relation to both *Sceloporus* and *Holbrookia*. The former genus it resembles in having the upper surface of the head covered with similar scales, and in being provided with auditory apertures. On the other hand, the body is covered with scales, like those in *Holbrookia*, while on the tail they are much large than in any of the above genera, thus contrasting greatly with those of the back. The genus *Uta*, moreover, has a subgular fold of skin, constituting a neck-ring similar to that in *Holbrookia*. Its elongated tail would recall to mind the genus *Crotaphytus*, were not the palatine teeth absent. Femoral pores exist, while anal ones are wanting.

Besides the species described below, this genus embraces two others, one of which is entirely new to science, and was sent in by Colonel J. D. Graham from the boundary-line, and which we call *Uta ornata*; while the other was described as a *Sceloporus*, and first as a mere variety of *S. grammicus*, afterward, however, separated under the specific name of *S. microlepidotus*. The minuteness of

Pl V.

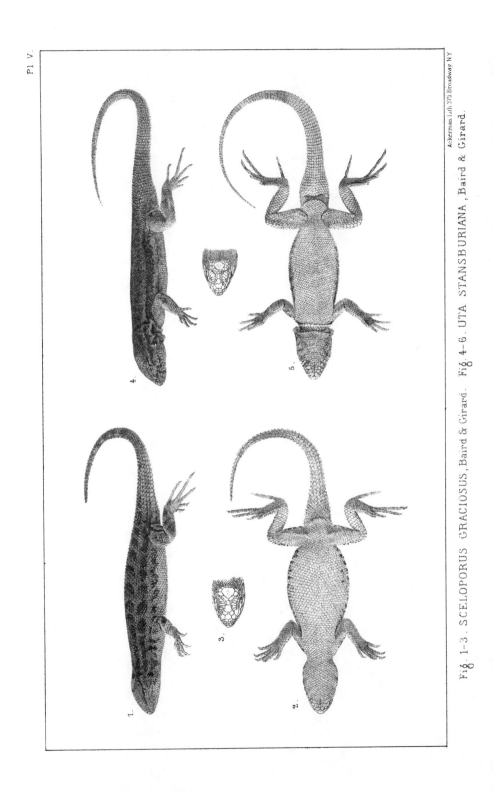

Fig. 1–3. SCELOPORUS GRACIOSUS, Baird & Girard. Fig. 4–6. UTA STANSBURIANA, Baird & Girard.

the scales to which it makes allusion becomes now a generic character. Thus the species included in the genus *Uta* are, generally speaking, of a smaller size than the sceloporī proper.

UTA STANSBURIANA, Baird and Girard.

PL. V. FIG. 4–6.

SPEC. CHAR.—Tail slender, elongated, and conical, provided with large scales arranged in verticils; a subgular fold in addition to the pectoral one.

This species is one of the handsomest and most graceful among the small saurian forms peculiar to North America. In its general aspect it recalls to mind the cnemidophorī, having, like the latter, the body covered with small polygonal scales, while on the tail the scales are large, elongated, and verticillated. The proportions in length between the body and tail, and the fold under the throat, are likewise similar in both *Cnemidophorus* and *Uta*. But when we compare the shape and structure of the head in the two, we detect differences which are not merely generic, but cause them to belong to different families. The upper surface of the head is covered with small and polygonal scales, as in *Sceloporus*, *Crotaphytus*, and *Holbrookia;* its shape is rather rounded than conical or elongated, and is broad and flattened, while it is narrower and higher than broad in cnemidophorī and allied genera. The body is subfusiform, the tail slender, conical, and nearly one and a-half times the length of the body and head together.

The occipital plate is polygonal and comparatively large; three or four superciliaries, the vertical and frontal plates, are a little larger than the many others by which they are surrounded. The nostrils are very conspicuous, and approximated to the end of the snout; they are situated interior to the prolongation of the superciliary ridge, and composed of elongated and narrow plates. The rostral plate is narrow, and is scarcely to be seen when viewed from above, but much more conspicuous than in *Holbrookia* when looked at in front. The plates lining the margin of the jaws are quadrangular, elongated, and much narrower on the upper than on the lower jaw. Under the chin, three or four pairs of polygonal scales are considerably the largest. Between the latter and those on the margin of the lower jaw two other rows may be seen, composed of scales a little larger than the subgular ones. The auditory aperture is moderate, surrounded by irregular folds of the skin which extend under the throat; from its anterior edge proceed three or four conical and acute scales; the posterior pectoral fold is provided along its margin with a row of large, smooth, and subquadrangular scales.   The anterior and upper surface of the locomotive members are covered with scales nearly of the same size of those of the belly, but carinated and a little narrower posteriorly.   Scales, similar to those of the belly, extend on the lower part of the hind legs, are somewhat larger, especially on the anterior margin.   The toes are slender and terminated by short, pointed, and slightly recurved nails.   The small scales which cover the middle region of the back, from the anterior limbs to the origin of the tail, are somewhat longer than those of the occiput and sides from the ear to the hind limbs.   The posterior part of the thigh and groins are covered with minute scales similar to those of the sides of the body.   The largest scales are seen on the tail, as already observed; they are verticillated and strongly carinated.

The colour below is uniform greenish-yellow, except under the head, where the green predominates, intermingled with brownish, narrow bands.   Above it is blackish-brown, marbled with greenish-yellow, or whitish-yellow irregular dots.   Sometimes a double row of dorsal patches of a deeper black may be seen along the back in some individuals, recalling to mind a similar distribution of colour in *Sceloporus scalaris*, *S. graciosus*, and *Holbrookia maculata*.

This species is from the valley of the Great Salt Lake, where it was collected by Captain Howard Stansbury; in remembrance of whose services to the country and to science we have designated it under the name which it now bears.

SCELOPORUS GRACIOSUS, Baird and Girard.

PL. V.   FIG. 1–3.

SPEC. CHAR.—Head subconical; scales of the back proportionally large; tail of medium size, slender and conical.

This small and graceful species has a much greater affinity with the Mexican *Sceloporus scalaris* than with *S. undulatus* of the United States.   The most striking character, as compared with *S. scalaris*, consists in the marked difference in size between the scales of the back and those of the base of the tail.   The latter is proportionally longer than in *S. scalaris*, and shorter than in *S. undulatus*.   The body of our species is subcylindrical, and rather short; the specimen figured being a female, the abdomen is represented in a state of too great expansion. The head is ovoidal, depressed, subconcave above. The occipital plate is heptagonal, broad, and linear posteriorly, pointed and very acute anteriorly. It is surrounded by twelve smaller plates, six of which, very small, line the posterior edge, while the other six are distributed on the remaining circumference, three to the right and three to the left. There are two vertical plates, the anterior one the largest and pentagonal. In advance of the latter, seven or eight polygonal frontal plates form a conspicuous group, while near the extremity of the snout the plates are as minute as the scales on the neck. The plates which line the margin of the jaws are small, narrow, elongated, and inconspicuous. On the chin there are three pairs comparatively larger and conspicuous. The scales on the back are spade-shaped and strongly carinated from the neck to the tip of the tail. On the latter region they are a little more acute posteriorly and vérticillated. On the sides of the abdomen they are smaller, and their outline less regular. The abdominal scales are smooth, irregularly lozenge-shaped, bidentated posteriorly as in *S. scalaris*. The opening of the ear is subtriangular, protected by several projecting scales arising from its anterior edge. The toes and nails are very slender; the latter are proportionally long and slightly curved. When the fore legs are stretched backward, the tip of their toes will reach to the knees of the hind ones when the latter are brought forwards.

The brilliancy of the general hue having disappeared by immersion in alcohol of the specimens collected, we are not prepared to describe this accurately. As to the markings, they differ somewhat from those of *S. scalaris*. The row of the large crescent spots along the back is more compact, and not so distinctly bordered with white. The yellowish band that runs from behind the eyes backward to the middle of the tail is much broader; and besides, there is a second similar band extending from below the snout, and passing under the eye and above the auditory aperture, to the insertion of the hind locomotive limbs; the sides, therefore, are not ornamented with vertical, slightly undulating dark stripes; the irregular patches that are seen on that region are entirely deprived of any white margin. The abdomen in the male is blue indigo, as in most species of the same genus. The neck and throat are unicolor in both sexes.

This species inhabits the valley of the Great Salt Lake, where it was collected by Captain Stansbury and Lieutenant Gunnison.

Elgaria scincicauda, Baird and Girard.

Pl. IV. Fig. 1–3.

Syn. *Tropidolepis scincicaudus.*—Skilt. Amer. Jour. of Sc. VII. 1849, 202, fig. 1–3.

Spec. char.—Dusky green above; light ash colour below. Eleven transverse black bands on the back, interrupted on the dorsal line; white dotted posteriorly, six or more on the tail. Thirteen to fourteen rows of scales, well carinated.

The individual of this species which we have had figured, although not quite full-grown, exhibits, nevertheless, all the essential characters for its identification and specific distinction. A much younger specimen was figured by Mr. Skilton, in the seventh volume of the second series of the American Journal of Sciences and Arts, where it is given as a species of *Tropidolepis*. The scales, indeed, are carinated, but this is not a character peculiar to the genus *Tropidolepis*. A closer examination soon reveals the characteristic features of the gerrhonoti, of which the genus *Elgaria* is a mere subdivision. The conical and tapering tail, which is longer than the body and head together, forms the prominent distinctive mark of the genus in which we place the present species. The longitudinal area of minute scales, which extends from behind the ears to the insertion of the hind legs, belong to gerrhonoti generally, and distinguishes them from *Tropidolepis* or *Sceloporus*. In elgaria and gerrhonoti, in general, there are neither femoral nor anal pores, while their existence in *Sceleporus* will enable any one to distinguish between them.

The hind legs of *E. scincicauda* are slightly longer and stouter than the anterior, not taking the toes into consideration, as those of the hind feet are generally much the longest. The head is flattened, and has the shape of an acute triangle, the summit of which would be rounded. The snout therefore is rather elongated, with the end conical. The plates which cover its upper surface are smooth, and faithfully represented in fig. 3. The scales of the back constitute twelve or thirteen rows, each of which is provided with a medial carina, or ridge, extending over the tail. The scales of the belly and lower surface of the tail are smooth; on the abdomen they form twelve rows, the middle one being composed of larger scales. Fig. 2 exhibits the differences of the scales under the head, throat, belly, and tail. The scales form transverse as well as longitudinal rows, not only on the tail, as is often the case, but likewise on the body itself. Those on the throat and

Pl. IV.

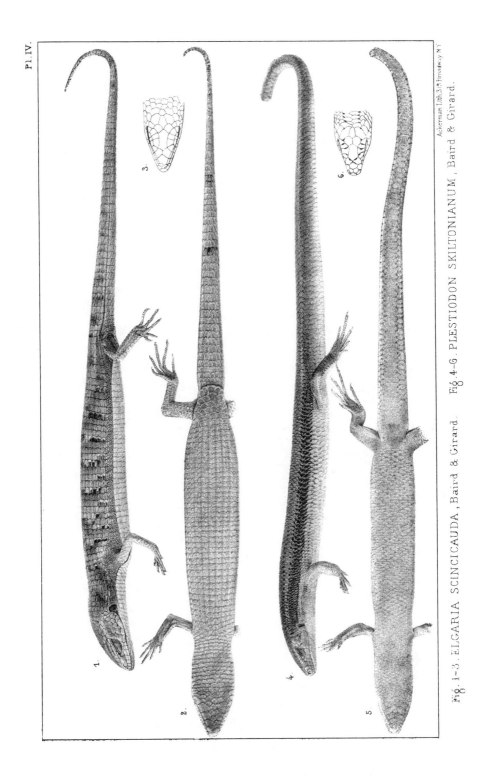

Ackerman Lith.3.ʳᵈ Broadway N.Y.

Fig. 1-3. ELGARIA SCINCICAUDA, Baird & Girard.   Fig. 4-6. PLESTIODON SKILTONIANUM, Baird & Girard.

lower surface of the head alone seem not subjected to any serial order.

Possessing only specimens that have been immersed in alcohol, and therefore have lost their general hue, we can only, in allusion to the colour, remark that the upper part of body and tail have transverse and irregular, sometimes undulating, and sometimes angularly broken bands of deep brown or black. Ten of these bands belong to the body from the occiput to the origin of the tail. On the tail itself they extend more or less toward the tip, according to the size of the specimen.

This species inhabits Oregon, about the Dalles of the Columbia River, where it has been collected by Rev. George Geary. A specimen in our possession, from California, was collected by Colonel Frémont. That which is represented on our plate we owe to the kindness of Dr. Avery J. Skilton.

PLESTIODON SKILTONIANUM, Baird and Girard.

PL. IV. FIG. 4–6.

SPEC. CHAR.—Head small, continuous with the body; tail stout, very long, and subquadrangular; olivaceous brown, with four broad bands of black.

This is a species of skink which must strike any one familiar with the general appearance of the other species of the same genus inhabiting North America. The tail, although considerably developed in all the skinks of the genus *Plestiodon*, acquires in this species much greater proportions. In the specimen figured, the tip of that organ is wanting, but when restored, the whole organ would be nearly twice the length of the rest of the body and head. Its form is rather subquadrangular than conical, and preserves a general stoutness which is not seen in the other species, in which it tapers more suddenly from its origin to its tip. The body is subcylindrical, and nearly of the same thickness from the occiput to the tail, into which it passes almost imperceptibly. The head itself is rather small, subconical, rounded on the snout; it is continuous with the body, the neck being but slightly contracted. The plates of its upper surface are represented in figure 6, which will serve as a good term for comparison with the other species. The locomotive members are very short; the fore ones rather slender, the hind ones stouter. The toes are terminated by delicate and slender nails, curved at their tip. The scales have a very smooth appearance; when examined attentively, those of the back and tail, however, exhibit four or more longitudinal furrows or stripes on each of them.

The lower part of the head and throat is whitish, the belly bluish. Above, olivaceous brown, with two broad bands of black on each side, and perhaps two narrow ones on the back extending from the head to the anterior region of the tail. A whitish or perhaps yellowish stripe extends from the opening of the ear to behind the hind legs, and a similar one from the occiput to the origin of the tail.

This species inhabits the same location in Oregon as *Elgaria scincicauda.* The specimen figured, together with several others, were collected by Rev. George Geary, and sent by him to Dr. Avery J. Skilton, to whom we are indebted for their examination, and to whom we have dedicated it, as a slight acknowledgment of gratitude.

Genus CHURCHILLIA, Baird and Girard.

GEN. CHAR.—Three pairs of frontal plates; a very small loral, and several postorbitals. Scales carinated.

In spite of the great uniformity in the plan of structure of ophidian reptiles, and especially of the genera *Coluber* and *Tropidonotus*, we do not hesitate in separating generically from both of these, the species hereon described.

The genus *Churchillia* has three pairs of frontal plates, one more than in both *Coluber* and *Tropidonotus;* the middle pair, however, is subjected to some irregularities, by which, instead of one pair, there is only an odd plate. In either case it is a constant character proper to our genus. There is a small loral plate and several postorbitals.

The scales of the upper part of the body are carinated, as in tropidonotus, but the lateral row, which is contiguous to the ventral shields, is scarcely larger than the other—while in *Tropidonotus*, the scales composing that row are much the largest.

CHURCHILLIA BELLONA, Baird and Girard.

SPEC. CHAR.—Body yellowish, with a series of large subhexagonal patches of brown, bordered with black, and two or three rows of smaller patches on the sides. A brownish black band across the eyes, from top of head to the angle of the mouth.

This snake attains a considerable size. The tail, properly so called, is comparatively very short, forming only the ninth part of the length. The head is moderate, conical, detached from the body by a somewhat contracted neck. The eyes are comparatively large, occupying the middle of the length of the head. There are two anterior orbital plates, the uppermost very large, vertically elongated, reaching the upper surface of the head; the lower one, on the other hand, is very minute, situated between the third and fourth labial shields. The postorbitals are four in number, of medium, but nearly of equal size, the upper ones, however, being slightly the largest. The lower one is separated from the small anterior orbital by the fourth labial shield, which reaches the orbit.

The scales of the back and sides are keeled, elliptical in form, and a little more pointed posteriorly than anteriorly. On the occiput they are smaller, polygonal, and smooth.

The coloration of this snake resembles at first glance that of *Coluber eximius;* the ground colour is a light yellowish-brown, maculated with large patches of a deeper brown, margined with black, and much smaller patches of pure black. The dorsal row of brown patches is considerably the largest, as in *Coluber eximius.* On the abdomen there are two rows of small and semilunar black dots, the convexity of which is turned forward. A narrow band of black is seen on the upper surface of the head, in advance of the eyes, extending obliquely to the angle of the mouth, being only interrupted by the eye itself.

This species was collected by General Churchill, on his march to Mexico, on the left bank of the Rio Grande, at the crossing near Presidio del Norte, in 1846; and it is with much satisfaction that we embrace the occasion to pay a tribute of respect to one, who, during the exercise of his arduous official labours, has always found time for the advancement of natural history, by securing specimens of whatever new or interesting species of animals might fall in his way.

COLUBER MORMON, Baird and Girard.

SPEC. CHAR.—Posterior frontal plates very large; vertical plate long and very narrow on its middle; eyes very large.

The only specimen which we have seen of this snake may prove hereafter to be a young individual, as it is only one foot and a half long; but we are satisfied it will also prove to be a very distinct species. The slender and conical tail forms between a third and a fourth of the total length. The head is elongated and ovoidal, separated from the body by a contracted neck. The vertical plate is elongated and contracted on its middle. The posterior pair of frontal plates has almost twice the size of the anterior pair. The eyes are proportionally very large, protected below by the fourth and fifth labial shields, anteriorly by a large and a small orbital plate, and posteriorly by two of nearly the same size, if not of the same shape. The loral is proportionally very much developed. The nostrils are prominent. There are eight labial plates to the upper jaw and seven to the lower. The scales are smooth, elongated on the back, and posteriorly pointed, while on the sides they are broader, and the row contiguous to the ventral shield is composed of scales broader than long. On the posterior part of the head, as usual, the scales are subcircular, or polygonal, and much the smallest. On the tail they assume rather a lozenge shape. There are one hundred and seventy-five ventral shields from the throat to the vent.

The colour is brown above and yellow underneath, with a bluish tint along the sides of the abdominal region. On the back there is a row of transversely elongated patches of deep brown, bordered with black. The sides are spotted with three indistinct rows of small spots of brown and black intermixed.

This species was found by Captain Howard Stansbury's party, in the valley of the Great Salt Lake.

HETORODON NASICUS, Baird and Girard.

SPEC. CHAR.—Minute and numerous frontal plates instead of two large pairs; two brown stripes over the head; temporal patch very broad.

The essential character which distinguishes this species from the *H. platyrhinos* and *H. simus*, which it most resembles, consists in the presence of numerous small scales between the vertical and rostral plates; that is, on the space which is occupied by the two pairs of frontal plates. In *H. simus*, it is true, very minute scales may be occasionally observed on the middle line between the vertical, rostral, and frontal plates; but when this is the case, the latter are not reduced to the small size which they have in the species which we here describe.

The vertical plate in *H. nasicus* is circularly subhexagonal. The superciliaries are longer than the vertical, and thus longer than broad, while the occipital are broader than long. The nasal is proportionally large, and so is the lower loral plate, as there exists a second loral above the first, much smaller than any of those of the orbital circle. A specimen of *H. simus* examined by us has shown a second similar small loral on one side of the head, while on the other it evidently did not exist, so that it may prove either not to be constant in *H. nasicus*, or to be likewise found in other species of the same genus. The rostral plate is directed upward, as in *H. simus*, having the same general shape as in the latter.

The tail has the same proportions with regard to the body as in *H. platyrhinos*, that is about the sixth of the entire length. The eyes are considerably smaller than in *H. platyrhinos*, as we have compared specimens of both species, having the same length and size of body. The only specimen of *H. nasicus* which we have seen is not a foot long, so that we have had to compare with it the young of *H. platyrhinos*. Now, if our *H. nasicus* be immature, it is the young of a species which differs from those already known of the genus, as shown by the very great difference in size of the eyes, and those other characters which we have just described.

In coloration, our species resembles more that of *H. platyrhinos* than that of *H. simus*. The ground colour appears to be the same. There are in both species three rows of blackish-brown patches, bordered with a line of light yellow or white; but while these patches are elongated in *H. platyrhinos*, they assume a more circular shape in *H. nasicus*, although there is no regularity or symmetry about them. Two indistinct and much smaller rows exist on the sides. The lower part of abdomen and tail is almost entirely black. The throat and lower surface of head are unicolor, of the same hue as the ground colour of the body above. On the occiput, immediately behind the occipital plate, there is a lanceolated patch, and on both sides of this a much greater irregularly oval one. Two brown stripes are seen on the top of the head, one over the anterior half of the eyes, extending vertically to the mouth, and another over the posterior half of the eye, hence obliquely backward, forming over the temples an elongated but much broader patch than in *H. platyrhinos* and *H. simus*.

This species was collected in Texas by General Churchill: a specimen is preserved at the Smithsonian Institution.

23

A MONOGRAPHIC ESSAY ON THE GENUS PHRYNOSOMA.

By CHARLES GIRARD.

THE numerous specimens of nearly all the known species of this genus which are now preserved in the Smithsonian Institution, together with those at the Academy of Natural Sciences of Philadelphia, have enabled us carefully to study and compare the different members of that most remarkable group, the result of which we propose here to present.

Indeed, there are no genera in the saurian order that can so readily be distinguished as that of *Phrynosoma*. The body more or less circular in shape, always depressed, sometimes flattened, scattered all over with irregular and spine-like scales; the solid and subtriangular head provided with acute spines or tuberculous knobs, the short and conical tail covered with scales similar to those of the body, sometimes even more prominent, are as many conspicuous features, which must strike any one at the very first glance. Their general aspect, perhaps their sluggishness, may recall to mind a frog or a toad: hence the vulgar name of horned toads or frogs. But the naturalist, with no hesitation, recognises in them true saurians, inasmuch as the body, instead of being smooth, like that of either toads and frogs, is covered, as just stated, with scales of a peculiar character. Besides the spines of the head, the tail, although short, is another feature by which they disagree from both toads and frogs. So much when these animals are at rest: as soon as they move, the observer cannot fail to be struck with the fact that phrynosomas never jump or leap, as is the case with the batrachians, to which they have been compared.

If we look now more closely at the zoological peculiarities proper to the genus *Phrynosoma* we will see that the vertex is a prominent feature of the head, subtriangular or cordiform, with a sharp and projecting margin, forming a carina which overlaps the orbits; sometimes it is terminated posteriorly by two spines, one on each side. The occipital region generally presents the largest spines in those species in which these exist as a prominent feature. The temporal region is very much developed and projects over the auditory aperture, and is provided along its projecting margin with spines or conical plates, the largest of which is most approximated to the occiput. The eyes seem as if situated in the middle of a groove extending from the snout to the occiput, on account of the projection of the superciliary ridge and temporal region. The lower jaw is generally bordered with a row or two of large plates, which vary in structure and shape according to the species, and furnish good discriminating characters between them. The snout is either truncated or acute. The nostrils are conspicuous, and situated near the extremity of the snout, either within the inner margin of the superciliary ridge, or on its direct prolongation. The upper surface of the head and sides not occupied by the spines or tuberculous knobs, are covered with small polygonal plates, varying in size according to the area over which they extend. The surface of these plates is rugose, wrinkled or keeled, as is also the surface of the spines themselves. They are exceedingly small in advance and behind the orbits. The whole surface of the eyelids is covered with minute scales of a granular appearance; the margin of the eyelid itself is ornamented with a double row of subquadrangular plates, a little larger than the granules of its surface. The lower part of the head from the chin to the breast is covered with small scales, characteristic in each species. The neck is generally very short, appearing as if contracted, the result of which contraction would be the presence of several folds of the skin, concealing the auditory apertures in conjunction with the temporal projection of the head.

The scales on the upper surface of the body are very irregular in size and shape; on the neck, above and below, on the pits, along the sides of the back, and on the groins, they assume a granular appearance, while along the middle of the back and on the tail they appear like thin lamellæ, very irregular still, and carinated or subcarinated. All over the back, sides, tail, and hind legs, there are large, irregularly pyramidal scales, with an acute point and a wrinkled or carinated surface. The margins of the abdomen exhibit one or two horizontal rows of these pyramidal but soft scales, bent backward, extending from the fore legs to the hind ones. The species in which the scales of the back are the largest, is *Phr. coronatum*, which strikes every one by its rough appearance; while those in which the scales are the least developed are *Phr. platyrhinos* and *Phr. modestum*, whose external appearance is in great measure destitute of that roughness which is generally associated with the idea of these reptiles.

The abdominal scales are subquadrangular or lozenge-shaped, either smooth or slightly keeled, according to the species. On the breast and anterior portion of the shoulders several rows of the largest scales are seen, very prominent, very acute posteriorly, and strongly carinated or keeled. The anterior and upper portion of the thigh is likewise provided with large scales, but much less conspicuously keeled than on the shoulders.

The tail is stout, always depressed at its base : it diminishes very rapidly posterior to the vent, and becomes cylindrical toward its tip. The pyramidal and raised scales are sometimes more conspicuous on its sides and upper surface than on the body itself. The scales below the tail, in the vicinity of the vent, have the general appearance of those of the belly ; in the post-anal groove some larger scales may occasionally be seen. Here the scales assume a subverticillated arrangement. On the conical portion of the tail they are carinated, while they are generally smooth about the vent.

The anterior and posterior legs are nearly of equal size ; the latter, however, are slightly stouter. The toes, five in number, are neither short nor very long ; the first and fifth are the shortest and either of equal length, or the fifth may be a little longer ; the second and fourth somewhat longer than the first and fifth, and likewise either of equal length, or the fourth somewhat longer than the second ; the third is always the longest. The scales extend all over the toes, overlapping even the base of the nails : they assume a subtriangular shape, with a very acute posterior summit, and a very distinct carina on their middle. The nails themselves are curved, compressed at the base, and very acute at the tip. On the inferior surface of the hind legs, along the thigh, a series of pores is observed, the femoral pores varying in number and conspicuousness according to the species. The anal pores are totally absent in phrynosomas.

We are thoroughly acquainted with six species of the genus *Phrynosoma*, viz. *Phr. coronatum*, *Phr. cornutum*, *Phr. douglassii*, *Phr. modestum*, *Phr. orbiculare*, and *Phr. platyrhinos*.

Phr. harlani is identical with *Phr. cornutum* ; *Phr. wiegmanni*, with *Phr. orbiculare* ; and *Phr. blainvillei*, with *Phr. coronatum*.

After a mature examination of Prof. Holbrook's description of

Phr. orbiculare, we have been led to the belief that the species described under that name is neither the *Phr. orbiculare* of Wiegmann, nor any of the other just mentioned, and indicates a species the characters of which cannot be properly defined, since the original specimens were not preserved. The species is said to occur in Arkansas, Louisiana, and Texas, that is, within the geographical range of *Phr. cornutum.* Now it is remarkable that among the numerous phrynosomas which have been received from these regions, all of them were found to belong to *Phr. cornutum;* unless the species be very rare, this circumstance cannot well be accounted for. *Phr. orbiculare* is exclusively Mexican, and *Phr. cornutum* North American. If any other species be found with *Phr. cornutum* within the limits ascribed in the United States to *Phr. orbiculare* by the author of the North American Herpetology, we do not hesitate in pronouncing it distinct from *Phr. orbiculare* of Wiegmann.

Dr. Wiegmann has indicated another species of the genus *Phrynosoma*, under the name of *Phr. bufonium*, and Surinam was first given as its home. But in his "Herpetologia Mexicana," he is in doubt as to the locality whence that species comes. *Phr. bufonium* is identified with *Phr. cornutum* by John Edward Gray in the catalogue of the British Museum. If *Phr. bufonium* be an inhabitant of South America, we doubt the correctness of this identification.

In the absence of authentic data in reference to *Phr. bufonium*, we would lay that species aside, and come back to the six ones the characters of which are well ascertained, and five of them represented with great skill on the accompanying plates. The different views of the head of these species have been made in similar attitudes in order to facilitate the comparisons.

A glance at plate VIII, will show at once the specific differences between *Phr. cornutum* (fig. 1–6) and *Phr. coronatum* (fig. 7–12). The profile, the position of the eyes and nostrils, the polygonal plates of the head, the direction of the spines, need scarcely to be alluded to, to render the differences apparent. The scales of the inferior surface of the head (fig. 3 and 9) exhibit a still more striking difference of form and arrangement in the two species. The femoral pores in *Phr. cornutum* (fig. 6) are but little conspicuous; they are much more so in *Phr. coronatum* (fig. 12), although the figure does not represent them as such. The only specimen on hand at the time at which this figure was made being in a dried state, the fleshy parts had shrunk and the femoral pores were thus

reduced and concealed.   On specimens preserved in alcohol they
are found as distinctly marked as in *Phr. douglassii* of plate VII,
fig. 10.

If we compare now *Phr. douglassii* with the two preceding ones,
its rounded and anteriorly truncated head gives to it a peculiarly
different aspect.   The reduced cephalic spines constitute another
feature quite as striking, especially when combined with the aspect
of the upper surface (fig. 6).   The lower surface of the head being
covered with uniform scales, there is no possibility of mistaking it
either for *Phr. cornutum*, which has a row of larger scales extending from the chin to the throat, or for *Phr. coronatum*, in which the
dissimilarity in the shape of these scales is still greater.

Phrynosoma platyrhinos seems at first very similar to *Phr.
douglassii*, on account, no doubt, of the small development of the
cephalic spines and the uniformity of the scales of the lower surface of the head.   But we need only compare the vertex, the occipital plates (fig. 1 and 6), the margin of the lower jaw (fig. 3
and 9), the profile (fig. 2 and 7), and the position of the nostrils
(fig. 4 and 9), in order to become satisfied of the specific distinction
between these two species.

The chief difference between *Phr. modestum* and *Phr. platyrhinos*
are not to be found prominent in the head, but rather in the general structure of the body and tail.   'The specimen which we have
had figured being a young one, these differences might appear too
trifling.   But recently we have received from Colonel J. D. Graham, a series of full-grown individuals, by which it can be shown
that this species, which we had distinguished from the others upon
an immature specimen, appears still more distinct upon the examination of the adults.   In comparing attentively the figures
which we now give of *Phr. modestum*, the differences will appear
evident.   The vertex is much more inclined forward in *Phr. modestum*
(Pl. VII. fig. 2) than in *Phr. platyrhinos*, (Pl. VI. fig. 6).   The plates
which line the margin of both the upper and lower jaws are likewise
different, as well as the scales of the inferior surface of the head,
which are proportionally smaller in *Phr. modestum* than in *Phr.
platyrhinos*.

Of *Phr. orbiculare* we have seen only two specimens, and these
were young individuals.   But there is something so striking in its
features as to enable us at once to distinguish it from its congener.
Its snout is flattened, and the extremities of the jaws much more
protruded than in any other species; it therefore differs greatly

in that respect from *Phr. platyrhinos, modestum,* and *douglassii,* with which it has in common the small and uniform scales on the inferior surface of the head. In the mean while, that same character distinguishes it from *Phr. cornutum* and *coronatum.* The femoral pores are very conspicuous. The plates which line the jaws are proportionally much smaller than in any other species.

The genus *Phrynosoma* is a truly American type. The distribution of its species over the continent is as follows :—*Phr. orbiculare* in the vicinity of the city of Mexico and in Sonora; *Phr. cornutum,* from Texas to Arkansas as far as the Rocky Mountains; *Phr. platyrhinos,* in the valley of the Great Salt Lake; *Phr. modestum,* in the valley of the Rio Grande del Norte ; and *Phr. coronatum* and *Phr. douglassii,* in Oregon and California; the latter species extending as far eastward as the valley of the Great Salt Lake, where it has been observed in company with *Phr. platyrhinos.*

The division of phrynosomas into two groups, according to the position of the nostrils, whether situated within the internal margin of the superciliary ridge or at its extremity, would bring into one group *Phr. orbiculare, coronatum,* and *douglassii,* and into another *Phr. cornutum, platyrhinos,* and *modestum.* On the other hand, if we subdivide the species according to the shape of the profile, we would have on one side : *Phr. orbiculare, cornutum,* and *coronatum,* and on the other *Phr. douglassii, platyrhinos,* and *modestum.* *Phr. douglassii* is the only species in which the cephalic spines remain in an undeveloped state. *Phr. coronatum* and *cornutum* have a double series of horizontal pyramidal scales on the periphery of the abdomen, while in *Phr. orbiculare, douglassii,* and *platyrhinos;* there is only one series of these, very small already in the latter, and totally absent in *Phr. modestum.* The difficulty of establishing subdivisions in this genus is thus plainly evident, and shows how natural and well circumscribed it is when considered as a whole by itself.

We give now the diagnostic characters by which the six species of Phrynosoma may be distinguished.

I. PHRYNOSOMA ORBICULARE, Wiegm.—Profile declive, tips of of jaws protruded, nostrils situated at the anterior extremity of the superciliary ridge. Occipital and temporal spines strong and well developed. One row of pyramido-horizontal and abdomino-peripheral scales. Scales on the inferior surface of head, small, of a general uniformity, although irregular in shape. The plates on the margin of the jaws are inconspicuous, and very little larger than the others: the lower jaw is bordered with a double row of plates, the small size of which is the most striking feature in this species. The scales on the belly are subtriangular, posteriorly acute, and slightly keeled in the young individual under consideration; they are smooth in the adult. Femoral pores well developed. Lower surface of the body maculated with irregularly elongated blackish spots.

II. Phrynosoma cornutum, Gray.—(Pl. VIII, fig 1–6.)—Same general profile as preceding. Nostrils situated within the internal margin of the superciliary ridge. Occipital and temporal spines longer and more acute than in the preceding species (fig. 1, 2, and 4). A double row of pyramido-horizontal and abdomino-peripheral scales. Scales on the inferior surface of the head small and slightly keeled, of a general uniformity, except one row on each side somewhat larger, pyramidal, acute, slightly raised and directed horizontally outward and backward (fig. 3). A series of very large, inframaxillary plates, sharp on their outer edge, the posterior one of which is transformed into a spine. The plates lining the margin of the jaws are not prominent. The scales of the belly are proportionally small, subquadrangular, posteriorly very acute and keeled. Femoral pores undeveloped or else rudimentary (fig. 6). Inferior surface of the body, unicolor.

III. Phrynosoma coronatum, Blainv.—(Pl. VIII, fig. 7–12.)—Profile declive; snout protruding; nostrils situated at the extremity of the superciliary ridge (fig. 7). Occipital and temporal spines perhaps less acute, but stouter than in *Phr. cornutum* (fig. 8). A double row of pyramido-horizontal and abdomino-peripheral scales. On the lower surface of the head (fig. 9), there exist two double series (four rows) of quite large pyramidal, posteriorly acute, slightly raised scales, inside of which, two double series of much smaller scales are observed, the two innermost rows the smallest. The remaining portion of the lower surface of the head is covered with minute polymorphal scales. The plates of the inframaxillary row are strong, flattened horizontally, and very acute posteriorly: they are very much approximated to the margin itself of the jaw. The scales of the belly are of medium size, smooth, sometimes subtriangular, pointed posteriorly, while others are subquadrangular. Femoral pores very conspicuous, the series of either side coming nearly into contact on the middle line of the belly, forming there a curve, the convexity of which is turned forward. Lower surface of body maculated as in *Phr. orbiculare.*

Pl. VIII.

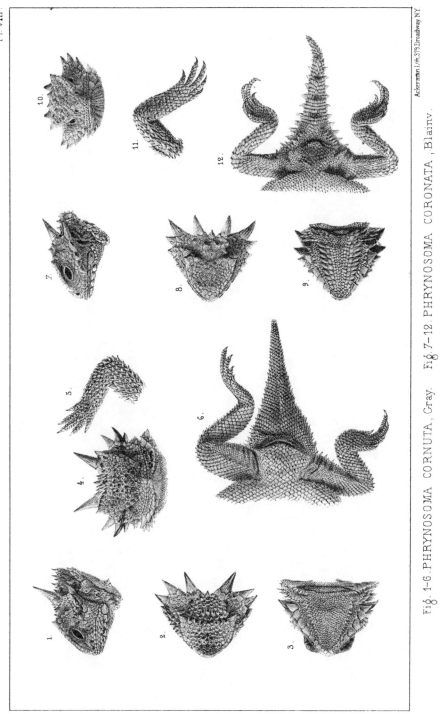

Fig. 1-6. PHRYNOSOMA CORNUTA, Gray.   Fig. 7-12. PHRYNOSOMA CORONATA, Blainv.

IV. Phrynosoma douglassii, Gray.—(Pl. VII, fig. 6–10.)—
Profile subtruncated (fig. 7). Nostril openings situated at the
extremity of the superciliary ridge (fig. 9). Occipital and temporal
spines reduced to blunt knobs (fig. 6 and 7). One row only of
pyramido-horizontal and abdomino-peripheral scales. Lower surface of head (fig. 8) covered with small and uniform scales. Marginal series of scales of the lower jaw large and conspicuous, flattened, with a sharp horizontal edge. An inframaxillary row
likewise conspicuous in their size (fig. 7, 8, and 9). Scales of
the belly smooth, acute posteriorly. Femoral pores very conspicuous (fig. 10). The series, from either side, are separated on the
middle region of the belly by a free space. The lower surface of
body appears as if unicolor, but, when examined carefully, numerous and crowded dots are seen.

V. Phrynosoma platyrhinos, Girard.—(Pl. VII, fig. 1–5.)
—Snout truncated, flattened, concave (fig. 2). Nostrils situated
within the internal margin of the superciliary ridge (fig. 4). Occipital and temporal spines of middle size (fig. 1 and 2). One
row of pyramido-horizontal and abdomino-peripheral scales, much
smaller than in the preceding species (compare fig. 1 to 6, on pl.
VII). Lower surface of head covered with small, nearly uniform
scales; on both sides, and near the neck, a series appears a little
more conspicuous, slightly raised and acute. Inframarginal series
of plates, large, of stout appearance, sharp and acute (fig. 3),
above which two rows of small plates are seen lining the margin
of the lower jaw (fig. 4). Scales of the belly smooth and of middle size. Femoral pores very conspicuous, but more apart than in
the preceding species (fig. 5). A free space is left on the middle region between the right and left series. The lower surface
of the body is unicolor.

VI. Phrynosoma modestum, Girard. (Pl. VI, fig. 4–8.)—Snout
truncated, flattened, but not concave (fig. 6). Nostrils opening within
the internal margin of the superciliary ridge (fig. 7). Occipital
and temporal spines of middle development (fig. 4 and 6). No
pyramido-horizontal scales at the periphery of the abdomen.
Lower surface of head with minute, generally uniform scales; a
row lining the inframaxillary plates, distinguishing itself by its
serial arrangement and its slightly increased size (fig. 5). Row
of inframarginal plates resembling that of *Phr. platyrhinos*,
(fig. 5); above which only one series of smaller plates is observed,
lining the margin of the lower jaw (fig. 6 and 7). Scales of the

belly proportionally larger than in any other species, smooth, quadrangular, and trapezoidal. Femoral pores conspicuous; the series from right and left coming into contact on the middle line of the belly, and forming a curve, the convexity of which is turned backward toward the vent. The lower surface of the body is unicolor.

PHRYNOSOMA DOUGLASSII, Gray.

PL. VII. FIG. 6–9.

Syn. PHRYNOSOMA DOUGLASSII, Gray, Synops. Rept. in *Griff.* Anim. Kingd. IX. 1831, 44.—WAGL. Nat. Syst. Amph. 1830, 146.—WIEGM. Herp. Mex. 1834, 54.—HOLBR. N. Amer. Herp. I. 1842, 101, Pl. XIV.—GRAY, Cat. Brit. Mus. 1845, 227.

Agama douglassii, BELL, Trans. Linn. Soc. L. XVI. (1828), 1833, 105, Pl. X.— HARL. Med. and Phys. Research. 1835, 141, fig. 3.

The specimen figured is not the largest of the species, but being the only one secured at Salt Lake, we took it in preference to any of those which we have from California and Oregon. It is about three inches and a-half long; the head is a little less than a fifth of the entire length. The body, from the neck to the origin of the hind legs, is about of the same length as the remaining posterior portion. The body is suborbicular, being nearly as broad as long. These dimensions may vary to some degree among different individuals, but, generally speaking, they give to the species its specific character as far as the form and outlines of the body are concerned. Viewed from above (fig. 6), the body is subtriangular, as broad behind as long; acuminated, but rounded in front. The vertex is cordiform, a little depressed in the middle, forming over the eyes a prominent carina, composed of four or five elongated plates, and posteriorly terminated by a blunt spine or acute knob. The occipital region, immediately behind, is depressed, and provided with three acute knobs, the central one inconspicuous. The temporal region is bordered posteriorly by three or four spines or subpyramidal plates. The auditory aperture is vertically oblong or semilunated. The nostrils are proportionally very large, and situated at the anterior prolongation of the superciliary ridge. The polygonal plates are very minute on the nasal region and all along the upper jaw; the marginal row, however, being a little more conspicuous. The profile (fig. 7) exhibits the characters just alluded to, and gives a perfect picture of the physiognomy of this species. The eyes are oval. The same figure 7 exhibits the double row of large scales of the lower jaw.

Fig. 1-5. PHRYNOSOMA PLATYRHINOS Girard.   Fig. 6-10. PHRYNOSOMA DOUGLASSII Gray.

Ackerman Lith 379 Broadway N.Y.

Pl. VI

Both of these rows meet in front of the symphysis of the jaw and behind the angle of the mouth, but leave between them a narrow area covered with very small scales. The inferior surface of the head (fig. 8) is very uniform; the scales which cover this region are small, some subovate, others subquadrangular. The pyramidal scales of the back constitute several irregular rows. One distinct and crowded row borders the outline of the abdomen. The scales on the belly are smooth, subquadrangular or lozenge-shaped, a little larger on the middle than toward the sides. The femoral pores are quite conspicuous (fig. 10), from fifteen to seventeen on each side.

The general hue of the specimen before us, preserved in alcohol, is olivaceous-green above, lighter below. Behind the occiput, on each side of the neck, there is an elongated patch of black, behind which a very small patch is seen, and, farther backward three or four others in pairs, triangular or quadrangular, the last of which is placed above and in advance of the hind legs. Four or five pairs of spots, diminishing gradually in size, may be followed along the tail. The dorsal patches are bordered with a line of light yellow. The abdomen appears unicolor, but, on careful examination, numerous brownish dots can be observed. The upper portion of the legs has a few small blackish spots.

The specimen figured is from the valley of the Great Salt Lake, where it was collected by Captain Stansbury.

PHRYNOSOMA PLATYRHINOS, Girard.

PL. VII. FIG. 1–5.

The general form of this species is more elongated than usual, the neck not so much contracted, and the head, consequently, more detached from the rest of the body. The shape of the head is as much a characteristic of this species as its structure. We allude to its circular form when viewed from above (fig. 1), and to the flattening of the nose, as exhibited in the profile (fig. 2). The upper surface exhibits two strong occipital spines, and a row of smaller ones on the temporal region, five on each side. The polygonal plates of the cordiform and flat vertex assume a symmetrical arrangement on both sides, so as to divide the space into two ovoidal areas, the outer row of which is composed of larger plates, while those enclosed are smaller and more irregular. Thus, the two posterior angles of the vertex, instead of being acutc, as in *Phr. douglassi*, are rounded, without any prominent knob or spine. Along the superciliary ridge which overlaps the eyes, the plates are the largest, at least, five of them, there being two very small ones nearly above the middle of the eye. The occipital area exhibits three subcircular plates in its centre, larger than the surrounding ones. A group of large subspinous plates is likewise observed at the base and in advance of the occipital spines. The plates on the snout and along the upper jaw are small and inconspicuous, except the marginal row, on account of an acute projection of each of them. The nose is flattened to excess, slightly concave, and the nostrils are situated at the inside of the superciliary ridge; thus placed in front (fig. 4). The eyes are circular. The lower jaw wants the first row of large plates which we have seen in *Phr. douglassii*, but the one which exists is so much more developed than in the latter, and composed of six very conspicuous plates on each side and two small ones (fig. 2 and 3). Between this row of plates and the margin of the jaw there is an area, covered, on its anterior portion, with two, and, near the angle of the mouth, with three rows of small and polygonal scales. On the lower surface of the head, from the chin to the throat, the scales are small and irregular; on the sides, however, and only for the posterior half of that distance, a row of from five to seven acute-edged scales may be seen. The folds of the neck do not exhibit any thing peculiar under the throat, but, on the sides and behind the ear, they are surmounted with pyramidal and raised scales. The auditory aperture is comparatively small—much smaller than in *Phr. douglassii*. The pyramidal and raised scales of the back are but little prominent. There is but one abdominal series of the latter, as in *Ph. douglassii*, originating behind the fore legs, but not extending so far backward as in others. The plates in the post-anal groove form two rows, the first composed of six, the second and posterior one of four only. The femoral pores are but few, from six to seven on each side, and quite distant from each other.

The head and tail are brown above, the upper part of the body ash-coloured; yellowish and unicolor below. On the sides of the neck is a large patch of black, and two similar ones, but narrow and undulating, on the back. Faint indications of transverse bands of black are observed on the tail.

Collected by Captain Stansbury about the Great Salt Lake.

PHRYNOSOMA MODESTUM, Girard.

PL. VI. FIG. 4–8.

The most striking characters by which this species can be distinguished from its congeners consists in the want of the peripheral abdominal row of pyramidal scales, and also in the slight development of the scales on the upper region of the body, which loses considerably that rough appearance so characteristic in the other species. The tail affords another character peculiar to *Phr. modestum;* it tapers more suddenly, and is perfectly cylindrical beyond the dilated portion of its base. The head has the same general appearance as in *Phr. platyrhinos,* although it is not so much truncated, and still less so in the adult than in the young (fig. 6). The vertex is more circular than in the latter, but the occipital and temporal spines do not differ much in the two species. The nostrils have the same position within the superciliary ridge, (fig. 7). The lower jaw exhibits one row of large plates, with one single series of very small ones above, forming the edge of the jaw, while we have seen two rows of the latter in *Phr. platyrhinos.* Below the head the scales are exceedingly small—much smaller than in *Phr. platyrhinos.* They are uniform among themselves, except a row of a little more conspicuous ones forming one series along the inside of the maxillary plates (fig. 5). The scales on the belly are smooth, subquadrangular, and larger than in any other species. The femoral pores are smaller, and even more apart than in *Phr. platyrhinos,* but there is no separation on the middle line of the belly, and the series from both sides meet in advance of the vent, forming a convex curve turned backward (fig. 8).

The coloration is uniform yellowish-brown above, with two lateral patches of black on the sides of the neck. Transversal and narrow bands of black are seen on the tail. The black spot seen on the left side of fig. 4 is accidental; that is, it exists on the specimen figured, but is not found on any others which have since come to hand.

Brought from the Rio Grande, west of San Antonio, by General Churchill. A series of adult specimens were collected from San Antonio to El Paso, by the party under Colonel J. D. Graham, late of the United States and Mexican boundary survey.

INSECTS.

By PROF. S. S. HALDEMAN.

THERE were but few facilities for collecting, preserving, and transporting insects upon the journey, and those which were brought home are few in number and in bad condition. Under these circumstances, Captain Stansbury has allowed other species to be introduced, which have been collected by Lieutenant Horace Haldeman, U. S. A., chiefly at Fredericksburg and Fort Gates, on the western frontier of Texas; and by Mr. Richard Kern, in a journey across the plains to Santa Fé. In the latter case, the specimens were thrown into bottles of spirits as collected, so that there is nothing to distinguish those which were found upon the route from those of Santa Fé; but as the greater part probably appertain to the latter locality, this has been used to Mr. Kern's species.

LEPIDOPTERA.

PAPILIO ASTERIAS, Cramer.

A specimen with the patagia yellow, and forming a continuous lateral yellow line with the spots upon the thorax and head.

CYNTHIA CARDUI, Linnæus.

A specimen of this species, which is common in Europe and the United States, and one of the most widely spread species known, occurring in India and Africa. On this continent it has been found among the Rocky Mountains and in California.

PIERIS PROTODICE.

DEILEPHILA LINEATA, Fabr.

(—*daucus*, Cramer). Harris, Am. Journal Sci., vol. 36.

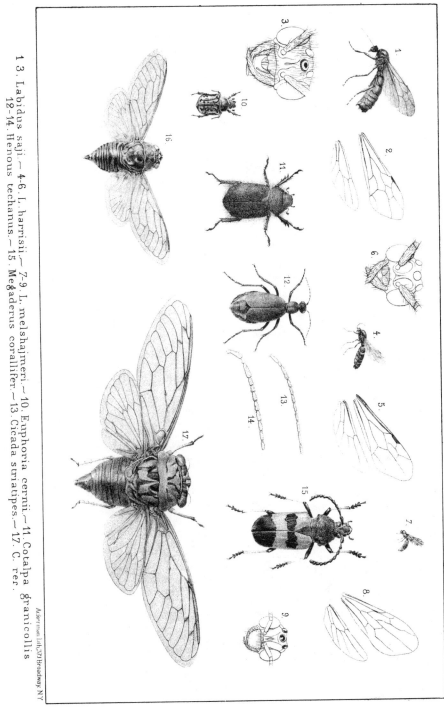

PL.IX.

1 3. Labidus saji.— 4-6. L. harrisii.— 7-9. L. melshajmeri.—10. Euphoria cernii.—11. Cotalpa granicollis
12-14. Henous techanus.—15. Megaderus corallifer.—13. Cicada striatipes.—17. C. rer.

Ackerman lith, 379 Broadway N.Y.

HYMENOPTERA.

Among the most interesting entomological discoveries in the imperfectly explored parts of the United States territory, that of the three new species of the genus *Labidus* must be included. This is a tropical form, and almost exclusively confined to Brazil, the most northern species hitherto described being from the West Indian Island of Saint Vincent. The three species were discovered at Fort Gates by Lieutenant Haldeman.

LABIDUS SAJI, Hald.

Pl. IX. Fig. 1–3.

Luteous, head brown above, and having (with the mandibles and basal articulation of the antennæ) piliferous punctures; stemmata large, and the posterior ones twice as far from each other as from the eyes; face excavated below the antennæ, with the lateral carinæ sharp or angular, and the medial line impressed; mandibles large, tapering slowly, and curved from the base. Thorax convex and shining, with numerous piliferous punctures; dorsal line narrow and distinctly impressed from the most prominent part to the anterior margin. Peduncle triangular, excised posteriorly with well-developed exterior angles. Abdomen indistinctly pubescent, with piliferous punctures posteriorly. Feet slender, simple, and uniformly coloured; base of the anterior tarsi excavated beneath for the tibial spur; ungues bifid; posterior feet extending beyond the abdomen; tibial spurs small. Wings with the stigmata long and narrow, posterior half indistinctly sanguineous, the nervures of the colour of the body, the membrane a pale tint of the same colour, and translucent. Length eight and a-half, wing seven and a-half, posterior tarsus two and a-half lines.

LABIDUS HARRISII, Hald.

Pl. IX. Fig. 4–6.

Polished and pubescent, above black, abdomen rufous. Head black, pubescent; stemmata large, posterior ones three times farther from each other than from the eyes; antennæ pale fulvous, base pilose; mouth rufous; mandibles pilose, robust, curved at the base only, the inner edge rectilinear, and the apex acute but not incurved. Thorax convex in front, with piliferous punctures, brown, and pilose; wings very pale dusky, translucent, nervures pale yellowish-brown. Feet slender and short, anterior tarsi medial line narrow and impressed; sides and feet dark reddish, curved at the base, the outer side being parallel with the internal excavation; anterior tibial spine curved, and rather robust, posterior feet not reaching the end of the abdomen. Peduncle of the abdomen black above, pubescent, transversely quadrangular, the anterior angles rounded. Abdomen compressed, thinly clothed with fulvous hair. Length five, expanse nine and a-half, posterior tarsus one line.

Labidus melshaemeri, Hald.

Pl. IX. Fig. 7–9.

Pale polished amber-coloured and pilose; head nearly quadrate, with the vertex black; the two posterior stemmata are distant, being nearly in contact with the eyes; mandibles pilose, sickle-shaped, curved from the base and diminishing rapidly to a slender incurved point. Wings very pale dusky, with the nervures pale brown; a black point upon the thorax at their insertion. Base of the anterior tarsi slightly curved; anterior tibial spine small and slightly curved; posterior feet not extending beyond the abdomen. Abdominal peduncle pilose, transverse, basal angles strongly rounded, apex concave; abdomen compressed. Length about three and a-half, wing three lines.

Ammophila aberti, Hald.

A large black and rufous species, the head and anterior wings of which are wanting in the only specimen collected. Thorax black cinereous primrose; patagia and feet (except the coxæ and trochanters) rufous; basal half of the posterior femora black, which extends in a line toward the apex upon the upper side; posterior tibial with the inner side darker than the outer side; posterior wings hyaline, nervures rufous. Abdomen rufous, peduncle and a blotch upon the apex above, black. Length fourteen, abdomen nine, to the constriction four lines. General form of *Ammophila sabulosa*. Named after Colonel Abert, chief of the Topographical Bureau, for his efforts toward the development of the natural history of the country, under various exploring expeditions.

HEMIPTERA.

CICADA REI, Hald.

PL. IX. FIG. 17.

Yellow, varied with black, sericeous beneath. Head yellow, pypostoma brown; the medial line yellow, and unimpressed, and the transverse ridges undulate; eyes connected by a broad transverse band. Pronotum yellow, with a narrow Y-shaped line divided to the base, a narrow transverse lateral spot on each side posteriorly, and another anteriorly, immediately behind the lateral stemmata. Mesonotum black, with a large lateral elongated yellow spot, and a pair of similarly coloured medial spots in the shape of the Hebrew letter *resh* inverted, and the points converging anteriorly upon the medial line; tergum dark brown. Wings with the nervures yellow to beyond the middle, when they become dark brown or blackish. The usual W-shaped mark is present; beneath and feet yellow; metasternal spines rather large; spines of the feet and apex of the tibial tinged with brown. Length of the body fourteen, to the end of the upper wings twenty-two lines; width of the prothorax seven lines. A large and handsome species, from the Great Salt Lake Valley.

CICADA STRIATIPES, Hald.

PL. IX. FIG. 16.

Above black, varied with a little yellow; beneath yellow, more or less primrose, particularly beneath. Head black, with a small yellow spot above the antennæ; hypostoma prominent, with the medial line yellow, and strongly impressed. Pronotum black, margined with yellow posteriorly, primose, and indistinctly lateral. Mesonotum black, with four small yellow spots, two connected with the scutel, and two central, one on each side of the medial line; lateral margins and scutel yellow, two raised yellow lines extending laterally from the latter. Tergum black, with the apex and margins of the segments yellow. Elytra and wings with the nervures yellowish-white; those of the exterior cells blackish; the basal portion, which is doubled beneath in repose, is orange. That of the posterior alulet extending half its length and ending in a narrow fuscous band; base of the superior wings with a black

24

point above. W spot near the apex wanting. Beneath, yellow; end of the haustellum a few points near the joints of the feet, and a transverse line at the base of the abdomen, black. Medial and posterior femora with an impressed stria along the inferior surface. Entire length thirteen, of the body nine and a-half, expanse of the wings twenty-three lines. This small species seems to be allied to *C. rimosa* of Say. It belongs to the section of *C. septemdecim*, in which the drums are exposed so as to render their action visible in the living insect.

ZAITHA RETICULATA, Hald.

Dark brown, haustellum stout, and curved, scutel longitudinally rugose, elytra with distinct raised reticulations; wings white, abdomen black, apex beneath paler, pectus varied with yellowish, and the external margin of the posterior femora of the same colour. Length eight and a-half, breadth four and a-half lines. This species is allied to *Z. testacea* and *Z. aurantiaca* of Leidy, (who described them under the generic name of *Perthostoma*,) in the Journal of Acad. Nat. Sci. of Philadelphia, 1847, p. 60; but the colour is deeper, and it is at once distinguished by the raised reticulations upon the elytra.

ZAITHA BIFOVEATA, Hald.

PL. X. FIG. 1.

Brownish-yellow, scutel and beneath darker; head much advanced in front, haustellum very long, and curved nearly in a quadrant; antennæ hairy, the three terminal articulations parallel, curved, and of equal length, the apical one thickest, but scarcely differing in shape. Pronotum punctate, the anterior two-thirds finely, and the posterior third more coarsely and confluently; a fovea without punctures upon each side, about a line from the anterior or lateral margins; scutel punctate, with the disk longitudinally rugose. Feet maculate with brown; margin of the venter maculate with flavous. Length sixteen, breadth seven, head nearly three, haustellum three and a-half lines. Fort Gates, Texas. This is the largest species of the genus, but it has the characters of the antennæ and rostrum, the long anterior coxæ, slender feet, and terminal nervures of the elytra without anastomoses, which distinguish this genus from *Belostoma*.

In *Belostoma*, the wing when folded has four nervures (omitting that of the fold) which reach the margin; in *Zaitha* there are but

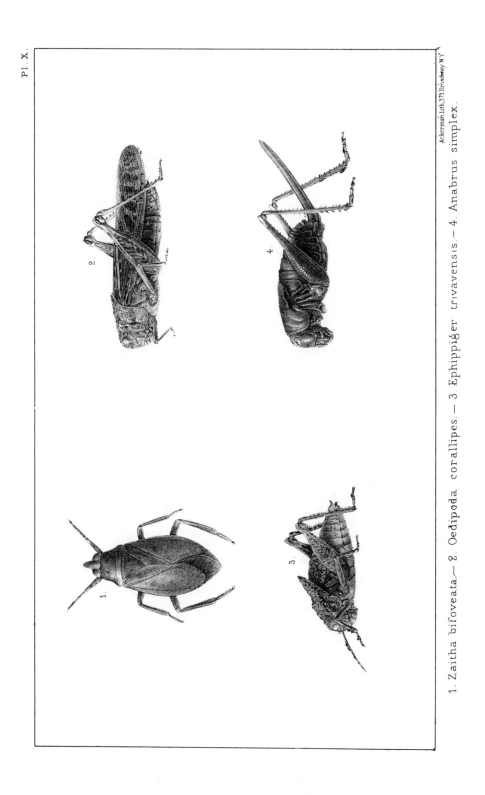

Pl. X.

1. Zaitha bifoveata.— 2. Oedipoda corallipes. — 3. Ephippiger trivavensis.— 4. Anabrus simplex.

two, the intermediate ones being evanescent. In the former, the first and second (from the fold) unite at the margin, but in the latter, the evanescent line representing the second reaches the margin parallel to the first nervure.

ORTHOPTERA.

EPHIPPIGERA TɾIVAVENSIS, Hald.

PL. X. FIG. 3.

Robust, dull brown, beneath yellowish; head rough, antennæ deep set, filiform, shorter than the pronotum, inserted opposite the lower canthus of the eyes, upon each side of a double vertical frontal carina; labrum transverse, and with the palpi flavous. Pronotum ample, coarsely scabrous, blackish, changing to yellowish posteriorly; elytra and wings rudimentary, the former gray, mottled with black. Inside of the posterior femora and tibiæ black, the former interrupted near the apex. The posterior tibiæ have a row of spines upon each above. Length fifteen, antennæ six, pronotum seven, width four and a-half, elytra four, posterior femora seven, and tibiæ seven lines. Chihuahua.

ŒDIPODA CORALLIPES, Hald.

PL. X. FIG. 2.

Yellowish-gray, conspicuously varied with brown, mostly in blotches, and upon the elytra and exterior side of the posterior femora. Vertex and pronotum scabrous and dark brown, the latter margined with flavous, its surface nearly flat, and the medial line but little raised. Angle of the elytra marked with a yellow line; a narrow line upon the internal margin. Wings bright yellow, margined with black. Inside of the posterior femora, tibiæ and tarsi, bright vermilion, a paler tint extending to the outside of the tarsi and lower half of the tibiæ. Length twenty-four lines, (two and a-half inches,) pronotum five, posterior femora ten, and tibiæ nine lines.

This fine large grasshopper is probably the species which has been destructive to vegetation in the Valley of the Great Salt Lake. It is nearly as large as the destructive *Œdipoda migratoria*, (with which it is congeneric.) The last-named species is known under the English name of migratory locust.

ANABRUS, Hald.

This new generic name is derived from the Greek *abros*, with
the negative prefix *an*, in allusion to the unprepossessing appearance of the insect. This genus has .broad articulate tarsi, the
soles concave, and the third articulation cordate. It resembles *Phalangopsis* in general appearance, the form of the head and labrum,
the high position of the antennæ, the narrow sternum, and the position and probably the form of the feet. It has, however, a distinct selliform pronotum extending over the basal articulation of
the abdomen, and concealing rudimentary elytra. Excepting the
tarsi, the posterior feet resemble those of a *Phalangopsis* and have
the spines distributed in the same manner. The ovipositor is
nearly straight, sword-shaped, unlike that of *Phalangopsis*, and
it is two-thirds the length of the body. A single specimen was
brought from the Valley of the Great Salt Lake, and of this the
antennæ, palpi, and anterior and medial feet are wanting.

ANABRUS SIMPLEX, Hald.

PL. X. FIG. 4.

Dark shining brown, posterior femora with an external and
internal row of small spines beneath upon the posterior extremity;
tibiæ angular, with a row of spines upon each side above, and two
approximate rows beneath with the spines alternating. Length
fifteen lines, pronotum six, ovipositor twelve, posterior femora and
tibiæ, each eleven, and tarsi three and a-half. This seems to be
one of the species which is eaten by the aborigines of the Valley
of the Great Salt Lake.

STENOPELMATUS FUSCUS, Hald.

Shining dark brown, abdomen darker. One specimen, seven
lines long, is from Santa Fé; another is eight lines long, and from
Chihuahua: the latter has the labrum and tibiæ darker than the
general colour.

It is possible that these small specimens may be immature, and
they would not have been characterized but for the fact that in
the allied genera the colour remains remarkably uniform during
the various transformations, which renders it probable that they
are not the larvæ of the rufo-testaceous Mexican *S. talpa*, which
my brother has brought from Jalapa. The tibial springs of *S.
fuscus* are well developed, a character by which the adult of

Phalangopsis can be distinguished from the pupæ of the same size and general appearance.

PHALANGOPSIS.

There is a larva of this genus in the collection from the Valley of the Great Salt Lake, which bears a close resemblance to *P. lapidicola.*

COLEOPTERA.

CICINDELA AUDUBONII, Le Conte.

Ann. Lyceum, N. Y. Valley of the Great Salt Lake and Sante Fé.

PANAGÆUS DISTINCTUS, Hald.

Rufous, sparsely hirsute, elytra with a fascia behind the middle, interrupted at the suture, apex blackish. Head scabrous and rather large, prothorax coarsely punctured, wider anteriorly than posteriorly, sides regularly rounded, posterior angles small and acute; dorsal line and region of the posterior angles impressed; elytra striate, with large impressed punctures. Length, three and a-half lines. Colour and general appearance of *P. fasciatus,* but smaller, with a larger head, the prothorax very different in shape, and the elytra more strongly marked. Sante Fé.

CARABUS FINITIMUS, Hald.

Allied to *C. sylvosus,* but somewhat wider. Blank slightly bluish on the margin. Prothora; less narrowed behind than in *sylvosus,* with the reflex margin and that of the elytra wider. Elytra more convex, very shining, finely punctured in lines, with three rows on each of distant impressed foveæ. Destitute of the scabrous appearance of *C. sylvosus.* Fort Gates.

PANGUS CALIGINOSUS.
DICÆLUS SPLENDIDUS.
CALOSOMA SCRUTATOR.
PLOCHIONUS TIMIDUS.

Occurring at Fort Gates.

STETHOXUS TRIANGULARIS, Say.

At Tampico.

MELOPS CONSTRICTUS.

CHLÆNIUS SERICEUS.

"   VICINUS.

AGONUM ERYTHROPUM.

PŒCILUS SCITULUS.

Were collected by Mr. Kern.

TROCHALUS EXPLANATUS, Le Conte.

Or a closely allied species, was brought by Captain Stansbury.

COTALPA GRANICOLLIS, Hald.

PL. IX. FIG. 11.

Hirsute, dark green, elytra reddish castaneous, feet black. Head, pronotum, scutel, and pygidium, green, and densely and confluently punctured. Elytra each with four indistinct impressed striæ; surface irregular punctured, punctures confluent toward the sutures. Under parts, including the femora, green, and densely punctate; tibiæ and tarsi, black. Length, eight lines. The body, above and below, with the elytra and feet, are irregularly hirsute, with whitish hairs. Valley of the Great Salt Lake.

EUPHORIA CERNII, Hald.

PL. IX. FIG. 10.

Dark brown elytra, varied with pale flavous. Head and pronotum densely and coarsely punctured; antennæ, palpi, and feet reddish-brown. Pronotum margined laterally and posteriorly with a narrow band of flavous; scutel black, with elongated shallow punctures, mostly toward the margin. Elytra each with a wide sutural and medial groove, irregularly maculated with dark brown and flavous in nearly equal proportions, the lateral and terminal with three sub-sutural spots; surface slightly punctate with longitudinal striæ near the suture, and fine transverse rugosities laterally. Pygidium faintly rugulose, pectus blackish. Length, five lines. Collected by Mr. Kern, after whom it is named.

MELOLONTHA DECEMLINEATA, Say.

Valley of the Great Salt Lake.

PELIDNOTA TRIPUNCTATA.

Fort Gates.

AREODA LANIGERA.

Santa Fé.

APHODIUS STRIGATUS, Say, which is common in the United States, occurs in Western Texas and as far south as Jalapa, in Mexico.

HYDROCHUS FOVEATUS, Hald.

Silvery-gray, varied with curious reflexions. Head coarsely and densely punctate; the largest punctures between the eyes; palpi flavous, prothorax nearly quadrangular, widest before, produced posteriorly into an obtuse angle; surface punctate with three foveæ across the middle, the central forming a triangle with two others in contact with it posteriorly. Elytra each with ten rows of deep dilated punctures. Feet flavous, varied with brown; length less than two lines. Fort Gates, Texas. Allied to *H. scabratus* of Mulsant, 1844. Ann. Sci. Phys. Nat. Lyon, vol. vii. p. 373. *H. gibbosus*, Melsheimer.

STAPHYLINUS VILLOSUS, Crav.

Mr. Kern brought a specimen of the species, which is common in the United States, and is found in Mexico and Cuba.

PHILONTHUS COMPTUS, Hald.

Allied to *P. œneus* and *P. harrisii*. Polished black. Head rather narrower than the prothorax, with foveæ in a transverse line, the external one orbital and placed before the middle of the eye; the next midway between this and the medial one, which is more shallow than the others, and in advance of them. There are three additional orbital foveæ posterior to the first, and several upon the posterior angles, which are strongly and sparsely punctate. Mandibles strong and incurved, with a stout tooth near the base, external margin with a groove for about half its length. Pronotum with four distant punctures arranged longitudinally

upon each side of the middle, a second line of three exterior to
these, (two placed opposite the interstices of the posterior three,
and the third at the posterior margin,) a third row of three or
four exterior to the latter, followed by a single puncture in the
lateral angle: there are also several marginal punctures posteriorly. Scutel flat, oblong, triangular, with piliferous punctures.
Elytra longer than the prothorax, widest posteriorly, and rather
wider than long; black with piliferous punctures, lateral margin
yellowish brown, hair yellowish upon the disk, and fulvous upon
the lateral margin. Wings fuliginous irised. Tergum, under parts
and feet with piliferous punctures. Length, six lines. A single
specimen collected by Mr. Kern, of which the antennæ are broken.

NECROPHORUS OBSCURUS, Kirby.

Fauna Bor. Amer. p. 97.—Valley of Great Salt Lake.

ELEODES COGNATA, Hald.

Colour, size, and markings as in *E. extricata*, but the punctur-
ing is much finer, and that of the pronotum more sparse. The
elytra have distant, minute elevated points, (some of them connected with the punctures,) which are more evident posteriorly.
Valley of the Great Salt Lake.

ELEODES OBSCURA, Say.

Two specimens in Captain Stansbury's collection.

NYCTOBATES (IPHTHINUS) INTERMEDIA, Hald.

Allied to *N. barbata*, Knoch (Tenebrio) Neue Beytraege, p. 166,
fig. (*striato-punctatus*, Dejean, Catalogue, p. 225) and similarly
barbate with fulvous hair. Punctures of the head larger and
more crowded (especially upon the vertex.) Pronotum with the
sides more rounded and the surface more coarsely punctured.
Surface of the elytra minutely but more distinctly punctured, and
the nine lines of punctures less distinct than in *N. barbata*.
This species agrees in size and colour with *N. barbata*, and in
distinctness of the lines of punctures upon the elytra it stands
between that species and *N. pennsylvanica*, Western Texas.

ZOPHERUS VARIOLOSUS, Sturm.

Described from Mexican specimens ; is found at Fort Gates.

Horia stansburii, Hald.

Black, elytra sanguineous. Head pilose, and with the prothorax scabrous with confluent punctures. Pectus shining, and, with the feet, punctate. Abdomen of the female with a small fovea upon the middle of the three terminal segments. Elytra scabrous, with large irregular confluent punctures. Length of the male four, of the female six lines. Valley of the Great Salt Lake.

Meloe parvus, Hald.

Black, somewhat shining, head with numerous dilated punctures extending to the labrum, eyes uniform, a smooth fovea near them, and a smooth pustule between the fovea and the insertion of the antennæ. Antennæ eleven-articulate, filiform, extending a little beyond the prothorax, and apparently alike in both sexes; the second articulation is the smallest, and the third equal to the two following; beyond the third the length gradually increases to the apex. Prothorax subquadrate, but the anterior angles are rounded and the middle advanced so as to form a neck; posterior angles raised in an obtuse pustule; dorsal line interrupted, impressed before the middle, and forming a rima posteriorly. Scutel punctate with the disk impressed. Elytra scabrous and acute. Abdomen above and below with minute piliferous punctures. Feet slender. Length from four to five lines. Kern's collection.

Henous, Hald.

Form of *Epicanta*, with the elytra abbreviated, connate, and each obtusely rounded. Prothorax subglobular, lengthened anteriorly. Abdomen, with the middle part above, coriaceous, and the lateral parts membranous; that of the female inflated. Antennæ setaceous, third articulation longest; from the third to the sixth slightly dilated and compressed in the male. Ungues cleft, with the parts equal.

Henous techanus, Hald.

Pl. IX. Fig. 12-14.

Black, short, pubescent, minutely granulate. Head, thorax, and elytra scabrous, with confluent punctures; labrum and clipeus with dilated impressed punctures, more crowded upon the labrum and sides of the clipeus.   Length of the female ten, breadth three and a-half, length of the elytra nearly five lines.

ELAPHIDION MARILANDICUM.

CLYTUS IRRORATUS.

"   FLEXUOSUS.

CERASPHORUS GARGANICUS.

Fort Gates, Texas.

MEGADERUS CORALLIPES, Newm.

PL. IX. FIG. 15.

Was described from an imperfect Mexican specimen by Newman, (Charlesworth, Mag. Nat. Hist., vol. iv., p. 195.)   It is now figured for the first time, from a specimen taken at Fort Gates.

LETTER FROM T. R. PEALE, ESQ., UPON THE LARVÆ OF INSECTS
FOUND IN THE GREAT SALT LAKE.

WASHINGTON, *May 12th*, 1852.

MY DEAR SIR:—The exuviæ of insects which you have brought
from the shores of the Great Salt Lake proves, on examination, to
have been deposited by aquatic diptera.

In the mass, I can detect fragments of the larvæ shells of the
pupa, and small portions of a mature *Chironomus* and other
Tipulidæ. More than nine-tenths of the mass is composed of
larvæ and exuviæ of *Chironomus*, or some species of mosquito—
probably undescribed; the fragments being too imperfect to determine.

You are best able to determine, first, whether mosquitoes exist
at any time at the Great Salt Lake in such unparalleled numbers
as this organic matter indicates; or, secondly, whether the salt of
the lake water has preserved their exuviæ, so that it has accumulated through a great length of time.

A few fragments of insects I have been able to determine as
belonging to the Linnæan genus *Nepa*, which is aquatic, and a
very few others as Hymenopterous, &c.

In the hope of soon seeing your Report on the most interesting
portion of our continent,

I remain
Yours truly,

T. R. PEALE.

CAPTAIN H. STANSBURY,
   Corps Topographical Engineers,
   Washington.

I am not aware that mosquitoes exist in such unusual abundance
in the vicinity of the lake; but incline to the opinion of Mr. Peale,
that the accumulation of the immense masses of these exuviæ is to
be attributed to the preservative qualities of the lake water.

H. S.

APPENDIX D.

BOTANY.

CATALOGUE OF PLANTS COLLECTED BY THE EXPEDITION.

BY PROFESSOR JOHN TORREY.

APPENDIX D.

BOTANY.

BY JOHN TORREY.

CLEMATIS LIGUSTICÆFOLIA, Nutt.—East base of the Black Hills. In fruit, September 29th. Tails of the carpels more than an inch long, and very slender.

ANEMONE PENNSYLVANICA, Lin.—Great Salt Lake Valley.

DELPHINIUM AZUREUM, Mich.—With the preceding. Fl. May 2d–19th.

BERBERIS (MAHONIA) AQUIFOLIUM, Pursh.—With the preceding; on the sides of the mountains. Fl. May 19th.

ARGEMONE HISPIDA, Gray, Plant. Fendl., No. 16.—With the preceding. Called the "Thistly plant" by the inhabitants. In fruit May 19th.

VIOLA PEDUNCULATA, Torr. and Gray.—Borders of the Salt Lake.

CORYDALIS AUREA, Willd.—Stansbury's Island, Great Salt Lake. Fl. June 26th.

ERYSIMUM ASPERUM, D. C.—Shore of the Salt Lake and along Weber's River. May–June.

STREPTANTHUS CRASSICAULIS, Torr. (Sp. nov.)—Glaucus; caule glabro inflato fistuloso; foliis oblongis runcinato-pinnatifidis vel runcinatis longe petiolatis; floribus erecto-patulis; petalis (purpureis) linearibus obtusiusculis calyce villoso-lanato duplo longioribus.

Mountain side, on the east shore of the Salt Lake. Fl. May 30. Found also on the tributaries of the Uintah River, Utah Territory, by Colonel Frémont. Annual. This species is easily distinguished by its inflated hollow stem and very woolly calyx. The leaves are mostly radical and deeply pinnatified; the terminal lobe much larger than the others, and triangular or deltoid. The stem is simple, from one to two feet high, more or less inflated toward the base, and nearly naked above. The flowers are nearly sessile, in a long terminal raceme, erect when first expanded, but finally becoming patulous. Calyx about half an inch long, the sepals oblong-lanceolate and woolly externally. The petals are dark purple, with a pale waved margin. Filaments all free. The siliques are not known.

Plate I. *Streptanthus crassicaulis*, of the natural size. Fig. 1, a sepal, showing the inner face and part of the hairiness on the back. Fig. 2, a petal. Fig. 3, the stamens and pistil. Fig. 4, a separate stamen. All magnified.

S. SAGITTATUS, Nutt. in Jour. Acad. Nat. Sc. VII., p. 12; not Hook and Arn.—Shore of the Salt Lake, May 6.

SISYMBRIUM CANESCENS, Nutt.—West shore of Salt Lake.

PHYSARIA DIDYMOCARPA, Gray. Pl. Illustr. I., p. 162, (in a note.) *Vesicaria didymocarpa*, Hook.—On Green River. In fruit, September 12th.

CLEOME LUTEA, Hook. Fl. Bor. Amer. I., p. 70, t. 25. *C. aurea*, Nutt?—Carrington's Island, Salt Lake. Fl. June 18.

Except in the greater length of the stipe and the large size of the plant, I see nothing to distinguish *C. aurea* of Nuttall from this species.

SIDALCEA MALVÆFLORA, Gray, mss. *S. orogana*, Gray, pl. Fendl., p. 20. *Sida malvæflora*, Lindl. *S. orogana*, Nutt.— Antelópe Island, Salt Lake. Fl. June 18–30. A white-flowered variety occurred in the same locality.

MALVASTRUM COCCINEUM, Gray, Gen. Ill. t. 121, pl. Fendl. p. 24. *Cristaria coccinea*, Pursh. *Sida coccinea*, D. C., Torr. and Gr., fl. 1, p. 682.

Var. β GROSSULARIÆFOLIUM. *M. grossulariæfolium*, Gray, l. c. *Sida grossulariæfolia*, Hook. and Arn.—Islands and shore of the Salt Lake. May and June.

Except in the larger size of the plant and in the less divided leaves, the var. β does not differ from the ordinary form of *M. coccineum*.

CALLIRRHOE INVOLUCRATA, Gray, Gen. Ill. 2, t. 117; Pl.

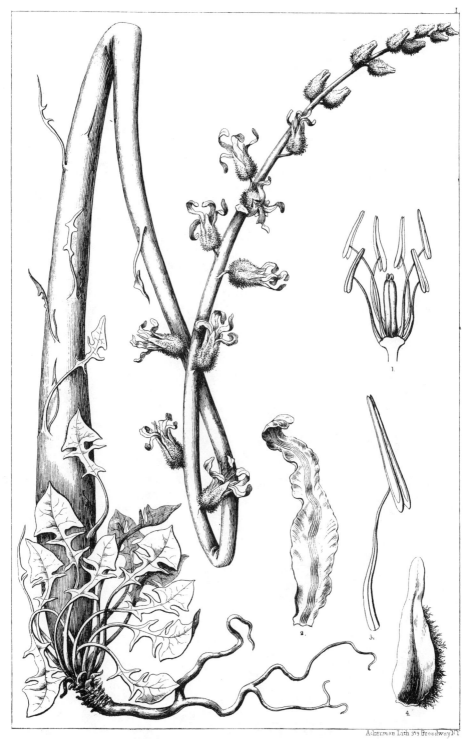

STREPTANTHUS CRASSICAULIS, Torr & Frem.

PHACA MOLLISSIMA β Torr.

Fendl. p. 16. *Malva involucrata*, Torr. and Gr. Fl. 1, p. 226. Upper waters of the Platte. The large tapering root is said to be edible.

VICIA AMERICANA, Muhl.—Valley of Salt Lake, June 1.

CICER ARIETINUM, Lin.—Sandy bottom land in the Valley of Salt Lake; probably introduced. This plant has also been found by Dr. Pickering on the banks of the Kooskooskee, or Clear Water, in Oregon; and I have received it from Southern California, where it was doubtless taken by the Spaniards. It is a little remarkable that it should now be found apparently wild in the interior of Oregon and in the valleys of Utah.

PHACA MOLLISSIMA, Nutt. in Torr. and Gr. Fl. 1, p. 350. *Astragalus purshii*, Dougl. in Hook. Fl. Bor., Amer. 1, p. 152.

Var. β UTAHENSIS; foliolis. 6–8, jugis, obovatis; pedunculis folio longioribus. Shores and islands of the Salt Lake. This plant is abundant in the Territory of Utah, and I have not received it from any other region. It differs from the ordinary form of *P. mollissima:* and if there were not what appear to be intermediate states of it, I should consider it a distinct species. It is less branched, and has more numerous leaflets than the var. β. The flowers are violet, four to six in number, in a short spiked raceme. The nearly mature legume is densely clothed with long woolly cream-coloured hairs, and very closely resembles that of *P. mollissima*. Our plant has much the appearance of *Astragalus glareosus*, Dougl. (*A. argophyllus*, Dougl.,) and which, I suspect, is a *Phaca*, but the leaves and fruit are different.

Plate II. *Phaca mollissima*, var. *utahensis* of the natural size. Fig. 1, a flower. Fig. 2, the wings and heel. Fig. 3, the stamens. Fig. 4, mature fruit of the var. α. Fig. 5, cross section of the same. Fig. 6, immature fruit of var. *utahensis*.

ASTRAGALUS ADSURGENS, Pall. ?—West shore of the Salt Lake, in sandy soil. Flowers white, shaded with purple. This plant seems intermediate between *A. adsurgens* and *A. striatus*, Nutt. The legumes were not found. May 1.

OXYTROPIS LAMBERTI, Pursh.—Upper waters of the Platte, &c.; frequent.

HEDYSARUM MACKENZII, Richards. App. Frankl. Journ. ed. 2, p. 28.—Promontory Range, Utah. Fl. May 1.

LUPINUS ALBICAULIS, Dougl. ?—High grassy land, Antelope
Island, Salt Lake. Fl. June 30. A suffrutescent species densely
clothed with short appressed almost silvery hairs. The leaflets
are mostly in sevens, oblanceolate and acute. The flowers are
nearly as large as in *L. perennis*, in rather dense, somewhat ver-
ticillate spikes; and the upper lip of the calyx is strongly soccate
or slightly spurred.

COWANIA STANSBURIANA, Torr. (Plate III.) C. foliis pin-
natifido 5–7-lobatis, lobis oblongis; floribus flavis. *C. plicata ?*
Torr. in Frém. 2d Report, p. 314; not of Don. Stansbury's
Island, Salt Lake. Colonel Frémont collected this plant in the
mountains of California, along the Virgin River, a tributary of
the Colorado. It is nearly related to *C. mexicana*, Don, (in Linn.
Trans. 14, p. 574, t. 22, f. 1,) which has also yellow flowers; but
the leaves in that species are three parted, with linear segments,
and they have a long narrowly cuneate base.

A third species of this genus, *C. plicata*, Don, was introduced
into England from Mexico in 1835, and figured in Sweet's British
Flower Garden, (t. 400.) This is clearly the plant afterward described and beautifully figured by Zuccarini in his Plant. Nov. v.
minus cognit, under the name of *Cowania purpurea*. It is also
Greggia rupestris of Englemann, in Wislizenius's Jour.

The *C. stansburiana* is a shrub attaining the height of from
six to twelve feet. It is much branched, and the young twigs are
glandular. The leaves grow mostly from short spurs. They are
ovate in outline, 4–6 lines long, deeply cut into five or seven
lobes, and whitish tomentose underneath, except the strong green
midrib, but green and somewhat glabrous above. They are revo-
lute on the margin, of a coriaceous texture, and sparingly dotted
with conspicuous glands. The flowers are solitary, terminal, and
on short peduncles. The calyx-tube is turbinate and glandular;
the segments are broad and obtuse. Petals sulphur-yellow, broadly
obovate, two or three times the length of the calyx-segments.
Styles persistent, beautifully plumose, and in fruit an inch or more
in length. Achenium linear-oblong, striate, and clothed with short
appressed hairs. For further remarks on the genus Cowania, see
Plantæ Fremontianæ, in the Smithsonian Contributions, vol. 5.

Plate III. *Cowania stansburiana;* a branch of the natural
size. Fig. 1, a leaf of the natural size. Fig. 2, upper surface
of a leaf magnified. Fig. 3, under surface of the same. Fig. 4,

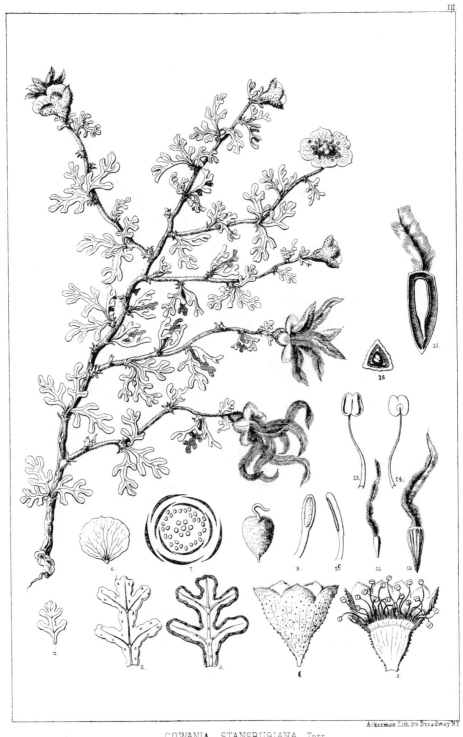

Ackerman Lith. 379 Broadway N.Y.

COWANIA STANSBURIANA. Torr.

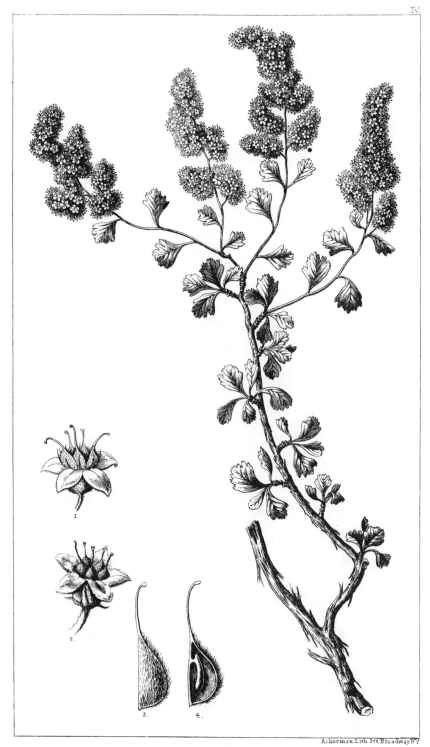

1.

2.

3.   4.

Ackerman Lith 379, Broadway N.Y.

SPIRÆA DUMOSA Nutt.

a flower-bud. Fig. 5, a flower laid open. Fig. 6, a petal. Fig. 7, plan of the flower. Fig. 8, a pistil. Fig. 9, front view of the style and stigma. Fig. 10, side view of the same. Fig. 11, a carpel of the natural size. Fig. 12, the same magnified. Fig. 13, a stamen seen in front. Fig. 14, the same seen from behind. Fig. 15, longitudinal section of a ripe carpel, showing the erect seed. Fig. 16, transverse section of the same. All the figures except No. 1 are more or less magnified.

SPIREA DUMOSA, Nutt. Mss.; Hook. Lond. Jour. Bot. 6, p. 217; Gray, pl. Fendl. p. 40. *S. discolor*, Torr. in Ann. Lyc., N. York, 2, p. 195; not of Pursh.—Stansbury's Island, Salt Lake. Fl. June 26.

Plate IV. *Spiræa dumosa;* a branch of the natural size. Fig. 1, the fructiferous calyx. Fig. 2, a carpel. Fig. 3, the same laid open.

S. OPULIFOLIA, var. PAUCIFLORA, Torr. and Gr. Fl. 1, p. 414.— Summit of a mountain on Stansbury's Island, Salt Lake. Fl. June 26. A tall, much branched shrub, with leaves scarcely more than half an inch in diameter.

ŒNOTHERA CÆSPITOSA, Nutt.—Shore and islands of the Salt Lake. May and June. Usually acaulescent, but sometimes throwing up a branching stem about six inches high. The flower is from two to three inches in diameter, white and fragrant. *S. montana*, of Nuttall, is hardly distinct from this species, and, perhaps, *Œ. marginata* should be regarded as a variety of the same.

Œ. SCAPOIDEA, Nutt. in Torr. and Gr. Fl. 1, p. 506.—Western shore of the Salt Lake. Fl. and fr. May.

Œ. ALBICAULIS, Nutt.; Torr. and Gr. Fl. p. 495.—Islands of the Salt Lake. Fl. June. Stem about a foot high; the flowers small, white, and inodorous.

GAYOPHYTUM RAMOSISSIMUM, Torr. and Gr. Fl. 1, p. 513.— Antelope Island, Salt Lake. Stem about eighteen inches high, with very slender branches, and flowers even smaller than in Mr. Nuttall's specimen of this plant. The pedicles are about twice as long as the ripe pod.

MENTZELIA ORNATA, Torr. and Gr., and Gray, Pl. Fendl. p. 47. *Bartonia ornata*, Nutt.—Islands of the Salt Lake. In our speci-

mens there are only five petals; and the filaments of the five
outermost stamens are only a little dilated, while the anthers are
perfect: but in other specimens, collected by Colonel Frémont,
there are ten petals, of which five inner ones are rather smaller
than the others; and so they are described by Mr. Nuttall. Sir
William Hooker thinks that *M. lævicaulis* is not distinct from
this species; but Dr. Gray states (l. c.) that it differs in its yellow
flowers, which open in the sunny hours, while in *M. ornata* they
are white, and open toward sunset.

M. ALBICAULIS, Dougl.; Torr. and Gr. l. c.—Valley of the
Salt Lake.

ERODIUM CICUTARIUM, L'Herit.—Islands of the Salt Lake.
Fl. June. This plant is widely spread over the western part of
North America, from the Rocky Mountains to the Pacific, and is
doubtless indigenous.

HEUCHERA RUBESCENS, Torr. (sp. nov.)—Scapo nudo glabro vel
scabriusculo; foliis suborbicularibus breviter 5–7-lobatis glabrius-
culis, lobis crenato-dentatis, dentibus setoso-mucronatis, vel obturis;
panicula oblongo; thyrsoidea sublaxa; staminibus exsertis; petalis
linearibus calyce æquali longioribus.

Stansbury's Island, Salt Lake. Fl. June 26. Rhizoma thick
and somewhat ligneous, clothed with brown vestiges of leaves.
Leaves an inch or an inch and a-half in diameter, nearly orbicular,
mostly cordate at the base, somewhat coriaceous, either wholly glabrous or very sparingly strigose-pubescent, moderately 5–7-lobed,
and the lobes crenate, or broadly toothed. The teeth usually
mucronate and sometimes ciliolate. Petioles 2–4 inches long.
Scapes varying from a span to fifteen inches high, entirely naked,
except a few remote appressed scales. Panicle rather loose and
few (15–20) flowered. Flowers about one-third larger than in
H. americana. Blacts lanceolate and often toothed. Calyx purplish red, campanulate, pubescent; the segments linear-oblong,
obtuse, and nearly equal. Petals narrowly linear, persistent, about
as long as the stamens. Styles much exserted.

This species has the foliage of *H. parvifolia,* the inflorescence of
H. hispida, and the calyx of *H. americana.*

Plate V. *Heuchera rubescens,* of the natural size. Fig. 1, a
flower. Fig. 2, the same laid open. Fig. 3, transverse section
of a capsule. Fig. 4, a seed. All the figures are magnified.

HEUCHERA RUBESCENS Torr.

PEUCEDANUM CITERNATUM, (var. ? PLATYCARPUM.)—Fructibus obovatis, alis membranaceis disci sesquilatioribus.—With the preceding. Except in the broadly-winged fruit, this plant does not appear to differ essentially from *P. biternatum*, Nutt.

THASPIUM MONTANUM, Gray.—Fl. Fendl. p. 57? On a mountain bordering the Salt Lake. Fl. May 25. One specimen has a perennial root, crowned with several spreading scapiform stems, which are (in the flowering state) from five to eight inches long. The whole plant is very glabrous and somewhat glaucous. The leaves are bi-tripinnatifidly cut, with oblong, acute, entire, or incised lobes. The yellow flowers are in dense umbels, with numerous rays. There is no involucre, and the involucels consist of 7–9 linear lanceolate leaflets. The carpels of the young fruit are furnished with five broad, undulate wings. The vittæ in the intervals seem to be solitary, or sometimes double.

ASTER OBLONGIFOLIUS, Nutt.—Stansbury's Island, Salt Lake, June 26.

ERIGERON CONCINNUM, Torr. and Gray, Fl. 2, p. 174.—Valley of Salt Lake, May 30.

DIETERIA PULVERULENTA, Nutt. in Torr. and Gray, Fl. 1, p. 101.—Green River, Sept. 12.

SOLIDAGO MISSOURIENSIS, Nutt.—With the preceding.

LINOSYRIS SERRULATA, Torr. (nov. sp.)—Ramulis scabriusculis; foliis anguste linearibus trinervibus rigidiusculis acutis, margine serulatis; capitulis fastigiato-corymbosis subquadrifloris; squamis oblongo-lanceolatis glabris subquinquefariam, imbricatis laxiusculis, exterioribus multo brevioribus, coroliis glabris.—Valley of the Salt Lake.

GRINDELIA SQUARROSA, Dunal.—Bear River, near the Hot and Cold Springs. Fl. May 10.

STENOTUS CÆSPITOSUS, Nutt. in Torr. and Gray, Fl. 2, p. 238.—Valley of the Salt Lake.

AMBROSIA CORONOPIFOLIA, Torr. and Gray, Fl. 2, p. 291.—Table land at the northern extremity of Salt Lake Valley, Sept. 19.

MONOTHRIX, Torr. (nov. gen.)—Capitulum hemisphericum, radiatum. Involucrum subtriseriale; squamis subæqualibus oblongo-linearibus. Receptaculum, nudum. Flores radii fœminei, uniseriales ligulati; ligula oblonga, apice tridentata. Flores disci hermaphroditi 4-dentati. Styli rami lineares, appendice elongato-lanceolata terminati. Achenia radii et disci conformia. Pappus uniaristatus; arista scabra corolla breviore; squamulæ, nullæ, suffrutices e basi ramosissimi. Folia opposita, vel alterna, ovata petiolata dentata vel sublobata. Pedunculi terminales, elongati, monocephali. Flores lutei.

M. STANSBURIANA, Torr.—Crevices of limestone rocks on Stansbury's Island, Salt Lake. Fl. June 26.

The lower part of the stem is thick and ligneous, but the branches are herbaceous. These are about a span high and are minutely glandular-pubescent. The leaves are scarcely half an inch in diameter, broadly ovate, or almost orbicular in outline, often subcordate at the base, with a few coarse, obtuse teeth, or almost lobed; the lower ones mostly opposite, but the upper ones often alternate. Heads 6–8 lines in diameter. Scales of the involucre in two or three series lanceolate, acute, glandularly puberulous, somewhat villous at the tip. Rays 6–10; the limb longer than the tube, and nearly twice as long as the involucral scales. Disk flowers constantly 4-toothed in all my specimens. Achenium obovate-oblong, compressed, slightly hispid-ciliate on the margin, crowned with a single rigid, upwardly scabrous bristle.

This genus is nearly related to *Perityle* of Bentham (Bot. Sulph. p. 23,) but differs in the absence of squamellæ on the achenium; the pappus consisting of a single bristle. A second species exists in Lindheimer's Texan collection of 1850, (No. 314.)

Plate VI. *Monothrix stansburiana,* of the natural size. Fig. 1, a leaf. Fig. 2, A head of flowers. Fig. 3, an involucrum laid open, the flowers removed to show the receptacle. Fig. 4, the same divided longitudinally. Fig. 5, an inner and an outer scale of the involucrum. Fig. 6, a ray flower. Fig. 7, a disk flower. Fig. 8, corolla of the disk flower laid open. Fig. 9, branches of the style and their appendages.

CHENACTIS STEVIOIDES, Hook. and Arn.; Torr. and Gray, Fl. 2, p. 371.—Strong's Knob, Salt Lake, June 10. Several of the ray flowers have the corolla dilated, but the lobes still nearly equal, and, as is the pappus, considerably shorter than in the disk flowers.

C. tenuifolia of Nutt. is scarcely distinct from this species.

C. ACHILLEÆFOLIA, Hook. and Arn.; Torr. and Gray, Fl. l. c.— Stansbury's Island, June 20. Stems about a span high, several

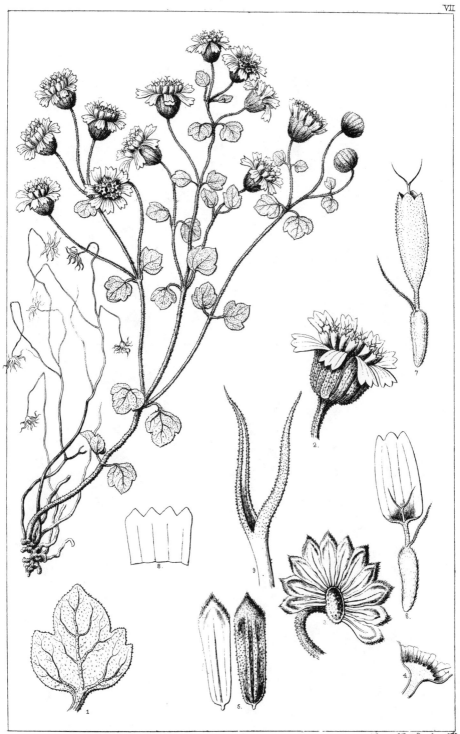

Ackerman,Lith.379 Broadway.NY

MONOTHRIX STANSBURIANA, Torr.

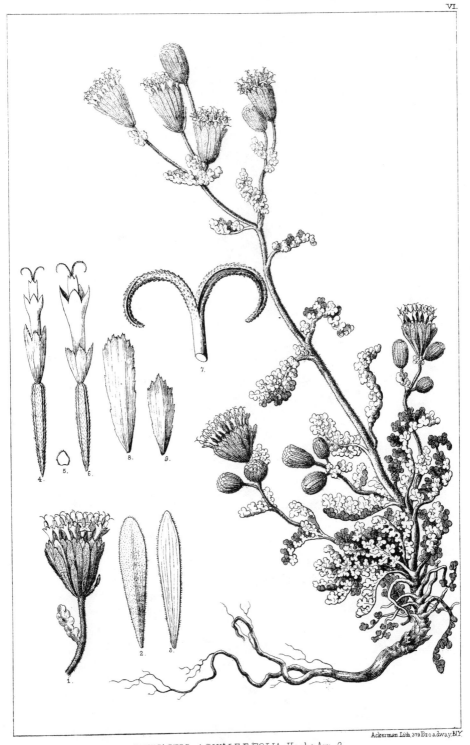

CHENACTIS ACHILLEÆ FOLIA. Hook & Arn. β.

from one root. Leaves somewhat fleshy, densely clothed with a white tomentum; the lobes very small, obtuse, and much crowded. Heads few (3–6) in a terminal corymb. Flowers of the ray and disk nearly alike, funnel-form. Pappus of about ten oblong, obtuse, denticulate scales; five of which, in the disk flowers, are nearly as long as the tube of the corolla, and the five other about half as long. Scales in the ray flowers much shorter than the corolla tube.

Plate VII. *Chenactis achilleæfolia*, of the natural size. Fig. 1, a head of flowers. Fig. 2, an exterior scale of the involucrum. Fig. 3, an interior scale of the same. Fig. 4, a disk flower. Fig. 5, cross section of an achenium. Fig. 6, a ray flower. Fig. 7, branches of the style and appendages. Fig. 8 and 9, scales of the pappus from a disk flower.

LAYIA GLANDULOSA, Hook. and Arn., Torr. and Gray, Fl. 2, p. 394.—Valley of the Salt Lake, east side.

ACHILLEA MILLEFOLIUM, Lin.—Islands of the Salt Lake, June.

ARTEMISIA TRIDENTATA, Nutt. in Trans. Amer. Phil. Soc. (n. ser.) 7, p. 398.—Green River, Sept. 12. Many of the larger species of the genus are called "Sage" by the hunters and emigrants.

A. FRIGIDA, Willd.; Torr. and Gray, Fl. 2, p. 424.—With the preceding.

A. LUDOVICIANA, Nutt., gen. 2, p. 143.—With the preceding.

A. CANADENSIS, Mich., Fl. 2, p. 129.—With the preceding.

SENECIO FILIFOLIUS, Nutt. in Trans. Amer. Phil. Soc. (n. ser.) 7, p. 414.—Green River, September.

S. HYDROPHILUS, Nutt. l. c.—Valley of the Salt Lake.

S. HOOKERI, Torr. and Gray, Fl. 2, p. 438.—Weber River, May 16. Scales of the involucre with black villous tips.

TETRADYMIA NUTTALLII, Torr. and Gray. *T. spinosa*, Nutt., l. c.—Shore of the Salt Lake, May 5. A thorny shrub, about four feet high.

CIRSIUM UNDULATUM, Spreng.—Stansbury's Island, Salt Lake. Fl. June 24.

STEPHANOMERIA RUNCINATA, Nutt. in Trans. Amer. Phil. Soc. 7, p. 427.—Carrington's Island, Salt Lake.

LYGODESMIA JUNCEA, Don.; Hook., Fl. Bor. Amer. 1, p. 295.—
Stansbury's Island, Salt Lake, June 23. The heads in our specimens are quite as large as in *L. grandiflora.* Captain Stansbury
states that the flowers are purple.

MALACOTHRIX SONCHOIDES, Torr. and Gray, Fl. 2, p. 486.—Shore
of the Salt Lake, and on Carrington's Island, May 30. The pappus is decidedly double in this species. The outer series consists
of five slender, nearly glabrous, and somewhat persistent bristles;
the inner of about fifteen scabrous capillary bristles, which are
caducous, and separate in a ring. I have seen the same character
in two or three other species. Dr. Gray, in his *Plantæ Fendleri-
anæ*, (p. 113, No. 453,) says that he noticed in "*M. sonchoides,
M. coulteri,* and especially in *M. californica,* that two (opposite)
bristles of the pappus are naked, instead of barbellate, and rather
stronger and less deciduous than the others." In *M. sonchoides*
I believe the outer series always consists of *five* bristles; but in
some species they are variable in number, and in others are entirely
wanting.

CREPIS ACUMINATA, Nutt. l. c.; Torr. and Gray, Fl. 2, 489.—
Stansbury's Island, Salt Lake, June 23. This is the tallest of our
indigenous species of crepis. Some of our specimens are about
three feet high. The radical leaves (including the petioles) are
more than a foot in length.

Plate VIII. *Crepis acuminata,* of the natural size. Fig. 1, a
separate flower magnified, as are the following. Fig. 2, an achenium with its pappus. Fig. 3, one of the hairs of the pappus.

FROXIMON CUSPIDATUM, Pursh. Fl. 2, p. 742.—Valley of the
Salt Lake.

CASTILLEJA HISPIDA, Benth. in Hook. Fl. Bor. Amer. 2, p. 105.
—Shore of the Salt Lake, May.

C. MINIATA, Dougl. in Hook. Fl. Bor. Amer. l. c.—With the
preceding.

C. SESSILIFLORA, Pursh. Fl. 2, p. 738.—Weber River.

PENSTEMON·GRANDIFLORUM, Nutt. in Fras. Catal., 1813.—On
the Arkansas River.

ERITRICHIUM GLOMERATUM, D. C. Prodr. 10, p. 131. *Myosotis
glomerata,* Nutt.—Near Salt Lake City. Fl. April 29.

Ackerman, Lith.379 Broadway NY

CREPIS ACUMINATA. Nutt.

ECHINOSPERMUM FLORIBUNDUM, Lehm.; Hook. Fl. Bor. Amer. 2, p. 84.—Valley of the Malade, Sept. 25. Near *E. deflexum.*

AMSINCKIA LYCOPSOIDES, Lehm.; D. C. Prodr. 10, p. 117.— Shore of the Salt Lake. Fl. May 5th.

MERTENSIA DRUMMONDII, G. Don.; D. C. Prodr. 10, p. 86.— Salt Lake Valley.

LITHOSPERMUM? CIRCUMSCISSUM, Hook. and Arn., Bot. Beech. Voy., suppl. p. 370.—On Green River. In my account of the plants collected in California and Oregon by the United States Exploring Expedition, I have made this plant the type of a new genus, (*Piptocalyx*,) allied to Eritrichium, from which it differs in its naked corolla and deciduous calyx.

HYDROPHYLLUM CAPITATUM, Dougl.; Benth. Trans. Lin. Soc. 17, p. 273.—Ogden's Pass, May 15.

EUTOCA HETEROPHYLLA, Torr. (n. sp.)—Erecta, scabro-pubescens; foliis oblongo-linearibus subsessilibus, integris vel ad basin utrinque unilobatis, lobis oblongis v. linearibus; floribus brevi-pedicellatis; lobis calycinis spathulata linearibus obtusiusculis; corolla patenti-campanulatâ calyce sesquilongiore; placentis multiovulatis.—Valley of the Salt Lake, on the eastern side.

Annual; about a foot high. Radical leaves spatulate; the cauline ones broadly linear, 1–1½ inch long; either entire or furnished on each side at the base (sometimes only on one side) with a spreading, narrow, acute lobe, so that the leaves appear somewhat halberd-form. Racemes short, terminating the branches. Lobes of the calyx about three and a-half lines long. Corolla widely campanulate, almost rotate, about five lines long; the lobes short and rounded. Appendages ten, narrow, connivant in pairs between the bases of the filaments. Stames nearly equal, a little shorter than the corolla. Style somewhat exserted; 2-lobed at the summit. Ovary with 15–20 ovules attached to each placenta. This species resembles *E. phacelioides*, Benth., but differs in the nearly sessile narrower leaves, the larger and broadly campanulate corolla, many-ovuled placentæ, &c.

GILIA (IPOMOPSIS) PULCHELLA, Dougl. in Hook. Fl. Bor. Amer. 2, p. 74.—Ogden Pass, May 15.

COLLOMIA LINEARIS, Nutt. Gen. Amer. pl. 1, p. 126.—With the preceding.

PHLOX HOODII, Richards, in Frankl. Jour. app. ed. 2, p. 6, t. 28.
—Mountains near the Salt Lake, April and May.

P. LONGIFOLIA, Nutt. Jour. Acad. Philad. 7, p. 41.—North-west shore of the Salt Lake, and near the mouth of Bear River, May 10.

PHYSALIS. LANCEOLATA, Mich.—Salt Lake Valley, June.

GENTIANA AFFINIS, Griseb., Gent. p. 289.—Moist places, Aug.18.

ACERATES DECUMBENS, Decaisne in D. C. Prod. 8, p. 522. *Anantherix decumbens*, Nutt.—Mountain on Stansbury's Island, Salt Lake, June 26. Stems often assurgent. Calyx and corolla green. Crown dark purple.

COMANDRA UMBELLATA, Nutt., Gen. 1, p. 157; Hook. Fl. Bor. Amer. 2, p. 139 t. 179.—Stansbury's Island, Salt Lake. Fr. June 20.

RUMEX VENOSUS, Pursh. Fl. 2, p.? Green River. Fr. September 12.

ERIGONUM UMBELLATUM, Torr. in Annal. Lyc. Nat. Hist. New York, 2, p. 241.—Valley of the Salt Lake.

E. FREMONTII, Torr.—With the preceding.

SARCOBATUS VERMICULARIS, Torr. in Emory's Report, p. 149. *S. maximiliani*, Nees. *Fremontia vermicularis*, Torr. in Fremont's first and second Reports. "Pulpy Thorn" of Lewis and Clark's travels.—Strong's Knob, Salt Lake, Fl. June 10.

GRAYIA POLYGONOIDES, Hook. and Arn. Bot. Beech. Voy. suppl. p. 338, Hook. ict., 271. *G. spinosa*, Mog. in D. C. Prodr. 11, p. 110.—Carrington's Island, Salt Lake.

CHENOPODINA LINEARIS, Mog. in D. C. Prodr. 11, p. 164, excl. syn. Ell. and Michx.—Mountain on the west shore of the Salt Lake. Fl. May 30. This plant attains the height of about three feet. The lower part of the stem is stout and shrubby. It differs entirely from the *C. maritima* of the Atlantic States; yet the authors who describe it as *not* shrubby are quoted by Moquin under *C. linearis*.

ARTHROCNEMUM FRUCTICOSUM, Moq. Chenop. Enum. p. 111, and in D. C. Prodr. 11, p. 151?—North shore of the Salt Lake. A common plant in all the salines of New Mexico and California. It is a shrub about one foot high, and much branched. The joints of the branches are more or less compressed, and emarginately bifid at the summit. The spikes are cylindrical and are not jointed; the flowers being alternate, and immersed in deep excavations of the rachis. The calyx is quadrangular, and consists of four cohering sepals, which are cucullate, spongy at the summit, and at length separate from each other. There is but a solitary stamen. The seed is loose in the utricle, oblong, and the embryo forms about half of an ellipse.

OBIONE CANESCENS, Moq. Chenop. p. 74, and *O. occidentalis*, Moq. in D. C. Prodr. 11, p. 112. *Pterochiton occidentale*, Torr. and Frém., in Frém. second Rep. p. 318. *Obione tetraptera*, Benth. Bot. Voy. Sulph. p. 48.—On Green River. Fr. September 10. This is a variable species, especially in the characters of the mature fructiferous calyx. Sometimes it is furnished with short, irregular-toothed wings, and at other times the wings are very broad and nearly entire.

O. CONFERTIFLORA, Torr. and Frém. l. c.—With the preceding.

ABRONIA MELLIFERA, Doug. Miss. Hook. Fl. Bor. Amer. 2, p. 125, Bot. Mag. l. 2879.—Strong's Knob, Salt Lake. Fl. June 10. Easily distinguished from *A. umbellata* by its broad involucral leaves and green flowers. *A. micranthus*, Torr. in Frémont's first Report, p. 96, and in Emory's Report, p. 149, seems to be a particular state of the plant, in which it bears very small but perfect flowers. In those works I noticed the peculiarity of the embryo; the inner cotyledon being constantly abortive. The same character exists in all the species of this genus: but I have not observed it in any other nyctagineous plant.

SHEPHERDIA ARGENTEA, Nutt. Gen. Amer. Pl. 2.—Black's Fork of the Green River. Fr. September 12.

EPHEDRA AMERICANA, Willd. Spec. Pl. 4, p. 860? Endl. Synops. Conif. p. 254.—Shore of the Salt Lake. A leafless shrub with very numerous branches, growing about four feet high. It is very doubtful whether it be the same as Willdenow's plant, which is a native of Quito. Although it is not uncommon in the interior of California and in New Mexico, I have never received the female flower or the fruit. All my specimens are males. *E. americana* is described as monœcious. The *Ephedra* noticed in Emory's Report under the name of *E. occidentalis*, (a mistake for *E. americana*), differs from this species in its three-parted sheaths with long subulate points.

TRIGLOCHIN MARITIMUM, Lin.—Pursh. Fl. 1, p. 257.—Stansbury's Island, Salt Lake, June 24.

POLYGONATUM CANALICULATUM, Pursh. Fl. 1, p. 235.—Valley of the Salt Lake?

AMIANTHIUM NUTTALLII, Gray, Melanth. in Ann. Lyc. Nat. Hist. N. York, IV., p. 123. *Helonias angustifolia,* and *H. paniculata,* Nutt.—Valley of the Salt Lake. Fl. May 1.

AMBLIRION, Rafin. in Journ. de Phys. 89, p. 102; Bernhardi, Bot. Zeit. 1835, p. 395? (ex Kth. Enum. 4, p. 255.) *Lilium* § *Amblirion,* Endl. gen. sub. No. 1098. *Fritillaria* § *Eucrinum,* Nutt.

A. PUDICUM, var. BIFLORUM, Torr. *Lilium pudicum,* Pursh. Fl. 1, p. 228, f. 1.; Schult. Syst. 7, p. 401. *Fritillaria pudica,* Spreng. Syst. 2, p. 64; Nutt. in Journ. Acad. Phil. 7, p. 54. Hook. Fl. Bor. Amer. 2, p. 182; Kunth Enum, l. c.—Promontory Range, Valley of Salt Lake. Fl. April 12.

This rare and interesting plant was long ago proposed as a distinct genus by the late Mr. Rafinesque. It is allied both to *Fritillaria* and to *Lilium.* It differs from both in the want of nectaries. Unfortunately the fruit is not known, so that it cannot be compared with those genera in an important character. Our specimens are all two-flowered. The root is flat, orbicular, and toothed round the border, with a cluster of little tubers on the upper side at the base of the stem. The leaves are linear, and from two to four inches long. The flowers are yellow, nodding, about an inch in length, somewhat obconical or funnel-form, and entirely destitute of a nectariferous groove. The stigma is simple and undivided.

According to Mr. Nuttall, *Fritillaria tulipæfolia* of Caucasus is another species of this genus. I have also specimens of what may prove to be a third species, collected by Colonel Frémont on the Feather River, California; for the style, though thickened at the summit, is undivided, and the nectary is wanting: but there are several flowers in a loose racemose panicle.

Plate IX. *Amblirion pudicum,* of the natural size. Fig. 1, a sepal magnified, as are all the following. Fig. 2, a stamen showing the back of the anther. Fig. 3, a front view of the same. Fig. 4, the pistil. Fig. 5, a cross section of the ovary.

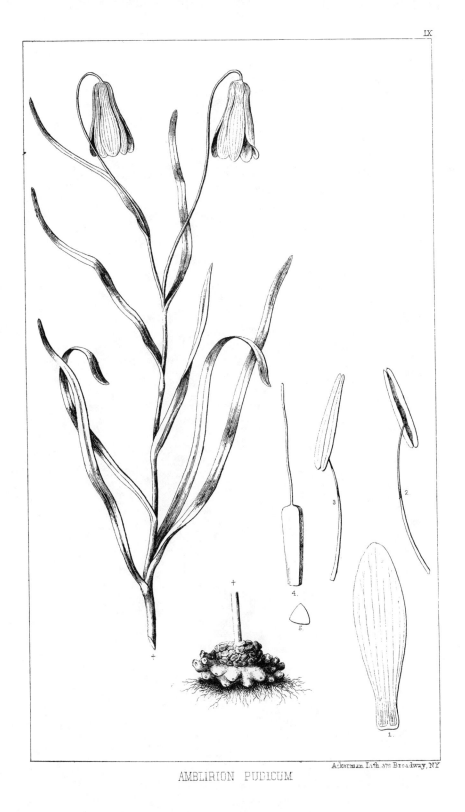

AMBLIRION PUDICUM

ALLIUM STELLATUM, Fraser, Bot. Mag. t. 1576.—Weber River, May 23.

A. RETICULATUM, Fraser, Bot. Mag. t. 1840.—Wahsatch Mountains, June.

CALOCHORTUS LUTEUS, Nutt. in Jour. Acad. Phil. 7, p. 53; probably not of Douglass.—Valley of Salt Lake. The root is called "sego" by the natives, and is much esteemed by them as food. It is bulbous, and varies in size from that of a pea to that of a filbert. Our plant agrees exactly with the description of Nuttall, who was probably mistaken as to the colour of the flower. The inner sepals seem to be *white*, except at the claw, which is yellow. I have not been able to institute a comparison between this plant and Douglass's *C. luteus;* but if ours proves to be distinct, it may be called *C. nuttallii.*

ERYTHRONIUM GRANDIFLORUM, Pursh. Fl. 1, p. 231. Lindl. Bot. Reg. t. 1786.—With the preceding.

TRITELEIA GRANDIFLORA, Lindl. Bot. Reg. fol. 1293. Hook. Fl. Bor. Am. 2, p. 186, t. 198, B.—Valley of Salt Lake. Fl. May.

JUNCUS BALTICUS, Willd., Hook. Fl. Bor. Amer. 2, p. 189.—Antelope Island, Salt Lake, June 1.

SISYRINCHIUM BERMUDIANA, Lin. *S. anceps*, Cavan.—Walnut Creek.

HYPOXIS ERECTA, Lin.—Upper Arkansas.

SCIRPUS TORREYI? Olney.—Gray, Bot. N. States, p. 526?—Stansbury's Island, Salt Lake. Fr. June 26.

Differs from *S. torreyi* in its longer and larger spikes, and in shorter point of the achenium; but in other respects it agrees.

ERIOCOMA CUSPIDATA, Nutt. Gen. 1, p. 40.—Antelope Island, Salt Lake, June 18. A beautiful grass, which seems to be distinct from *Stipa.*

KOELERIA CRISTATA, Pers.—Gray, Gram. and Cyp. 1, No. 45.—With the preceding.

HORDEUM JUBATUM, Lin.—Torr. Fl. 1, p. 158.—Antelope Island, Salt Lake, June.

AGROPYRUM REPENS, Gaert.—With the preceding.

CLYMUS STRIATUS, Willd.—With the preceding.

APPENDIX E.

LETTER FROM PROFESSOR JAMES HALL, OF NEW YORK,

CONTAINING OBSERVATIONS ON THE

GEOLOGY AND PALÆONTOLOGY

OF THE

COUNTRY TRAVERSED BY THE EXPEDITION,

AND

NOTES UPON SOME OF THE FOSSILS
COLLECTED ON THE ROUTE.

APPENDIX E.

GEOLOGY AND PALÆONTOLOGY.

BY PROF. JAS. HALL.

ALBANY, *February*, 1852.

CAPTAIN STANSBURY:

DEAR SIR:—I have examined with care the specimens of rocks and fossils which you submitted to my inspection. I find them, with some few exceptions, to represent very clearly the products of four distinct geological periods, as follows:—The older are metamorphic rocks of silurian or devonian age, or perhaps both; the next in order, and recognisable by their fossil remains, are of the carboniferous period; the third are of the cretaceous period; and the fourth are of the tertiary. Besides these there are the products of ancient volcanic action in the basalts and amygdaloids, with some specimens of obsidian.

After a careful examination of the specimens, and a comparison with the notes and journal which you submitted to me, I have marked upon the map of your route, and upon the map of the Salt Lake region, the different colours indicating the character of the geology at the different points where the specimens were collected. I am aware that the specimens with the notes, together, would have warranted me in colouring in a more extended manner, but I have preferred to confine myself to the position and actual evidences furnished by specimens. By having the map in this condition nothing is hazarded, and every new fact obtained can be readily added to it, or it may be filled up to some extent from the indications furnished by the topographical features.

It will be the more satisfactory mode to follow your route in the remarks I shall make in this connection.

The first specimens furnished are from the west side of the Missouri River, near and above Fort Leavenworth. These are all from limestone of the carboniferous period, and apparently from the upper of the two great limestones of this period in the west. The most conspicuous fossils are *Productus, Terebratula,* &c.

26   401

The route from the Missouri westward shows a continuation of this limestone as far as the Big Blue.

Here it disappears, judging from specimens and remarks in the notes. It is soon succeeded by strata of cretaceous age, which, from the specimens preserved, I have been able to recognise as extending for a considerable distance on the route between Turkey Creek and Big Sandy.

Among the cretaceous fossils are a species of *Pholadomya*, and the *Inoceramus*, which is so common and abundant in numerous localities in this region.

It is quite probable that these beds extend much farther, but I find no specimens in the collection; and the notes indicate that there are heavy deposites of drift, which may have obscured the exposure of the formation below.

This drift formation, (judging from the descriptions given in the notes,) or the debris from the immediate geological formation, appears to have covered the older stratified deposites, since no mention is made of them till approaching the forks of Platte River on the 25th June. At this point were collected some specimens of clays with small marine shells, too imperfect for determination; but from the general character, and from the occurrence of bones in the same place, it is presumed that they are of tertiary age. Above the forks of the Platte River similar bones and shells are noticed, and, on the 1st of July, specimens of bones were collected. Numerous fragments of bones were collected on the 3d of July, apparently belonging to some mammalia of the herbivorous character. These bones are too imperfect for determination beyond their general character. From the description of the mode of occurrence, and their being imbedded in a matrix of considerable hardness and tenacity, one would be led to infer that they were of some tertiary deposite.

Among these specimens is a single ramus of the lower jaw, which apparently belonged to some carnivorous animal; but no teeth are preserved in it, nor were any teeth of any kind found in the collection.

From July 3d to 11th, the notes give no evidence of any thing of special interest. On the latter date, bones are mentioned as occurring in the locality examined, but no specimens having this date are preserved in the collection.

It would appear that the character of the country from near Fort Kearny to near Fort Laramie is uniform, and that no deposite of older date than the tertiary were observed. Of the specimens collected there is but a single individual indicating the character of a marine formation. From the condition of the bones it may even be questioned whether the deposite containing them is not of post tertiary age.

The specimens from the vicinity of Fort Laramie are all from limestone of the carboniferous period. Some of the fossils are identical with species collected between the Missouri and the Big Blue, and we can only suppose, from the great similarity of the specimens, that it is a continuation of the same formation. From the dates marked upon the specimens, it is evident that this limestone extends to some distance on the east and west of Fort Laramie.

The specimens bearing date of July 19th, two days' march northwest of Fort Laramie, are a feldspathic granite with little quartz or mica. The rocks in this locality are doubtless of metamorphic origin, probably rocks of silurian age. The specimens collected three days' march in advance of this place, on the North Fork of the Platte River, are shaly sandstone and thinly laminated sandstones containing fossils. The fossils are some brachiopods, with others similar to *Monotis*, and we may presume from the described position of the beds, and from the character of the fossils, that these beds are of devonian age. In the journal these beds are recorded as dipping at the rate of 15° to the north-east.

The specimens bearing the mark of July 24th, are precisely like those collected at Fort Laramie, and contain the same species of fossils. On the same date were seen (according to the journal) gray and red sandstones. On the following day is recorded a bed of coral, three or four feet thick, with *Sigillaria* and *Calamites*. The specimens of this date sent to me are those of bituminous coal and others of soft shale, but I have been unable to distinguish any well-marked vegetable remains.

From the proximity of limestone of the age of the coal, and the record of sigillaria and calamites occurring in the same connection, it may be presumed that this coal belongs to the true coal measures; and this locality is probably an exposure indicating the existence of a great basin. This point itself and the surrounding country are well worthy of a more extended examination, since the discovery of workable beds of coal in this region would be a matter of national importance.

The record of July 27th shows the occurrence of red shales and sandstones, which may be of the age of the coal, or beneath that formation.

From July 30th to August 2d, the notes of the Journal and the specimens show the existence of compact quartz rock, crystallized silicious limestone, and conglomerate.

From August 3d to August 6th, I have no specimens indicating the character of the formations passed over. From this date to August 11th, including the distance from the southern extremity of the Wind River Mountains to Fort Bridger, the collections are all of marine tertiary age, including many specimens of *Nautilus* and other marine shells.

From this time nearly all the records and collections pertain to the Salt Lake and its vicinity. Near Fort Hall several specimens of volcanic rocks were collected, and obsidian and lava about the Pannack and the head of the Malade.

South of Fort Hall the specimens collected are of granular sandstone, and of quartz rock resulting from an altered sandstone; to the west, and above these, are chert and limestone of carboniferous age. The limestone in this locality contains fewer shells than that in the more easterly localities, but has a large number of corals.

The specimens collected in the islands and shores of the Great Salt Lake are sufficient to give one a very good idea of the general geological features. The specimens are of metamorphic rocks, consisting of talcose and mica slates, hornblende rocks, and a few specimens of granitic or sienitic character.

Some specimens of the latter description occur along the valley of Ogden's River. Antelope Island, Frémont Island, a part of Promontory Point, and Mud Island, on the east side of the lake, judging from the numerous specimens, consist principally of talcose and mica slates, with hornblende rock. Carrington Island, Hat Island, a point north by west from Hat Island, name not known, and a part of Strong's Knob, consist of similar rocks with some of altered sandstone or quartz rock. In several localities, as at Promontory' Point and near Mud Island, the metamorphic strata appear to be overlaid by a coarse conglomerate, or coarse sandstone, which is partially altered, and assumes the character of a quartz rock.

From all the facts in my possession, it would appear that these metamorphic rocks are distinctly stratified and highly inclined, but do not attain any great elevation. The direction of the ranges, corresponding to that of the elevating force, appears to be nearly in the direction of north by west and south by east. From the form of the lake and the different localities at which rocks of this character occur, we may infer that there were two lines of elevation, corresponding with the divisions of the lake.

The more elevated portions of the lake shore, and the mountain ranges, consist of carboniferous limestone. In some localities this limestone is partially altered, losing its granular character and becoming sub-crystalline, or threaded by numerous veins of calcareous spar. In most localities, however, the limestone abounds with fossils, particularly corals of the cyathophyllideæ.

From the records in the journal of observation and from specimens, I have been able to indicate several localities of importance. The principal of these is Stansbury's Island, the summit of which is of limestone, and has an elevation of three thousand feet. The limestone is said to rest on coarse sandstone and conglomerate, specimens of which accompany the limestone. Limestone also occurs on the mountains of the Spring Valley range, to the southwest of the lake.

Stansbury's Island, from its position at the southern extremity of the lake, and from its isolated and elevated character, has been more fully exposed than the localities on the west side. Along the western shore, southward of Strong's Knob, the same limestone was examined and noted in three places, and in two it is marked as underlaid by sandstone. Limestone also occurs at Strong's Knob with the altered rocks. West of the knob, another point is indicated as limestone; and northward of this, Gunnison's Island is of the same rock. Dolphin Island, and also a considerable space on the shore west of this island, are indicated as limestone, both from specimens and the journal. On the eastern shore, opposite Dolphin Island, limestone occurs in close proximity to metamorphic strata.

It should not be omitted that the same limestone occurs to the north of Great Salt Lake City, and is quarried in that neighbourhood. It appears both from the specimens and the notes of observation that the limestone overlies a coarse sandstone, or conglomerate, which almost invariably accompanies it.

Although I have not felt at liberty to colour on the map any other points than those indicated both by the notes and by specimens examined, yet I can have no doubt but all the elevated ranges on the west, south, and north of the Great Salt Lake are capped by the carboniferous limestone. Judging from the relative position of the limestone, and the metamorphic rocks of Antelope and Frémont's Islands, the former occupies the position of low, synclinal basins, the valleys between being produced to a large extent, probably by erosion along the anticlinal axes, produced by the elevation of the metamorphic beds. We may expect, also, that the same limestone will be found on the elevated plateaus and mountains on the east side of the lake.

It will be seen from these facts that we have very satisfactory information that this limestone of the carboniferous period is widely distributed in the region around the Great Salt Lake.   Its position relative to the coal-bed on the North Fork of Platte River has not been determined; but since no beds of coal have been observed on the slopes of the mountains in the region of the Salt Lake, we are left to infer that the coal is to be sought (as elsewhere) above the limestone. ·Since the existence of coal is proved in one point, (admitting the evidence in favour of its age being that of the carboniferous period,) we are warranted in the conclusion that it has once existed over a much wider area, and can be sought with success in the proper situations.   The importance of this mineral in that distant region cannot be too highly estimated, and the geographical position and extent of the beds should be one of the first points ascertained in the location of any route of communication between the east and the west.

In comparing the notes and specimens with the map of your route and the large map of the Salt Lake and adjacent country, I have confined myself to indicating by a colour the kind of rock occurring at each point, scarcely in any case extending this colouring even when the topographical features of the country would warrant the conclusion that the same rock existed. Your knowledge of the character of the surface and the relative elevations will enable you in many instances to determine the limits of those formations marked; while, for myself, not fully understanding their features, I might fall into some error.

Hoping to see the investigations you have so well begun carried still further, until we can have a good geographical and geological map of this region,

I remain,

Very truly and respectfully,

Your ob't. serv't.

JAMES HALL.

Plate 1.

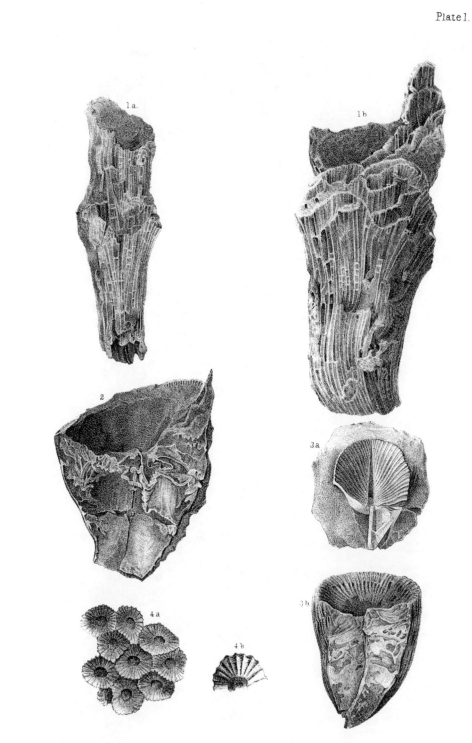

N. B. The colours on the map of the travelled route are—

Blue ....Carboniferous limestone.
Green...............Cretaceous formation.
Yellow..............Tertiary formation.
                     (In some places not indicated by colour.)
Black ....Coal-beds.
Red ....Metamorphic rock.

On the Great Salt Lake map are—

Red ....Metamorphic rock.
Blue.................Limestone.
Yellow..............Sandstone and conglomerate beneath the
                 limestone.

NOTES UPON SOME OF THE FOSSILS COLLECTED ON THE ROUTE FROM
THE MISSOURI RIVER TO THE GREAT SALT LAKE, AND IN THE VICI-
NITY OF THE LATTER PLACE, BY THE EXPEDITION UNDER THE
COMMAND OF CAPTAIN HOWARD STANSBURY, T. E.

THE species described in the following paragraphs are either
from limestone of the carboniferous period or from strata nearly
associated, and which, from their character and relations, are
clearly of the same age. The other fossils of the collection consist of a few cretaceous species, and of numerous fragments of
bones from the tertiary formation.

The brachiopods were collected to the eastward of the Salt Lake
region, and the corals are abundant in the limestone to the west
and north-west of the Salt Lake. The few acephala are from argillaceous beds between Fort Laramie and the Salt Lake.

CORALS.—CYATHOPHYLLIDEÆ.

FAVIPHYLLUM? RUGOSUM, (n. sp.)

PLATE I. FIG. 1 a AND 1 b.

Cells deep; structure of the centre unknown; external portion
cellular, with transverse septæ and vertical intermediate dissepi-
ments, giving a columnar structure.

The specimens are all silicified, and I have been unable to examine the central portion; the exterior, where weathered, presents the appearance of a bundle of the columns of *Favosites*, except that they are generally four-sided, and the inner sides necessarily narrower than the outer ones.

FAPHRENTIS? MULTILAMELLÆ.

PLATE I. FIG. 2.

Coral free, turbinate, somewhat rapidly expanding, cells deep; lamellæ numerous, thin; outer portion cellular.

From the specimens in my possession, it cannot be positively determined that this fossil is a true *Faphrentis*, but many features induce this reference.

Loc. Cloth Cap and Flat Rock, Great Salt Lake.

FAPHRENTIS STANSBURII, Hall, (n. sp.)

PLATE I. FIG. 3 a b.

Turbinate, free, or attached only by a pedicel nearly straight or but slightly curved; cup rather deep; margin (when entire) thin, lamellæ numerous, thin, intermediate ones extending from the margin one-third to one-half the semidiameter; fossett distinct.

Loc. Stanbury's Island, Cloth Cap, and Flat-rock Point, Great Salt Lake.

LITHOSTRONTION ———, (sp. indet.)

PLATE I. FIG. 4 a b.

Coral massive; cells of medium size, deep; lamellæ crenulate.

The specimen is much weathered, and, from the presence of an ochreous incrustation, the specific characters cannot be clearly described. It differs in the dimensions and other characters of the cells from two species of the carboniferous period known to me from localities east of the Mississippi River.

Loc. Top of Stansbury's Island, Great Salt Lake.

Plate II.

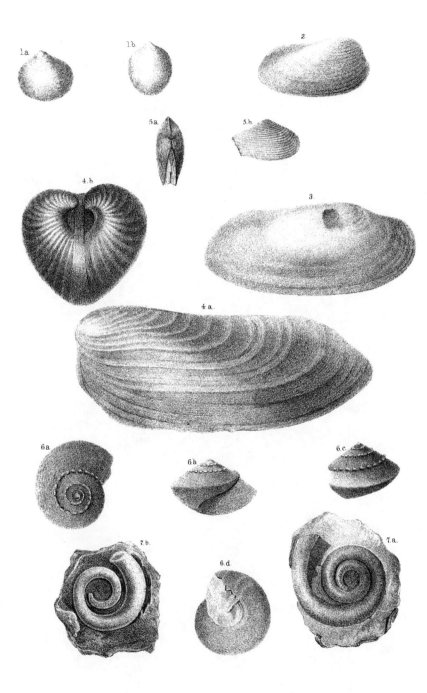

BRACHIOPODA.

TEREBRATULA SUBTILITA.

PLATE II. FIG. 1 a b, 2 a b.

Gibbous, obovoid; valves nearly equal, convex; beak of the dorsal valve elevated, incurved, and perforated at the apex; a mesial depression commencing just below the centre and extending to the front, which is produced and elevated, filling a broad sinus in the ventral valve; surface marked by strong concentric striæ, or lines of growth, with faint, often almost imperceptible radiating striæ.

Fig. 1 a, a young individual.

Fig. 1 b, an individual of the ordinary size and form.

Fig. 2 a, a more gibbous form.

Fig. 2 b, profile view of the preceding.

Fig. 2 c, front view of the same.

Loc. Missouri River, near Weston.

SPIRIFER HEMIPLICATA.

PLATE II. FIG. 3 a b.

Shell gibbous; ventral valve more elevated, beaks nearly equal; entire surface marked by finely radiating strata; each valve with about three plications on each side of the mesial sinus and elevation, which plications extend halfway from the base to the beak, leaving the upper half of the shell marked only by fine striæ; anterior portion of the dorsal valve produced in a long extension, which fills a deep angular sinus in the ventral valve.

Fig. 3 a, view of the dorsal valve, which, from distortion, shows the beak of the ventral valve projecting above it.

Fig. 3 b, front view of the same specimen.

Loc. Missouri River, near Weston.

SPIRIFER OCTOPLICATA?

PLATE II. FIG. 4 a b.

The specimens figured appear to be young individuals, and may probably belong to this characteristic carboniferous species.

Fig. 4 a, this specimen has suffered from lateral pressure, causing an unnatural extension of the beak.

Fig. 4 b, the dorsal valve of a larger individual, having six plications on each side of the mesial sinus.

The surface is marked by distinct, undulating, concentric striæ, which are again crossed by finer thread-like elevations, and which appear to have been the bases of short spines.

Loc. Missouri River, near Weston.

SPIRIFER TRIPLICATA, Hall, (n. sp.)

PLATE II. FIG. 5 a b c.

Shell subquadrangular; dorsal valve more gibbous than the ventral; area nearly linear; beak of dorsal valve small, acute, and closely incurved; mesial depression shallow in the upper part, but becoming deeper and expanded toward the base, and produced in front; entire surface, including the mesial sinus and elevation, covered with fine plications, which, being simple in their origin, soon divide into three, which are continued to the base without further division.

This species differs from the *S. striatus*, Sowerby, in its form, and in the circumstance that the plications are less subdivided toward the margin of the shell.

Fig. 5 a, ventral valve, and area of the dorsal valve.

Fig. 5 b, dorsal valve of the same individual.

Fig. 5 c, profile view of the same. The form is somewhat distorted by pressure.

Loc. Missouri River, above Weston.

CHONETES VARIOLATA, (D'Orb. sp.) De Koninck.

PLATE III. FIG. 1 a b.

This species bears the essential characteristics of those figured and described by De Koninck, though it is larger than most of his figures. The broad, scarcely defined mesial depression of the dorsal valve gives a straight or slightly sinuous outline in front.

This fossil is associated with several of the preceding species, near Weston on the Missouri River.

Plate III.

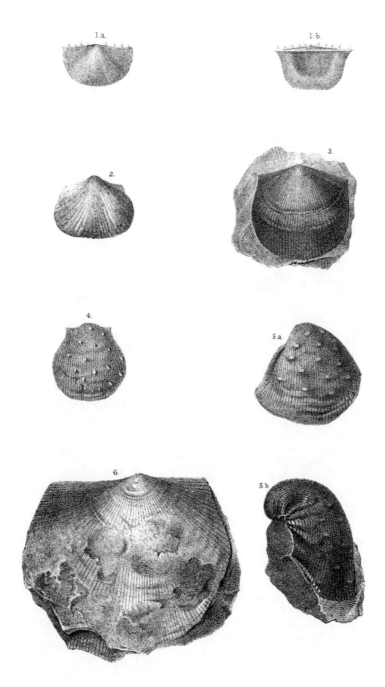

1.a.

1.b.

2.

3.

4.

5.a.

6.

5.b.

Ackerman Lith 379 Broadway N.Y

PRODUCTUS COSTATUS?

PLATE III. FIG. 2.

Reference, De Koninck, Recherches sur les Animaux Fossils, première partie, page 92, pl. VIII., fig. 3.

The specimen figured is apparently a young individual of this species, in a bad state of preservation. The species is also cited by De K., from the Missouri River, from whence the specimen figured was obtained. Some other fragments from the Platte River appear to belong to the same species.

PRODUCTUS SEMIRETICULATUS.

PLATE III. FIG. 3, 5 a and 5 b.

Reference, De Koninck, Recherches sur les Animaux Fossils, première partie, page 83, pl. VIII., IX., and X.

I refer, with some hesitation, the specimens here figured, to this very variable species. One or two of the specimens are very narrow and much elongated; the striæ are flexuous, sometimes preserving the bases of numerous spines, and at other times entirely free from these appendages. Other specimens are proportionally shorter and broader, and present the usual form of this species, though none of them are larger than those figured.

The specimens are all in limestone of a dark gray or brownish-gray colour, from near Fort Laramie. Some impressions of the same or a similar species occur in limestone from Flat-rock Point, and other places in the neighbourhood of the Great Salt Lake.

PRODUCTUS ——— (sp. indet.)

PLATE III. FIG. 4.

This species bears considerable resemblance to *P. costatus*, in the aspect and marking of its surface, but its form is quite different. It occurs on the Missouri River, near Weston, associated with Ferebratulæ and other species of *Productus*, *Spirifer*, &c.

A species of *Productus* resembling *P. punctatus* in the character of its surface, occurs on the Big Blue River, in soft shaly limestone; but the specimens are too imperfect for determination. The occurrence of this and other species, shows the existence of carboniferous strata at several points after leaving the Missouri River, and, in some instances, after crossing tracts of country that are probably of cretaceous beds.

ORTHIS UMBRACULUM?

PLATE III. FIG. 6.

The specimen corresponds with one from the carboniferous rocks of Kentucky and Tennessee, which is referred to this species. It is however somewhat distorted by pressure, and other specimens are necessary for a full determination.

Loc. Missouri River, above Fort Leavenworth.

ACEPHALA.

AVICULA? CUSTA.

PLATE IV. FIG. 1 a b.

Shell obliquely ovoid; hinge line much shorter than the width of the shell; beaks prominent, and the upper part of the shell gibbous; surface marked by fine even striæ.

This shell occurs, with a few other fossils, in thinly laminated gray sandstone, which, judging from the notes of observation, lies below the limestone of Fort Laramie.

TELLINOMYA PROTENSA, Hall, (n. sp.)

PLATE IV. FIG. 3.

Shell elongate-oval; beaks placed about one-third the width of the shell from the anterior extremity, somewhat pointed; surface marked by fine concentric striæ and some stronger lines of growth.

Loc. near Le Bonte, with the preceding species.

CYPRICARDIA OCCIDENTALIS.

PLATE IV. FIG. 2.

Shell rhomboid-ovate; anterior extremity rounded; posterior obliquely truncate; posterior slope with a distinct carina extending from the back to the posterior basal margin; beak near the anterior extremity; surface marked by concentric striæ and some more elevated ridges or lines of growth.

This species occurs in a gray argillaceous limestone, associated with *Productus, Chonetes,* etc.

Loc. from the Big Blue River.

Plate IV.

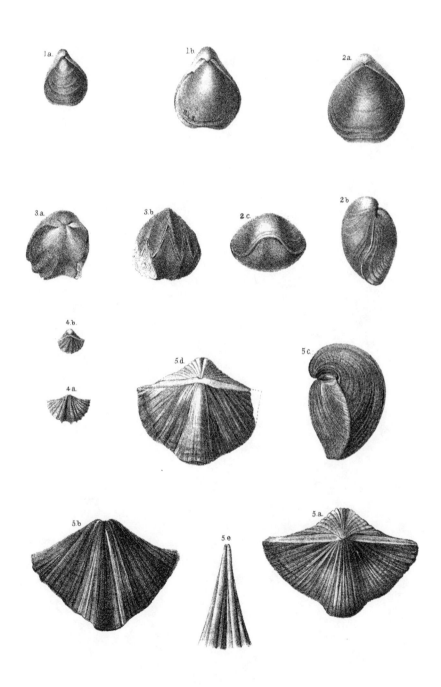

Ackerman Lith 379 Broadway N.Y.

ALLORISMA TERMINALIS, Hall, (n. sp.)

PLATE IV. FIG. 4 a b.

Shell elongate-ovoid, with the posterior extremity extended and sub-acute; beaks anterior, or in a line with the anterior extremity of the shell; surface marked by strong concentric ridges, which, diverging from the beak, are more prominent on the central portion of the shell, and gradually die out on the cardinal line. The shell is also quite smooth toward the basal margin, with the exception of the rather coarse concentric striæ which cover the entire surface.

Fig. 4 a, view of the left valve.

Fig. 4 b, anterior view of the shell.

Loc. from the Big Blue River.

NUCULA ARATA, Hall, (n. sp.)

PLATE IV. FIG. 5 a b.

Shell oval-ovate, rounded before, and gradually narrowing behind the beaks (posterior extremity broken off); beaks prominent, closely incurved; posterior lunule elongated and distinctly defined; surface marked by distinct (rather sharp where unworn) equal concentric ridges, scarcely so wide as the furrows between them. The ridges, when seen in a longitudinal direction, have an imbricated appearance.

Fig. 5 a, the right valve, showing the anterior extremity broken off.

Fig. 5 b, a cardinal view, showing the beaks and defined posterior lunule.

This beautiful species occurs with *Terebratula, Spirifer,* and *Productus,* in a decomposing limestone, on the east side of the Missouri River, below Weston.

GASTEROPODA.

PLEUROTOMARIA CORONULA, Hall, (n. sp.)

PLATE IV. FIG. 6 a b c d.

Depressed trochiform, volutions about five, angular, slightly convex on the upper side, and sloping almost uniformly from the suture to the margin; lower surface more rounded; aperture sub-quadrangular; striæ bent abruptly backward on the acute outer edge of the last volution, which has scarcely a distinct carina; upper margin of the volutions, along the suture, marked by an elevated nodulose ridge, giving a beautiful coronate feature to the upper part of the shell.   Umbilicus, none.

Fig. 6 a, view of the upper surface of the shell.

Fig. 6 b, view of the aperture, which is imperfect.

Fig. 6 c, anterior view of the shell.

Fig. 6 d, base of the shell.

This beautiful species was found with other carboniferous fossils.

EUOMPHALUS SUBPLANUS, Hall. (n. sp.)

PLATE IV. FIG. 7 a b.

Spiral, convolute; volutions about five, in contact, round, or very obtusely sub-angular on the upper outer margin of old specimens, surface evenly striated.

In young specimens the apex is depressed, but in the specimen figured it is slightly above the outer volution.   The specimen fig. 7 b is the under side of a cast of an individual of apparently the same species, the absence of the shell leaving the volutions not in contact.

Fig. 7 a, view of the upper side of a specimen from limestone on the top of Stansbury's Island, Great Salt Lake.

Fig. 7 b, a cast in limestone from between the Big and Little Blue Rivers.

APPENDIX F.

LETTER FROM L. D. GALE,

WITH

A CHEMICAL ANALYSIS OF THE WATER OF THE GREAT SALT LAKE,
AND OTHER MINERAL WATERS AND SALINE SUBSTANCES,
COLLECTED DURING THE JOURNEY.

APPENDIX F.

CHEMICAL ANALYSES, &c.

BY DR. L. D. GALE.

Sir:—I have carefully examined the specimens of water, and earthy and saline compounds, from the Valley of the Great Salt Lake, which you put into my hands for chemical analysis, and I herewith report the results.

I have inspected and tested all the specimens, and made a detailed analysis of such only as I deemed might be of some interest to know. Thus, the water of the Great Salt Lake, that of the Hot Spring, the Warm Spring, and the native salæratus, are all more or less important to the public.

The first of these is perhaps the most important of all. The water of this lake must vary considerably in its strength at different seasons of the year. It is important, hence, in stating the strength of the water to state the time when the water experimented on was collected. That fact, so far as it relates to these experiments, will be found, it is presumed, in the body of the work.

The specimens examined contain full twenty per cent. of pure chloride of sodium, and not more than two per cent. of other salts, and is one of the purest and most concentrated brines known in the world.

The strongest brine reported by Professor Beck, on the salines of the State of New York, is that of the new well at Syracuse, containing 17.35 per cent. of chloride of sodium.—The water of the Warm Spring is a sulphurous water, strongly impregnated with sulphuretted hydrogen, and has medicinal virtues that may render it valuable.

The native salæratus from Mud Plain, as well as that from the banks of the Sweetwater, is a valuable domestic salt.

Before stating the results of the analyses made, it is proper to say that the quantity of water from the several sources was too small to enable me to make so critical an analysis as I otherwise

would have done.—That from the Salt Lake being not more than
about two quarts, and that from the Warm Spring a little more
than half a pint, while that from the Hot Spring was about a pint
and a-half. I was compelled, therefore, to use the greatest possible
economy in the materials, and to confine my attention to the most
common materials generally found in salines. Besides this, I was
also obliged to confine myself mainly to the liquid contents of the
vessels, and neglect, except in one case, (namely, the water of the
Warm Spring,) the gaseous matters, and that in consequence of
the sealing of the bottles having been loosened by the severe agi-
tation in travelling, so that more or less of the contents of each
vessel had escaped before they arrived in this city. It was therefore useless to make any experiments on the supposed gaseous
matters as they may have existed at the sources.

The great importance of the waters of Great Salt Lake rendered
it justifiable, in my view, to make some experiments of a practical
character relative to the procuring from it of a good quality of
salt, even better than that usually found in this section of country,
and by which it seems to me the water may be a source of revenue
and convenience.

As will be seen in the detailed analysis below, the salt water
yields about twenty per cent. of pure common salt, and about two
per cent. of foreign salts; most of the objectionable parts of which
are the chloride of lime and the chloride of magnesia, both of
which, being very deliquescent, attract moisture from the damp
atmosphere, which has the effect to moisten and partially dissolve
the common salt, and then when the mass is exposed to dry air,
or heat, or both, a hard crust is formed. I believe I have found
a remedy for the caking, which is cheap and easily used. It consists in sprinkling over the salt obtained by the evaporation of the
water and heaped up in a bin or box containing a porous bottom
of blankets or other like material, a cold solution of the salt as it
is concentrated from the lake, till crystals begin to be deposited.
This concentrated brine, while it will dissolve none of the common
salt, will dissolve all the chlorides of calcium and magnesium, and
carry them down through the porous bottom, and thus leave the
salt purer and better than any now found in our markets. For
persons who are obliged to prepare temporarily the salt, as travellers passing through the country, the water of the lake, without
concentration, may be used for washing out the deliquescent chlorides, sprinkling the heap of salt by a watering pot, at intervals

of two or three hours during a single day, and allowing it to drain and dry at night, and be spread to the sun an hour or two the following morning.

This experiment is successful on a small scale, and will no doubt admit of extended application.

The water of the lake examined was perfectly clear, and had the specific gravity of 1.170, water being 1.000.

One hundred parts by weight were evaporated to dryness in a water-bath below the boiling point and then heated to about three hundred degrees of the thermometer, and retained at that heat till the mass ceased to lose any weight. It gave solid contents 22.422, and consisted of

Chloride of Sodium	20.196
Sulphate of Soda	1.834
Chloride of Magnesium	0.252
Chloride of Calcium	0. trace.

The water of the Warm Spring of Salt Lake City is a Harrowgate water, abounding in sulphur. The water is very limpid, having a strong smell of sulphuretted hydrogen, and contains the gas both absorbed in the water and also combined with bases.

The specific gravity of the water I found to be 1.0112, and, when opened, was highly charged with gas, although the cork had allowed much of the gas, and water even, to escape.

One hundred parts of the water were evaporated to dryness at a temperature of about 200° of Fahrenheit, and yielded solid matter 1.082000.

The heat necessary for this also carried off sulphuretted hydrogen per cent. 0.037454.

One hundred parts of the water gave an analysis of the following results:—

Sulphuretted hydrogen absorbed in the water	0.037454
" " combined with bases*	0.000728
Carbonate of lime, precipitated by boiling	0.075000
Carbonate of magnesia, " "	0.022770
Chloride of calcium	0.005700
Sulphate of soda	0.064835
Chloride of sodium	0.816600
	1.023087

* Probably combined with some of the bases and decomposed by the heat used to separate the water in solidifying the contents, as the gas could hardly be detected when the contents were dried.

The water of the *Hot Spring* was found to have the specific gravity of 1.0130, and one hundred parts yielded solid contents 1.1454.

Chloride of sodium	0.8052
Chloride of magnesium	0.0288
Chloride of calcium	0.1096
Sulphate of lime	0.0806
Carbonate of lime	0.0180
Silica	0.0180
	1.0602

NATIVE SALÆRATUS AND ALUM.

The specimen labelled *Efflorescence from a Salæratus Pond*, on the Sweetwater River, has been tested, and found to be composed of the sesquicarbonate of soda, mixed with sulphate of soda and chloride of sodium, and is one of the native salts called *Trona*, found in the Natron Lakes in Hungary, Africa, and other countries.

Three grammes of this salt in dry powder, cleared of its earthy impurities, gave carbonic acid 0.9030 of a gramme, which would indicate 1.73239 grammes of the sesquicarbonate. The other salts were found to be the muriate and sulphate of soda: the proportions were not determined.

The specimen of alum from *Alum Point, Great Salt Lake*, is a rare and interesting mineral. It is a true alum; but instead of being an alum with an alkaline base, as potash or soda alum, it is found to be an alum with a base of manganese, differing from all other true alums in crystallizing in needle-shaped quadrilateral (?) prisms. It is soluble in several times its weight of water. It has the taste of ordinary alum, though less strong, from the fact, perhaps, that it is less soluble.

The mineral is an effloresced mass, found on the surface of a slate rock abounding with a sulphuret (as is believed) of manganese, from the decomposition of which the sulphur, being oxidized, is converted into sulphuric acid, and combining directly with the base, manganese and the alumina of the slate, forms the alum in question.

The specimen, as it reached me, had lost nearly all of its water of crystallization; and, in order to make a fair analysis of it as a specific salt, a portion of the specimen was dissolved in water and recrystallized, and the crystals dried to the first appearance of efflorescence on the projecting points, and then a given weight of the crystals was heated to drive off the water of crystallization. Having previously learned that it was an alum, with the double base of manganese and alumina, I made a careful analysis and obtained the following result from the salt dried by blotting paper :—

100 grammes of the freshly crystallized salt gave—

Water	73.0
Protoxide of manganese	08.9
Alumina	04.0
Sulphuric acid	18.0

It is not easy to explain the relation of the acid to the two bases here in accordance with the usual constitution of alums, as there does not seem to be enough acid for the supply of an equivalent to each base, nor of alumina for the manganese. But as I have not the time to repeat my experiments, they must stand for what they are worth.

This salt may be substituted for common alum in nearly all its various uses for tanning, in combination with the salt brine of the Great Salt Lake, in what is called the process of tawing; and where tan bark is difficult to obtain, it is a valuable acquisition to the arts. And should the locality of alum at any time give out from exhaustion, the rock may be blasted and the alum made by artificial means, as the alum slates of England are worked.

The manganese alum is also susceptible of various uses as a mordant and a colouring agent in dyeing, where it is not only a substitute for common alum, but subserves other and additional purposes of communicating various tints of fancy colours to shades of red, brown, &c. Thus we have purples, lilacs, browns, and many other tints, from the use of manganese.

For details in this art, see Parnell's Applied Chemistry—Calico-printing.

Yours truly,

L. D. GALE.

HOWARD STANSBURY, ESQ.
Captain Corps of Topographical Engineers, U. S. Army.

WASHINGTON, *March* 25, 1851.

ALPHABETICAL INDEX.

The asterisks indicate the page of the appendices where the locality or object is especially referred to.

Finch, gray-crowned, 317*.
Finch, Lincoln's, 317*.
Fish in Warm Springs, 117.
Flat-head Indians, 214.
Flat-rock Point, 172.
Flowers on the prairie, 28.
Fort Bridger, 74, 228, 276*, 281*, 300*.
Fort Hall, 93.
Fort John, 53.
Fort Kearny, 30, 272, 290*, 301*.
Fort Laramie, 52, 273*, 288*, 301*.
Fort Leavenworth, 270, 292, 301*.
Fossils, 32, 34, 35, 56, 58, 60, 61, 68, 74, 89, 91, 116, 196, 211.
Fossil bones, 33, 34, 39, 402.
Fossils described, 407.
Fossil plants, 62, 72, 73.
Fossil trees, 72.
Fourche Boise River, 274*.
Fourth of July, celebration of, 42.
Fox, great-tailed, 309*.
Frappe's Creek, 250, 285*, 300*.
Frémont Island, 160, 297.
Fresh water on Salt Lake, 173, 178, 184.
Froximon cuspidatum, 392*.
Fuligula affinis, 324*.

G

Gasteropoda, 413*.
Gayophytum ramosissimum, 387*.
Gentiana affinis, 394*.
Geographical positions, table of, 300*.
Geology, 38, 69, 71, 75, 78, 79, 83, 89, 90, 96, 103, 111, 113, 159, 163, 223, 230, 232, 234, 244.
Geology of the route described, 401*.
Gilia pulchella, 393*.
Gnats, annoyance from, 174, 176, 190.
Golden Pass, 218, 278*.
Goose Creek, 89.
Goose, Canada, 321*.
Goose, white-fronted, 321*.
Government train, 28.
Grand Island, 29.
Grayia polygonoides, 394*.
Grayia spinosa, 209.
Grease-wood, 172.
Grease-wood Creek, 274*.
Great Basin, 227, 264.
Great Salt Lake, 101.
Great Salt Lake City, 84, 277*, 278*.
Green River, 72, 276*, 282*.
Grindelia squarrosa, 389*.
Gros Bois Creek, 94.
Grus canadensis, 319*.
Gulls, 102, 179, 188, 191, 205, 206.
Gulls' eggs, 197.
Gulo luscus, 311*.

Gunnison's Island, 197, 297*.
Gypsum, 243, 246.

H

Ham's Fork, 74, 231, 276*.
Hastings's Cut-off, 112.
Hat Island, 204.
Hawk, sharp shinned, 314*.
Hawk, red-tailed, 314*.
Hedspeth's Cut-off, 293*.
Hedysarum mackenzii, 385*.
Hemiptera, 369*.
Henous techanus, 377*.
Heterodon nasicus, 352*.
"   platyrhinos, 353*.
"   simus, 353*.
Heuchera, 210.
Heuchera rubescens, 388*.
High Fork, 94.
Hill Creek, 281*.
Holbrookia, 340*.
Holbrookia maculata 342*, 308.
Hordeum jubatum, 397*.
Horia stansburii, 377*.
Horned Frogs, 178.
Horned Frogs, monograph of, 354.
Horse Creek, 273*, 287*.
Horse-shoe Creek, 56, 273*.
Horses stolen by Indians, 22.
Hot Springs, 213, 215, 293*, 294*.
Hot Spring water, analysis of, 420*.
Hydrochus foveatus, 375*.
Hydrophyllum capitatum, 393*.
Hymenoptera, 367*.
Hypoxis erecta, 397*.

I

Independence Creek, 292*.
Independence Rock, 65.
Indians, 100, 103, 107, 251.
Indians, alarm of, 26.
Indian burial lodge, 40, 42.
Indian camp, 46.
Indian Creek, 270*.
Indian lodges, 111, 181.
Indian pottery, 182.
Indian Springs, 185, 192.
Indian traces, 244, 245, 248.
Inoceramus, 402.
Insects described, 366*.

J

Jealousy of the Mormons, 85.
Jordan River, 141, 156.

THE END.

STEREOTYPED BY L. JOHNSON & CO.
PHILADELPHIA.